CALL OF DUTY

BLACK OPS III

TONY PARKER

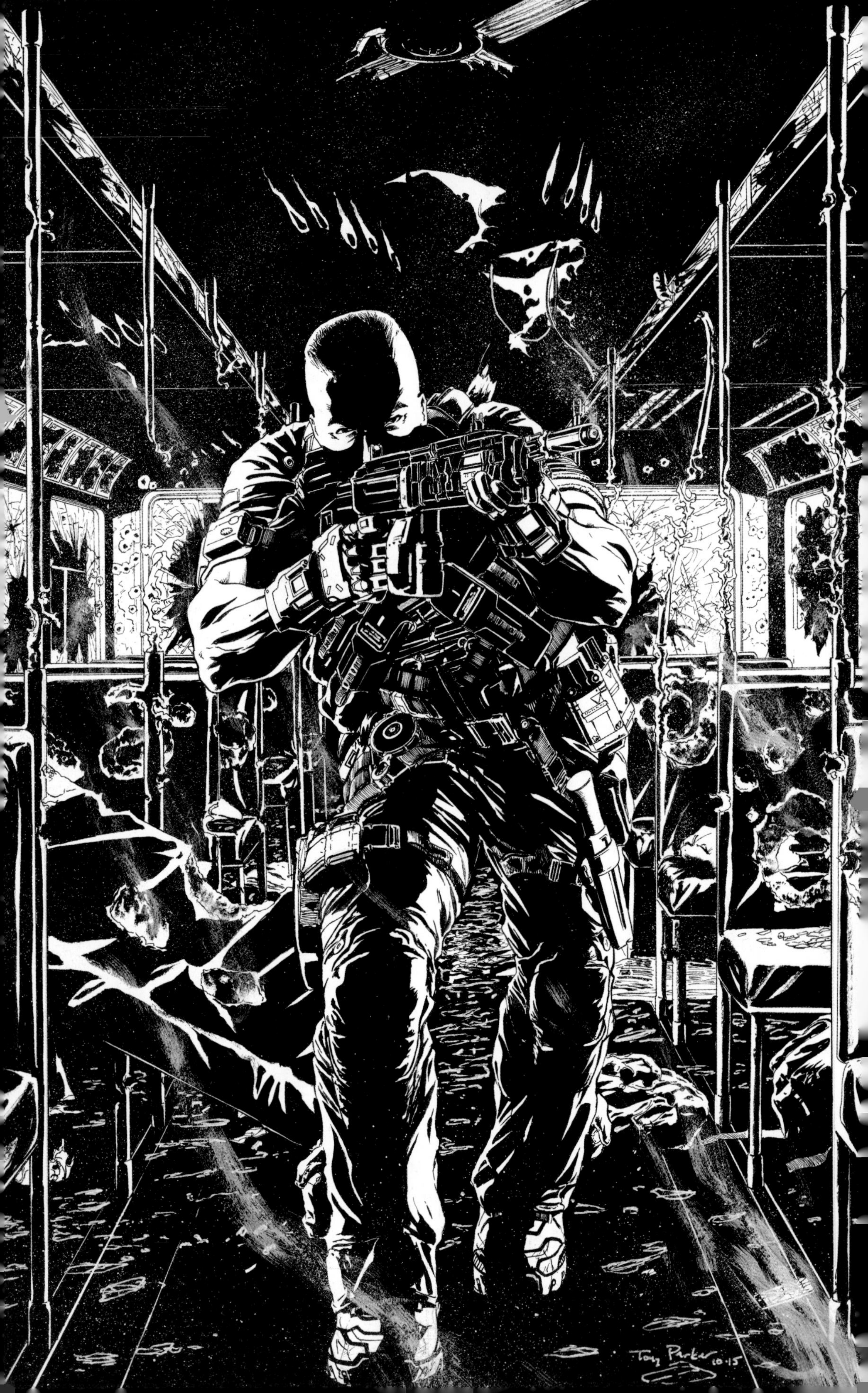
Tony Parker 10·15

CALL OF DUTY®
BLACK OPS III

STORY BY
LARRY HAMA

ART BY
MARCELO FERREIRA

COLORS BY
DAN JACKSON

LETTERS BY
MICHAEL HEISLER

COVER ART AND CHAPTER BREAKS BY
BENJAMIN CARRÉ   ANTHONY PALUMBO

TONY PARKER   FELIPE MASSAFERA   IBRAHIM MOUSTAFA

E. M. GIST   JASON FELIX

DARK HORSE BOOKS   treyarch   ACTIVISION®

PRESIDENT AND PUBLISHER
MIKE RICHARDSON

EDITOR
PATRICK THORPE

ASSISTANT EDITORS
EVERETT PATTERSON, CARDNER CLARK

DESIGNER
JACK THOMAS

DIGITAL ART TECHNICIAN
ALLYSON HALLER

Call of Duty: Black Ops III

This volume collects issues #1–#6 of the Dark Horse Comics series *Call of Duty: Black Ops III*.

Library of Congress Cataloging-in-Publication Data

Names: Hama, Larry, author. | Ferreira, Marcelo (Illustrator) illustrator. |
Jackson, Dan, 1971- illustrator. | Heisler, Michael, illustrator. |
Carré, Benjamin, illustrator. | Palumbo, Anthony, illustrator. | Parker,
Tony, 1973- illustrator. | Massafera, Felipe, illustrator. | Moustafa,
Ibrahim, illustrator. | Gist, E. M., illustrator. | Felix, Jason, 1973-
illustrator.
Title: Call of Duty : Black Ops III / story by Larry Hama : art by Marcelo
Ferreira : colors by Dan Jackson : letters by Michael Heisler : cover art
and chapter breaks by Benjamin Carré, Anthony Palumbo, Tony Parker, Felipe
Massafera, Ibrahim Moustafa, E. M. Gist, Jason Felix.
Description: First edition. | Milwaukie, OR : Dark Horse Books, 2017. | "This
volume collects issues #1-#6 of the Dark Horse Comics series Call of Duty:
Black Ops III"
Identifiers: LCCN 2016010224 | ISBN 9781616559663 (paperback)
Subjects: LCSH: Soldiers--Comic books, strips, etc. | Graphic novels. |
BISAC: GAMES / Video & Electronic. | COMICS & GRAPHIC NOVELS / Media
Tie-In.
Classification: LCC PN6728.C337 H36 2016 | DDC 741.5/973--dc23
LC record available at https://lccn.loc.gov/2016010224

Published by
Dark Horse Books
A division of Dark Horse Comics, Inc.
10956 SE Main Street
Milwaukie, OR 97222

DarkHorse.com

To find a comics shop in your area, call the
Comic Shop Locator Service toll-free at 1-888-266-4226.
International Licensing: (503) 905-2377

First edition: January 2017
ISBN 978-1-61655-966-3

1 3 5 7 9 10 8 6 4 2
Printed in China

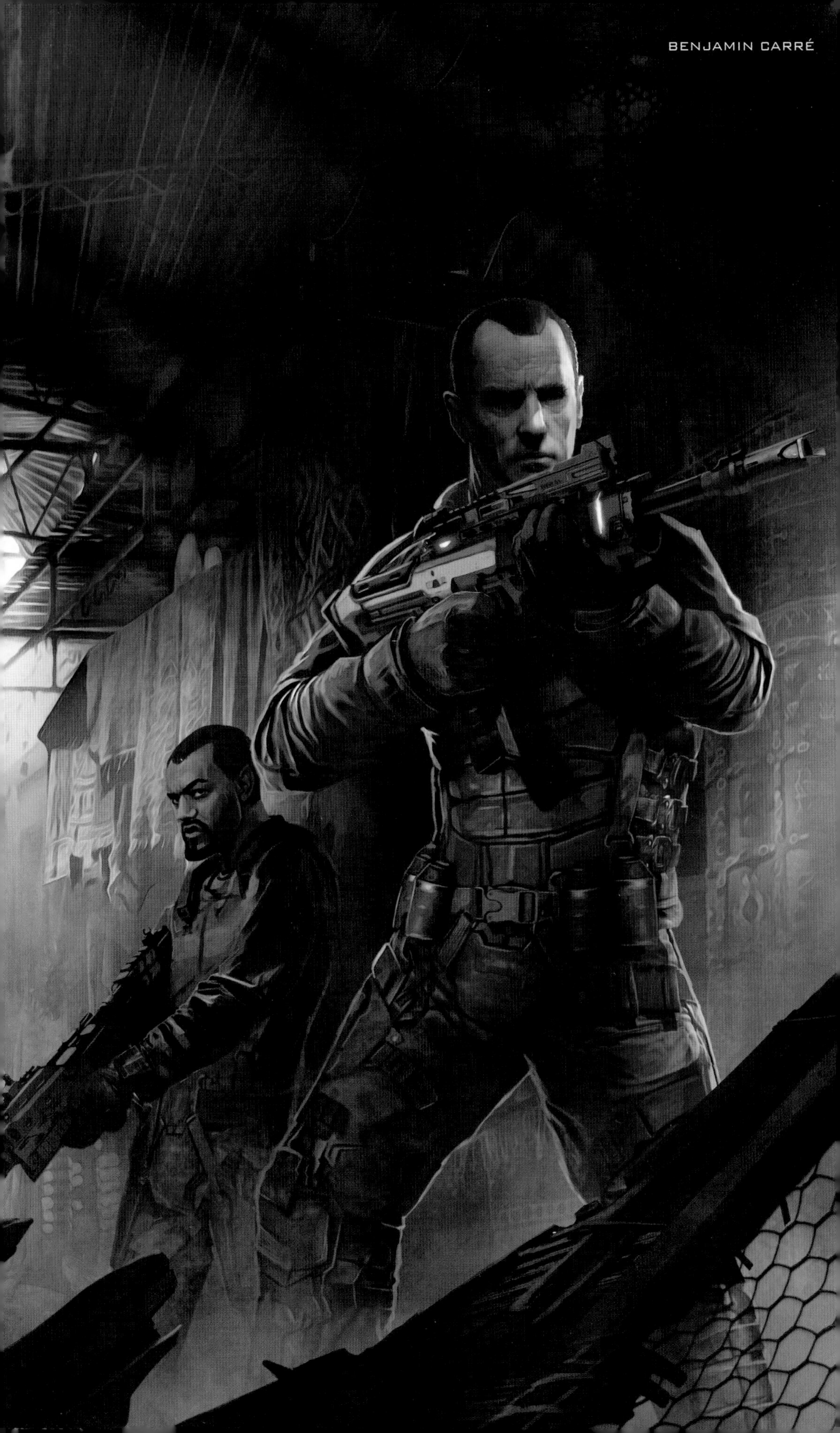
BENJAMIN CARRÉ

IBRAHIM MOUSTAFA

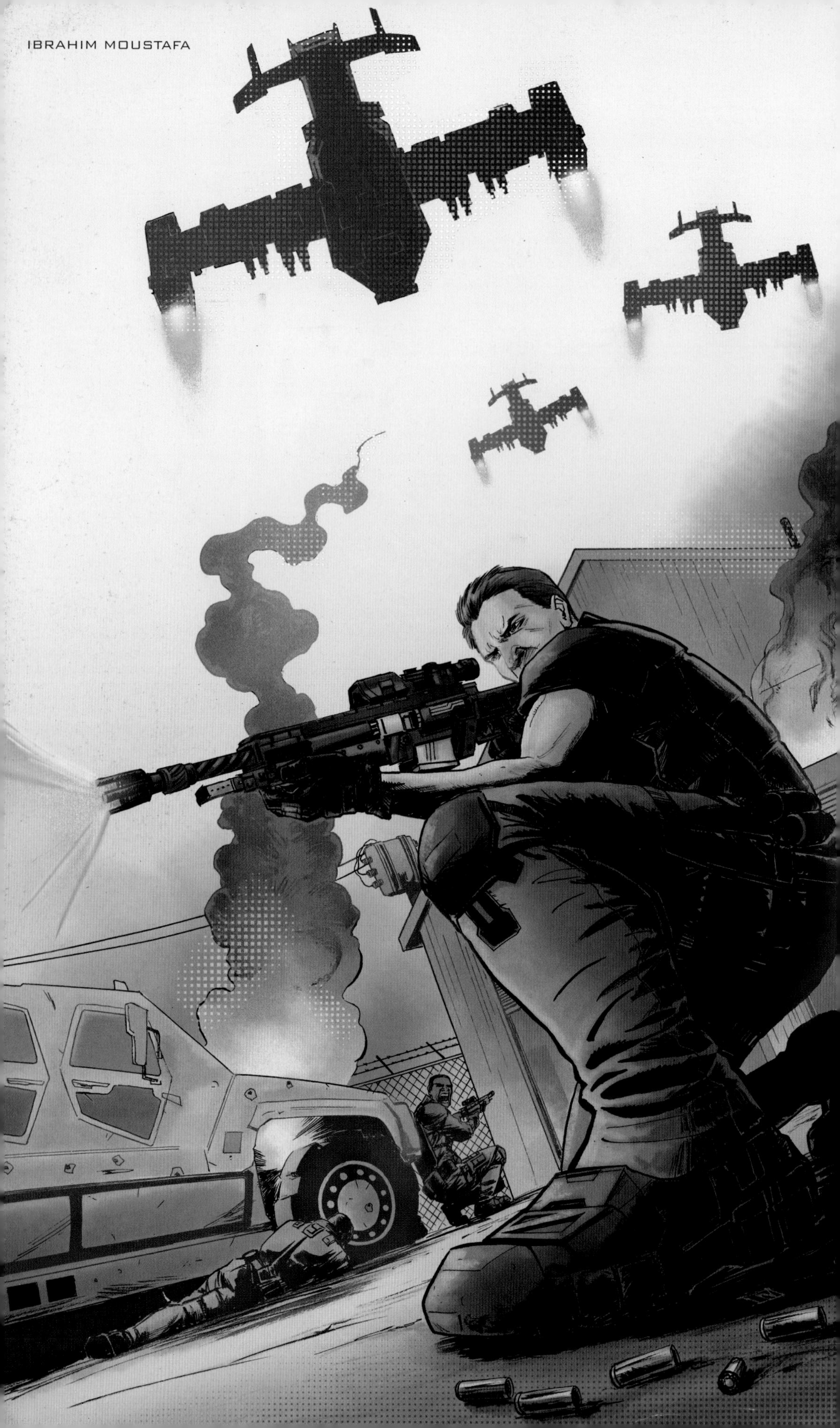

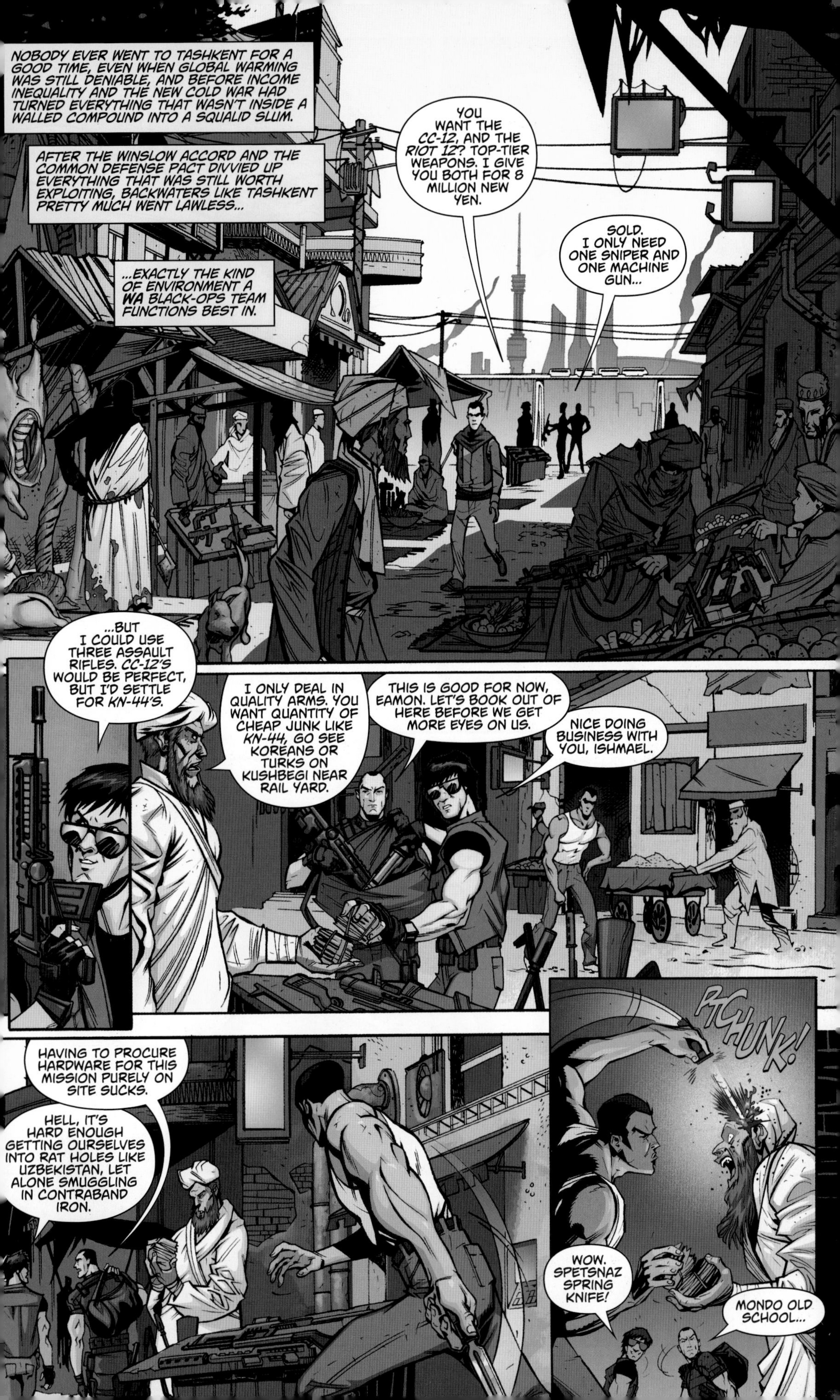
NOBODY EVER WENT TO TASHKENT FOR A GOOD TIME, EVEN WHEN GLOBAL WARMING WAS STILL DENIABLE, AND BEFORE INCOME INEQUALITY AND THE NEW COLD WAR HAD TURNED EVERYTHING THAT WASN'T INSIDE A WALLED COMPOUND INTO A SQUALID SLUM.
AFTER THE WINSLOW ACCORD AND THE COMMON DEFENSE PACT DIVVIED UP EVERYTHING THAT WAS STILL WORTH EXPLOITING, BACKWATERS LIKE TASHKENT PRETTY MUCH WENT LAWLESS...
...EXACTLY THE KIND OF ENVIRONMENT A WA BLACK-OPS TEAM FUNCTIONS BEST IN.
YOU WANT THE CC-12, AND THE RIOT 12? TOP-TIER WEAPONS. I GIVE YOU BOTH FOR 8 MILLION NEW YEN.
SOLD. I ONLY NEED ONE SNIPER AND ONE MACHINE GUN...
...BUT I COULD USE THREE ASSAULT RIFLES. CC-12'S WOULD BE PERFECT, BUT I'D SETTLE FOR KN-44'S.
I ONLY DEAL IN QUALITY ARMS. YOU WANT QUANTITY OF CHEAP JUNK LIKE KN-44, GO SEE KOREANS OR TURKS ON KUSHBEGI NEAR RAIL YARD.
THIS IS GOOD FOR NOW, EAMON. LET'S BOOK OUT OF HERE BEFORE WE GET MORE EYES ON US.
NICE DOING BUSINESS WITH YOU, ISHMAEL.
HAVING TO PROCURE HARDWARE FOR THIS MISSION PURELY ON SITE SUCKS.
HELL, IT'S HARD ENOUGH GETTING OURSELVES INTO RAT HOLES LIKE UZBEKISTAN, LET ALONE SMUGGLING IN CONTRABAND IRON.
PTCHUNK!
WOW. SPETSNAZ SPRING KNIFE!
MONDO OLD SCHOOL...

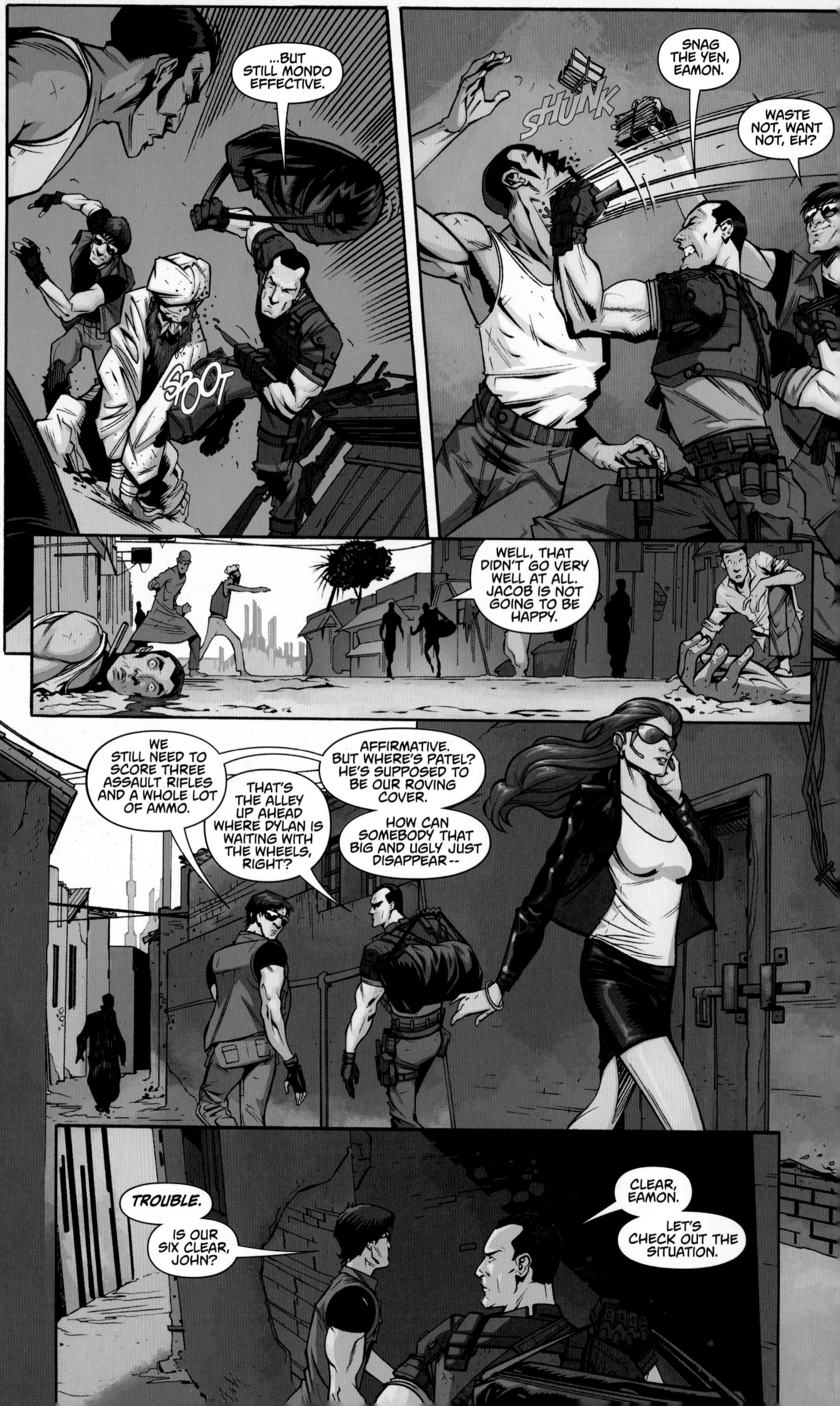

...BUT STILL MONDO EFFECTIVE.
SPOOT
SHUNK
SNAG THE YEN, EAMON.
WASTE NOT, WANT NOT, EH?
WELL, THAT DIDN'T GO VERY WELL AT ALL. JACOB IS NOT GOING TO BE HAPPY.
WE STILL NEED TO SCORE THREE ASSAULT RIFLES AND A WHOLE LOT OF AMMO.
AFFIRMATIVE. BUT WHERE'S PATEL? HE'S SUPPOSED TO BE OUR ROVING COVER.
THAT'S THE ALLEY UP AHEAD WHERE DYLAN IS WAITING WITH THE WHEELS, RIGHT?
HOW CAN SOMEBODY THAT BIG AND UGLY JUST DISAPPEAR --
TROUBLE.
IS OUR SIX CLEAR, JOHN?
CLEAR, EAMON.
LET'S CHECK OUT THE SITUATION.

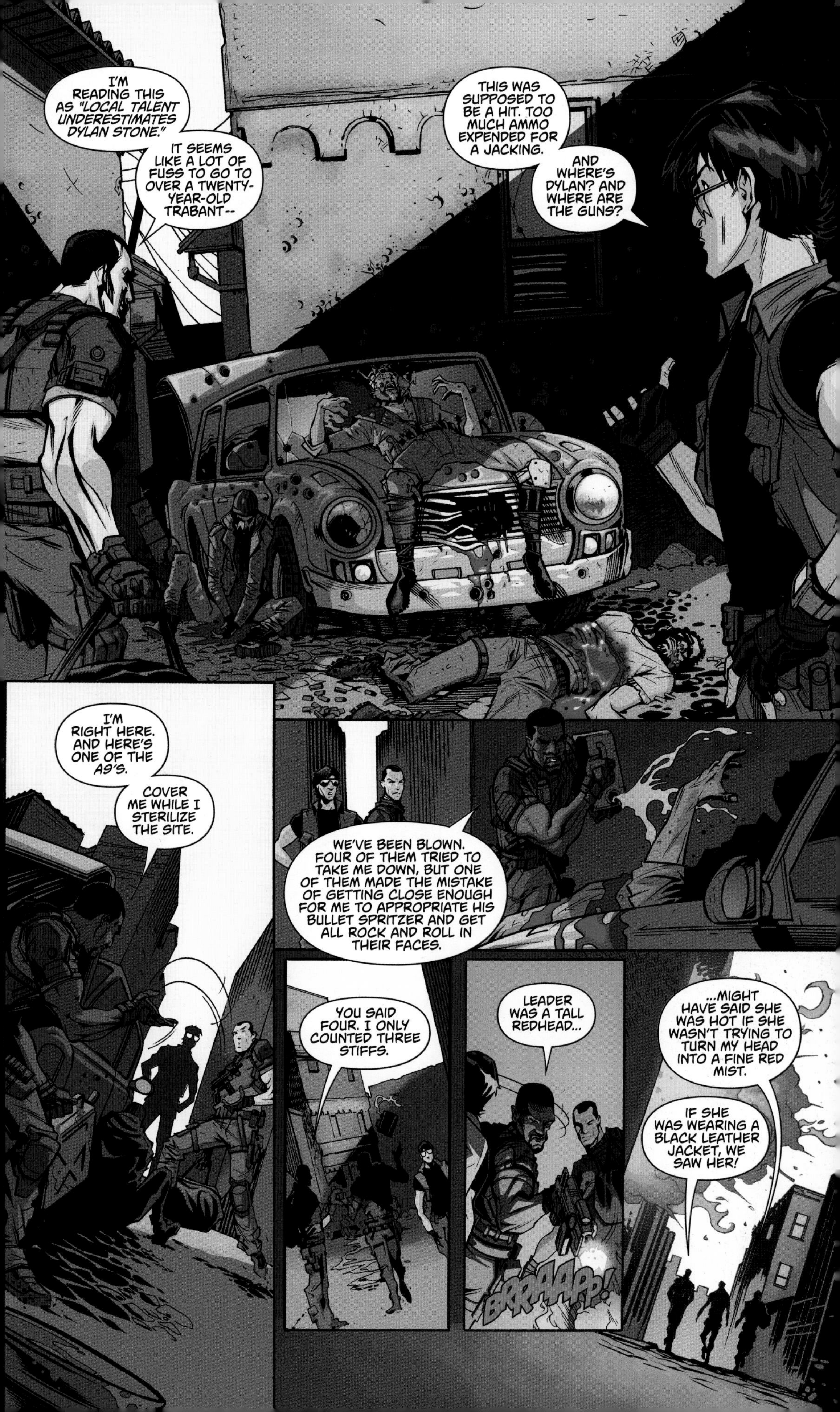
I'M READING THIS AS "LOCAL TALENT UNDERESTIMATES DYLAN STONE."
IT SEEMS LIKE A LOT OF FUSS TO GO TO OVER A TWENTY-YEAR-OLD TRABANT--
THIS WAS SUPPOSED TO BE A HIT. TOO MUCH AMMO EXPENDED FOR A JACKING.
AND WHERE'S DYLAN? AND WHERE ARE THE GUNS?
I'M RIGHT HERE. AND HERE'S ONE OF THE A9'S.
COVER ME WHILE I STERILIZE THE SITE.
WE'VE BEEN BLOWN. FOUR OF THEM TRIED TO TAKE ME DOWN, BUT ONE OF THEM MADE THE MISTAKE OF GETTING CLOSE ENOUGH FOR ME TO APPROPRIATE HIS BULLET SPRITZER AND GET ALL ROCK AND ROLL IN THEIR FACES.
YOU SAID FOUR. I ONLY COUNTED THREE STIFFS.
LEADER WAS A TALL REDHEAD...
BRRAAAPP!
...MIGHT HAVE SAID SHE WAS HOT IF SHE WASN'T TRYING TO TURN MY HEAD INTO A FINE RED MIST.
IF SHE WAS WEARING A BLACK LEATHER JACKET, WE SAW HER!

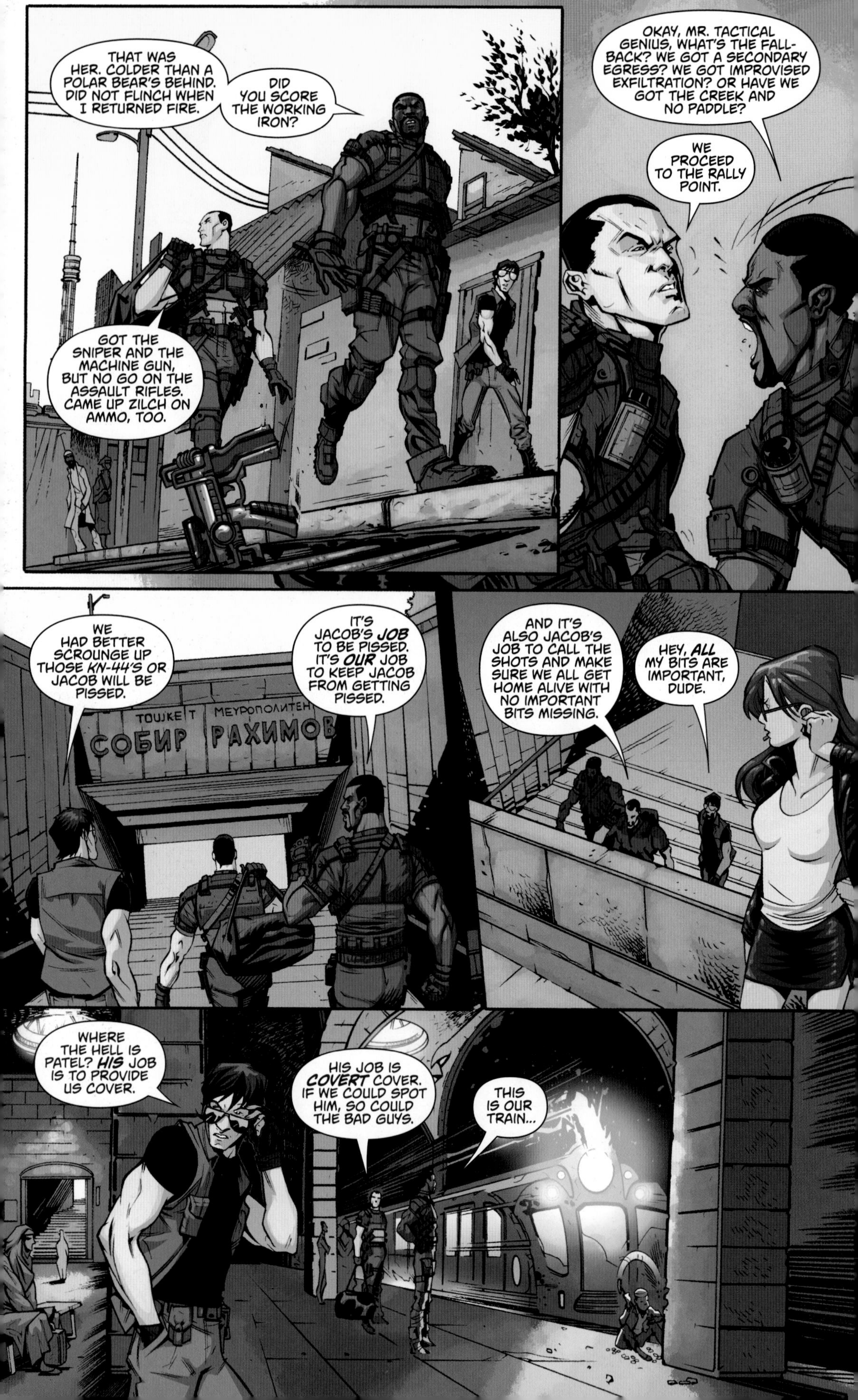
THAT WAS HER. COLDER THAN A POLAR BEAR'S BEHIND. DID NOT FLINCH WHEN I RETURNED FIRE.
DID YOU SCORE THE WORKING IRON?
GOT THE SNIPER AND THE MACHINE GUN, BUT NO GO ON THE ASSAULT RIFLES. CAME UP ZILCH ON AMMO, TOO.
OKAY, MR. TACTICAL GENIUS, WHAT'S THE FALL-BACK? WE GOT A SECONDARY EGRESS? WE GOT IMPROVISED EXFILTRATION? OR HAVE WE GOT THE CREEK AND NO PADDLE?
WE PROCEED TO THE RALLY POINT.
WE HAD BETTER SCROUNGE UP THOSE KN-44'S OR JACOB WILL BE PISSED.
IT'S JACOB'S JOB TO BE PISSED. IT'S OUR JOB TO KEEP JACOB FROM GETTING PISSED.
СОБИР РАХИМОВ
AND IT'S ALSO JACOB'S JOB TO CALL THE SHOTS AND MAKE SURE WE ALL GET HOME ALIVE WITH NO IMPORTANT BITS MISSING.
HEY, ALL MY BITS ARE IMPORTANT, DUDE.
WHERE THE HELL IS PATEL? HIS JOB IS TO PROVIDE US COVER.
HIS JOB IS COVERT COVER. IF WE COULD SPOT HIM, SO COULD THE BAD GUYS.
THIS IS OUR TRAIN...

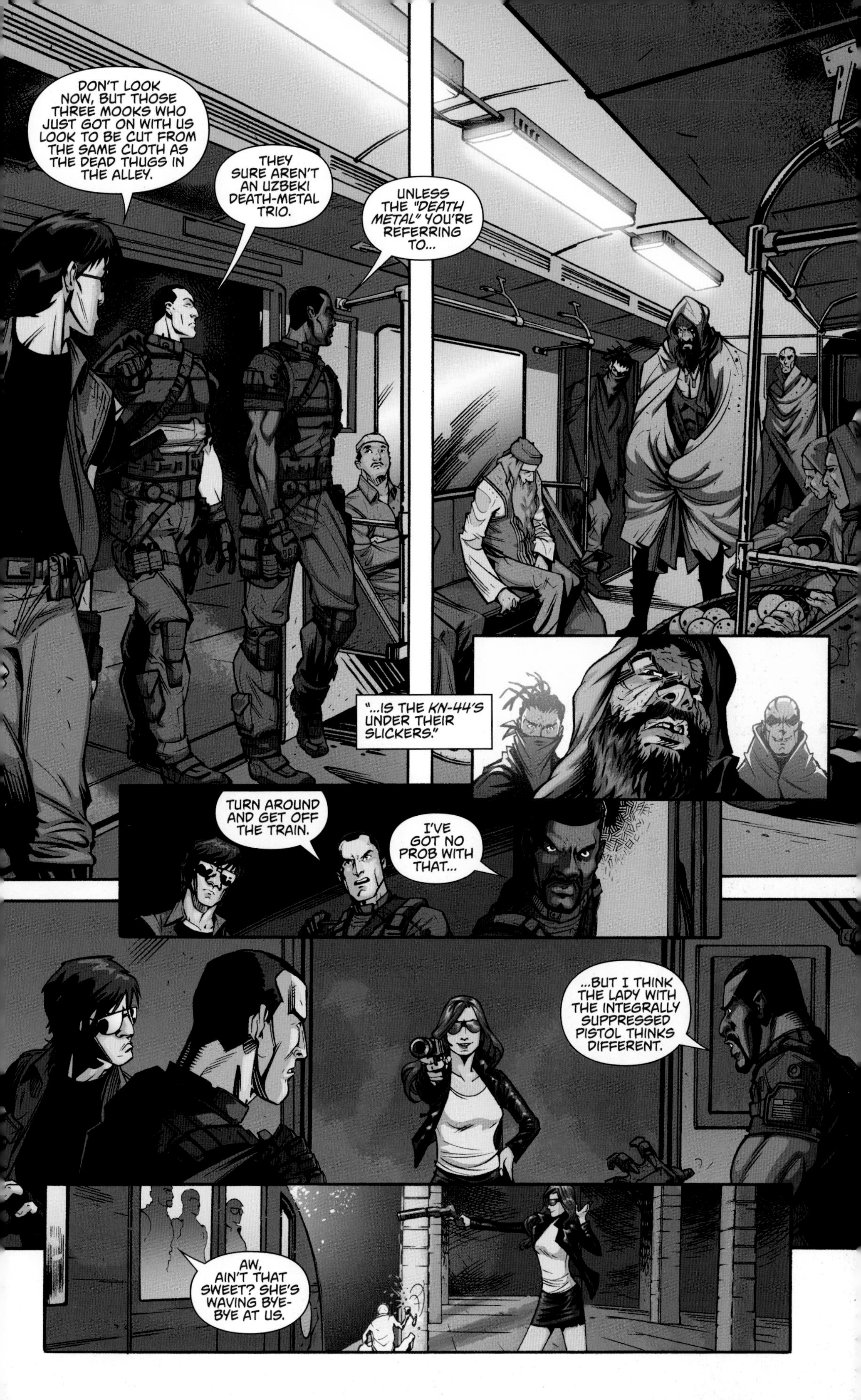
DON'T LOOK NOW, BUT THOSE THREE MOOKS WHO JUST GOT ON WITH US LOOK TO BE CUT FROM THE SAME CLOTH AS THE DEAD THUGS IN THE ALLEY.
THEY SURE AREN'T AN UZBEKI DEATH-METAL TRIO.
UNLESS THE "DEATH METAL" YOU'RE REFERRING TO...
"...IS THE KN-44'S UNDER THEIR SLICKERS."
TURN AROUND AND GET OFF THE TRAIN.
I'VE GOT NO PROB WITH THAT...
...BUT I THINK THE LADY WITH THE INTEGRALLY SUPPRESSED PISTOL THINKS DIFFERENT.
AW, AIN'T THAT SWEET? SHE'S WAVING BYE-BYE AT US.

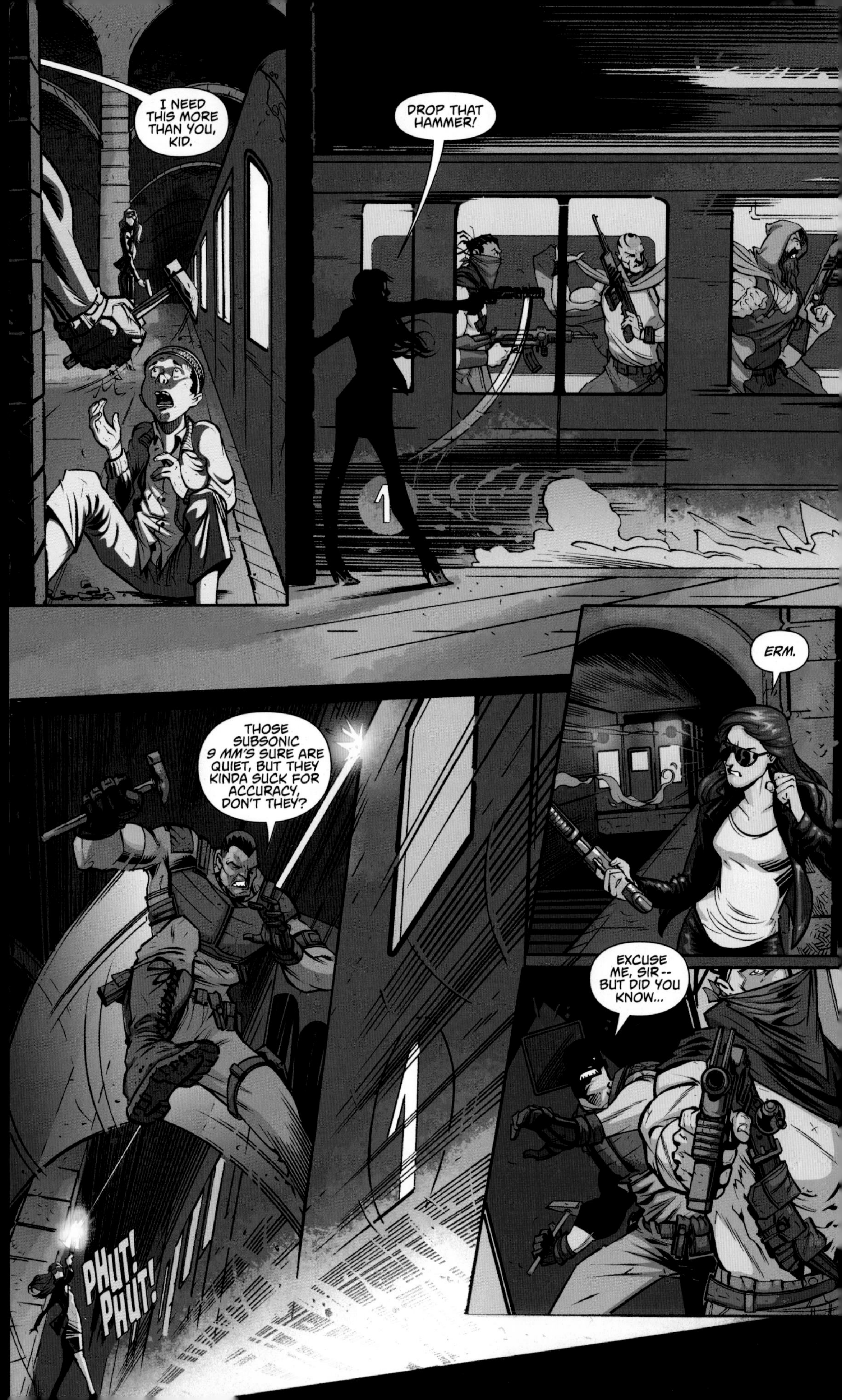
I NEED THIS MORE THAN YOU, KID.
DROP THAT HAMMER!
1
ERM.
THOSE SUBSONIC 9 MM'S SURE ARE QUIET, BUT THEY KINDA SUCK FOR ACCURACY, DON'T THEY?
EXCUSE ME, SIR-- BUT DID YOU KNOW...
PHUT! PHUT!

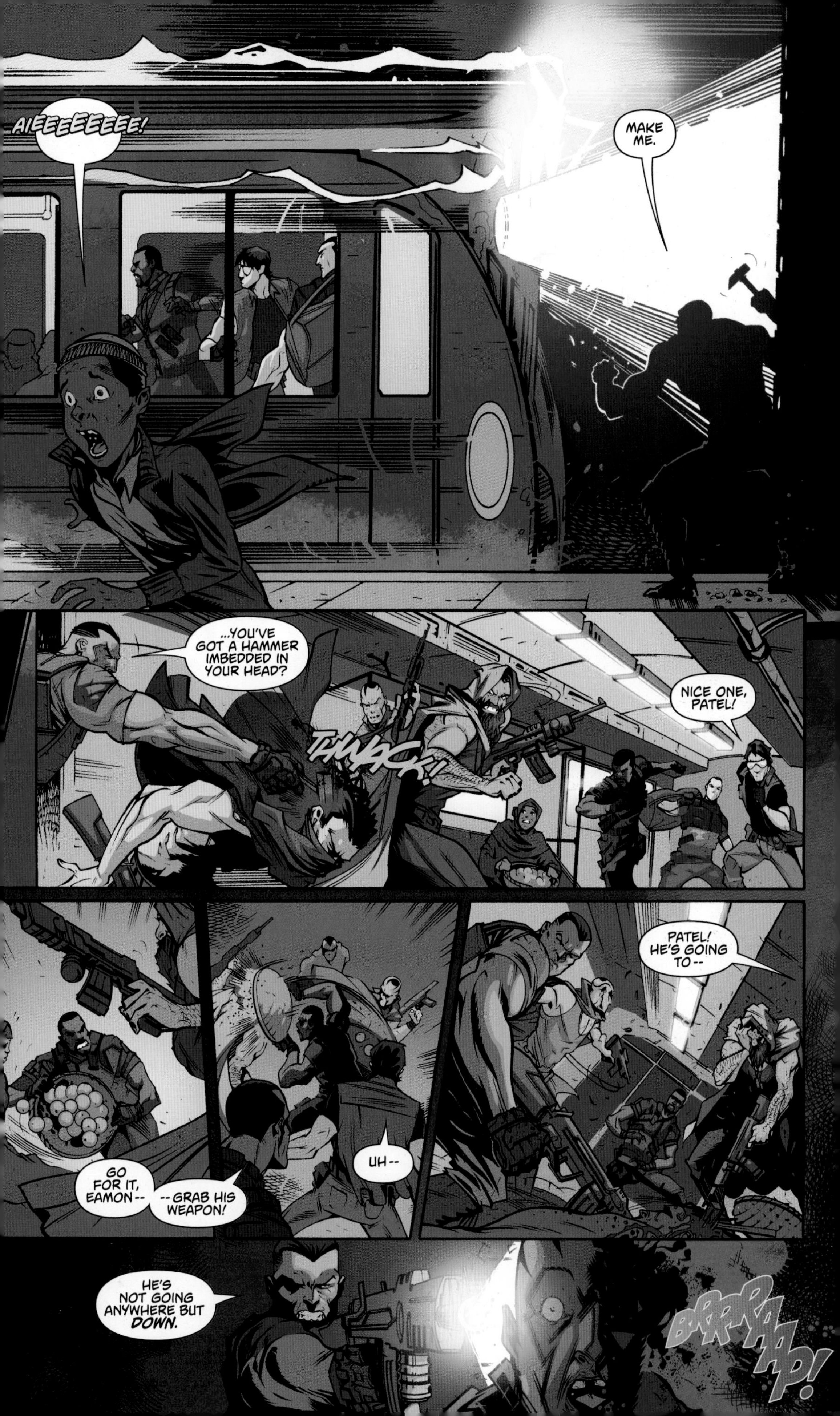
AIEEEEEEEE!
MAKE ME.
...YOU'VE GOT A HAMMER IMBEDDED IN YOUR HEAD?
THWACK!
NICE ONE, PATEL!
PATEL! HE'S GOING TO --
GO FOR IT, EAMON--
--GRAB HIS WEAPON!
UH--
HE'S NOT GOING ANYWHERE BUT DOWN.
BRRRAAAP!

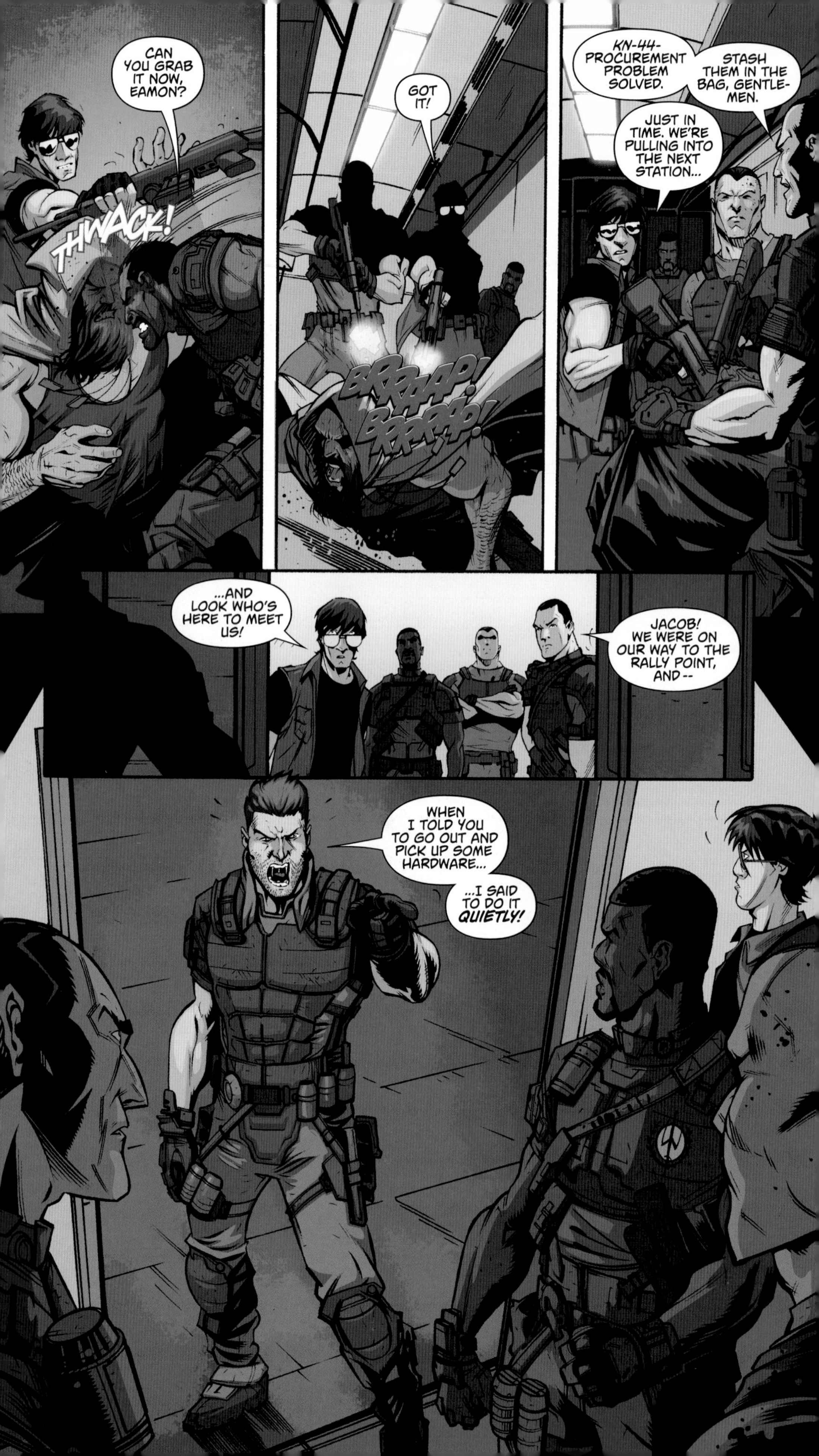
CAN YOU GRAB IT NOW, EAMON?
THWACK!
GOT IT!
BRRAAP! BRRRAP!
KN-44-PROCUREMENT PROBLEM SOLVED.
STASH THEM IN THE BAG, GENTLEMEN.
JUST IN TIME. WE'RE PULLING INTO THE NEXT STATION...
...AND LOOK WHO'S HERE TO MEET US!
JACOB! WE WERE ON OUR WAY TO THE RALLY POINT, AND --
WHEN I TOLD YOU TO GO OUT AND PICK UP SOME HARDWARE...
...I SAID TO DO IT QUIETLY!

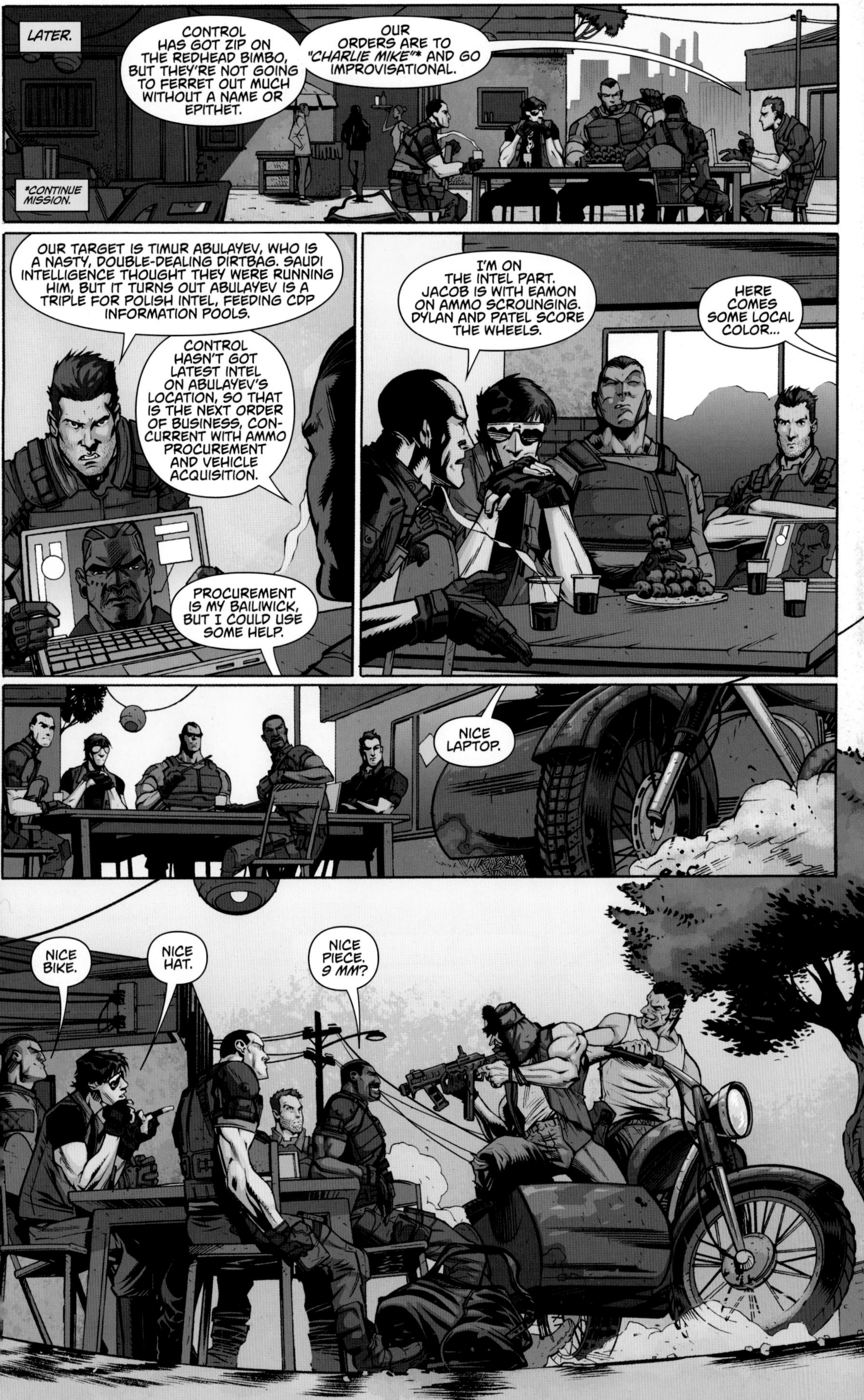
LATER.
CONTROL HAS GOT ZIP ON THE REDHEAD BIMBO, BUT THEY'RE NOT GOING TO FERRET OUT MUCH WITHOUT A NAME OR EPITHET.
OUR ORDERS ARE TO "CHARLIE MIKE"* AND GO IMPROVISATIONAL.
*CONTINUE MISSION.
OUR TARGET IS TIMUR ABULAYEV, WHO IS A NASTY, DOUBLE-DEALING DIRTBAG. SAUDI INTELLIGENCE THOUGHT THEY WERE RUNNING HIM, BUT IT TURNS OUT ABULAYEV IS A TRIPLE FOR POLISH INTEL, FEEDING CDP INFORMATION POOLS.
CONTROL HASN'T GOT LATEST INTEL ON ABULAYEV'S LOCATION, SO THAT IS THE NEXT ORDER OF BUSINESS, CONCURRENT WITH AMMO PROCUREMENT AND VEHICLE ACQUISITION.
PROCUREMENT IS MY BAILIWICK, BUT I COULD USE SOME HELP.
I'M ON THE INTEL PART. JACOB IS WITH EAMON ON AMMO SCROUNGING. DYLAN AND PATEL SCORE THE WHEELS.
HERE COMES SOME LOCAL COLOR...
NICE LAPTOP.
NICE BIKE.
NICE HAT.
NICE PIECE. 9 MM?

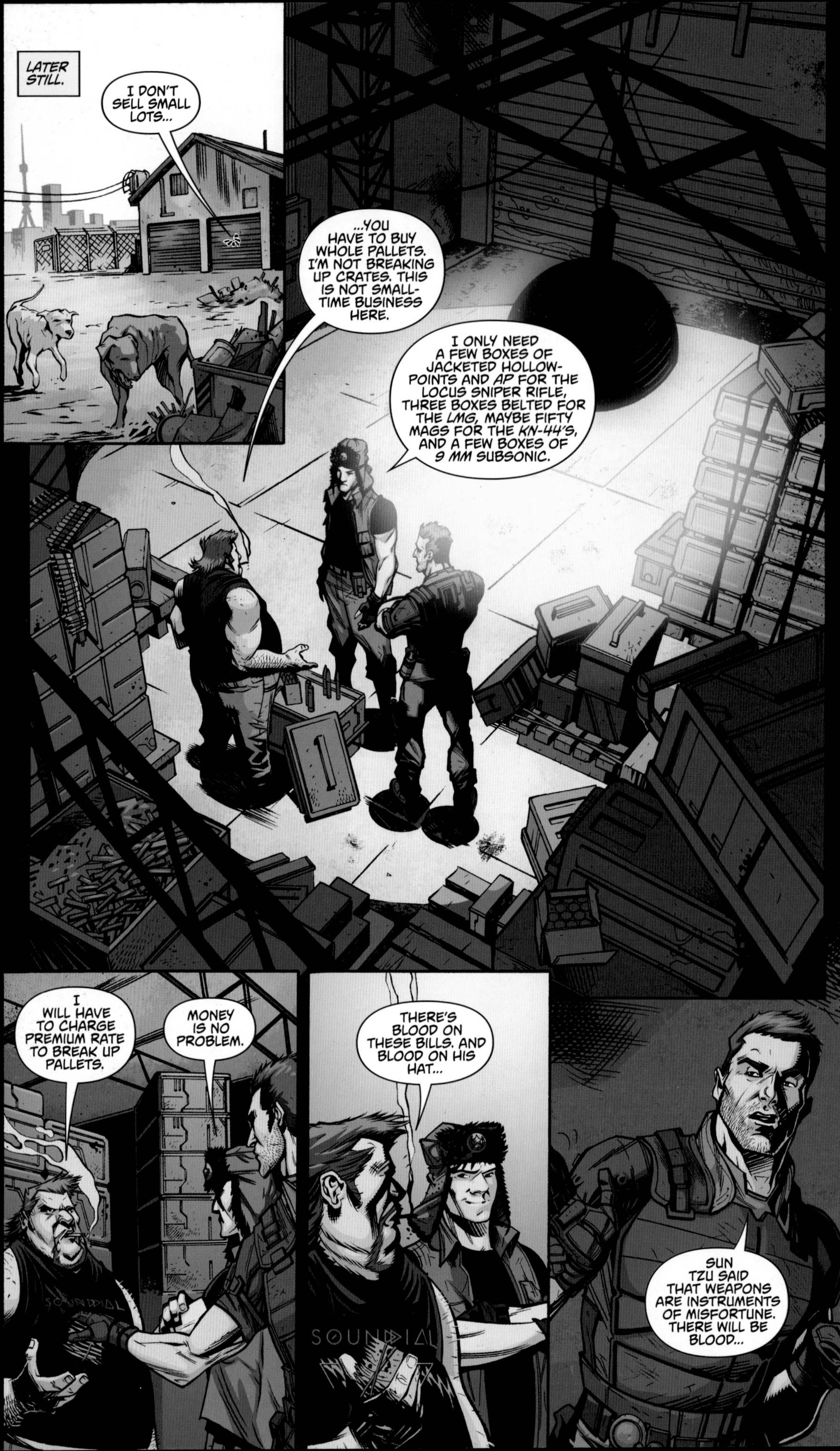
LATER STILL.
I DON'T SELL SMALL LOTS...
...YOU HAVE TO BUY WHOLE PALLETS. I'M NOT BREAKING UP CRATES. THIS IS NOT SMALL-TIME BUSINESS HERE.
I ONLY NEED A FEW BOXES OF JACKETED HOLLOW-POINTS AND AP FOR THE LOCUS SNIPER RIFLE, THREE BOXES BELTED FOR THE LMG, MAYBE FIFTY MAGS FOR THE KN-44'S, AND A FEW BOXES OF 9 MM SUBSONIC.
I WILL HAVE TO CHARGE PREMIUM RATE TO BREAK UP PALLETS.
MONEY IS NO PROBLEM.
THERE'S BLOOD ON THESE BILLS. AND BLOOD ON HIS HAT...
SUN TZU SAID THAT WEAPONS ARE INSTRUMENTS OF MISFORTUNE. THERE WILL BE BLOOD...

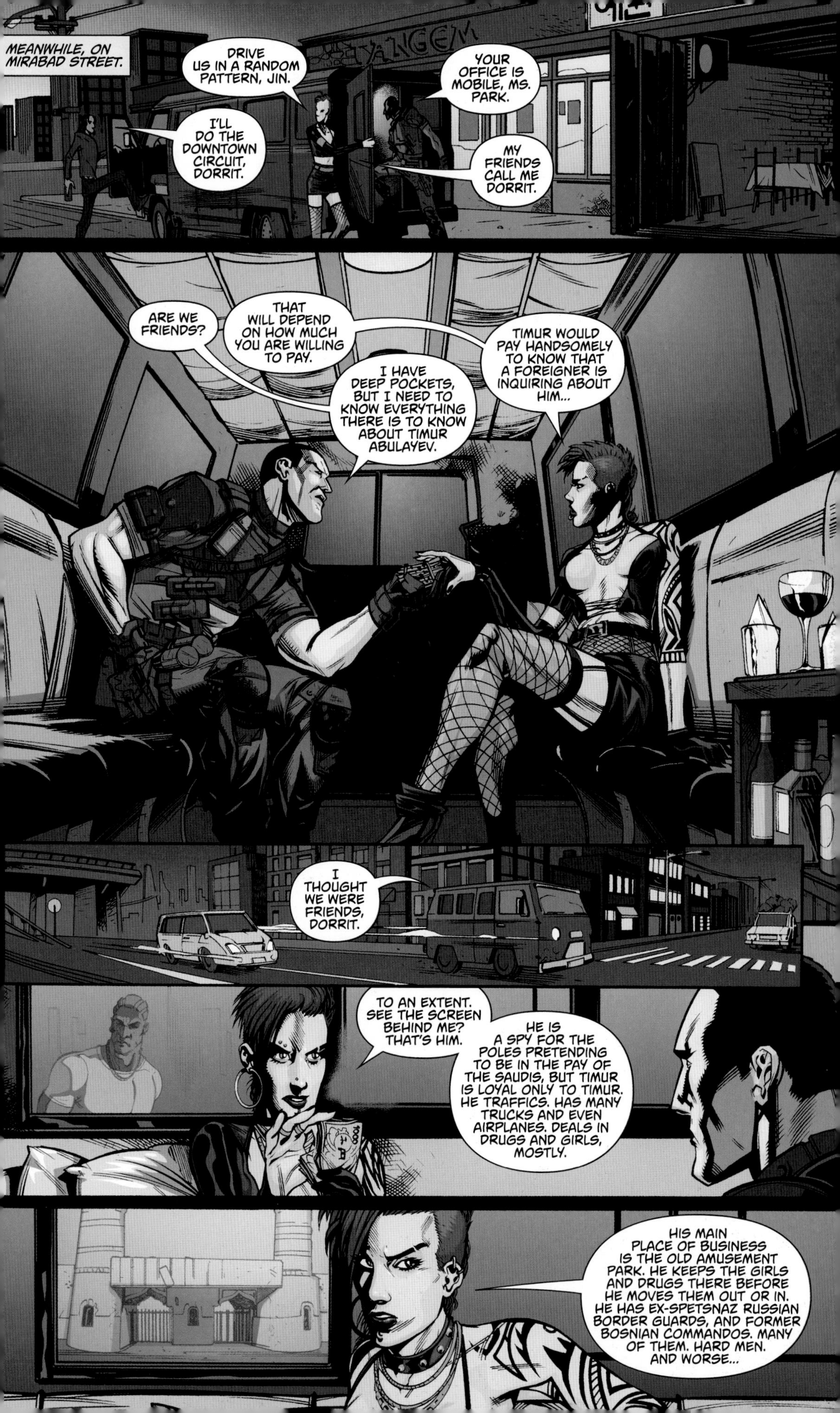
MEANWHILE, ON MIRABAD STREET.
DRIVE US IN A RANDOM PATTERN, JIN.
YOUR OFFICE IS MOBILE, MS. PARK.
I'LL DO THE DOWNTOWN CIRCUIT, DORRIT.
MY FRIENDS CALL ME DORRIT.
ARE WE FRIENDS?
THAT WILL DEPEND ON HOW MUCH YOU ARE WILLING TO PAY.
TIMUR WOULD PAY HANDSOMELY TO KNOW THAT A FOREIGNER IS INQUIRING ABOUT HIM...
I HAVE DEEP POCKETS, BUT I NEED TO KNOW EVERYTHING THERE IS TO KNOW ABOUT TIMUR ABULAYEV.
I THOUGHT WE WERE FRIENDS, DORRIT.
TO AN EXTENT. SEE THE SCREEN BEHIND ME? THAT'S HIM.
HE IS A SPY FOR THE POLES PRETENDING TO BE IN THE PAY OF THE SAUDIS, BUT TIMUR IS LOYAL ONLY TO TIMUR. HE TRAFFICS. HAS MANY TRUCKS AND EVEN AIRPLANES. DEALS IN DRUGS AND GIRLS, MOSTLY.
HIS MAIN PLACE OF BUSINESS IS THE OLD AMUSEMENT PARK. HE KEEPS THE GIRLS AND DRUGS THERE BEFORE HE MOVES THEM OUT OR IN. HE HAS EX-SPETSNAZ RUSSIAN BORDER GUARDS, AND FORMER BOSNIAN COMMANDOS. MANY OF THEM. HARD MEN. AND WORSE...

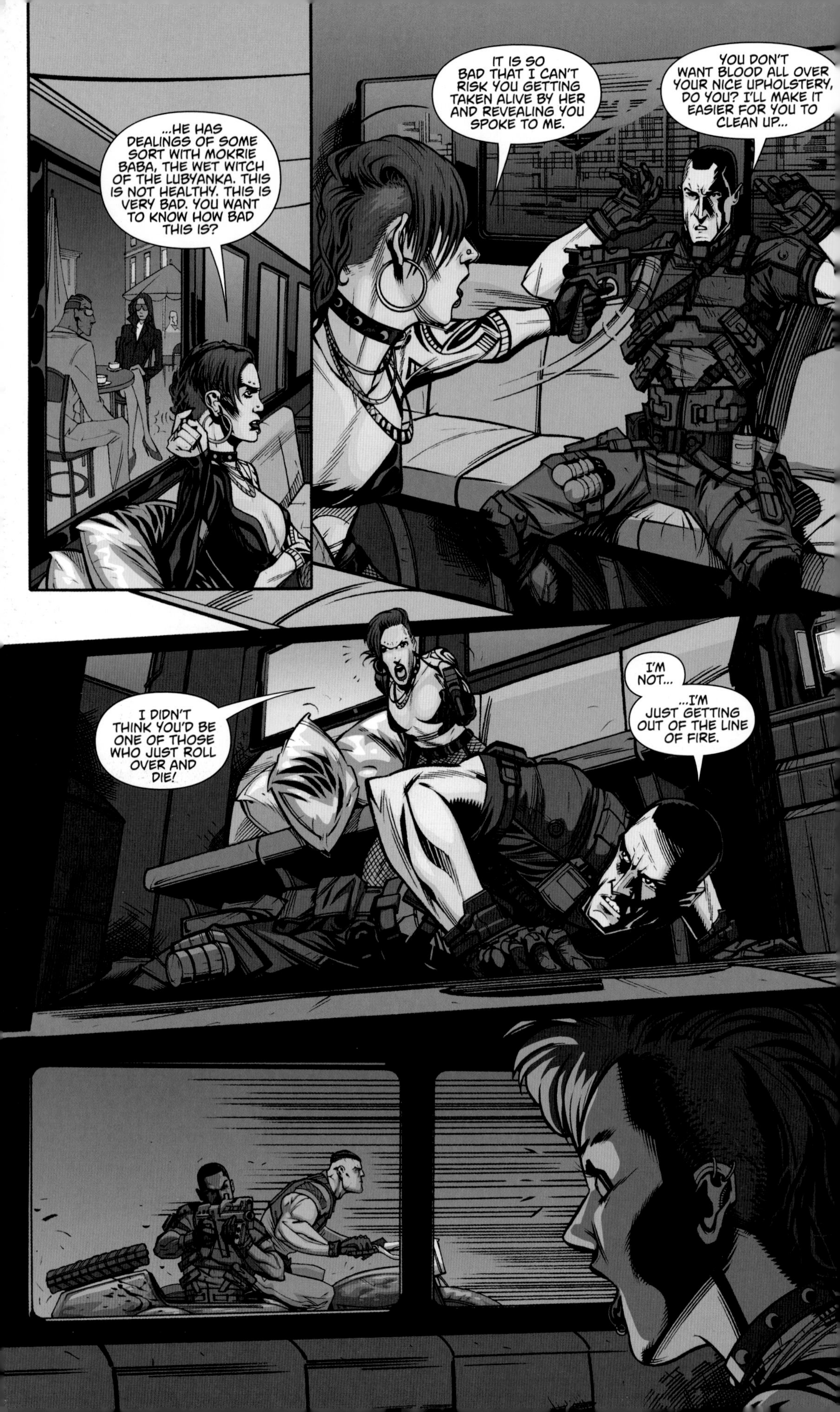
...HE HAS DEALINGS OF SOME SORT WITH MOKRIE BABA, THE WET WITCH OF THE LUBYANKA. THIS IS NOT HEALTHY. THIS IS VERY BAD. YOU WANT TO KNOW HOW BAD THIS IS?
IT IS SO BAD THAT I CAN'T RISK YOU GETTING TAKEN ALIVE BY HER AND REVEALING YOU SPOKE TO ME.
YOU DON'T WANT BLOOD ALL OVER YOUR NICE UPHOLSTERY, DO YOU? I'LL MAKE IT EASIER FOR YOU TO CLEAN UP...
I DIDN'T THINK YOU'D BE ONE OF THOSE WHO JUST ROLL OVER AND DIE!
I'M NOT...
...I'M JUST GETTING OUT OF THE LINE OF FIRE.

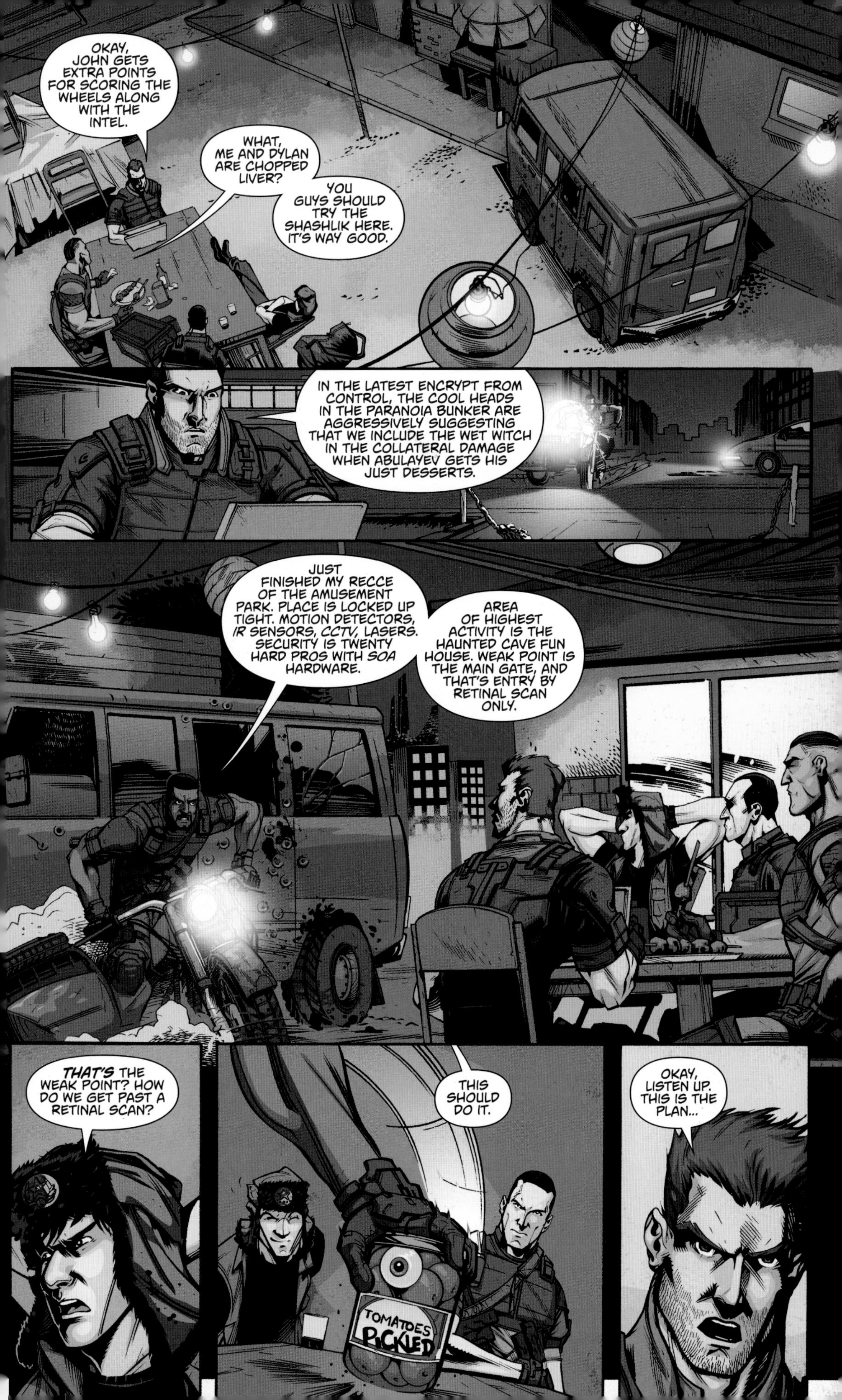
OKAY, JOHN GETS EXTRA POINTS FOR SCORING THE WHEELS ALONG WITH THE INTEL.
WHAT, ME AND DYLAN ARE CHOPPED LIVER?
YOU GUYS SHOULD TRY THE SHASHLIK HERE. IT'S WAY GOOD.
IN THE LATEST ENCRYPT FROM CONTROL, THE COOL HEADS IN THE PARANOIA BUNKER ARE AGGRESSIVELY SUGGESTING THAT WE INCLUDE THE WET WITCH IN THE COLLATERAL DAMAGE WHEN ABULAYEV GETS HIS JUST DESSERTS.
JUST FINISHED MY RECCE OF THE AMUSEMENT PARK. PLACE IS LOCKED UP TIGHT. MOTION DETECTORS, IR SENSORS, CCTV, LASERS. SECURITY IS TWENTY HARD PROS WITH SOA HARDWARE.
AREA OF HIGHEST ACTIVITY IS THE HAUNTED CAVE FUN HOUSE. WEAK POINT IS THE MAIN GATE, AND THAT'S ENTRY BY RETINAL SCAN ONLY.
THAT'S THE WEAK POINT? HOW DO WE GET PAST A RETINAL SCAN?
THIS SHOULD DO IT.
TOMATOES PICKLED
OKAY, LISTEN UP. THIS IS THE PLAN...

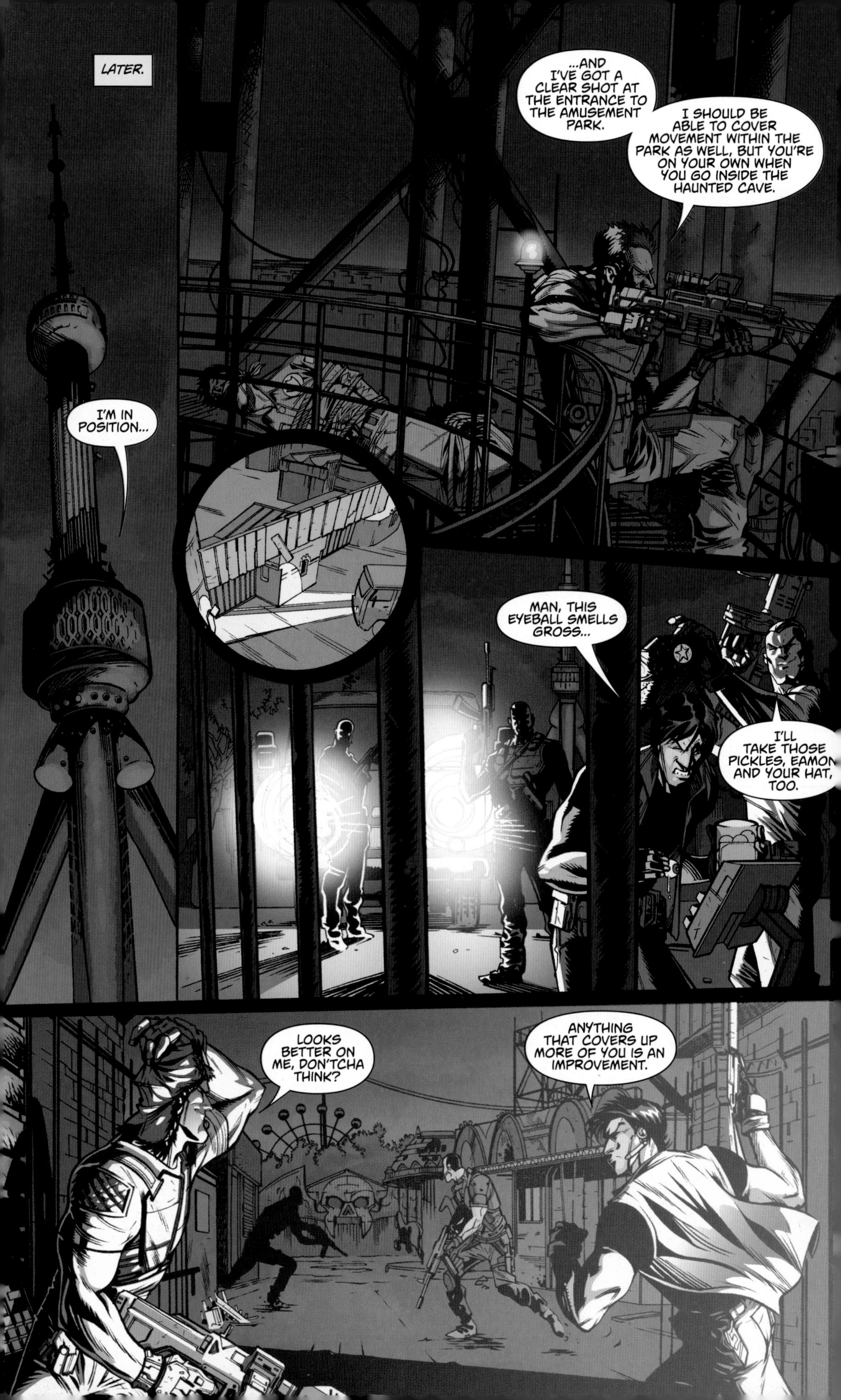
LATER.
I'M IN POSITION...
...AND I'VE GOT A CLEAR SHOT AT THE ENTRANCE TO THE AMUSEMENT PARK.
I SHOULD BE ABLE TO COVER MOVEMENT WITHIN THE PARK AS WELL, BUT YOU'RE ON YOUR OWN WHEN YOU GO INSIDE THE HAUNTED CAVE.
MAN, THIS EYEBALL SMELLS GROSS...
I'LL TAKE THOSE PICKLES, EAMON AND YOUR HAT, TOO.
LOOKS BETTER ON ME, DON'TCHA THINK?
ANYTHING THAT COVERS UP MORE OF YOU IS AN IMPROVEMENT.

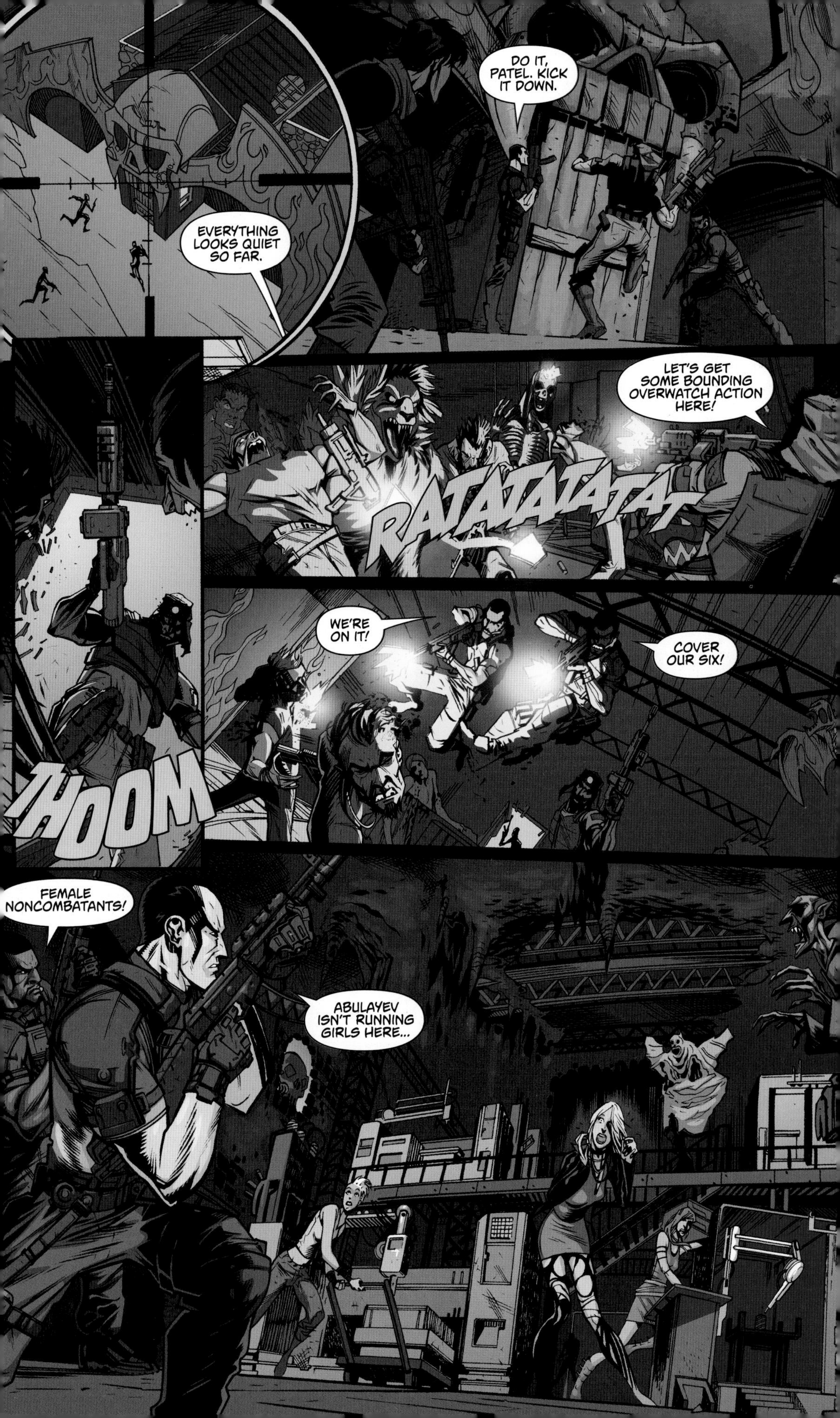
EVERYTHING LOOKS QUIET SO FAR.
DO IT, PATEL. KICK IT DOWN.
THOOM
LET'S GET SOME BOUNDING OVERWATCH ACTION HERE!
RATATATATAT
WE'RE ON IT!
COVER OUR SIX!
FEMALE NONCOMBATANTS!
ABULAYEV ISN'T RUNNING GIRLS HERE...

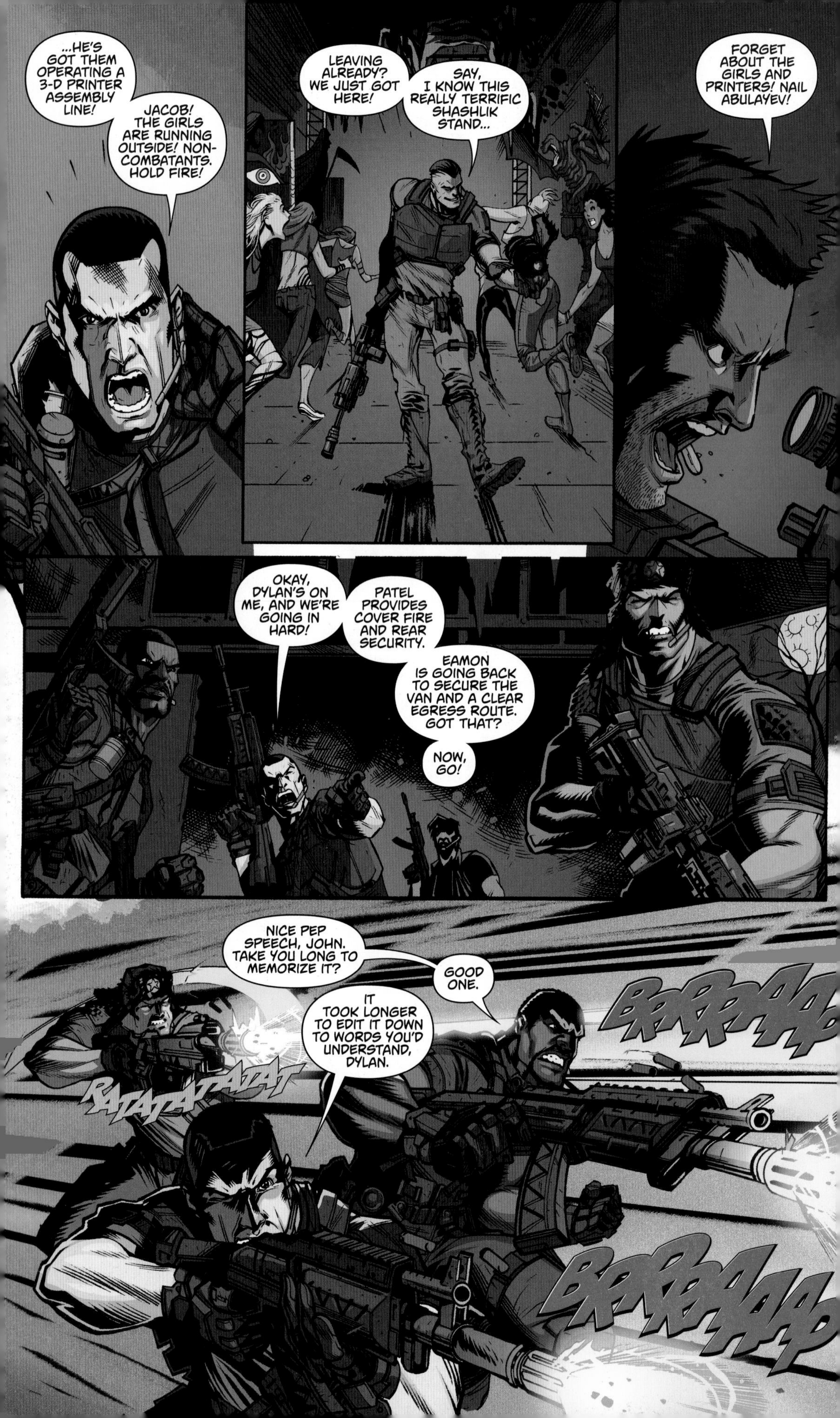
...HE'S GOT THEM OPERATING A 3-D PRINTER ASSEMBLY LINE!
JACOB! THE GIRLS ARE RUNNING OUTSIDE! NON-COMBATANTS. HOLD FIRE!
LEAVING ALREADY? WE JUST GOT HERE!
SAY, I KNOW THIS REALLY TERRIFIC SHASHLIK STAND...
FORGET ABOUT THE GIRLS AND PRINTERS! NAIL ABULAYEV!
OKAY, DYLAN'S ON ME, AND WE'RE GOING IN HARD!
PATEL PROVIDES COVER FIRE AND REAR SECURITY.
EAMON IS GOING BACK TO SECURE THE VAN AND A CLEAR EGRESS ROUTE. GOT THAT?
NOW, GO!
NICE PEP SPEECH, JOHN. TAKE YOU LONG TO MEMORIZE IT?
GOOD ONE.
IT TOOK LONGER TO EDIT IT DOWN TO WORDS YOU'D UNDERSTAND, DYLAN.
RATATATATAT

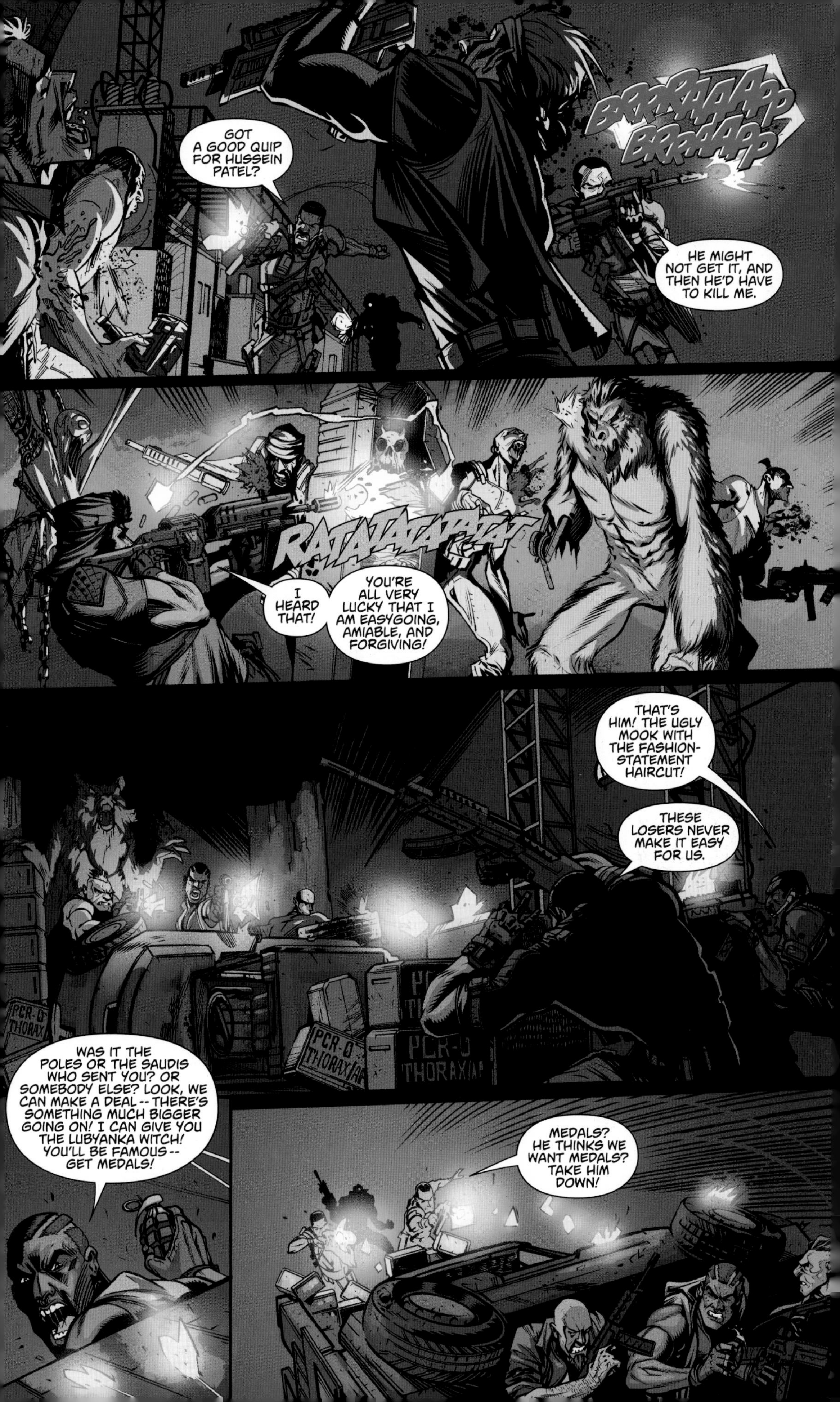
BRRRAAAAPP
BRRRAAPP
GOT A GOOD QUIP FOR HUSSEIN PATEL?
HE MIGHT NOT GET IT, AND THEN HE'D HAVE TO KILL ME.
RATATATATATAT
I HEARD THAT!
YOU'RE ALL VERY LUCKY THAT I AM EASYGOING, AMIABLE, AND FORGIVING!
THAT'S HIM! THE UGLY MOOK WITH THE FASHION-STATEMENT HAIRCUT!
THESE LOSERS NEVER MAKE IT EASY FOR US.
PCR-0 THORAX
WAS IT THE POLES OR THE SAUDIS WHO SENT YOU? OR SOMEBODY ELSE? LOOK, WE CAN MAKE A DEAL -- THERE'S SOMETHING MUCH BIGGER GOING ON! I CAN GIVE YOU THE LUBYANKA WITCH! YOU'LL BE FAMOUS -- GET MEDALS!
MEDALS? HE THINKS WE WANT MEDALS? TAKE HIM DOWN!

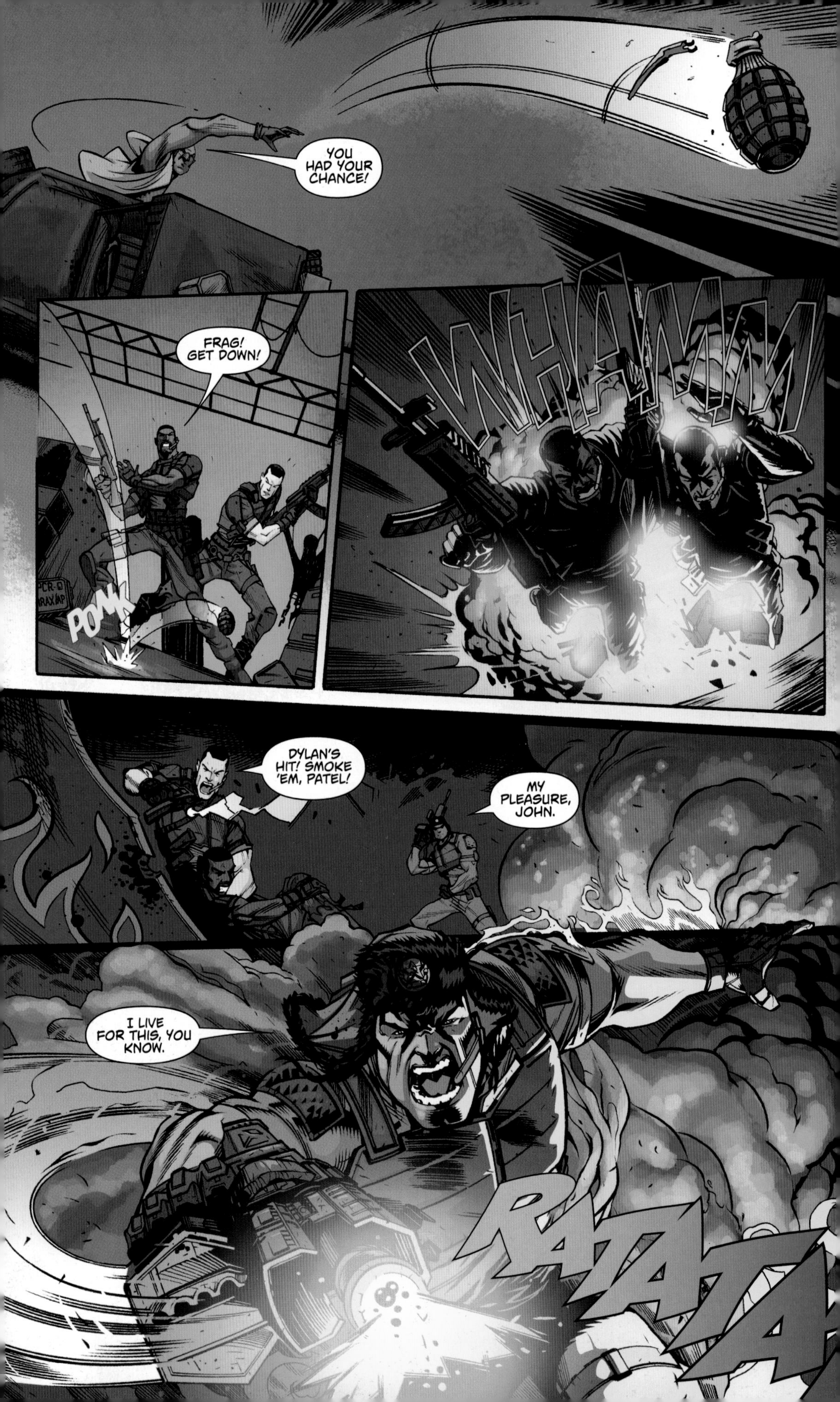
YOU HAD YOUR CHANCE!
FRAG! GET DOWN!
PONK
WHAMM
DYLAN'S HIT! SMOKE 'EM, PATEL!
MY PLEASURE, JOHN.
I LIVE FOR THIS, YOU KNOW.
RATAT

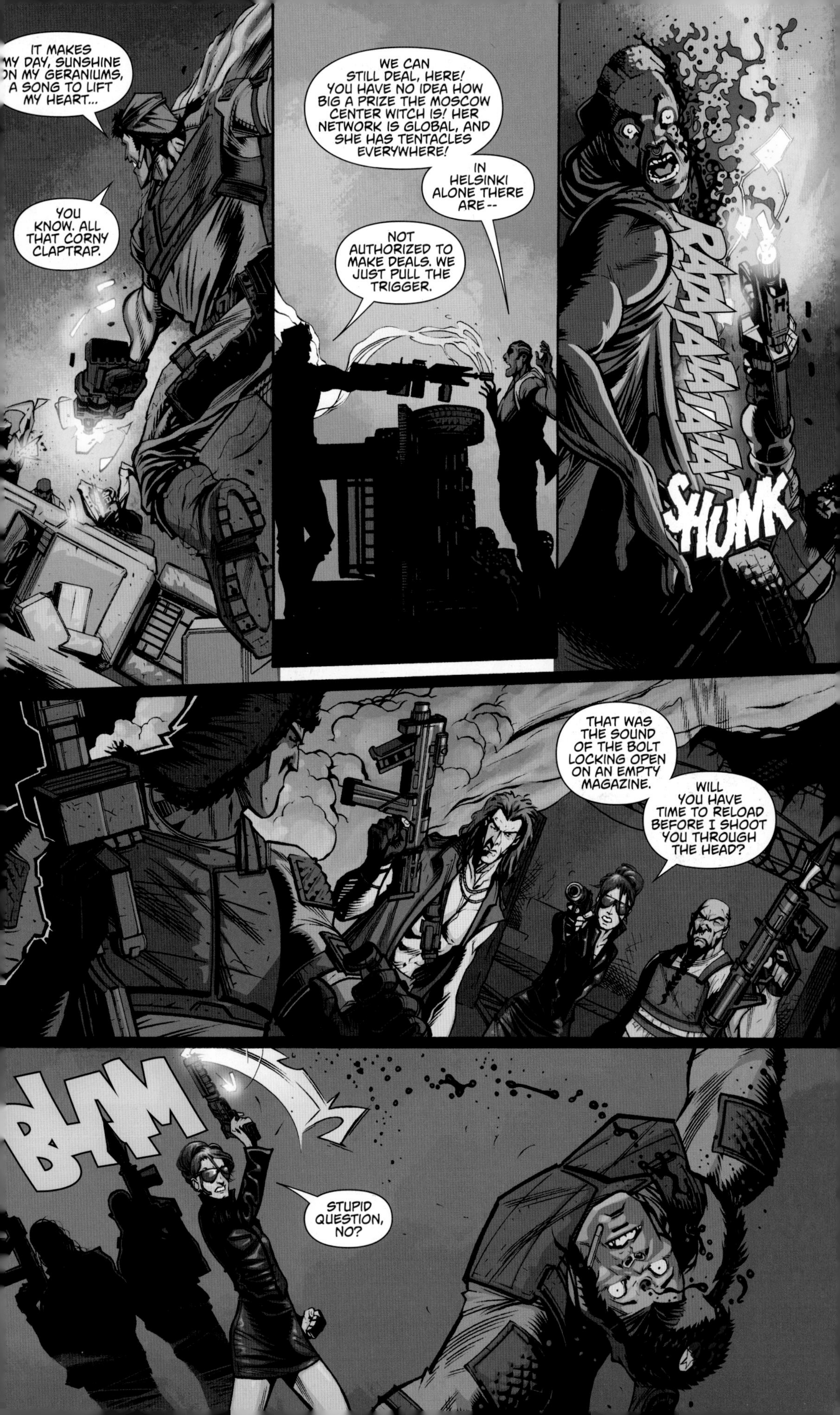
IT MAKES MY DAY, SUNSHINE ON MY GERANIUMS, A SONG TO LIFT MY HEART...
YOU KNOW. ALL THAT CORNY CLAPTRAP.
WE CAN STILL DEAL, HERE! YOU HAVE NO IDEA HOW BIG A PRIZE THE MOSCOW CENTER WITCH IS! HER NETWORK IS GLOBAL, AND SHE HAS TENTACLES EVERYWHERE!
IN HELSINKI ALONE THERE ARE --
NOT AUTHORIZED TO MAKE DEALS. WE JUST PULL THE TRIGGER.
SHUNK
THAT WAS THE SOUND OF THE BOLT LOCKING OPEN ON AN EMPTY MAGAZINE.
WILL YOU HAVE TIME TO RELOAD BEFORE I SHOOT YOU THROUGH THE HEAD?
BLAM
STUPID QUESTION, NO?

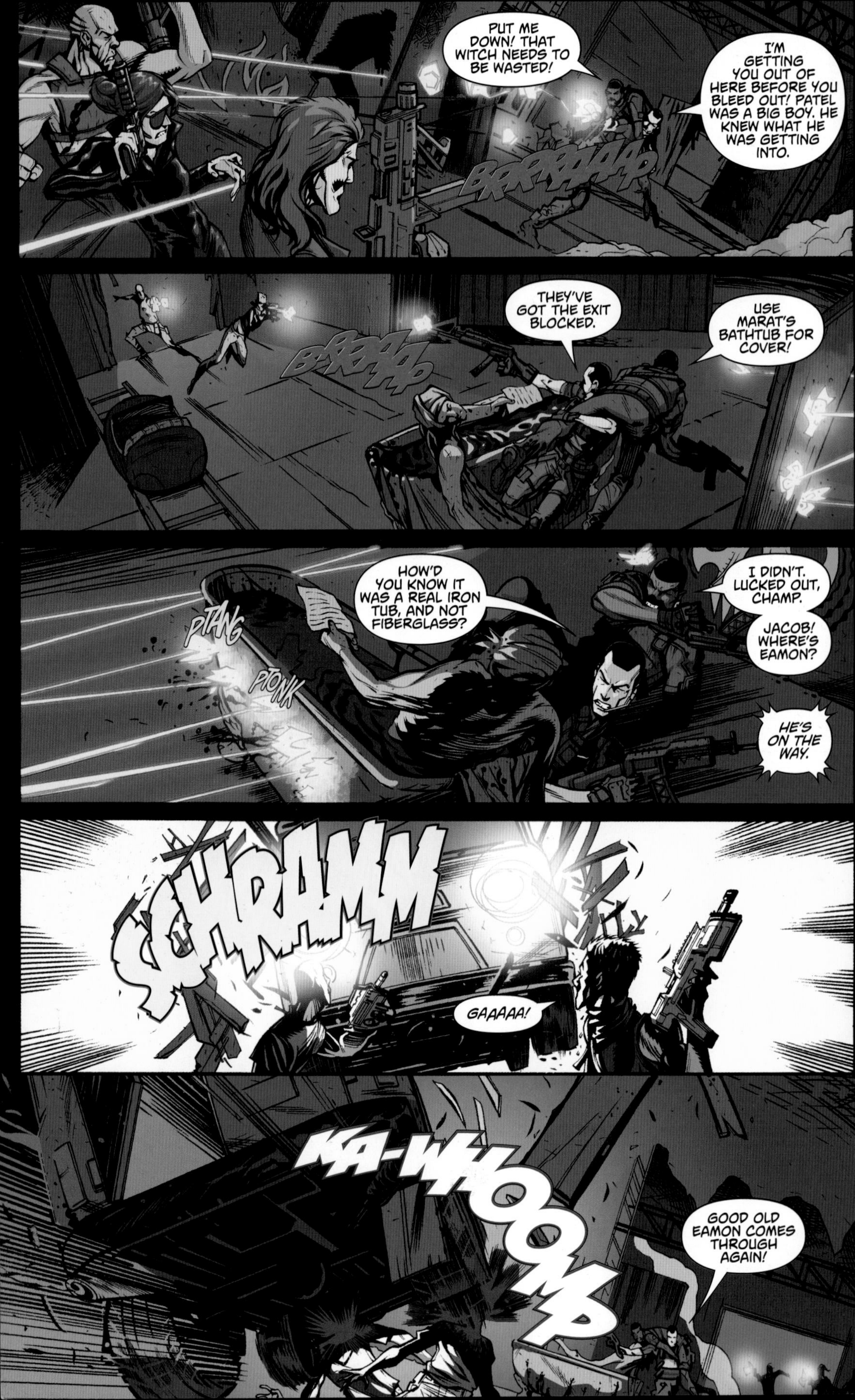
PUT ME DOWN! THAT WITCH NEEDS TO BE WASTED!
I'M GETTING YOU OUT OF HERE BEFORE YOU BLEED OUT! PATEL WAS A BIG BOY. HE KNEW WHAT HE WAS GETTING INTO.
BRRRAAAP
B-RRRAAAP
THEY'VE GOT THE EXIT BLOCKED.
USE MARAT'S BATHTUB FOR COVER!
HOW'D YOU KNOW IT WAS A REAL IRON TUB, AND NOT FIBERGLASS?
I DIDN'T. LUCKED OUT, CHAMP.
JACOB! WHERE'S EAMON?
PTANG
PTONK
HE'S ON THE WAY.
SCHRAMM
GAAAAA!
KA-WHOOMP
GOOD OLD EAMON COMES THROUGH AGAIN!

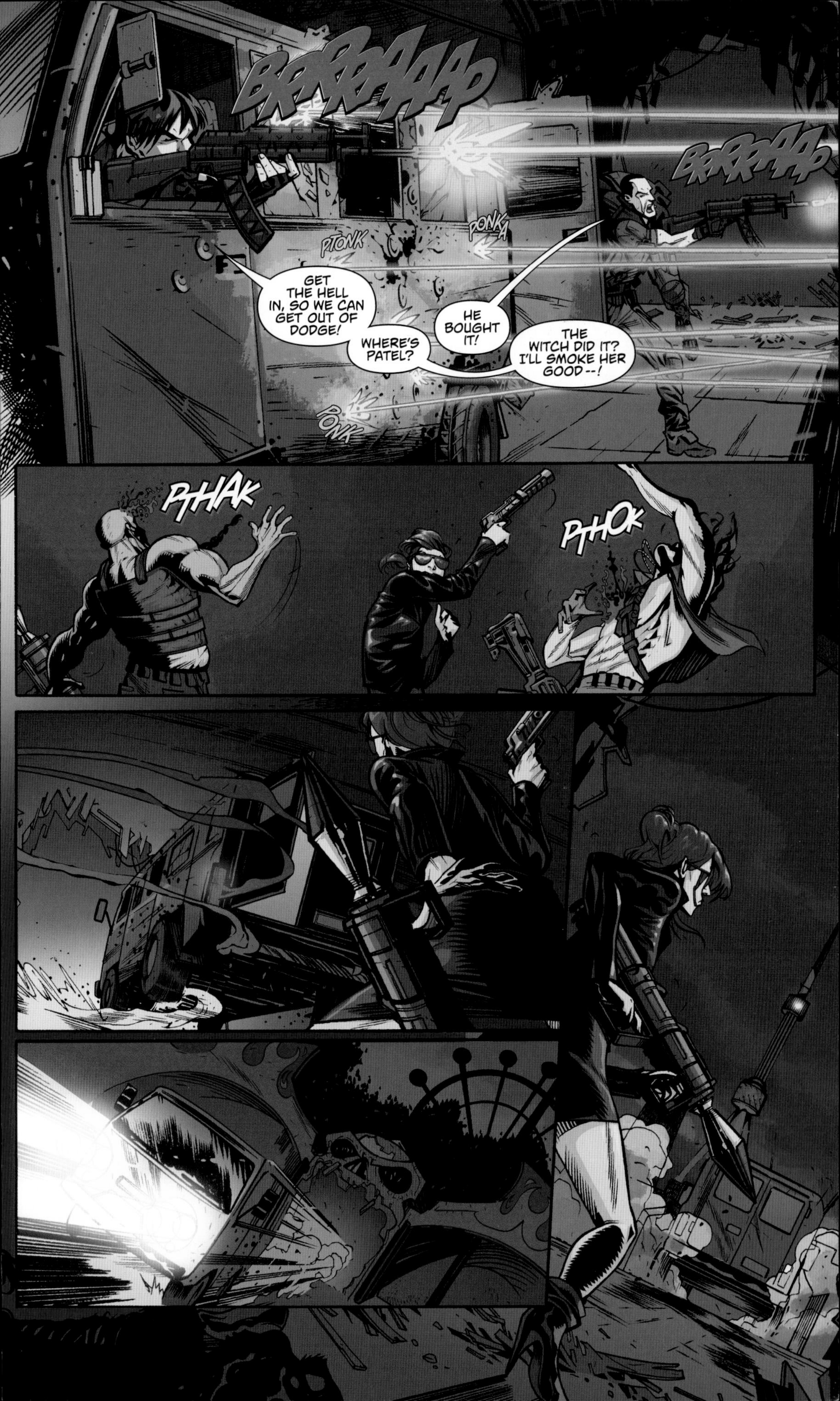
BRRRAAAP
BRRRAAP
PTONK
PONKA
GET THE HELL IN, SO WE CAN GET OUT OF DODGE!
WHERE'S PATEL?
HE BOUGHT IT!
THE WITCH DID IT? I'LL SMOKE HER GOOD--!
PONK
PTHAK
PTHOK

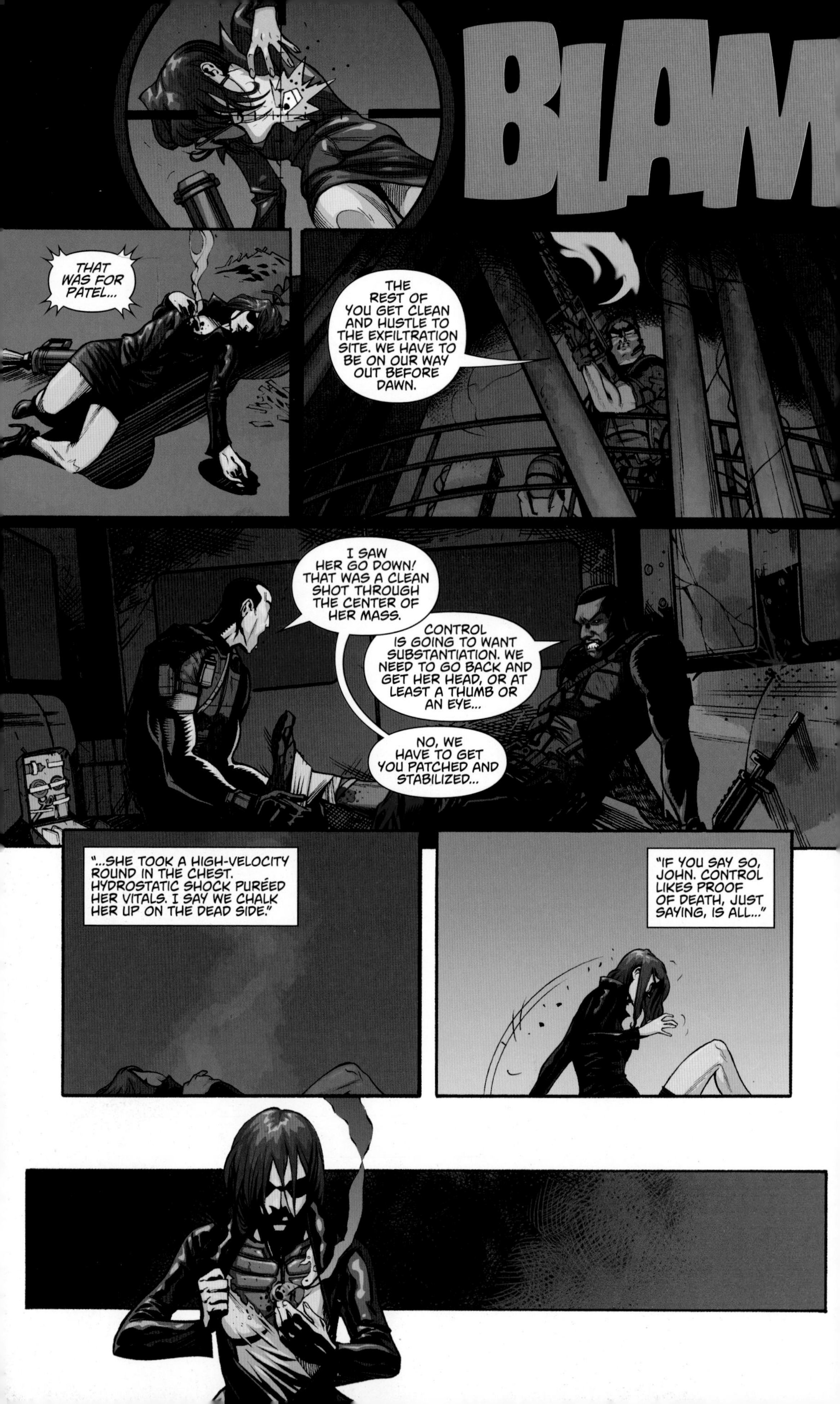

BLAM
THAT WAS FOR PATEL...
THE REST OF YOU GET CLEAN AND HUSTLE TO THE EXFILTRATION SITE. WE HAVE TO BE ON OUR WAY OUT BEFORE DAWN.
I SAW HER GO DOWN! THAT WAS A CLEAN SHOT THROUGH THE CENTER OF HER MASS.
CONTROL IS GOING TO WANT SUBSTANTIATION. WE NEED TO GO BACK AND GET HER HEAD, OR AT LEAST A THUMB OR AN EYE...
NO, WE HAVE TO GET YOU PATCHED AND STABILIZED...
"...SHE TOOK A HIGH-VELOCITY ROUND IN THE CHEST. HYDROSTATIC SHOCK PURÉED HER VITALS. I SAY WE CHALK HER UP ON THE DEAD SIDE."
"IF YOU SAY SO, JOHN. CONTROL LIKES PROOF OF DEATH, JUST SAYING, IS ALL..."

ANTHONY PALUMBO

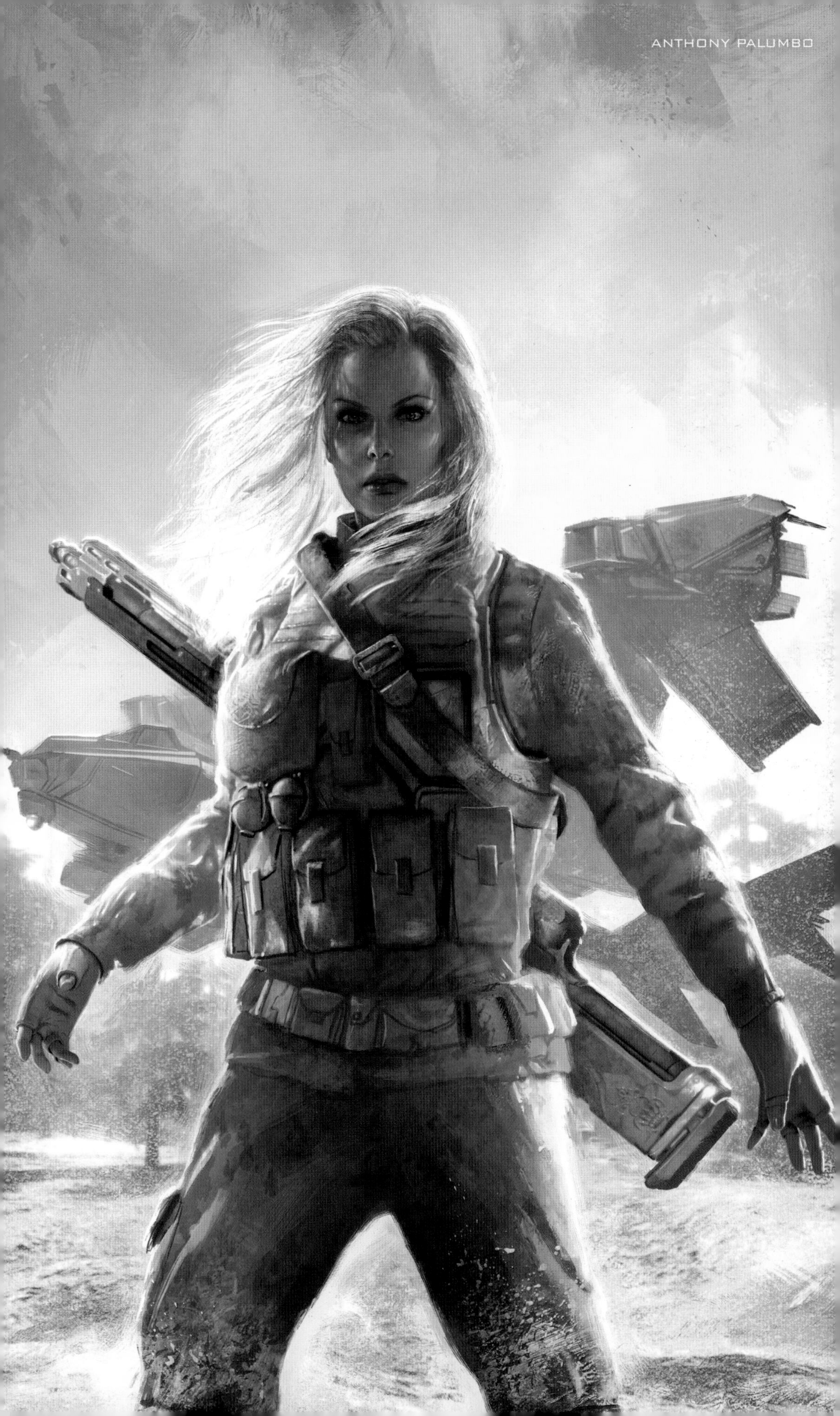

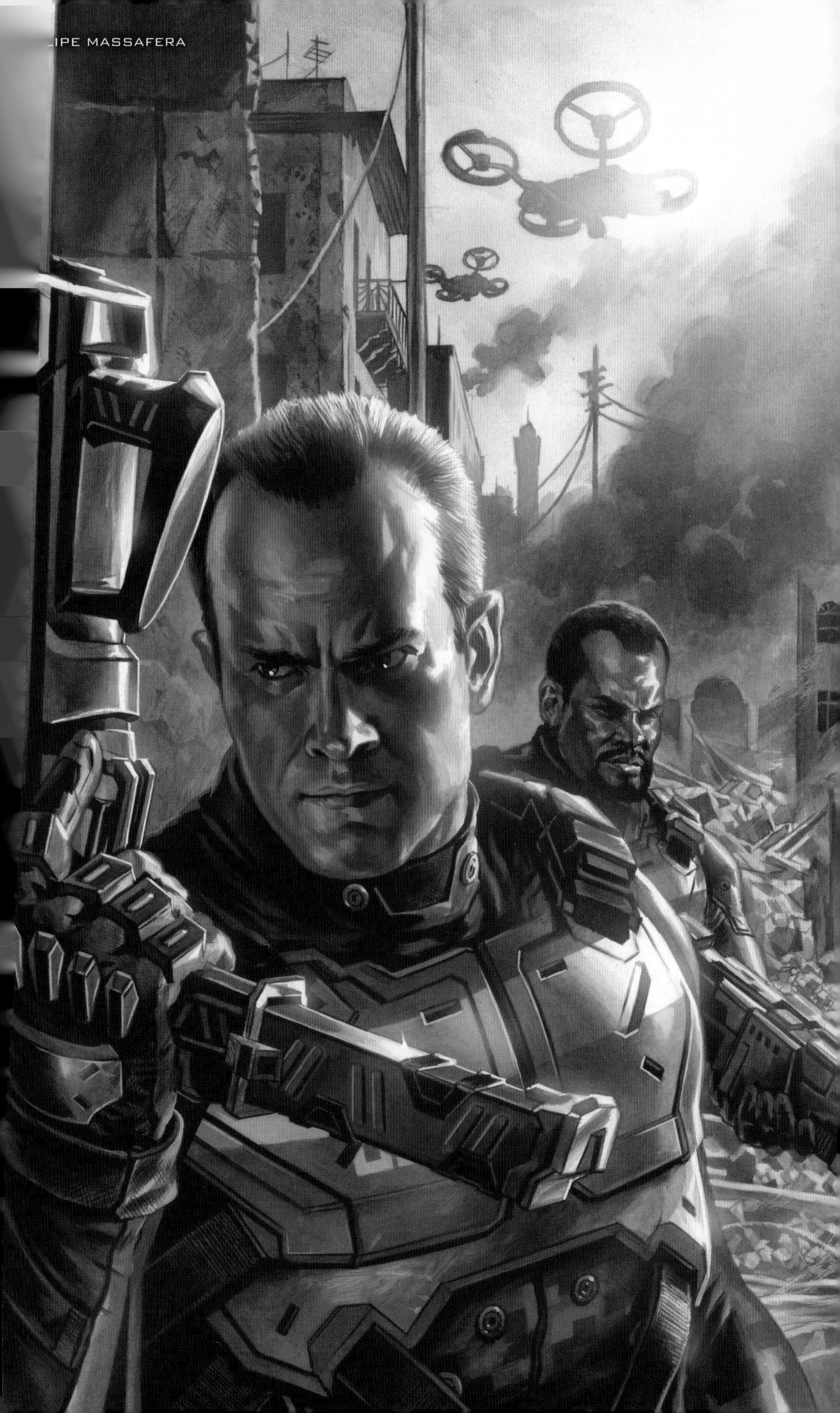

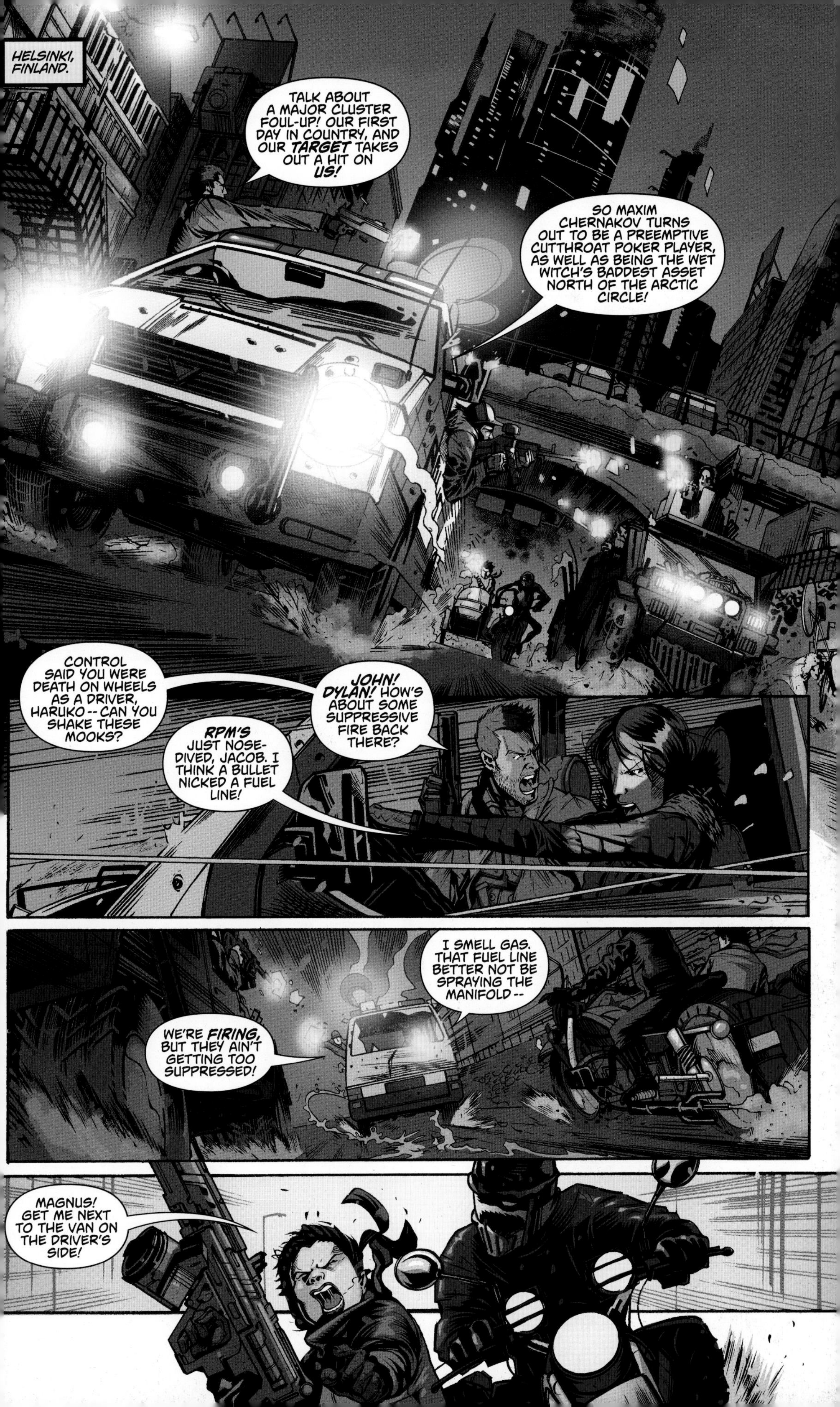
HELSINKI, FINLAND.
TALK ABOUT A MAJOR CLUSTER FOUL-UP! OUR FIRST DAY IN COUNTRY, AND OUR TARGET TAKES OUT A HIT ON US!
SO MAXIM CHERNAKOV TURNS OUT TO BE A PREEMPTIVE CUTTHROAT POKER PLAYER, AS WELL AS BEING THE WET WITCH'S BADDEST ASSET NORTH OF THE ARCTIC CIRCLE!
CONTROL SAID YOU WERE DEATH ON WHEELS AS A DRIVER, HARUKO -- CAN YOU SHAKE THESE MOOKS?
JOHN! DYLAN! HOW'S ABOUT SOME SUPPRESSIVE FIRE BACK THERE?
RPM'S JUST NOSE-DIVED, JACOB. I THINK A BULLET NICKED A FUEL LINE!
I SMELL GAS. THAT FUEL LINE BETTER NOT BE SPRAYING THE MANIFOLD --
WE'RE FIRING, BUT THEY AIN'T GETTING TOO SUPPRESSED!
MAGNUS! GET ME NEXT TO THE VAN ON THE DRIVER'S SIDE!

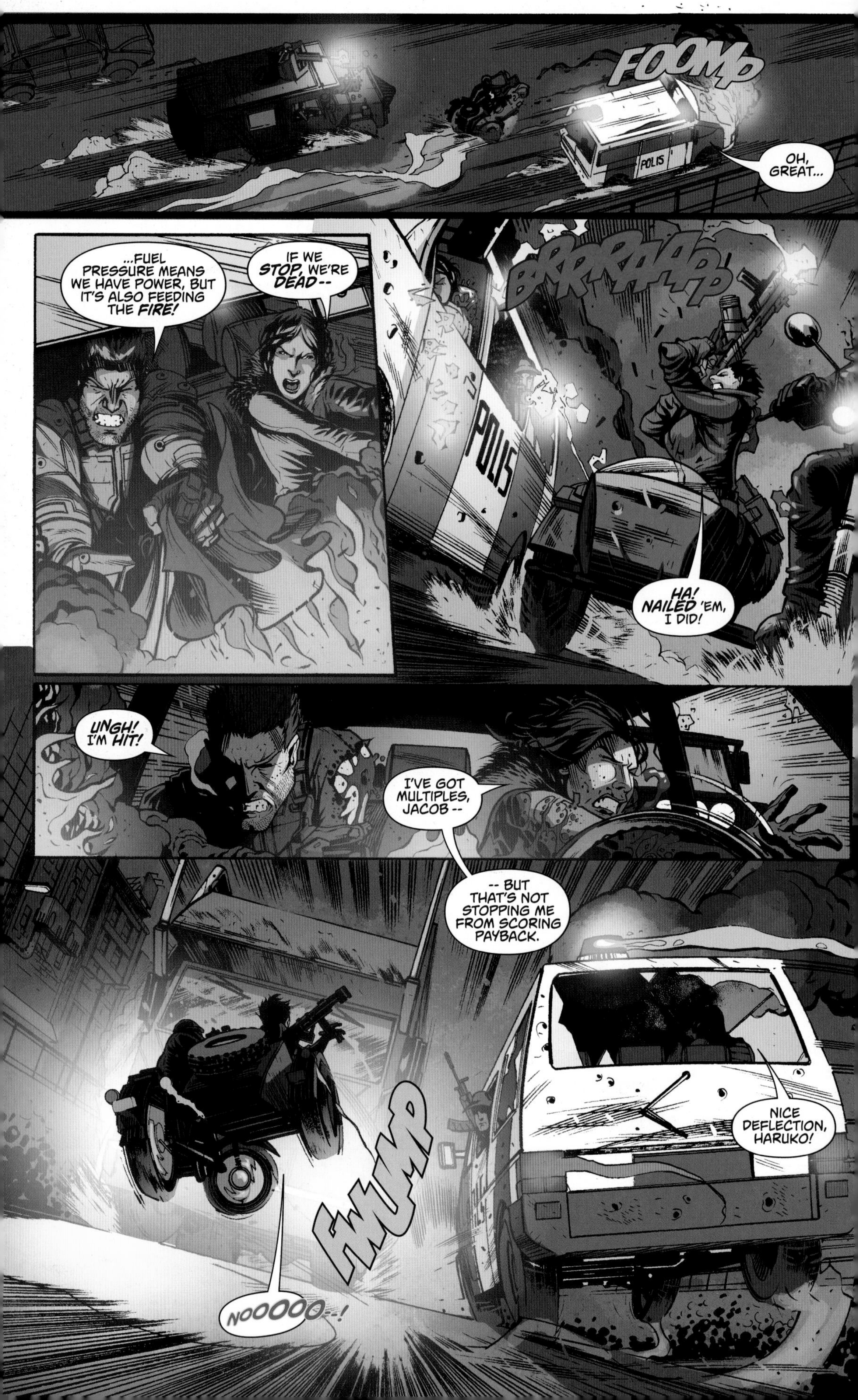
FOOMP
OH, GREAT...
POLIS
...FUEL PRESSURE MEANS WE HAVE POWER, BUT IT'S ALSO FEEDING THE FIRE!
IF WE STOP, WE'RE DEAD--
BRRRAAAP
POLIS
HA! NAILED 'EM, I DID!
UNGH! I'M HIT!
I'VE GOT MULTIPLES, JACOB --
-- BUT THAT'S NOT STOPPING ME FROM SCORING PAYBACK.
NICE DEFLECTION, HARUKO!
FWUMP
NOOOOO--!

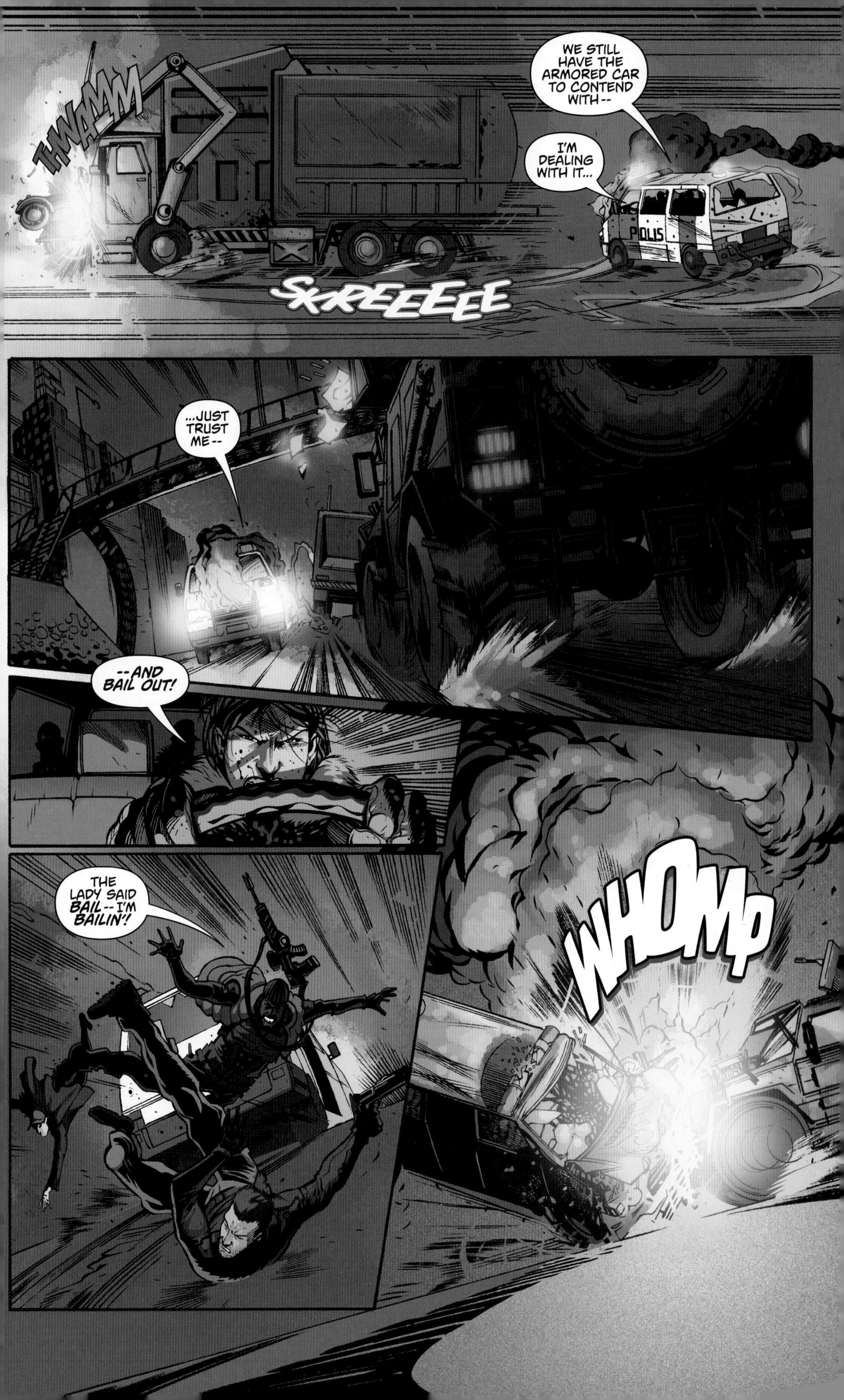
THWAAMM
WE STILL HAVE THE ARMORED CAR TO CONTEND WITH--
I'M DEALING WITH IT...
POLIS
SKREEEEEE
...JUST TRUST ME--
--AND BAIL OUT!
THE LADY SAID BAIL--I'M BAILIN'!
WHOMP

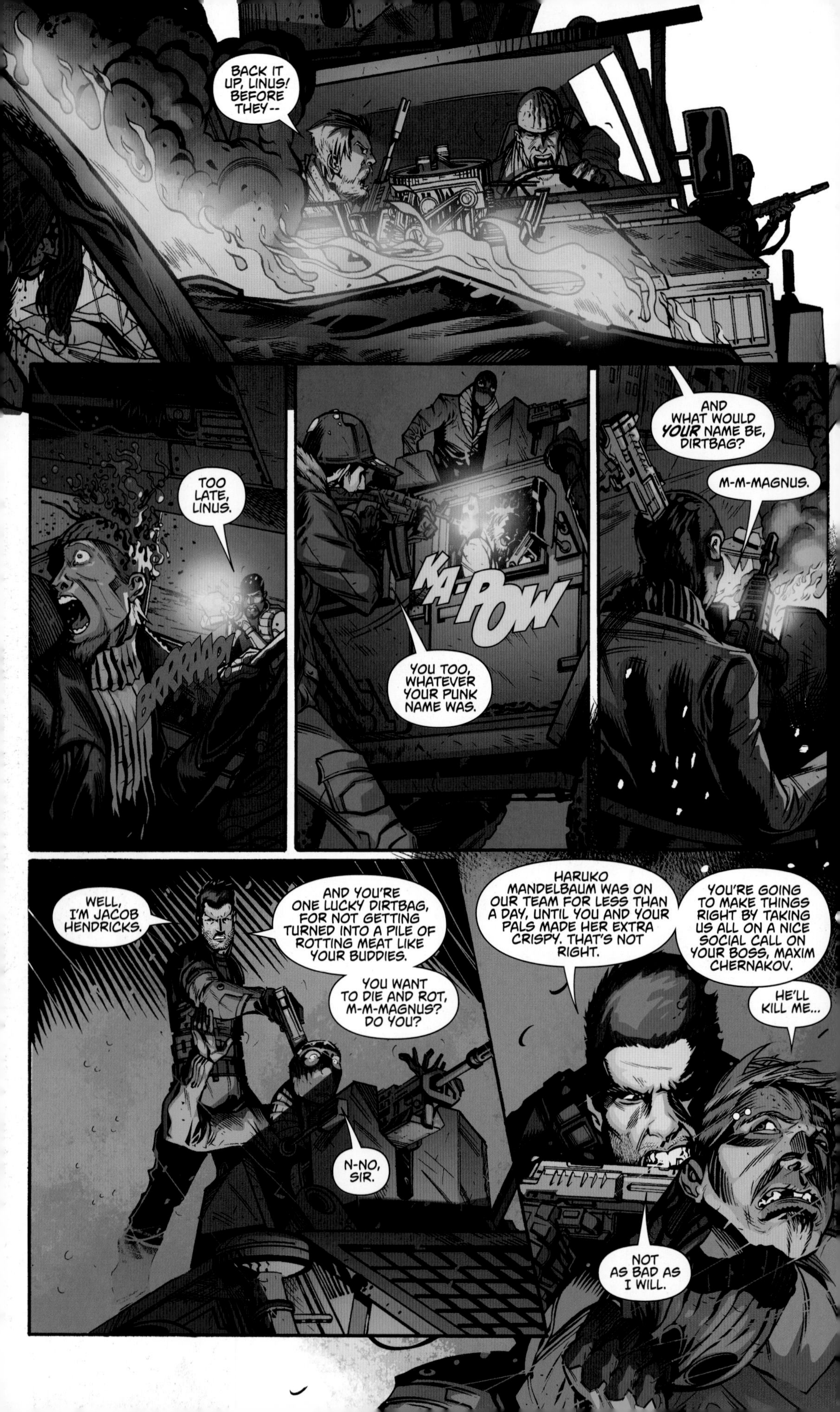
BACK IT UP, LINUS! BEFORE THEY--
TOO LATE, LINUS.
KA-POW
YOU TOO, WHATEVER YOUR PUNK NAME WAS.
AND WHAT WOULD YOUR NAME BE, DIRTBAG?
M-M-MAGNUS.
WELL, I'M JACOB HENDRICKS.
AND YOU'RE ONE LUCKY DIRTBAG, FOR NOT GETTING TURNED INTO A PILE OF ROTTING MEAT LIKE YOUR BUDDIES.
YOU WANT TO DIE AND ROT, M-M-MAGNUS? DO YOU?
N-NO, SIR.
HARUKO MANDELBAUM WAS ON OUR TEAM FOR LESS THAN A DAY, UNTIL YOU AND YOUR PALS MADE HER EXTRA CRISPY. THAT'S NOT RIGHT.
YOU'RE GOING TO MAKE THINGS RIGHT BY TAKING US ALL ON A NICE SOCIAL CALL ON YOUR BOSS, MAXIM CHERNAKOV.
HE'LL KILL ME...
NOT AS BAD AS I WILL.

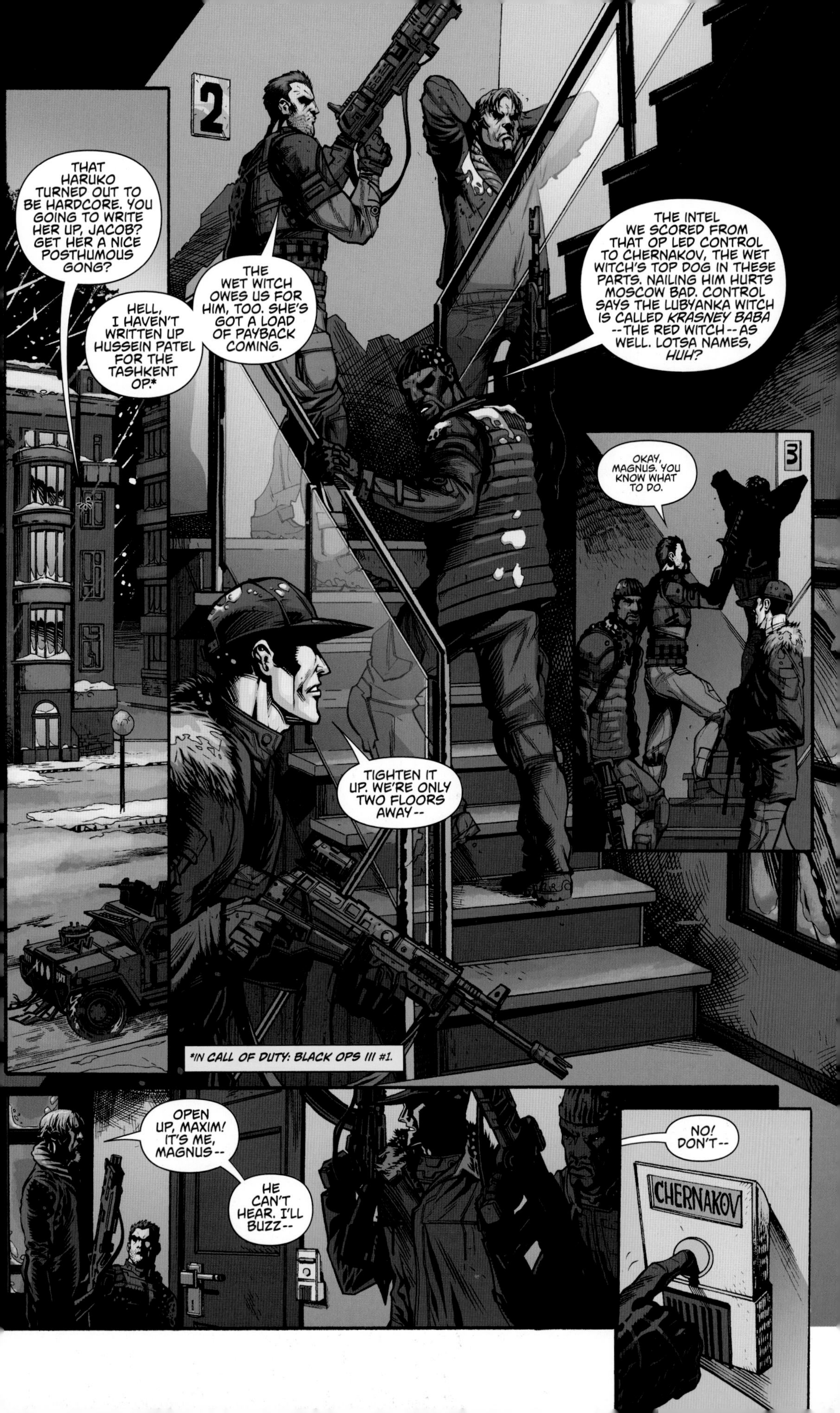
THAT HARUKO TURNED OUT TO BE HARDCORE. YOU GOING TO WRITE HER UP, JACOB? GET HER A NICE POSTHUMOUS GONG?
HELL, I HAVEN'T WRITTEN UP HUSSEIN PATEL FOR THE TASHKENT OP.*
THE WET WITCH OWES US FOR HIM, TOO. SHE'S GOT A LOAD OF PAYBACK COMING.
THE INTEL WE SCORED FROM THAT OP LED CONTROL TO CHERNAKOV, THE WET WITCH'S TOP DOG IN THESE PARTS. NAILING HIM HURTS MOSCOW BAD. CONTROL SAYS THE LUBYANKA WITCH IS CALLED *KRASNEY BABA* --THE RED WITCH--AS WELL. LOTSA NAMES, *HUH?*
TIGHTEN IT UP. WE'RE ONLY TWO FLOORS AWAY--
*IN CALL OF DUTY: BLACK OPS III #1.
OKAY, MAGNUS. YOU KNOW WHAT TO DO.
OPEN UP, MAXIM! IT'S ME, MAGNUS--
HE CAN'T HEAR. I'LL BUZZ--
NO! DON'T--
CHERNAKOV

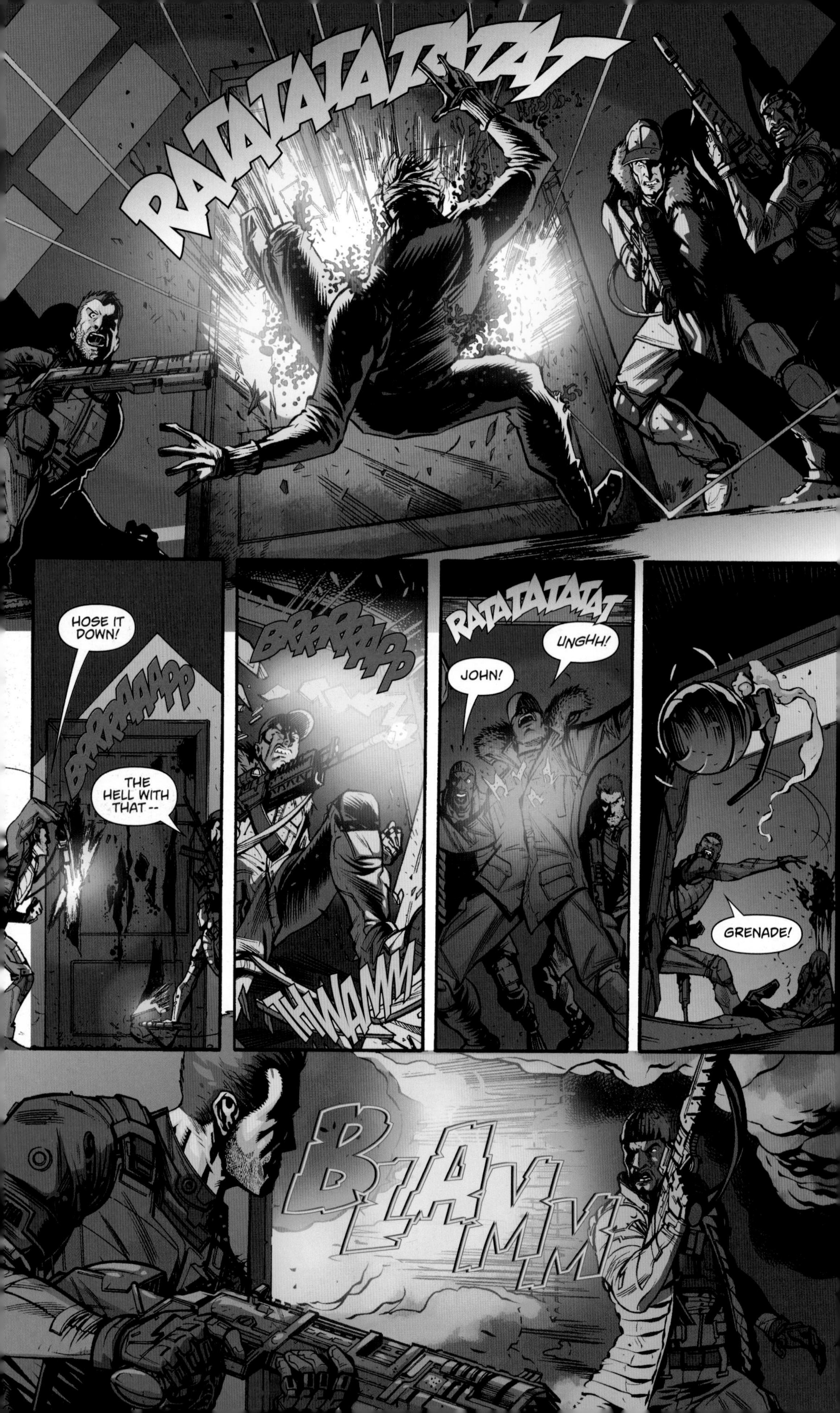
RATATATATATAT
HOSE IT DOWN!
BRRRAAAPP
THE HELL WITH THAT --
BRRRRAPP
THWAMM
RATATATATAT
UNGHH!
JOHN!
GRENADE!
BLAMMM

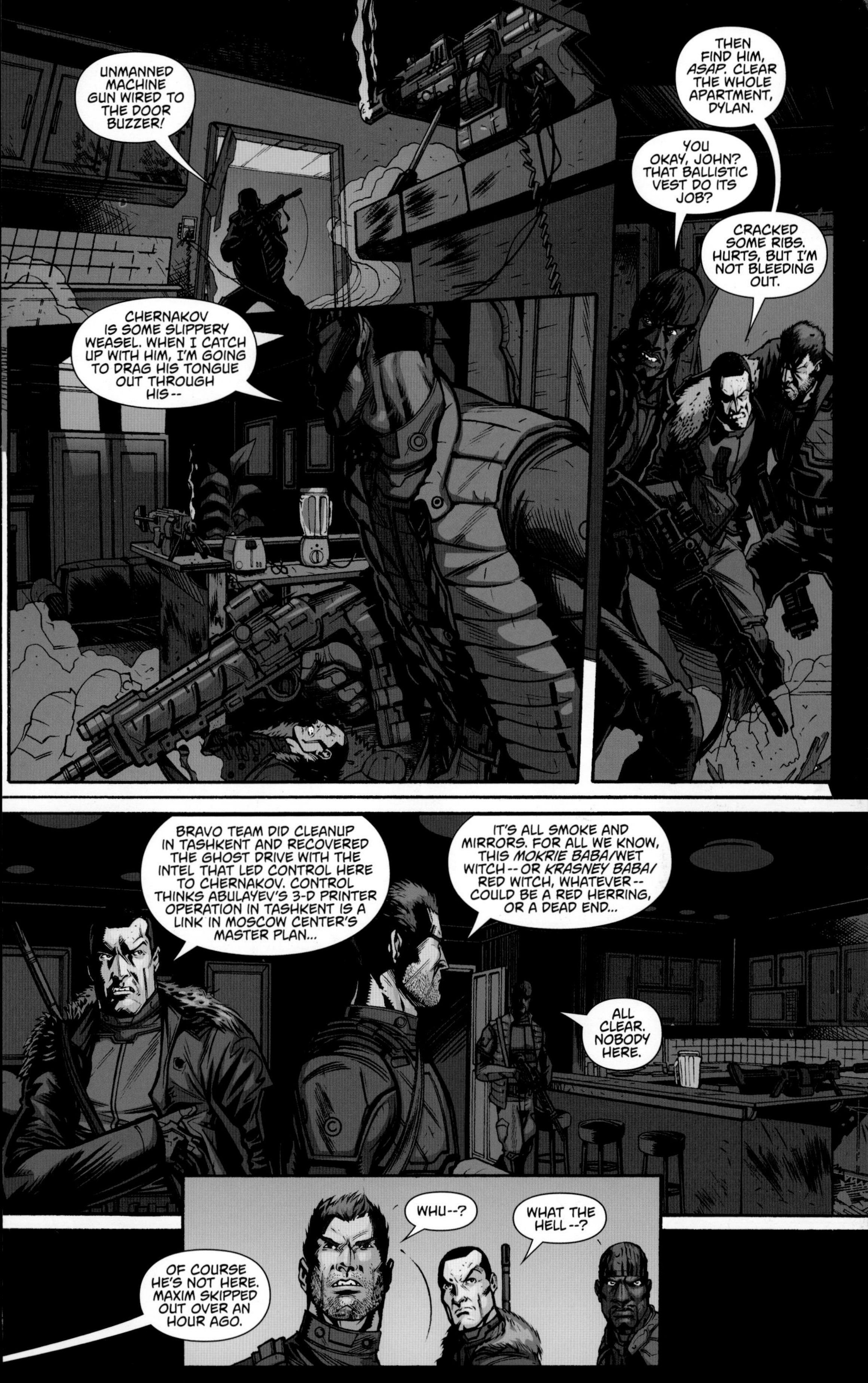

UNMANNED MACHINE GUN WIRED TO THE DOOR BUZZER!
THEN FIND HIM, ASAP. CLEAR THE WHOLE APARTMENT, DYLAN.
YOU OKAY, JOHN? THAT BALLISTIC VEST DO ITS JOB?
CRACKED SOME RIBS. HURTS, BUT I'M NOT BLEEDING OUT.
CHERNAKOV IS SOME SLIPPERY WEASEL. WHEN I CATCH UP WITH HIM, I'M GOING TO DRAG HIS TONGUE OUT THROUGH HIS--
BRAVO TEAM DID CLEANUP IN TASHKENT AND RECOVERED THE GHOST DRIVE WITH THE INTEL THAT LED CONTROL HERE TO CHERNAKOV. CONTROL THINKS ABULAYEV'S 3-D PRINTER OPERATION IN TASHKENT IS A LINK IN MOSCOW CENTER'S MASTER PLAN...
IT'S ALL SMOKE AND MIRRORS. FOR ALL WE KNOW, THIS *MOKRIE BABA*/WET WITCH -- OR *KRASNEY BABA*/ RED WITCH, WHATEVER -- COULD BE A RED HERRING, OR A DEAD END...
ALL CLEAR. NOBODY HERE.
OF COURSE HE'S NOT HERE. MAXIM SKIPPED OUT OVER AN HOUR AGO.
WHU--?
WHAT THE HELL--?

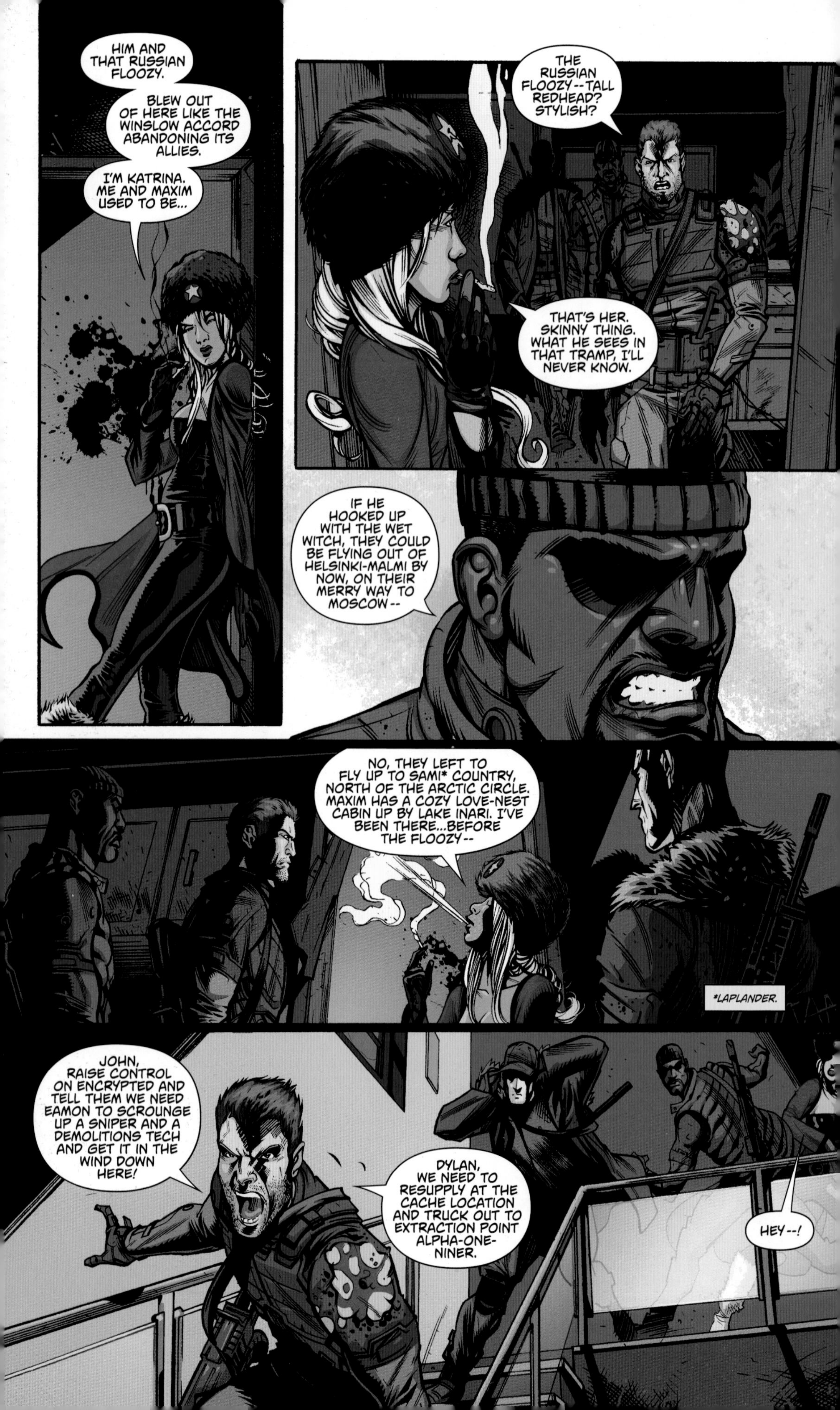

HIM AND THAT RUSSIAN FLOOZY.
BLEW OUT OF HERE LIKE THE WINSLOW ACCORD ABANDONING ITS ALLIES.
I'M KATRINA. ME AND MAXIM USED TO BE...
THE RUSSIAN FLOOZY--TALL REDHEAD? STYLISH?
THAT'S HER. SKINNY THING. WHAT HE SEES IN THAT TRAMP, I'LL NEVER KNOW.
IF HE HOOKED UP WITH THE WET WITCH, THEY COULD BE FLYING OUT OF HELSINKI-MALMI BY NOW, ON THEIR MERRY WAY TO MOSCOW--
NO, THEY LEFT TO FLY UP TO SAMI* COUNTRY, NORTH OF THE ARCTIC CIRCLE. MAXIM HAS A COZY LOVE-NEST CABIN UP BY LAKE INARI. I'VE BEEN THERE...BEFORE THE FLOOZY--
*LAPLANDER.
JOHN, RAISE CONTROL ON ENCRYPTED AND TELL THEM WE NEED EAMON TO SCROUNGE UP A SNIPER AND A DEMOLITIONS TECH AND GET IT IN THE WIND DOWN HERE!
DYLAN, WE NEED TO RESUPPLY AT THE CACHE LOCATION AND TRUCK OUT TO EXTRACTION POINT ALPHA-ONE-NINER.
HEY--!

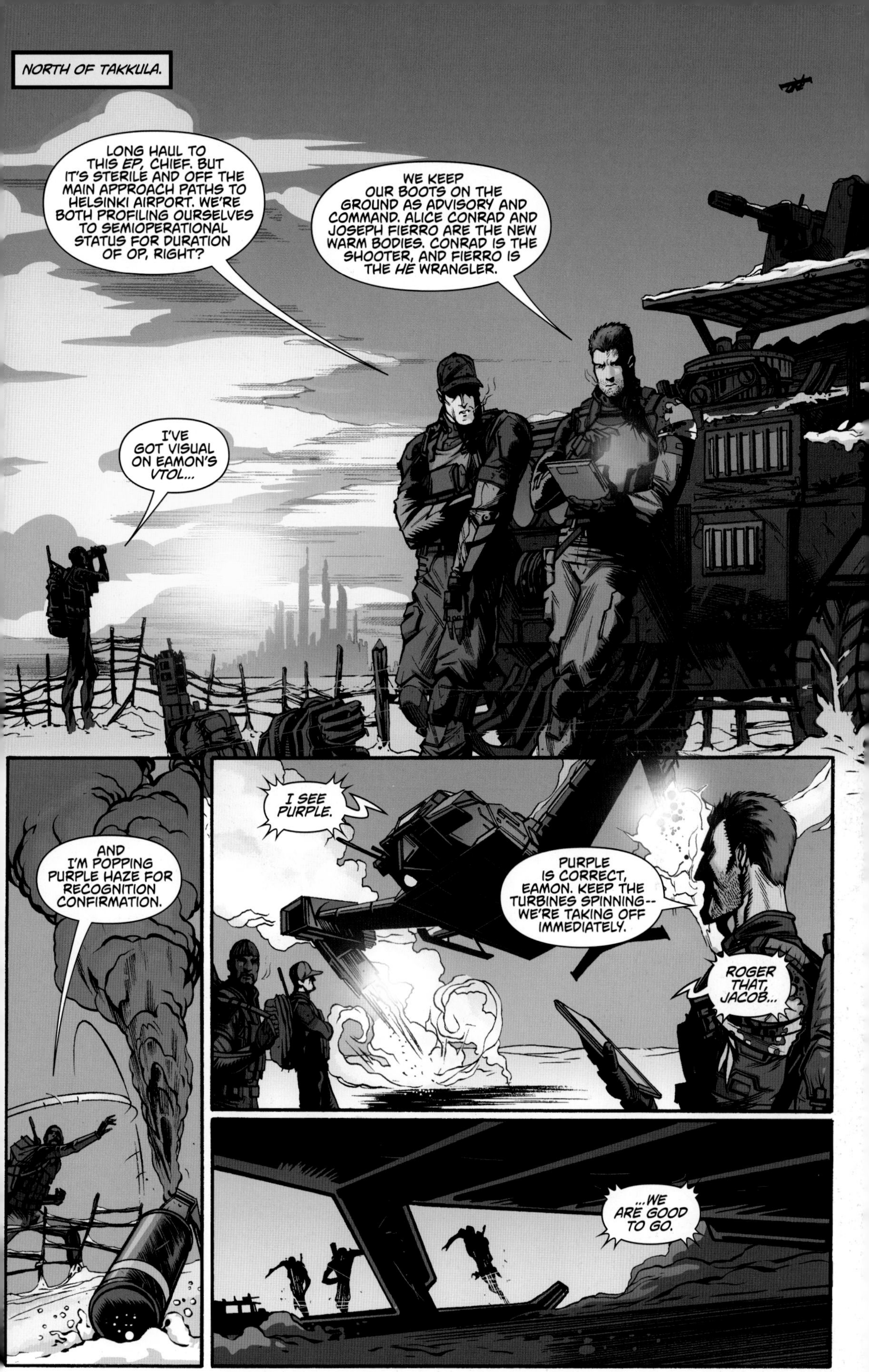
NORTH OF TAKKULA.
LONG HAUL TO THIS EP, CHIEF. BUT IT'S STERILE AND OFF THE MAIN APPROACH PATHS TO HELSINKI AIRPORT. WE'RE BOTH PROFILING OURSELVES TO SEMIOPERATIONAL STATUS FOR DURATION OF OP, RIGHT?
WE KEEP OUR BOOTS ON THE GROUND AS ADVISORY AND COMMAND. ALICE CONRAD AND JOSEPH FIERRO ARE THE NEW WARM BODIES. CONRAD IS THE SHOOTER, AND FIERRO IS THE HE WRANGLER.
I'VE GOT VISUAL ON EAMON'S VTOL...
AND I'M POPPING PURPLE HAZE FOR RECOGNITION CONFIRMATION.
I SEE PURPLE.
PURPLE IS CORRECT, EAMON. KEEP THE TURBINES SPINNING-- WE'RE TAKING OFF IMMEDIATELY.
ROGER THAT, JACOB...
...WE ARE GOOD TO GO.

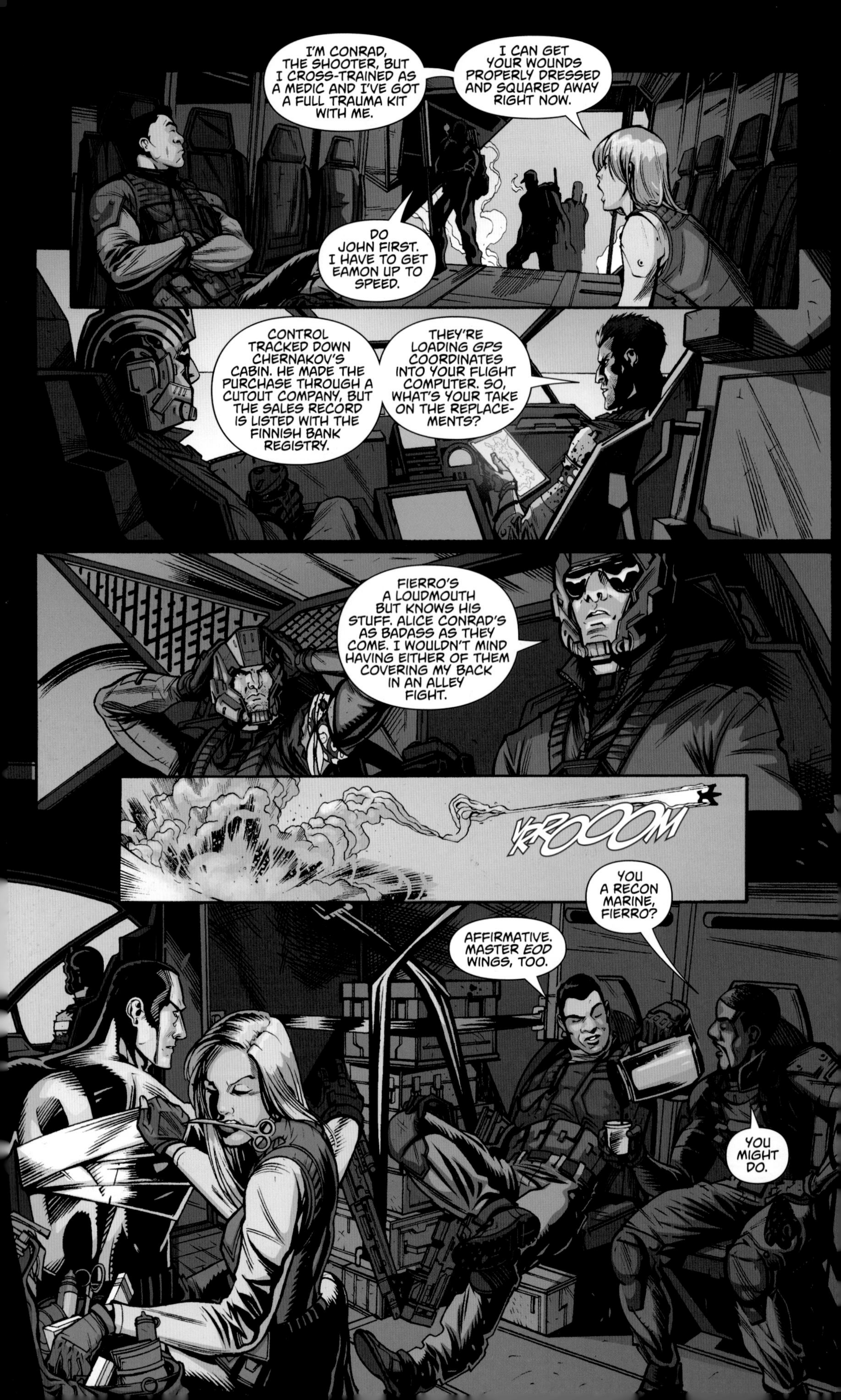

I'M CONRAD, THE SHOOTER, BUT I CROSS-TRAINED AS A MEDIC AND I'VE GOT A FULL TRAUMA KIT WITH ME.
I CAN GET YOUR WOUNDS PROPERLY DRESSED AND SQUARED AWAY RIGHT NOW.
DO JOHN FIRST. I HAVE TO GET EAMON UP TO SPEED.
CONTROL TRACKED DOWN CHERNAKOV'S CABIN. HE MADE THE PURCHASE THROUGH A CUTOUT COMPANY, BUT THE SALES RECORD IS LISTED WITH THE FINNISH BANK REGISTRY.
THEY'RE LOADING GPS COORDINATES INTO YOUR FLIGHT COMPUTER. SO, WHAT'S YOUR TAKE ON THE REPLACE-MENTS?
FIERRO'S A LOUDMOUTH BUT KNOWS HIS STUFF. ALICE CONRAD'S AS BADASS AS THEY COME. I WOULDN'T MIND HAVING EITHER OF THEM COVERING MY BACK IN AN ALLEY FIGHT.
VKROOOOM
YOU A RECON MARINE, FIERRO?
AFFIRMATIVE. MASTER EOD WINGS, TOO.
YOU MIGHT DO.

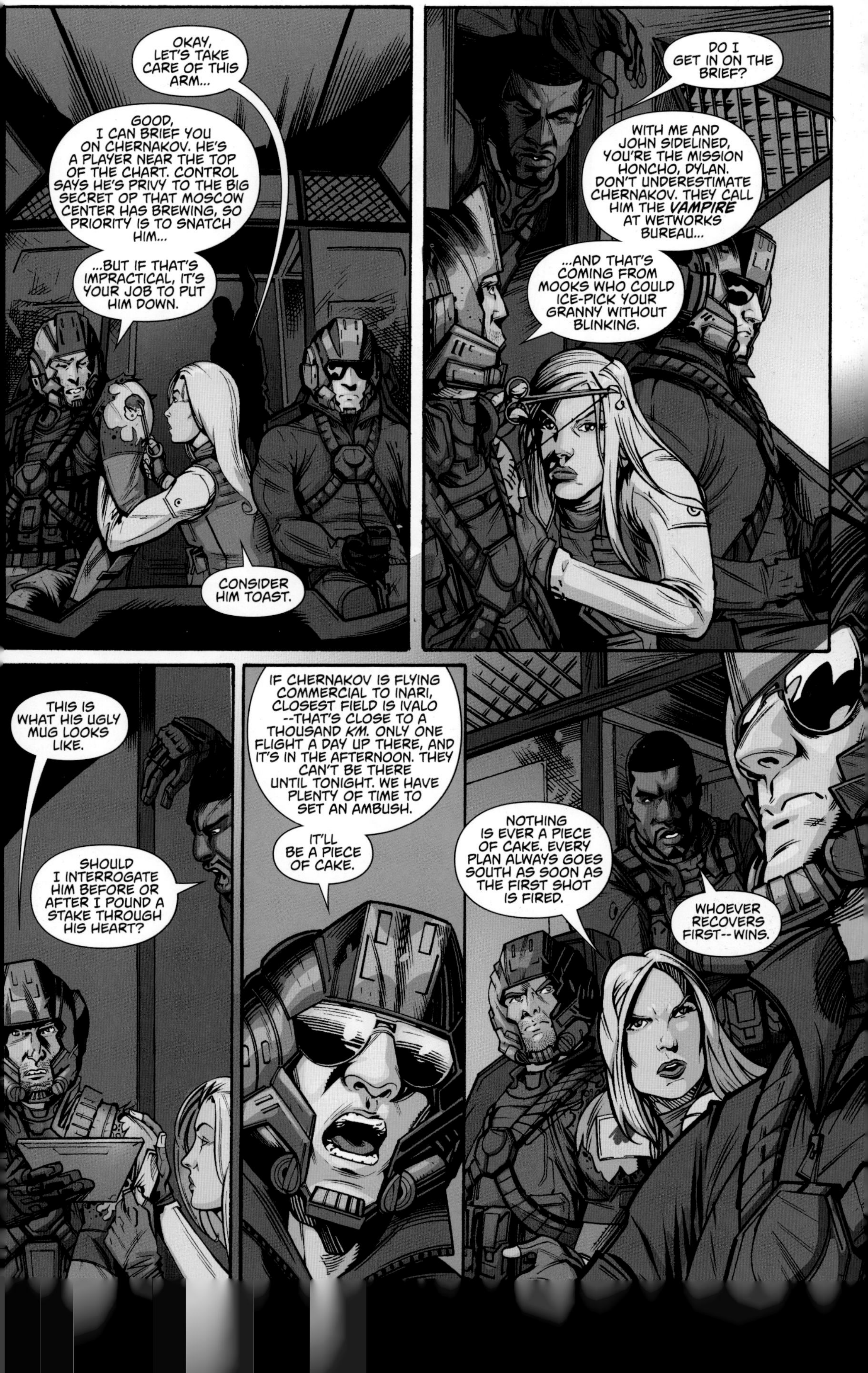
OKAY, LET'S TAKE CARE OF THIS ARM...
GOOD, I CAN BRIEF YOU ON CHERNAKOV. HE'S A PLAYER NEAR THE TOP OF THE CHART. CONTROL SAYS HE'S PRIVY TO THE BIG SECRET OP THAT MOSCOW CENTER HAS BREWING, SO PRIORITY IS TO SNATCH HIM...
...BUT IF THAT'S IMPRACTICAL, IT'S YOUR JOB TO PUT HIM DOWN.
CONSIDER HIM TOAST.
DO I GET IN ON THE BRIEF?
WITH ME AND JOHN SIDELINED, YOU'RE THE MISSION HONCHO, DYLAN. DON'T UNDERESTIMATE CHERNAKOV. THEY CALL HIM THE *VAMPIRE* AT WETWORKS BUREAU...
...AND THAT'S COMING FROM MOOKS WHO COULD ICE-PICK YOUR GRANNY WITHOUT BLINKING.
THIS IS WHAT HIS UGLY MUG LOOKS LIKE.
SHOULD I INTERROGATE HIM BEFORE OR AFTER I POUND A STAKE THROUGH HIS HEART?
IF CHERNAKOV IS FLYING COMMERCIAL TO INARI, CLOSEST FIELD IS IVALO --THAT'S CLOSE TO A THOUSAND *KM*. ONLY ONE FLIGHT A DAY UP THERE, AND IT'S IN THE AFTERNOON. THEY CAN'T BE THERE UNTIL TONIGHT. WE HAVE PLENTY OF TIME TO SET AN AMBUSH.
IT'LL BE A PIECE OF CAKE.
NOTHING IS EVER A PIECE OF CAKE. EVERY PLAN ALWAYS GOES SOUTH AS SOON AS THE FIRST SHOT IS FIRED.
WHOEVER RECOVERS FIRST--WINS.

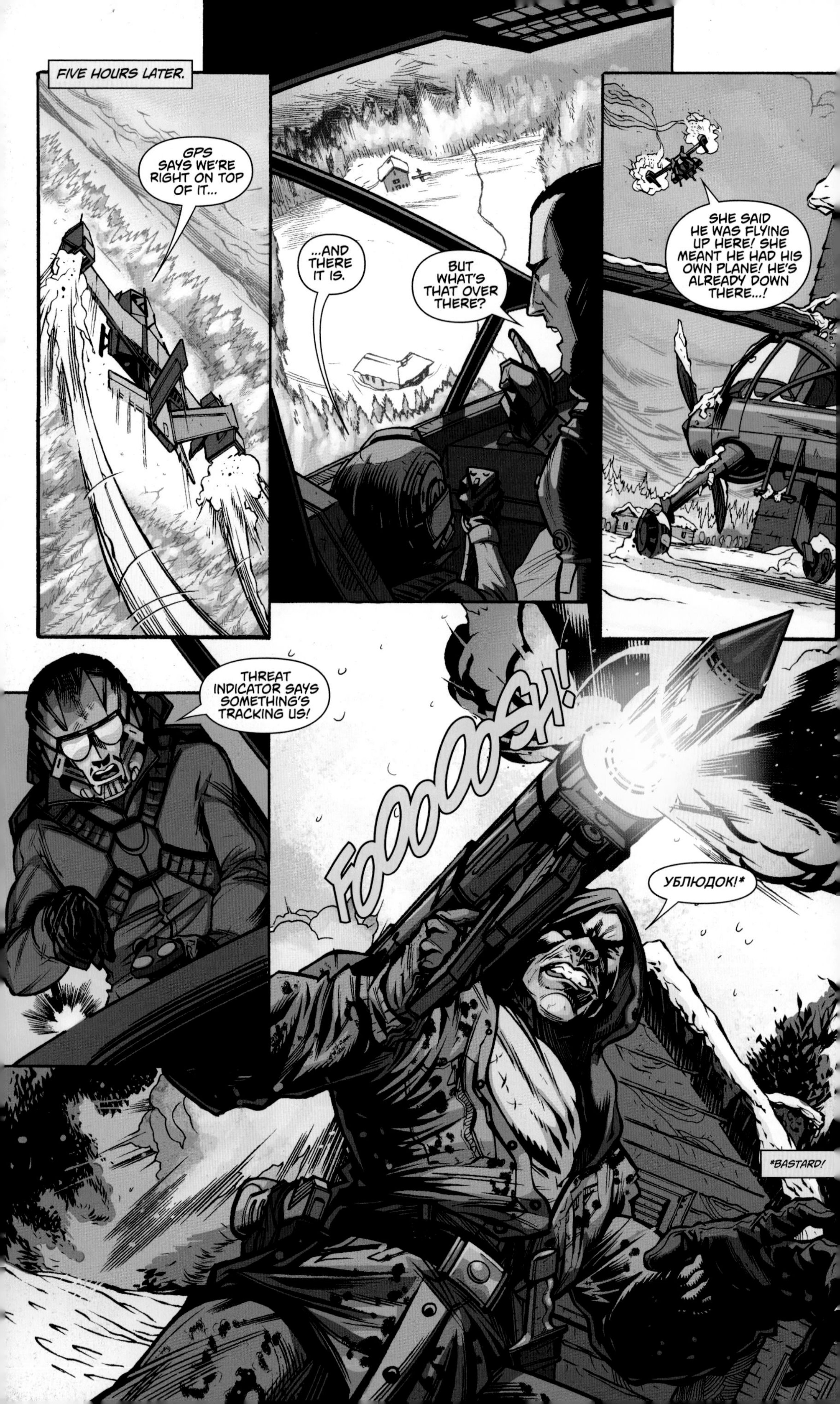
FIVE HOURS LATER.
GPS SAYS WE'RE RIGHT ON TOP OF IT...
...AND THERE IT IS.
BUT WHAT'S THAT OVER THERE?
SHE SAID HE WAS FLYING UP HERE! SHE MEANT HE HAD HIS OWN PLANE! HE'S ALREADY DOWN THERE...!
THREAT INDICATOR SAYS SOMETHING'S TRACKING US!
FOOOOOSH!
УБЛЮДОК!*
*BASTARD!

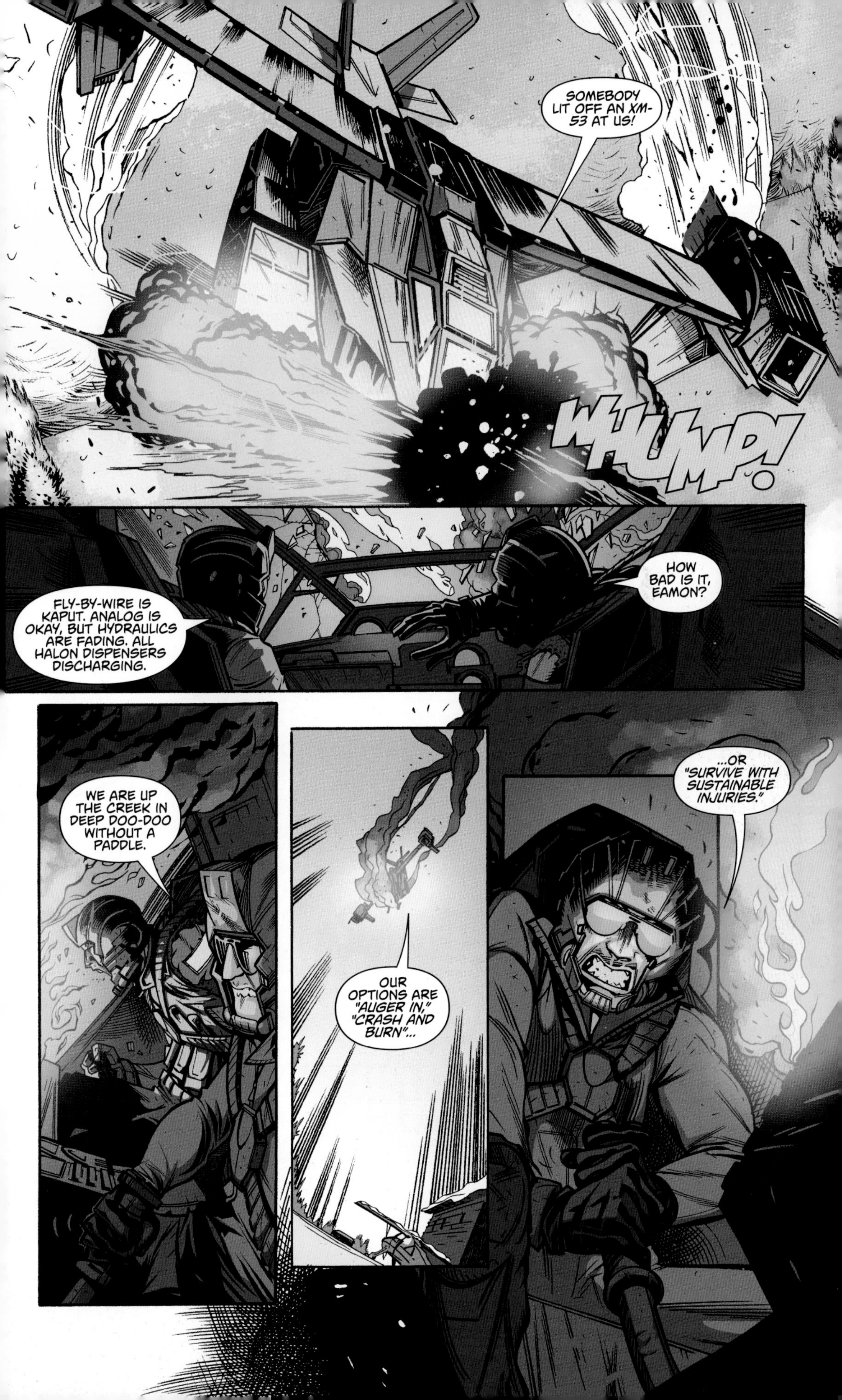
SOMEBODY LIT OFF AN XM-53 AT US!
WHUMP!
HOW BAD IS IT, EAMON?
FLY-BY-WIRE IS KAPUT. ANALOG IS OKAY, BUT HYDRAULICS ARE FADING. ALL HALON DISPENSERS DISCHARGING.
WE ARE UP THE CREEK IN DEEP DOO-DOO WITHOUT A PADDLE.
OUR OPTIONS ARE "AUGER IN," "CRASH AND BURN"...
...OR "SURVIVE WITH SUSTAINABLE INJURIES."

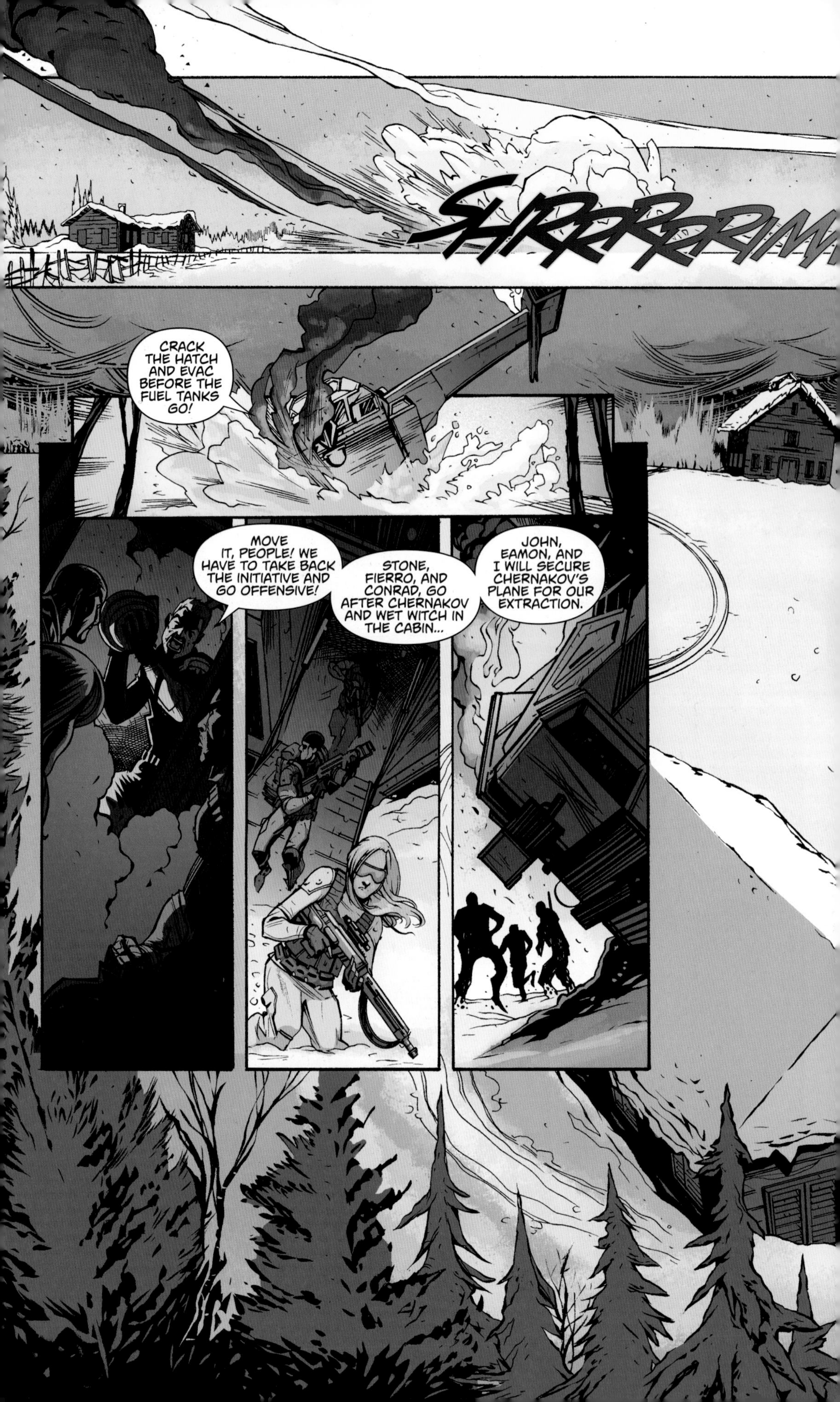
SHRRRRRIMM
CRACK THE HATCH AND EVAC BEFORE THE FUEL TANKS GO!
MOVE IT, PEOPLE! WE HAVE TO TAKE BACK THE INITIATIVE AND GO OFFENSIVE!
STONE, FIERRO, AND CONRAD, GO AFTER CHERNAKOV AND WET WITCH IN THE CABIN...
JOHN, EAMON, AND I WILL SECURE CHERNAKOV'S PLANE FOR OUR EXTRACTION.

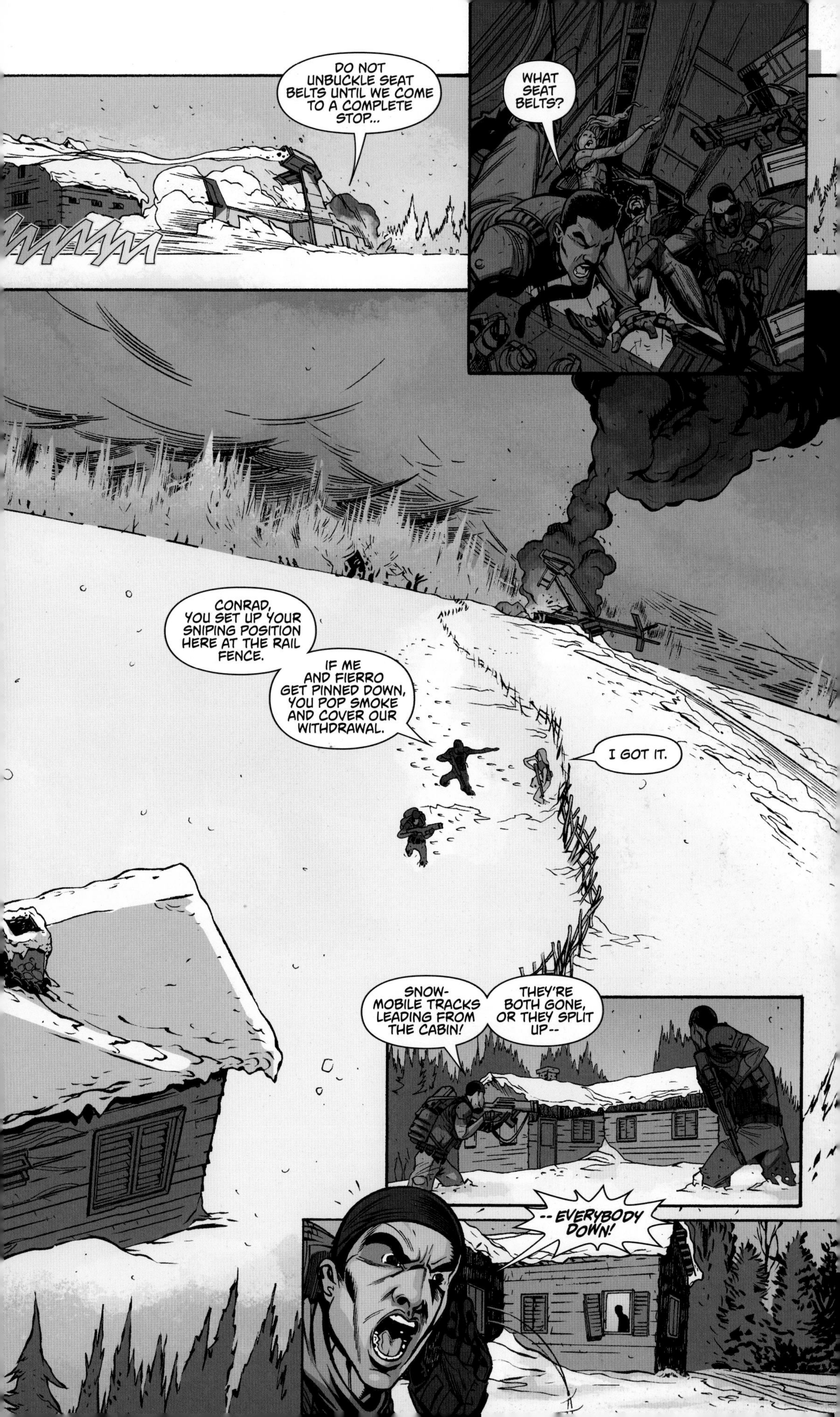
DO NOT UNBUCKLE SEAT BELTS UNTIL WE COME TO A COMPLETE STOP...
WHAT SEAT BELTS?
WMMM
CONRAD, YOU SET UP YOUR SNIPING POSITION HERE AT THE RAIL FENCE.
IF ME AND FIERRO GET PINNED DOWN, YOU POP SMOKE AND COVER OUR WITHDRAWAL.
I GOT IT.
SNOW-MOBILE TRACKS LEADING FROM THE CABIN!
THEY'RE BOTH GONE, OR THEY SPLIT UP--
--EVERYBODY DOWN!

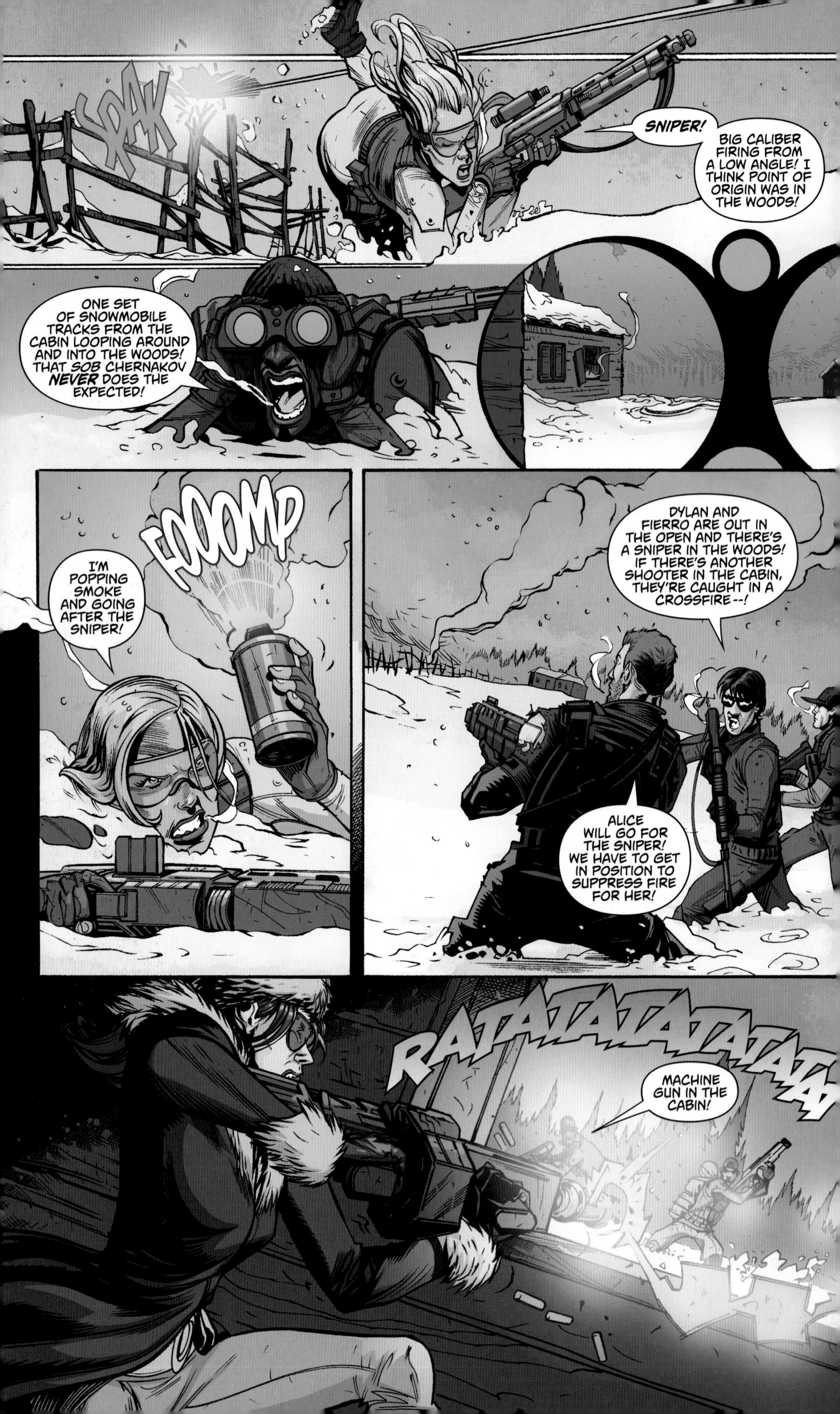
SPAK
SNIPER!
BIG CALIBER FIRING FROM A LOW ANGLE! I THINK POINT OF ORIGIN WAS IN THE WOODS!
ONE SET OF SNOWMOBILE TRACKS FROM THE CABIN LOOPING AROUND AND INTO THE WOODS! THAT SOB CHERNAKOV NEVER DOES THE EXPECTED!
FOOOMP
I'M POPPING SMOKE AND GOING AFTER THE SNIPER!
DYLAN AND FIERRO ARE OUT IN THE OPEN AND THERE'S A SNIPER IN THE WOODS! IF THERE'S ANOTHER SHOOTER IN THE CABIN, THEY'RE CAUGHT IN A CROSSFIRE--!
ALICE WILL GO FOR THE SNIPER! WE HAVE TO GET IN POSITION TO SUPPRESS FIRE FOR HER!
RATATATATATATAT
MACHINE GUN IN THE CABIN!

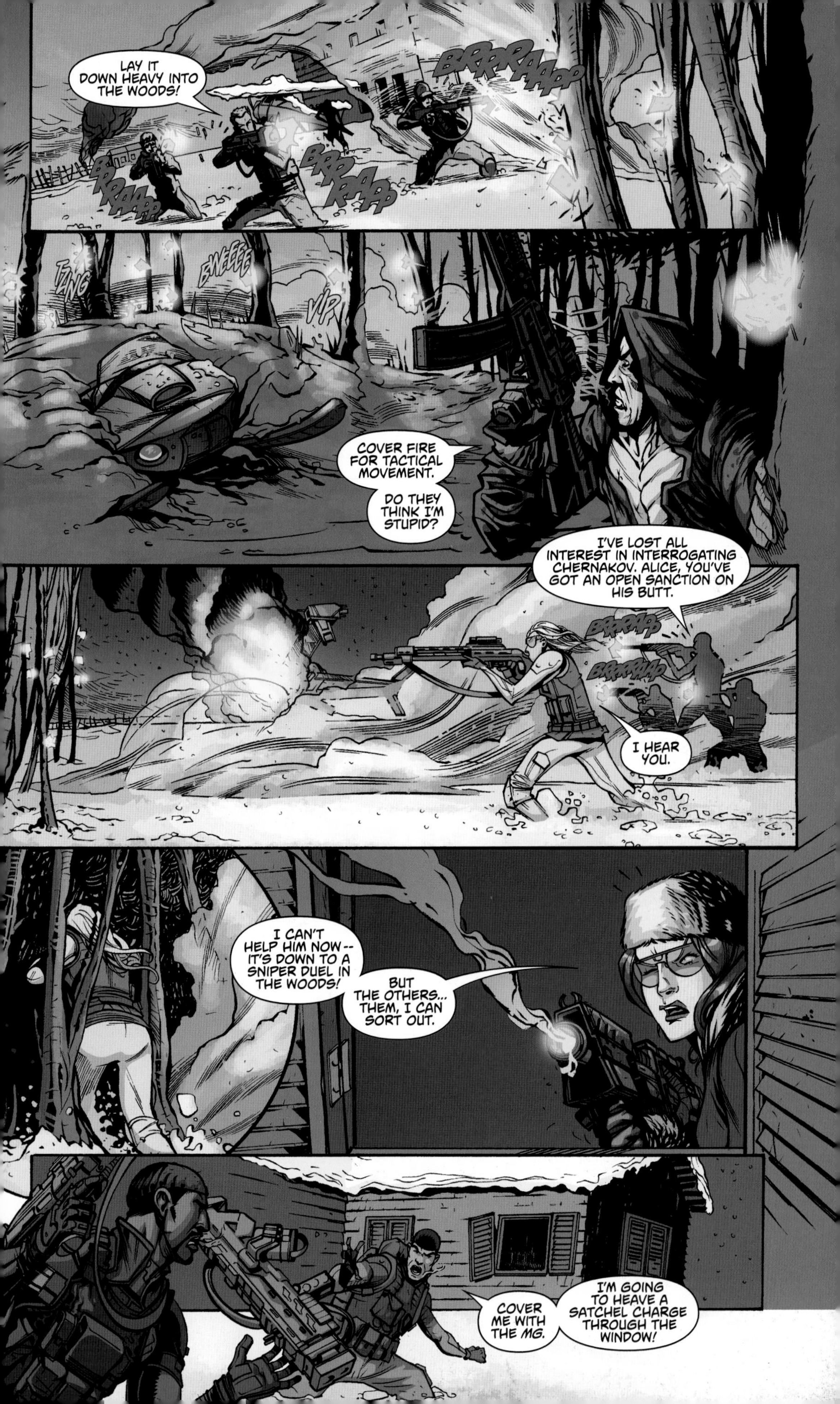
LAY IT DOWN HEAVY INTO THE WOODS!
BRRRAAPP
BRRRAAPP
BRRRAAPP
TZING
BWEEEEE
VIP
COVER FIRE FOR TACTICAL MOVEMENT.
DO THEY THINK I'M STUPID?
I'VE LOST ALL INTEREST IN INTERROGATING CHERNAKOV. ALICE, YOU'VE GOT AN OPEN SANCTION ON HIS BUTT.
BRRRAP
BRRRAAP
I HEAR YOU.
I CAN'T HELP HIM NOW -- IT'S DOWN TO A SNIPER DUEL IN THE WOODS!
BUT THE OTHERS... THEM, I CAN SORT OUT.
I'M GOING TO HEAVE A SATCHEL CHARGE THROUGH THE WINDOW!
COVER ME WITH THE MG.

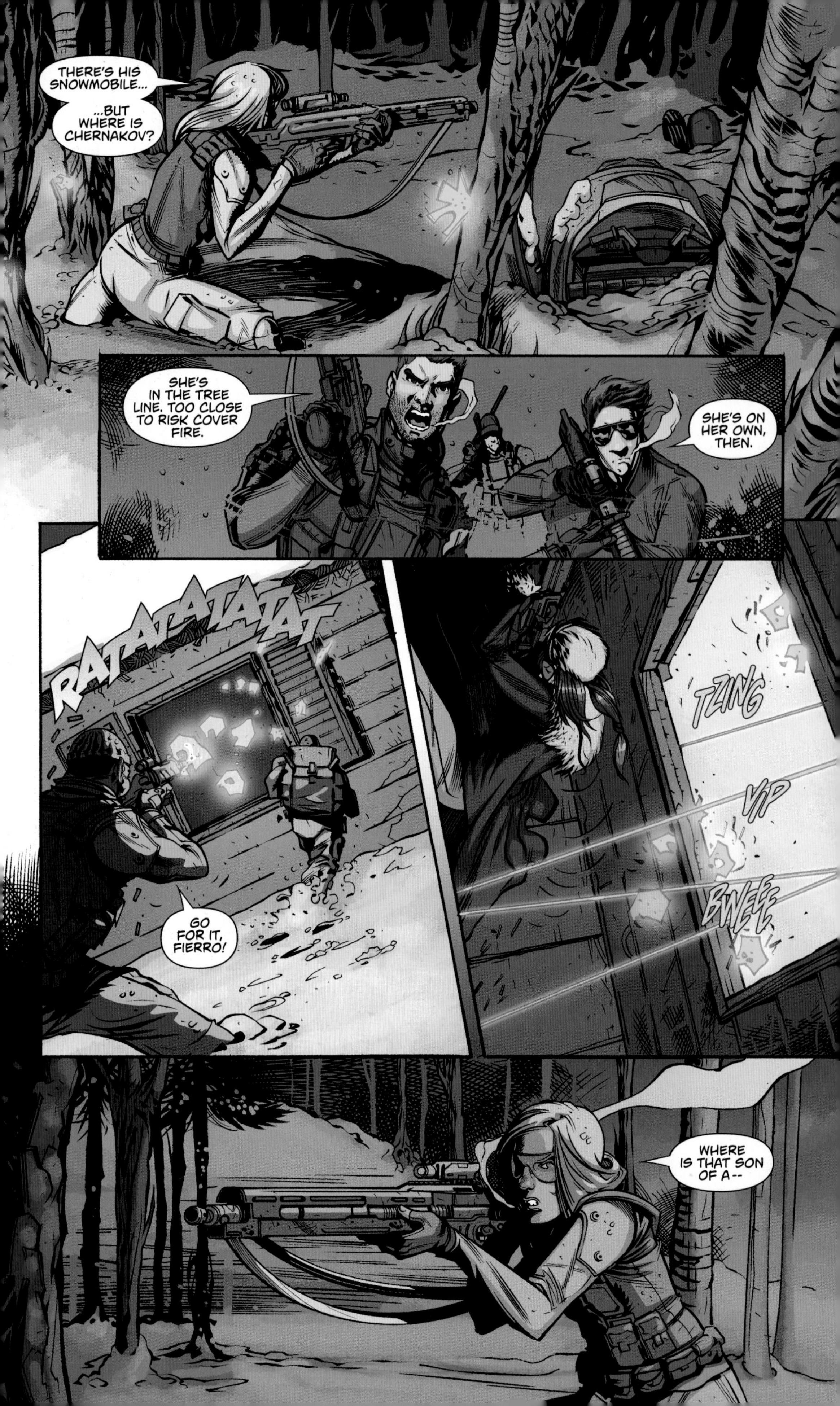
THERE'S HIS SNOWMOBILE...
...BUT WHERE IS CHERNAKOV?
SHE'S IN THE TREE LINE. TOO CLOSE TO RISK COVER FIRE.
SHE'S ON HER OWN, THEN.
RATATATATAT
GO FOR IT, FIERRO!
TZING
VIP
BWEEE
WHERE IS THAT SON OF A--

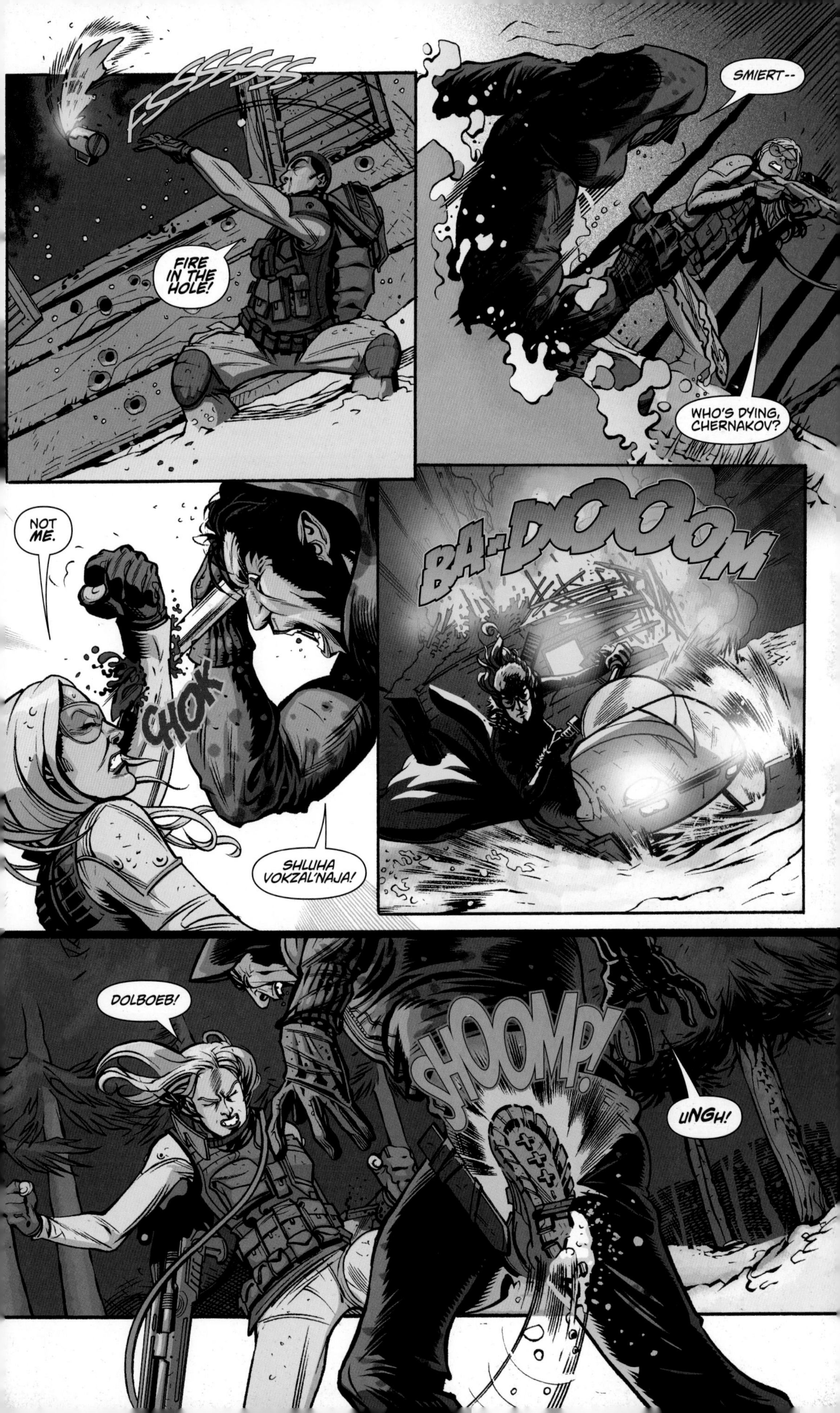
FSSSSSSSS
FIRE IN THE HOLE!
SMIERT--
WHO'S DYING, CHERNAKOV?
NOT ME.
CHOK
SHLUHA VOKZAL'NAJA!
BA-DOOOOM
DOLBOEB!
SHOOMP!
UNGH!

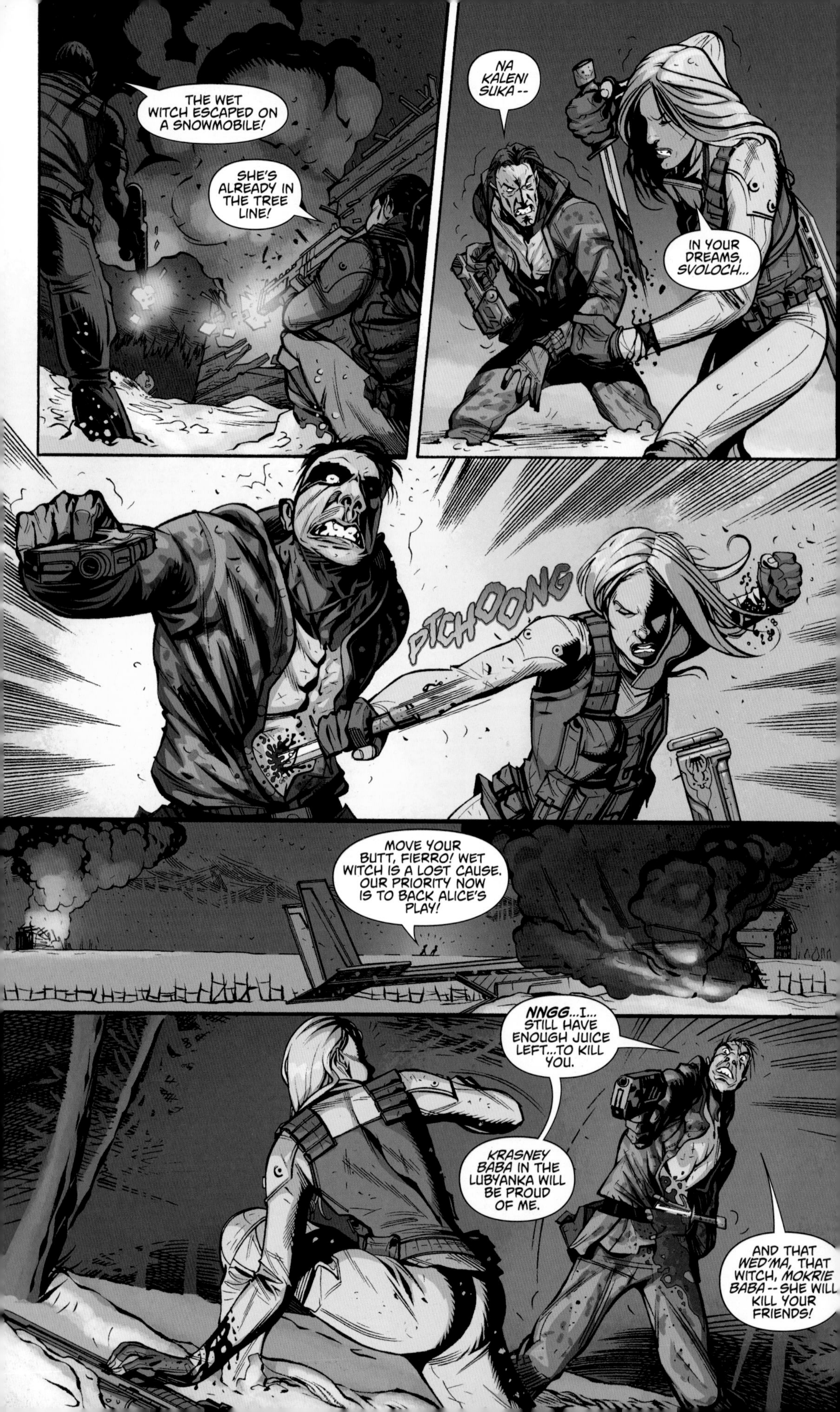
THE WET WITCH ESCAPED ON A SNOWMOBILE!
SHE'S ALREADY IN THE TREE LINE!
NA KALENI SUKA --
IN YOUR DREAMS, SVOLOCH...
PTCHOONG
MOVE YOUR BUTT, FIERRO! WET WITCH IS A LOST CAUSE. OUR PRIORITY NOW IS TO BACK ALICE'S PLAY!
NNGG...I... STILL HAVE ENOUGH JUICE LEFT...TO KILL YOU.
KRASNEY BABA IN THE LUBYANKA WILL BE PROUD OF ME.
AND THAT WED'MA, THAT WITCH, MOKRIE BABA -- SHE WILL KILL YOUR FRIENDS!

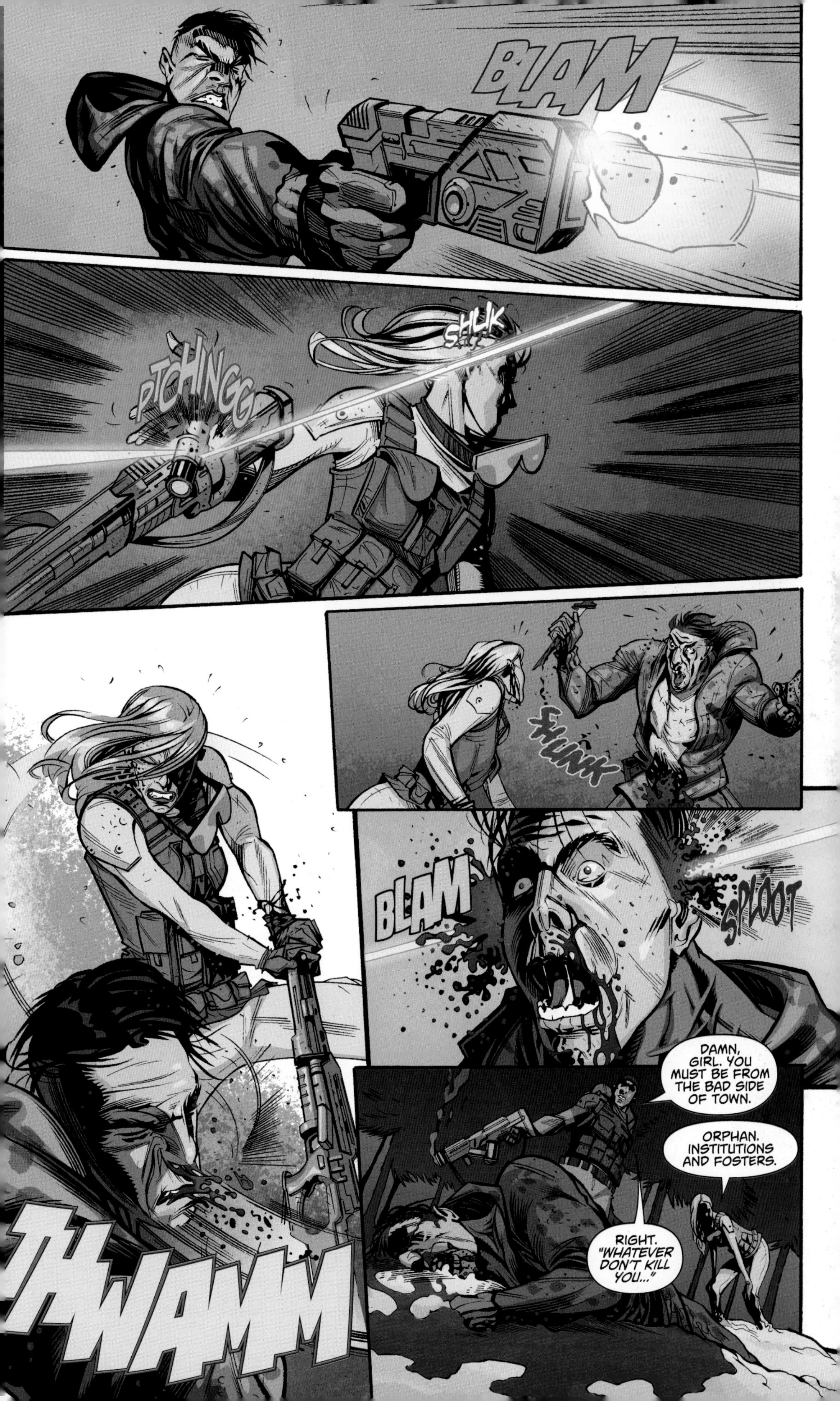
BLAM
SHLIK
PTCHINGG
SHUNK
THWAMM
BLAM
SPLOOT
DAMN, GIRL. YOU MUST BE FROM THE BAD SIDE OF TOWN.
ORPHAN. INSTITUTIONS AND FOSTERS.
RIGHT. "WHATEVER DON'T KILL YOU..."

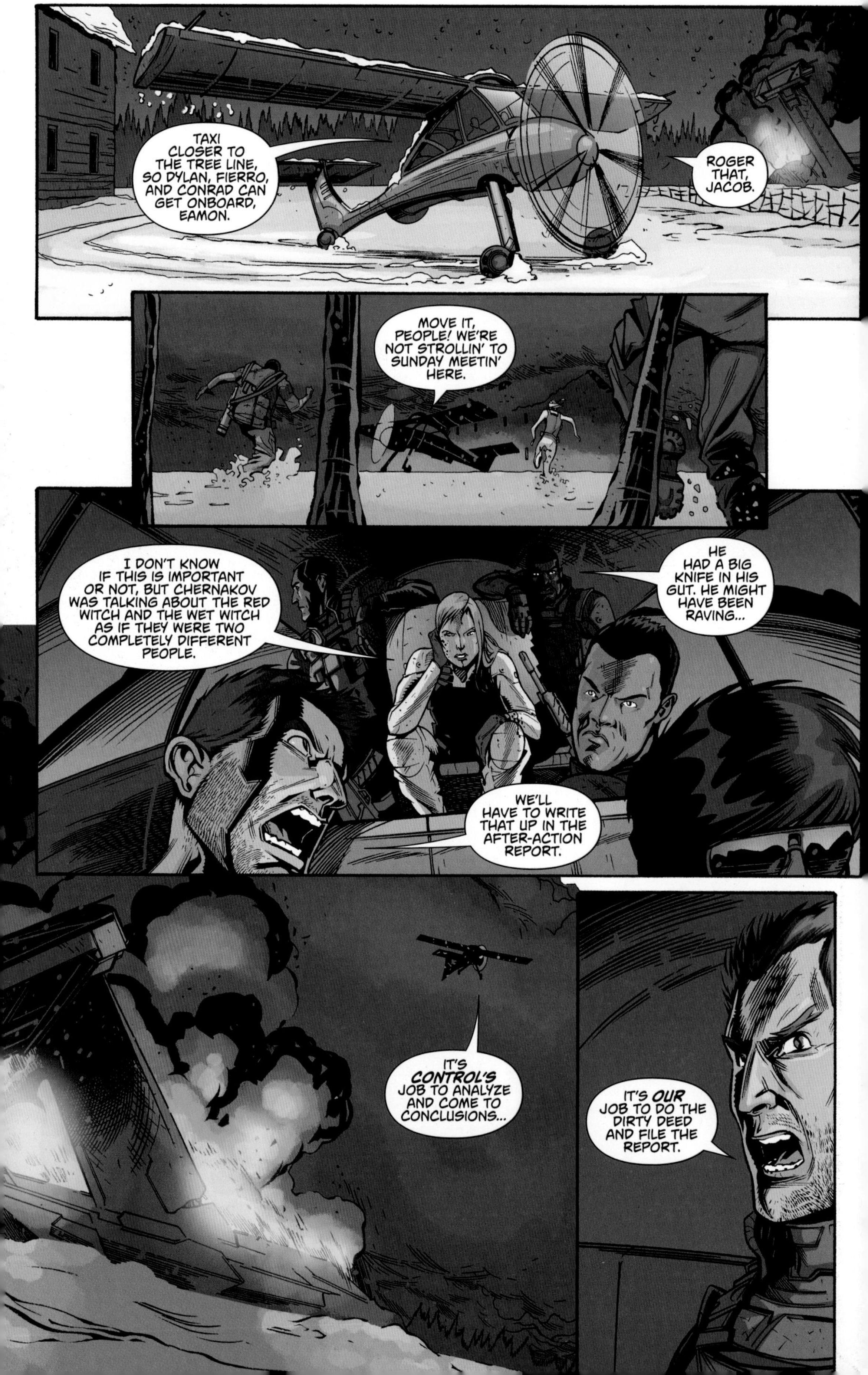
TAXI CLOSER TO THE TREE LINE, SO DYLAN, FIERRO, AND CONRAD CAN GET ONBOARD, EAMON.
ROGER THAT, JACOB.
MOVE IT, PEOPLE! WE'RE NOT STROLLIN' TO SUNDAY MEETIN' HERE.
I DON'T KNOW IF THIS IS IMPORTANT OR NOT, BUT CHERNAKOV WAS TALKING ABOUT THE RED WITCH AND THE WET WITCH AS IF THEY WERE TWO COMPLETELY DIFFERENT PEOPLE.
HE HAD A BIG KNIFE IN HIS GUT. HE MIGHT HAVE BEEN RAVING...
WE'LL HAVE TO WRITE THAT UP IN THE AFTER-ACTION REPORT.
IT'S *CONTROL'S* JOB TO ANALYZE AND COME TO CONCLUSIONS...
IT'S *OUR* JOB TO DO THE DIRTY DEED AND FILE THE REPORT.

ANTHONY PALUMBO

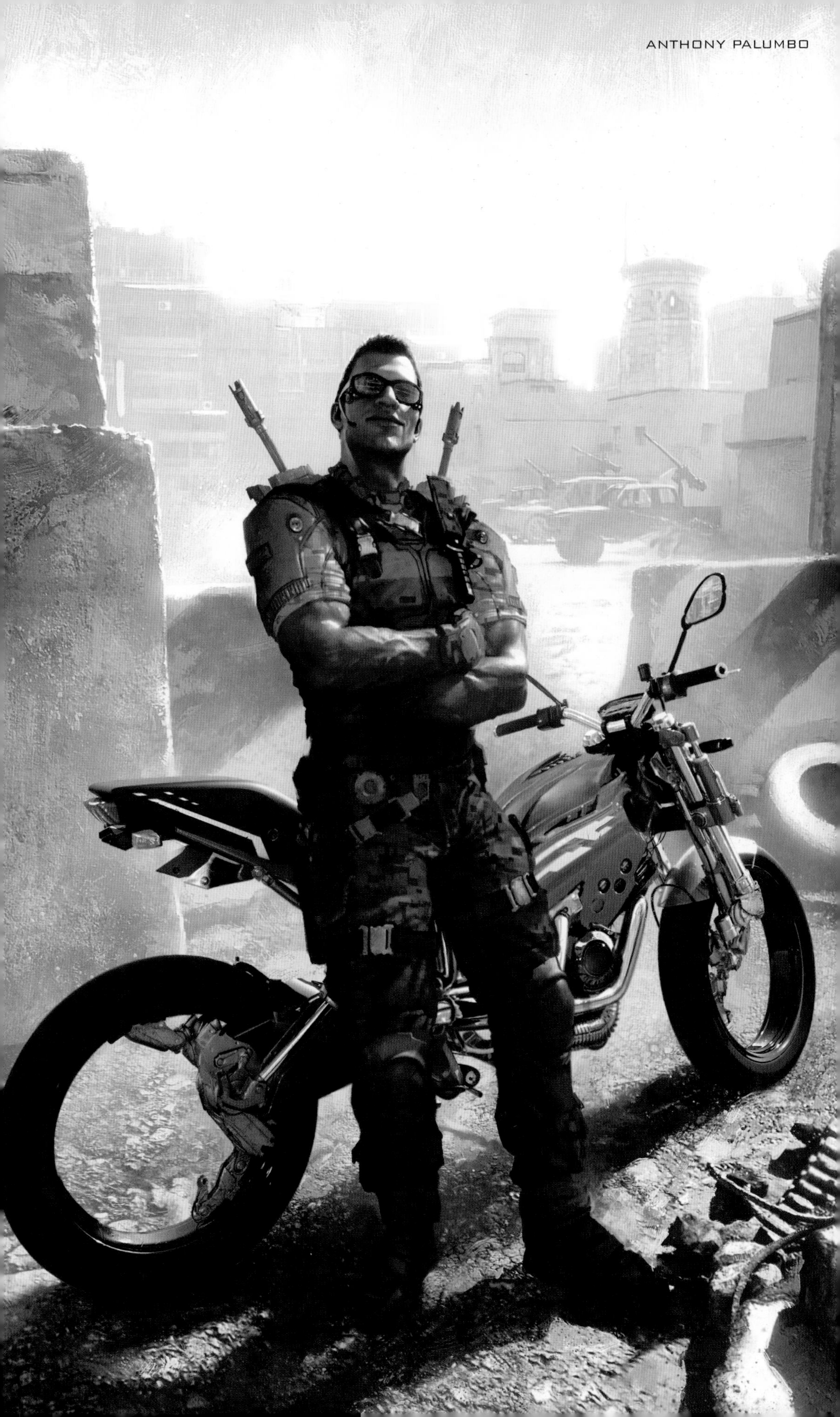

JASON FELIX

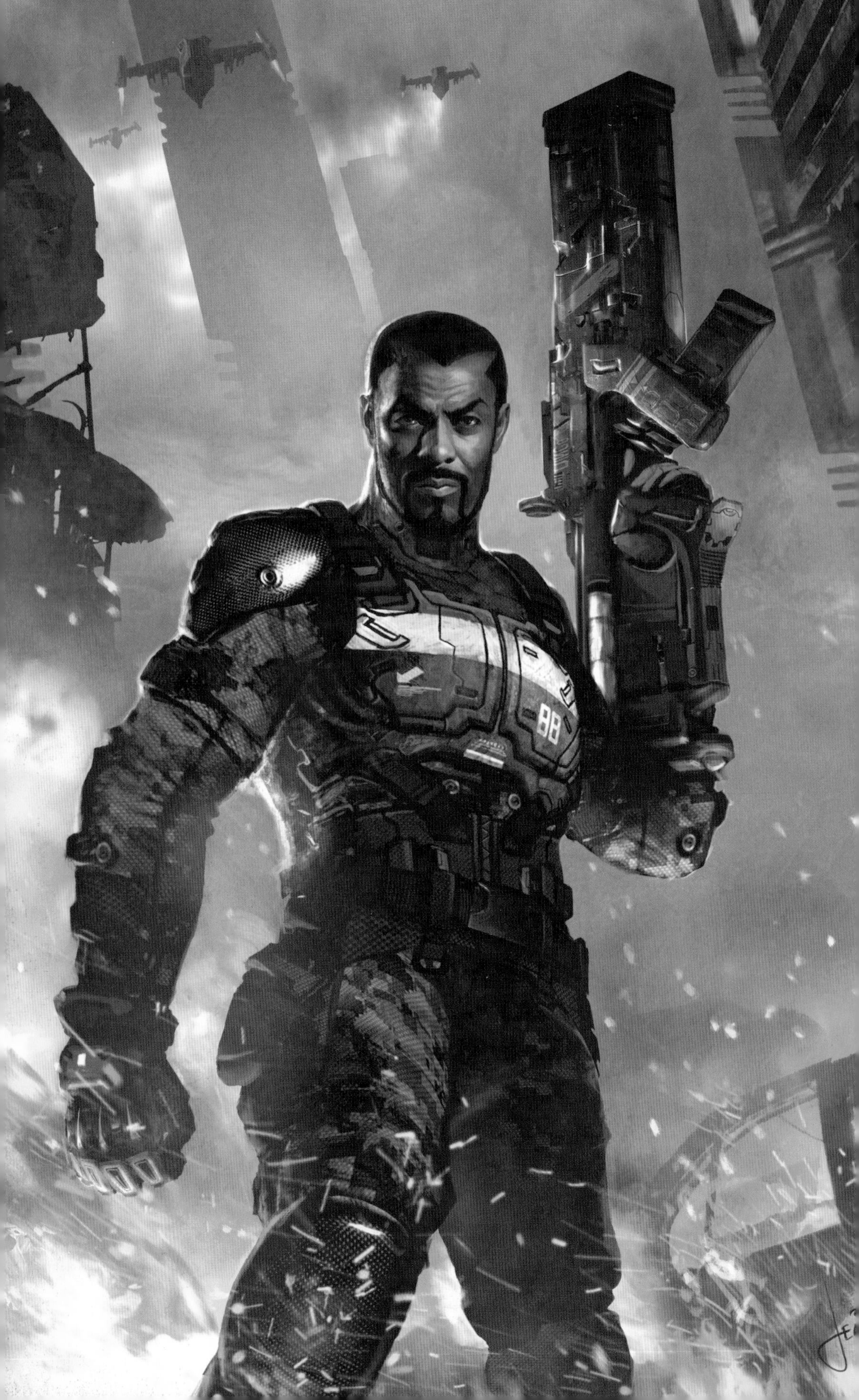

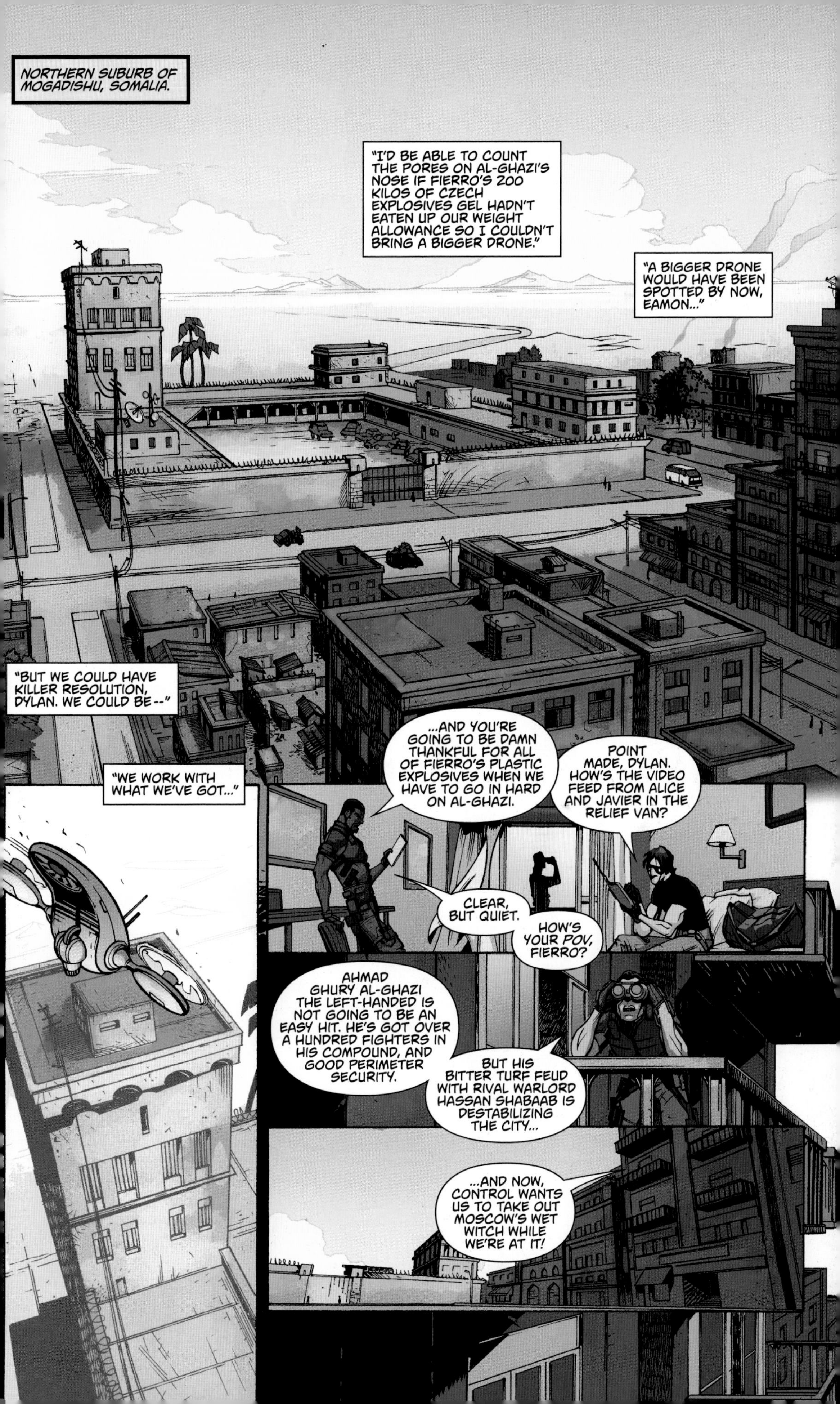
NORTHERN SUBURB OF MOGADISHU, SOMALIA.
"I'D BE ABLE TO COUNT THE PORES ON AL-GHAZI'S NOSE IF FIERRO'S 200 KILOS OF CZECH EXPLOSIVES GEL HADN'T EATEN UP OUR WEIGHT ALLOWANCE SO I COULDN'T BRING A BIGGER DRONE."
"A BIGGER DRONE WOULD HAVE BEEN SPOTTED BY NOW, EAMON..."
"BUT WE COULD HAVE KILLER RESOLUTION, DYLAN. WE COULD BE--"
"WE WORK WITH WHAT WE'VE GOT..."
...AND YOU'RE GOING TO BE DAMN THANKFUL FOR ALL OF FIERRO'S PLASTIC EXPLOSIVES WHEN WE HAVE TO GO IN HARD ON AL-GHAZI.
POINT MADE, DYLAN. HOW'S THE VIDEO FEED FROM ALICE AND JAVIER IN THE RELIEF VAN?
CLEAR, BUT QUIET.
HOW'S YOUR POV, FIERRO?
AHMAD GHURY AL-GHAZI THE LEFT-HANDED IS NOT GOING TO BE AN EASY HIT. HE'S GOT OVER A HUNDRED FIGHTERS IN HIS COMPOUND, AND GOOD PERIMETER SECURITY.
BUT HIS BITTER TURF FEUD WITH RIVAL WARLORD HASSAN SHABAAB IS DESTABILIZING THE CITY...
...AND NOW, CONTROL WANTS US TO TAKE OUT MOSCOW'S WET WITCH WHILE WE'RE AT IT!

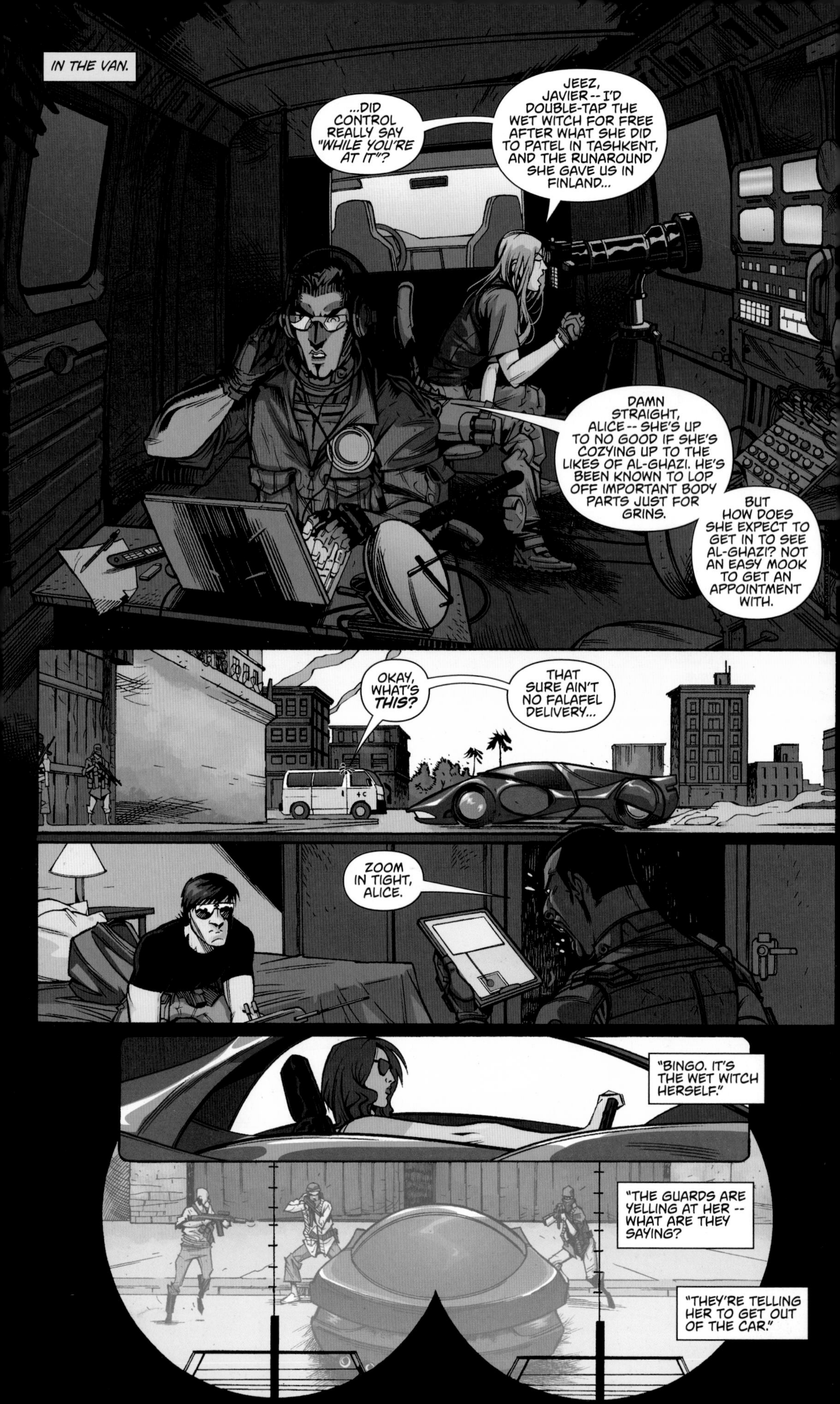
IN THE VAN.
...DID CONTROL REALLY SAY "WHILE YOU'RE AT IT"?
JEEZ, JAVIER -- I'D DOUBLE-TAP THE WET WITCH FOR FREE AFTER WHAT SHE DID TO PATEL IN TASHKENT, AND THE RUNAROUND SHE GAVE US IN FINLAND...
DAMN STRAIGHT, ALICE -- SHE'S UP TO NO GOOD IF SHE'S COZYING UP TO THE LIKES OF AL-GHAZI. HE'S BEEN KNOWN TO LOP OFF IMPORTANT BODY PARTS JUST FOR GRINS.
BUT HOW DOES SHE EXPECT TO GET IN TO SEE AL-GHAZI? NOT AN EASY MOOK TO GET AN APPOINTMENT WITH.
OKAY, WHAT'S *THIS?*
THAT SURE AIN'T NO FALAFEL DELIVERY...
ZOOM IN TIGHT, ALICE.
"BINGO. IT'S THE WET WITCH HERSELF."
"THE GUARDS ARE YELLING AT HER -- WHAT ARE THEY SAYING?
"THEY'RE TELLING HER TO GET OUT OF THE CAR."

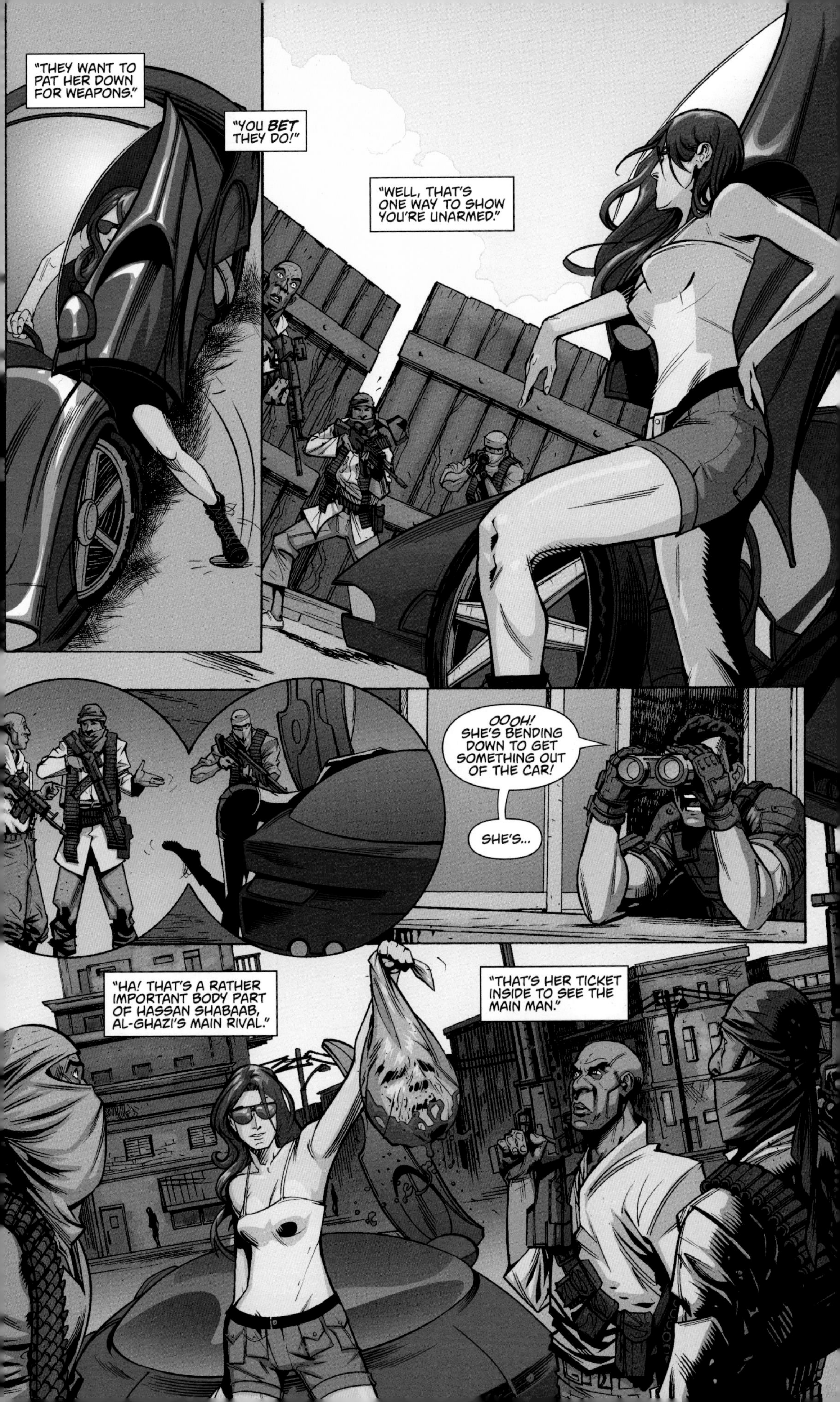
"THEY WANT TO PAT HER DOWN FOR WEAPONS."
"YOU BET THEY DO!"
"WELL, THAT'S ONE WAY TO SHOW YOU'RE UNARMED."
OOOH! SHE'S BENDING DOWN TO GET SOMETHING OUT OF THE CAR!
SHE'S...
"HA! THAT'S A RATHER IMPORTANT BODY PART OF HASSAN SHABAAB, AL-GHAZI'S MAIN RIVAL."
"THAT'S HER TICKET INSIDE TO SEE THE MAIN MAN."

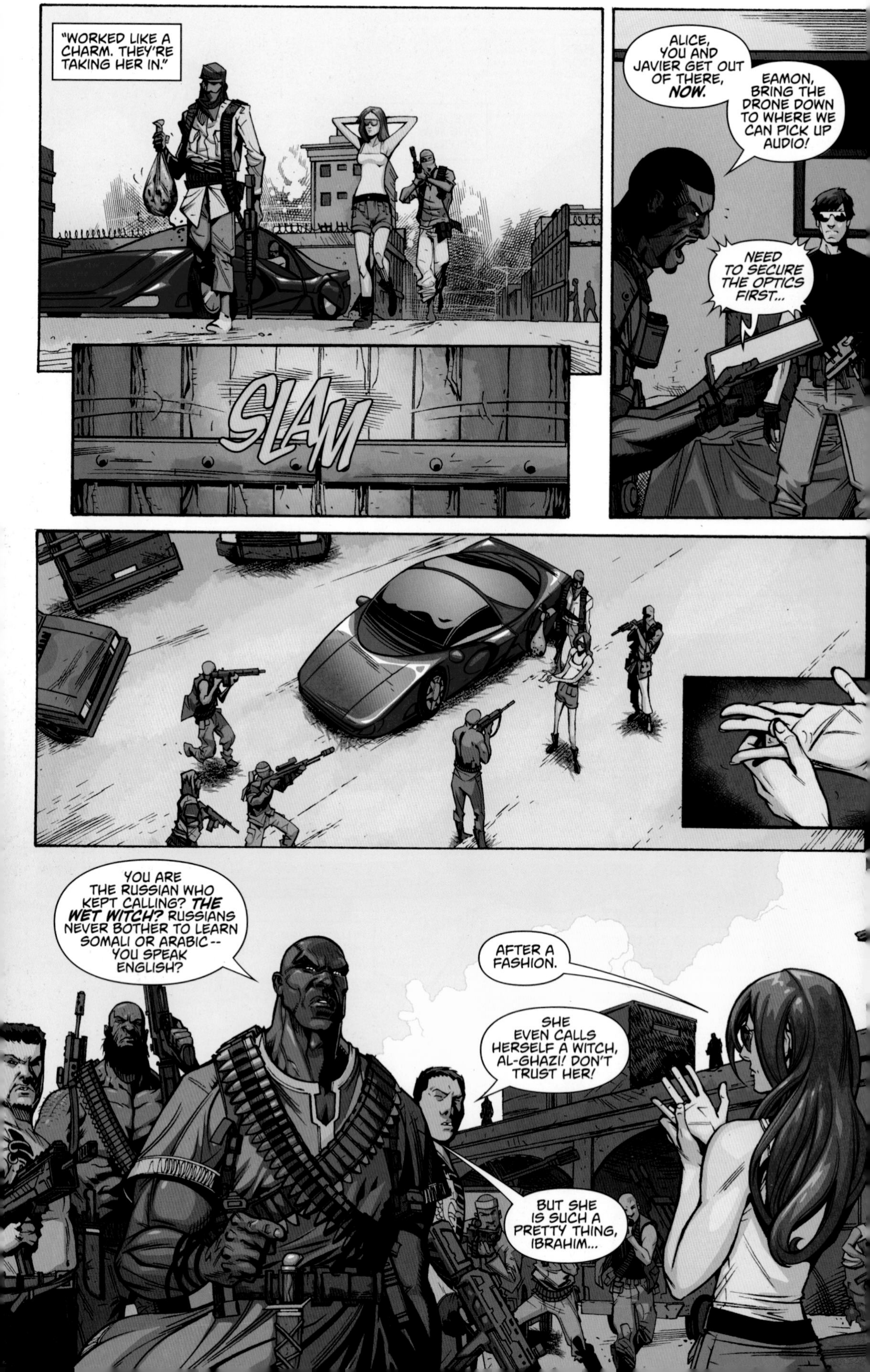
"WORKED LIKE A CHARM. THEY'RE TAKING HER IN."
SLAM
ALICE, YOU AND JAVIER GET OUT OF THERE, NOW.
EAMON, BRING THE DRONE DOWN TO WHERE WE CAN PICK UP AUDIO!
NEED TO SECURE THE OPTICS FIRST...
YOU ARE THE RUSSIAN WHO KEPT CALLING? THE WET WITCH? RUSSIANS NEVER BOTHER TO LEARN SOMALI OR ARABIC -- YOU SPEAK ENGLISH?
AFTER A FASHION.
SHE EVEN CALLS HERSELF A WITCH, AL-GHAZI! DON'T TRUST HER!
BUT SHE IS SUCH A PRETTY THING, IBRAHIM...

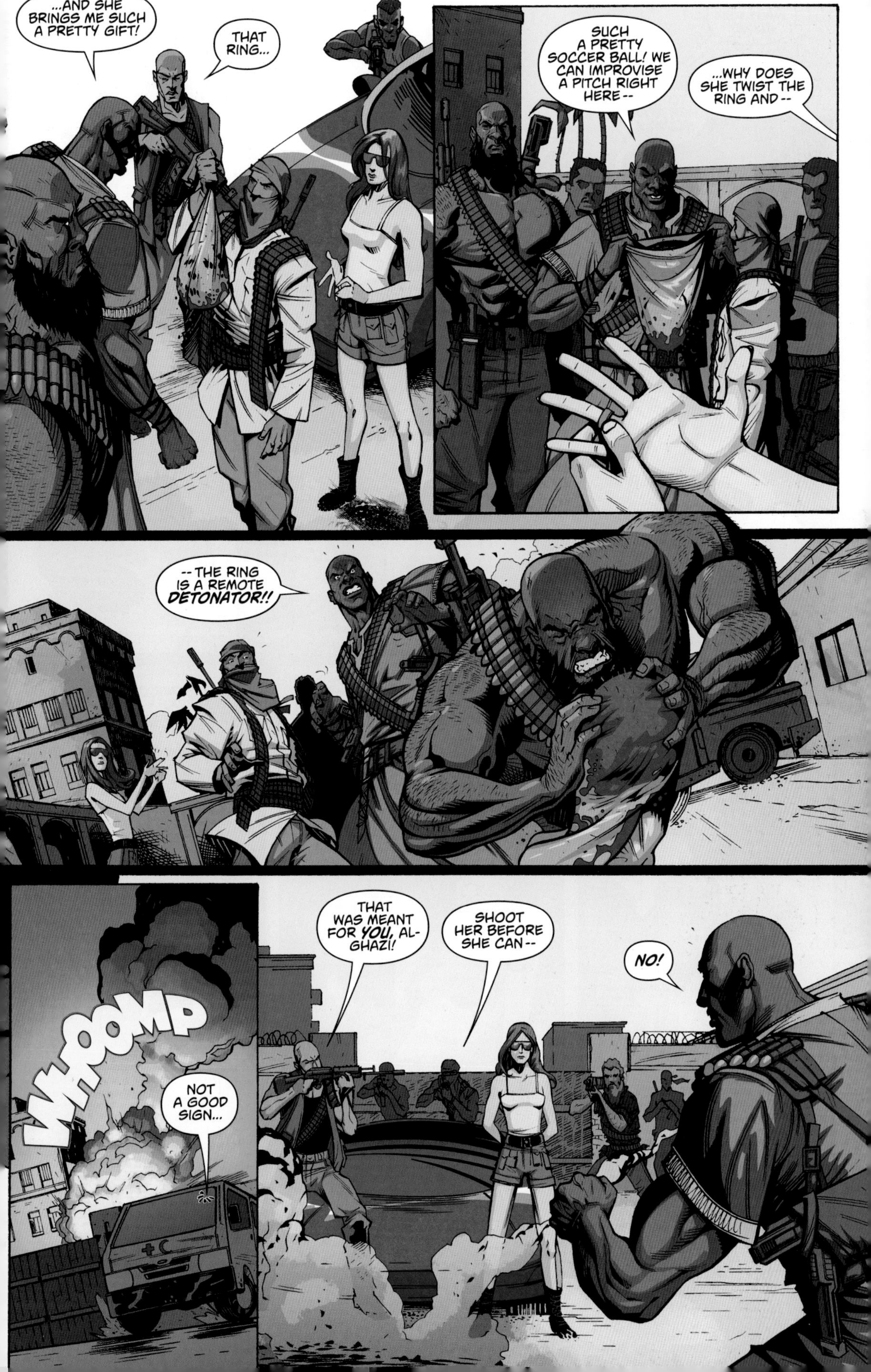

...AND SHE BRINGS ME SUCH A PRETTY GIFT!
THAT RING...
SUCH A PRETTY SOCCER BALL! WE CAN IMPROVISE A PITCH RIGHT HERE--
...WHY DOES SHE TWIST THE RING AND--
--THE RING IS A REMOTE DETONATOR!!
WHOOMP
NOT A GOOD SIGN...
THAT WAS MEANT FOR YOU, AL-GHAZI!
SHOOT HER BEFORE SHE CAN--
NO!

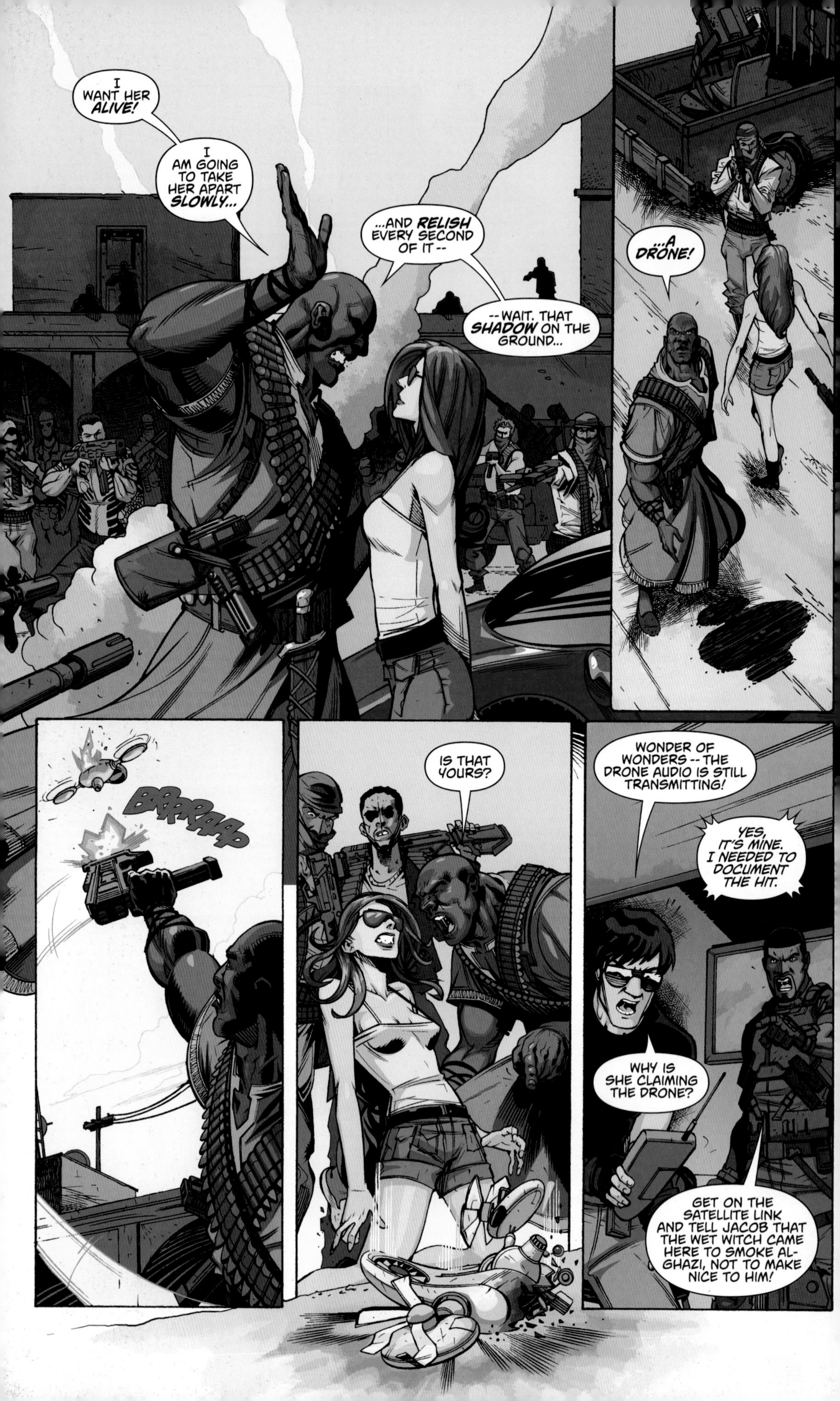
I WANT HER ALIVE!
I AM GOING TO TAKE HER APART SLOWLY...
...AND RELISH EVERY SECOND OF IT --
--WAIT. THAT SHADOW ON THE GROUND...
...A DRONE!
BRRRAAAP
IS THAT YOURS?
WONDER OF WONDERS -- THE DRONE AUDIO IS STILL TRANSMITTING!
YES, IT'S MINE. I NEEDED TO DOCUMENT THE HIT.
WHY IS SHE CLAIMING THE DRONE?
GET ON THE SATELLITE LINK AND TELL JACOB THAT THE WET WITCH CAME HERE TO SMOKE AL-GHAZI, NOT TO MAKE NICE TO HIM!

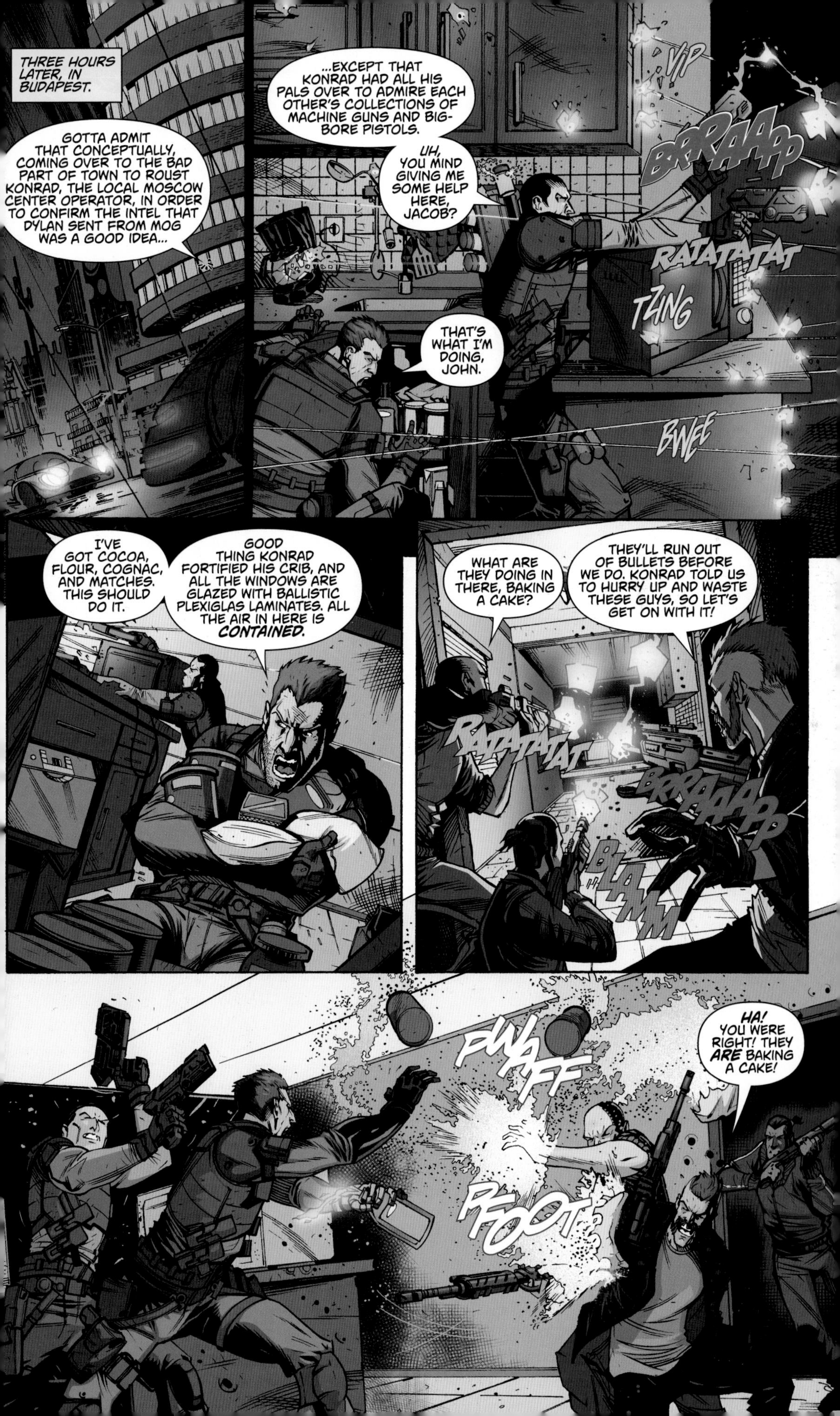
THREE HOURS LATER, IN BUDAPEST.
GOTTA ADMIT THAT CONCEPTUALLY, COMING OVER TO THE BAD PART OF TOWN TO ROUST KONRAD, THE LOCAL MOSCOW CENTER OPERATOR, IN ORDER TO CONFIRM THE INTEL THAT DYLAN SENT FROM MOG WAS A GOOD IDEA...
...EXCEPT THAT KONRAD HAD ALL HIS PALS OVER TO ADMIRE EACH OTHER'S COLLECTIONS OF MACHINE GUNS AND BIG-BORE PISTOLS.
VIP
BRRAAAPP
UH, YOU MIND GIVING ME SOME HELP HERE, JACOB?
RATATATAT
TZING
THAT'S WHAT I'M DOING, JOHN.
BWEE
I'VE GOT COCOA, FLOUR, COGNAC, AND MATCHES. THIS SHOULD DO IT.
GOOD THING KONRAD FORTIFIED HIS CRIB, AND ALL THE WINDOWS ARE GLAZED WITH BALLISTIC PLEXIGLAS LAMINATES. ALL THE AIR IN HERE IS CONTAINED.
WHAT ARE THEY DOING IN THERE, BAKING A CAKE?
THEY'LL RUN OUT OF BULLETS BEFORE WE DO. KONRAD TOLD US TO HURRY UP AND WASTE THESE GUYS, SO LET'S GET ON WITH IT!
RATATATATAT
BRRAAAPP
BLAMM
PWAFF
PFOOT
HA! YOU WERE RIGHT! THEY ARE BAKING A CAKE!

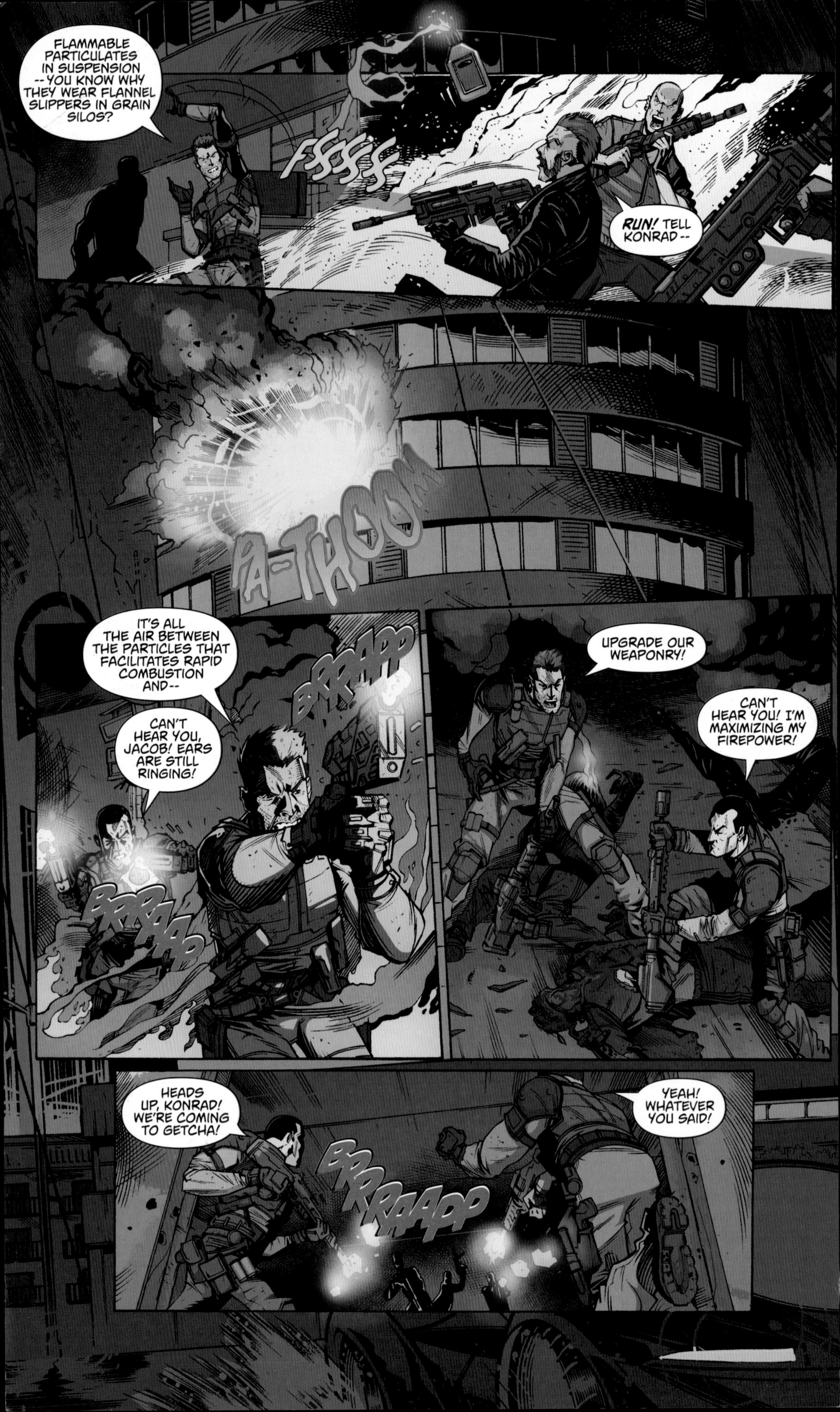
FLAMMABLE PARTICULATES IN SUSPENSION --YOU KNOW WHY THEY WEAR FLANNEL SLIPPERS IN GRAIN SILOS?
FSSSS
RUN! TELL KONRAD--
PA-THOOM
IT'S ALL THE AIR BETWEEN THE PARTICLES THAT FACILITATES RAPID COMBUSTION AND--
BRRAPP
CAN'T HEAR YOU, JACOB! EARS ARE STILL RINGING!
BRRAAAP
UPGRADE OUR WEAPONRY!
CAN'T HEAR YOU! I'M MAXIMIZING MY FIREPOWER!
HEADS UP, KONRAD! WE'RE COMING TO GETCHA!
YEAH! WHATEVER YOU SAID!
BRRRAAAPP

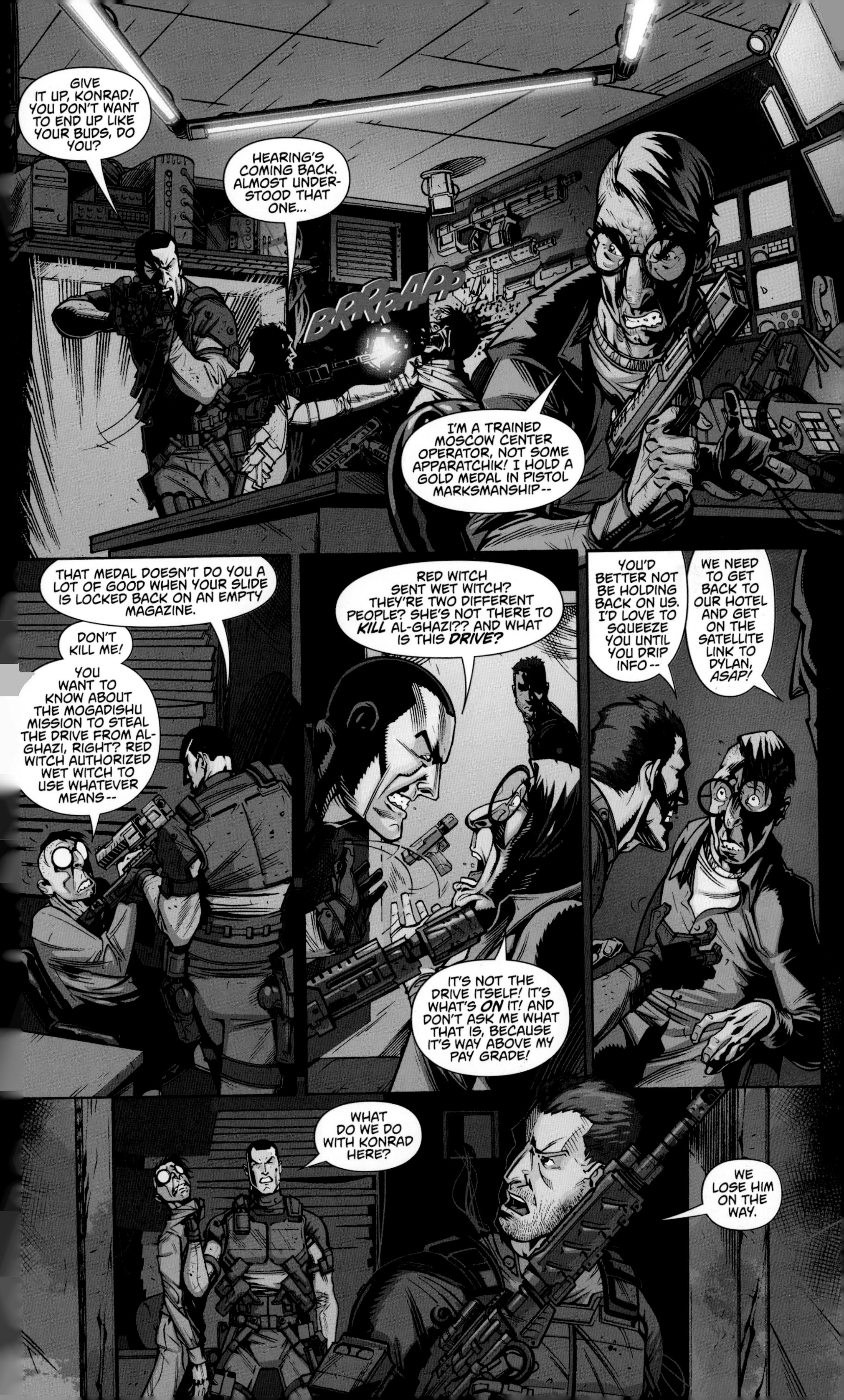
GIVE IT UP, KONRAD! YOU DON'T WANT TO END UP LIKE YOUR BUDS, DO YOU?
HEARING'S COMING BACK. ALMOST UNDER-STOOD THAT ONE...
BRRRAPP
I'M A TRAINED MOSCOW CENTER OPERATOR, NOT SOME APPARATCHIK! I HOLD A GOLD MEDAL IN PISTOL MARKSMANSHIP--
THAT MEDAL DOESN'T DO YOU A LOT OF GOOD WHEN YOUR SLIDE IS LOCKED BACK ON AN EMPTY MAGAZINE.
DON'T KILL ME!
YOU WANT TO KNOW ABOUT THE MOGADISHU MISSION TO STEAL THE DRIVE FROM AL-GHAZI, RIGHT? RED WITCH AUTHORIZED WET WITCH TO USE WHATEVER MEANS--
RED WITCH SENT WET WITCH? THEY'RE TWO DIFFERENT PEOPLE? SHE'S NOT THERE TO *KILL* AL-GHAZI?? AND WHAT IS THIS *DRIVE?*
IT'S NOT THE DRIVE ITSELF! IT'S WHAT'S *ON* IT! AND DON'T ASK ME WHAT THAT IS, BECAUSE IT'S WAY ABOVE MY PAY GRADE!
YOU'D BETTER NOT BE HOLDING BACK ON US. I'D LOVE TO SQUEEZE YOU UNTIL YOU DRIP INFO--
WE NEED TO GET BACK TO OUR HOTEL AND GET ON THE SATELLITE LINK TO DYLAN, *ASAP!*
WHAT DO WE DO WITH KONRAD HERE?
WE LOSE HIM ON THE WAY.

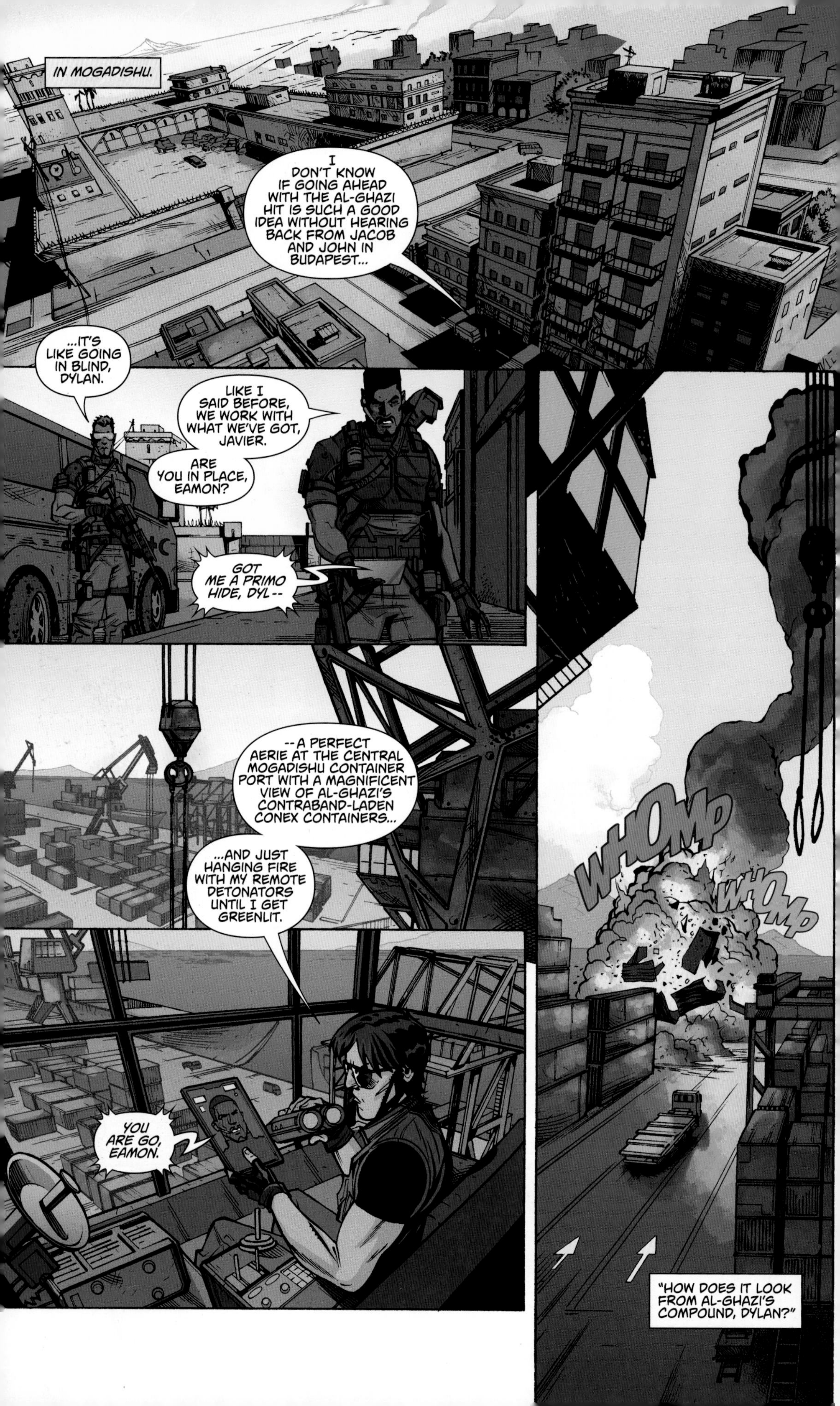
IN MOGADISHU.
I DON'T KNOW IF GOING AHEAD WITH THE AL-GHAZI HIT IS SUCH A GOOD IDEA WITHOUT HEARING BACK FROM JACOB AND JOHN IN BUDAPEST...
...IT'S LIKE GOING IN BLIND, DYLAN.
LIKE I SAID BEFORE, WE WORK WITH WHAT WE'VE GOT, JAVIER.
ARE YOU IN PLACE, EAMON?
GOT ME A PRIMO HIDE, DYL--
--A PERFECT AERIE AT THE CENTRAL MOGADISHU CONTAINER PORT WITH A MAGNIFICENT VIEW OF AL-GHAZI'S CONTRABAND-LADEN CONEX CONTAINERS...
...AND JUST HANGING FIRE WITH MY REMOTE DETONATORS UNTIL I GET GREENLIT.
YOU ARE GO, EAMON.
WHOMP
WHOMP
"HOW DOES IT LOOK FROM AL-GHAZI'S COMPOUND, DYLAN?"

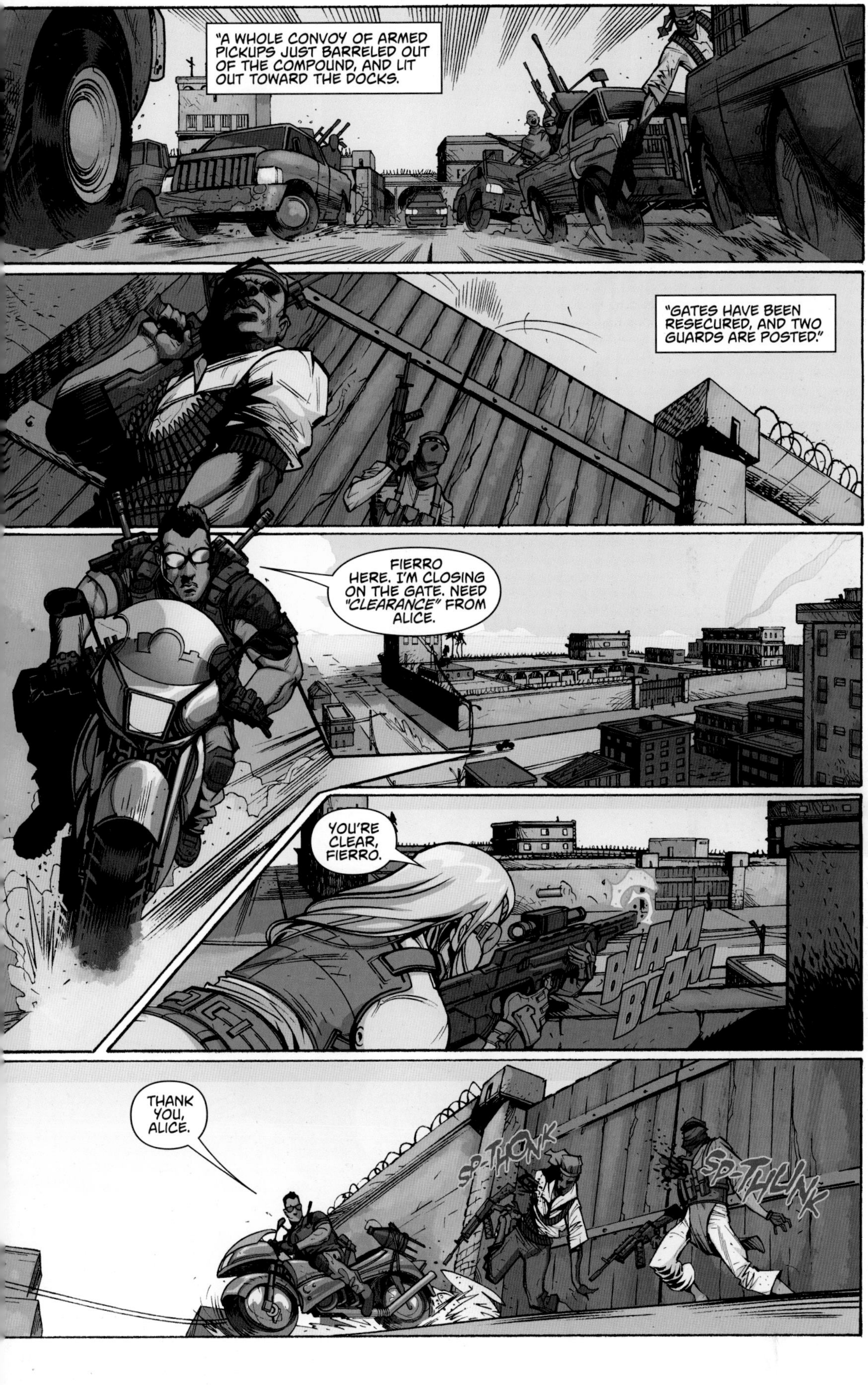

"A WHOLE CONVOY OF ARMED PICKUPS JUST BARRELED OUT OF THE COMPOUND, AND LIT OUT TOWARD THE DOCKS.
"GATES HAVE BEEN RESECURED, AND TWO GUARDS ARE POSTED."
FIERRO HERE. I'M CLOSING ON THE GATE. NEED "CLEARANCE" FROM ALICE.
YOU'RE CLEAR, FIERRO.
BLAM BLAM
THANK YOU, ALICE.
SP-THUNK
SP-THUNK

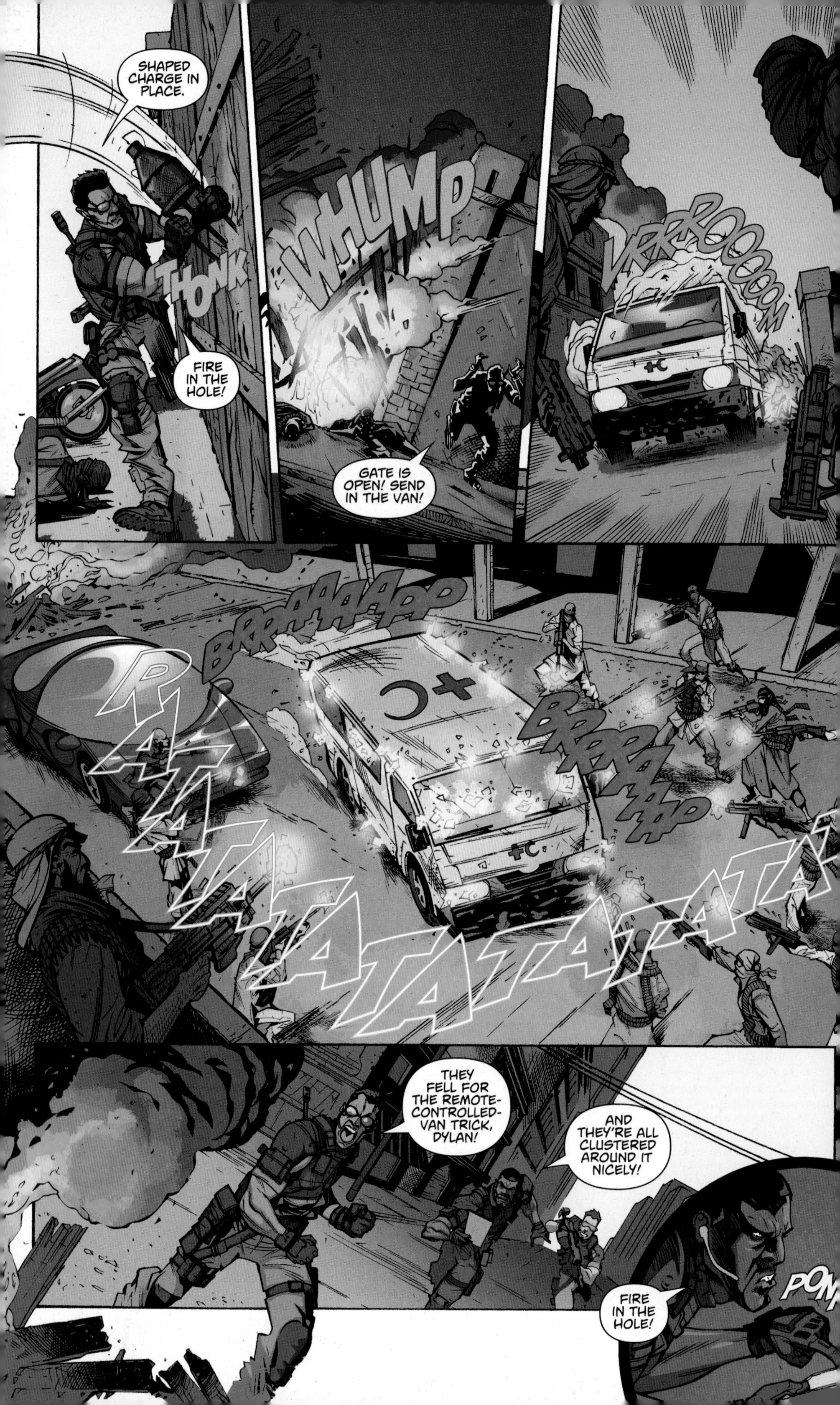
SHAPED CHARGE IN PLACE.
THONK
FIRE IN THE HOLE!
WHUMP
GATE IS OPEN! SEND IN THE VAN!
VRRROOOOOM
BRRAAAAPP
RATATATATATATATA
BRRRAAAP
THEY FELL FOR THE REMOTE-CONTROLLED-VAN TRICK, DYLAN!
AND THEY'RE ALL CLUSTERED AROUND IT NICELY!
FIRE IN THE HOLE!
POM

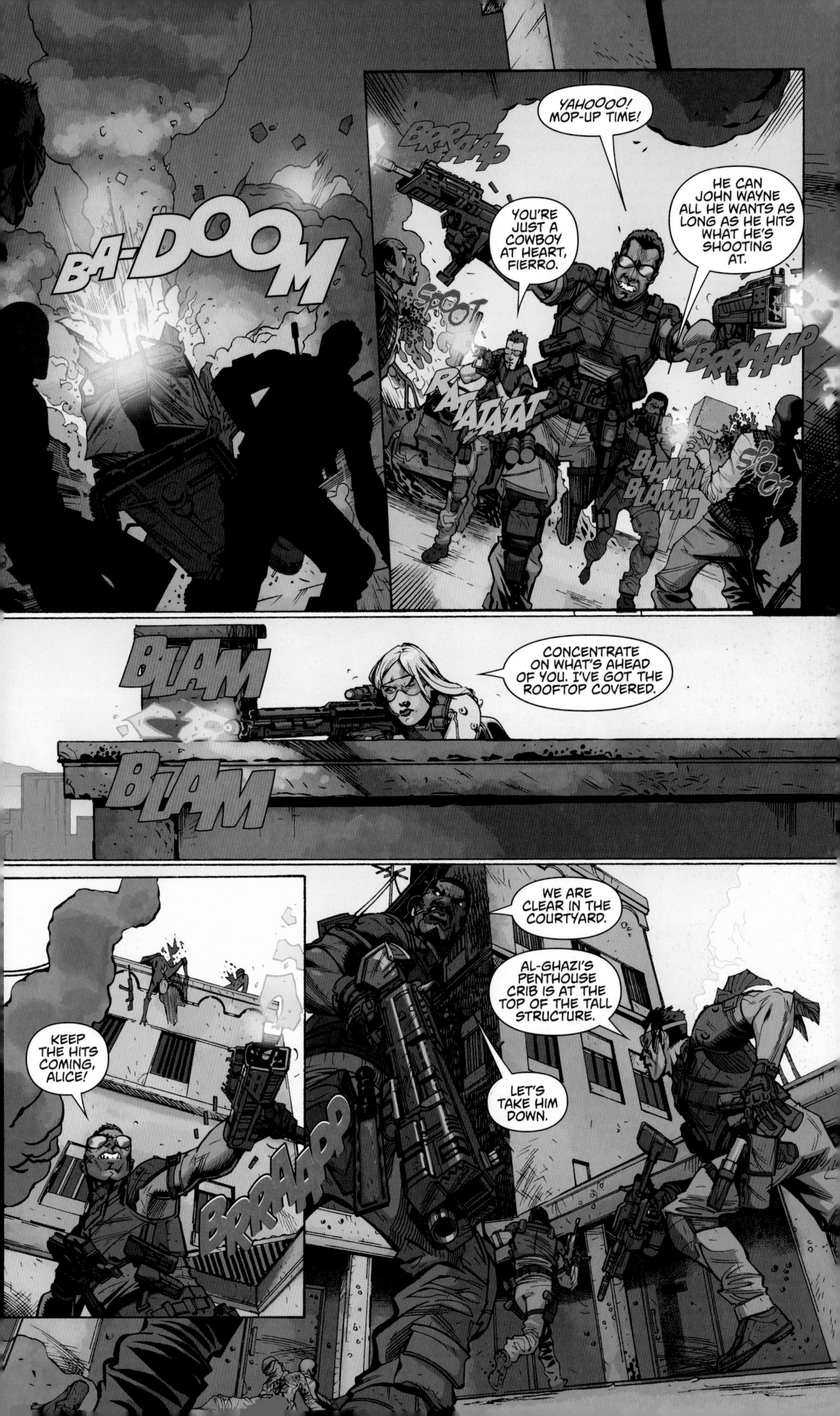
BA-DOOM
BRRAAAP
YAHOOOO! MOP-UP TIME!
YOU'RE JUST A COWBOY AT HEART, FIERRO.
HE CAN JOHN WAYNE ALL HE WANTS AS LONG AS HE HITS WHAT HE'S SHOOTING AT.
SPOOT
RATATATAT
BRRAAAP
BLAMM BLAMM
SPOOT
BLAM
CONCENTRATE ON WHAT'S AHEAD OF YOU. I'VE GOT THE ROOFTOP COVERED.
BLAM
KEEP THE HITS COMING, ALICE!
BRRAAAP
WE ARE CLEAR IN THE COURTYARD.
AL-GHAZI'S PENTHOUSE CRIB IS AT THE TOP OF THE TALL STRUCTURE.
LET'S TAKE HIM DOWN.

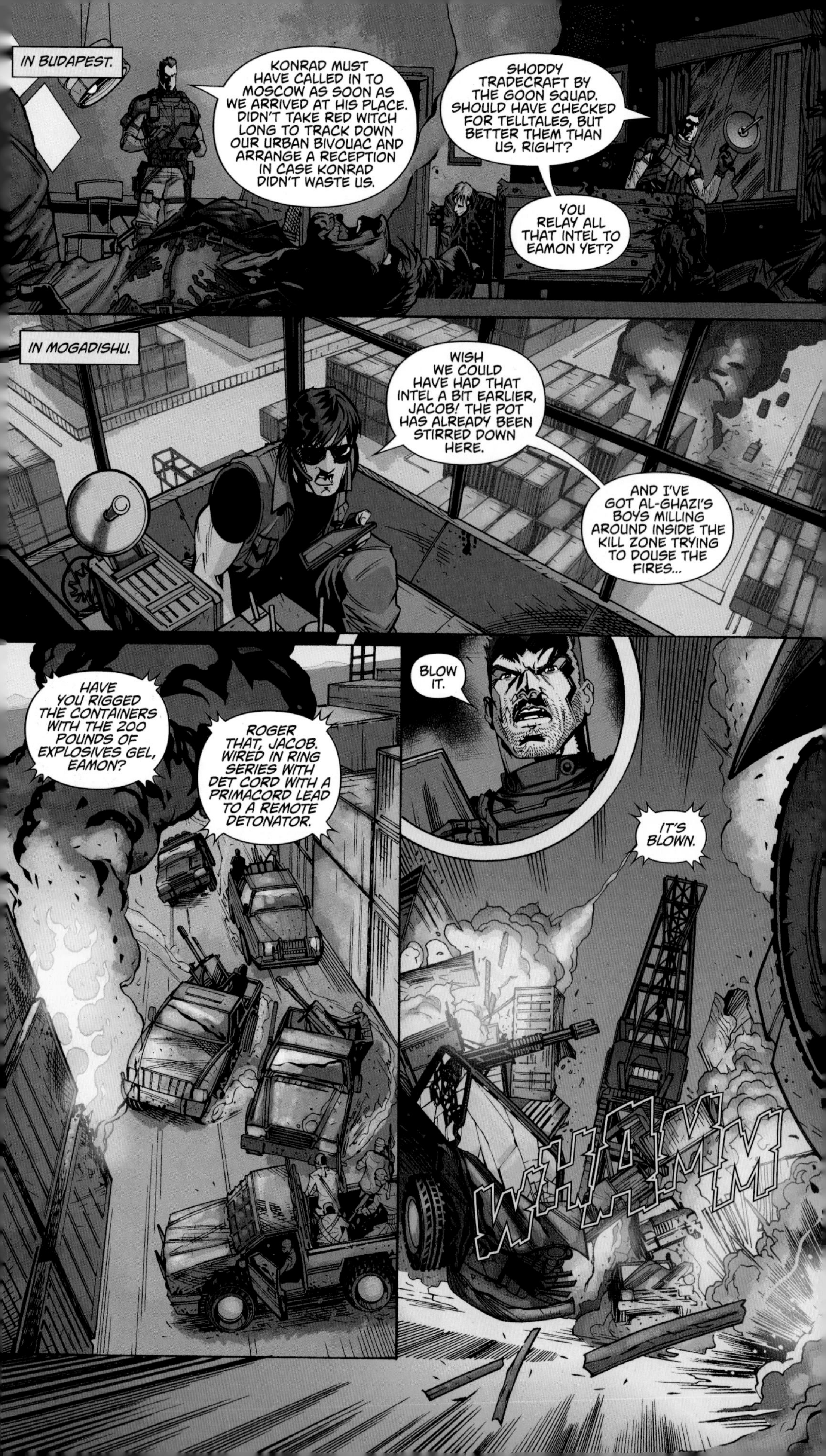
IN BUDAPEST.
KONRAD MUST HAVE CALLED IN TO MOSCOW AS SOON AS WE ARRIVED AT HIS PLACE. DIDN'T TAKE RED WITCH LONG TO TRACK DOWN OUR URBAN BIVOUAC AND ARRANGE A RECEPTION IN CASE KONRAD DIDN'T WASTE US.
SHODDY TRADECRAFT BY THE GOON SQUAD. SHOULD HAVE CHECKED FOR TELLTALES, BUT BETTER THEM THAN US, RIGHT?
YOU RELAY ALL THAT INTEL TO EAMON YET?
IN MOGADISHU.
WISH WE COULD HAVE HAD THAT INTEL A BIT EARLIER, JACOB! THE POT HAS ALREADY BEEN STIRRED DOWN HERE.
AND I'VE GOT AL-GHAZI'S BOYS MILLING AROUND INSIDE THE KILL ZONE TRYING TO DOUSE THE FIRES...
HAVE YOU RIGGED THE CONTAINERS WITH THE 200 POUNDS OF EXPLOSIVES GEL, EAMON?
ROGER THAT, JACOB. WIRED IN RING SERIES WITH DET CORD WITH A PRIMACORD LEAD TO A REMOTE DETONATOR.
BLOW IT.
IT'S BLOWN.
WHAMM

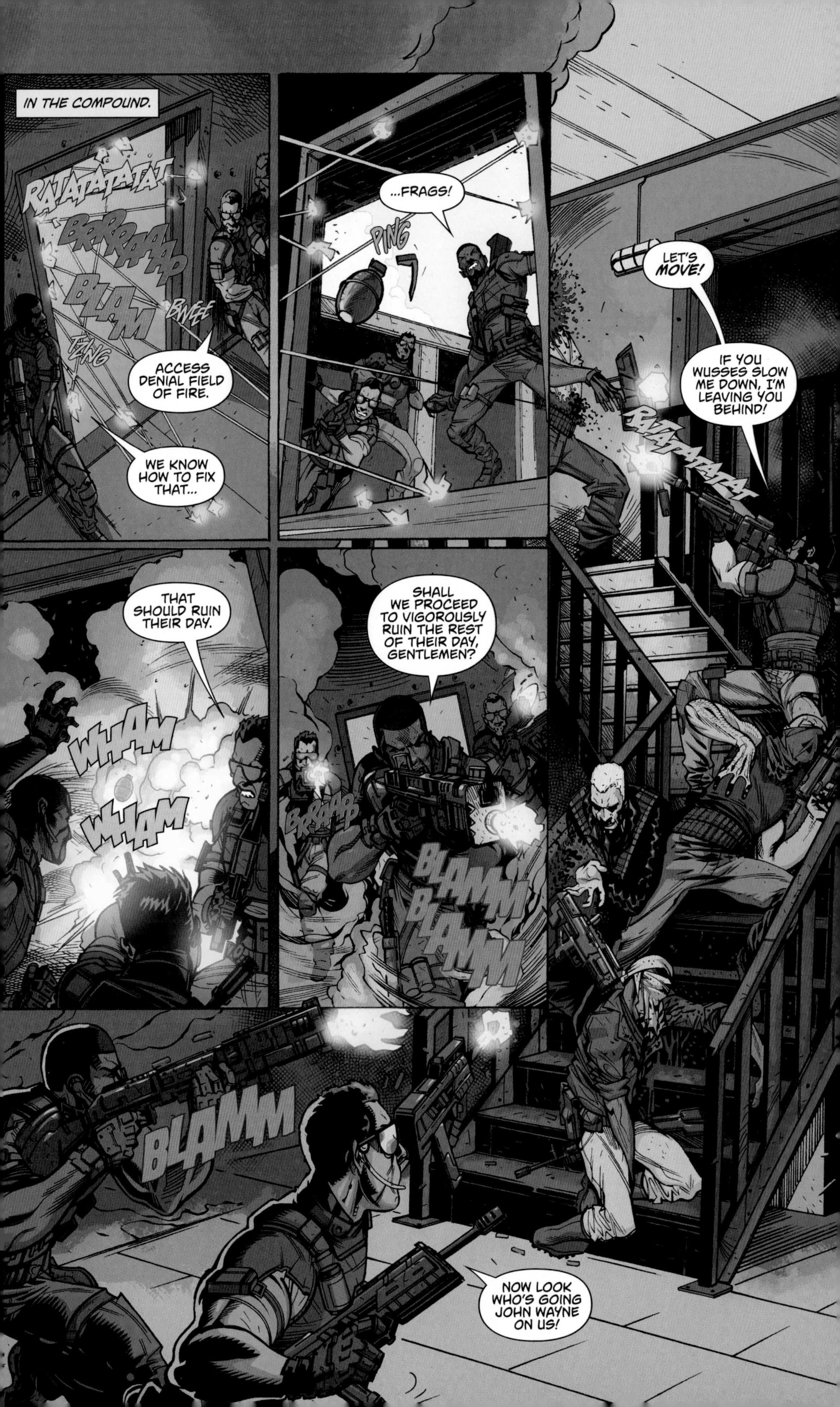
IN THE COMPOUND.
RATATATATAT
BRRRAAAP
BLAM
BWEEE
TZING
ACCESS DENIAL FIELD OF FIRE.
WE KNOW HOW TO FIX THAT...
...FRAGS!
PING
LET'S MOVE!
IF YOU WUSSES SLOW ME DOWN, I'M LEAVING YOU BEHIND!
RATATATATAT
THAT SHOULD RUIN THEIR DAY.
WHAM
WHAM
SHALL WE PROCEED TO VIGOROUSLY RUIN THE REST OF THEIR DAY, GENTLEMEN?
BRRAAP
BLAMM
BLAMM
BLAMM
BLAMM
NOW LOOK WHO'S GOING JOHN WAYNE ON US!

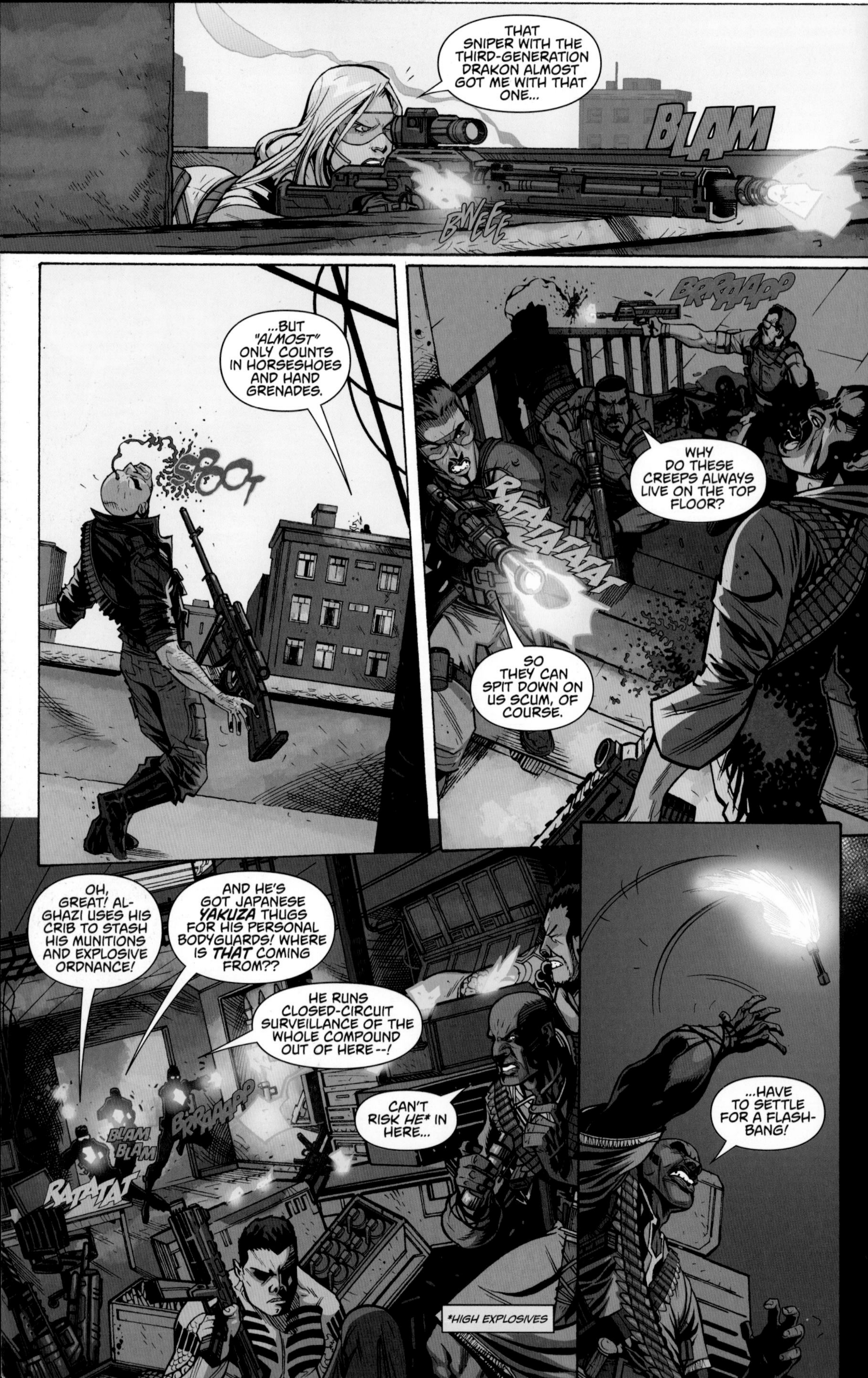

THAT SNIPER WITH THE THIRD-GENERATION DRAKON ALMOST GOT ME WITH THAT ONE...
BLAM
BWEEE
...BUT "ALMOST" ONLY COUNTS IN HORSESHOES AND HAND GRENADES.
SPOOT
BRRAAPP
WHY DO THESE CREEPS ALWAYS LIVE ON THE TOP FLOOR?
RATATATATAT
SO THEY CAN SPIT DOWN ON US SCUM, OF COURSE.
OH, GREAT! AL-GHAZI USES HIS CRIB TO STASH HIS MUNITIONS AND EXPLOSIVE ORDNANCE!
AND HE'S GOT JAPANESE YAKUZA THUGS FOR HIS PERSONAL BODYGUARDS! WHERE IS THAT COMING FROM??
HE RUNS CLOSED-CIRCUIT SURVEILLANCE OF THE WHOLE COMPOUND OUT OF HERE--!
BRRAAAPP
BLAM BLAM
RATATAT
CAN'T RISK HE* IN HERE...
...HAVE TO SETTLE FOR A FLASH-BANG!
*HIGH EXPLOSIVES

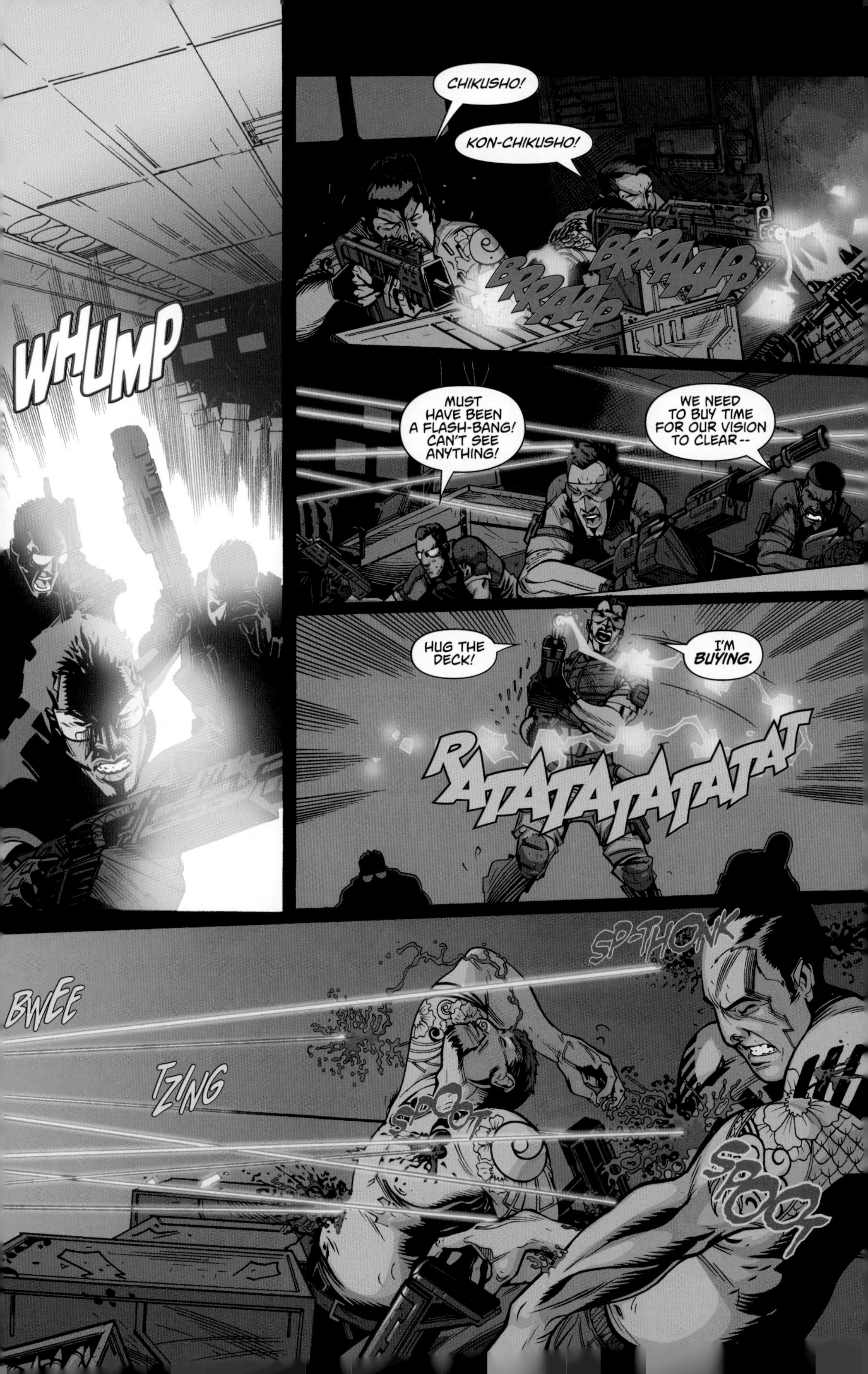
WHUMP
CHIKUSHO!
KON-CHIKUSHO!
BRRAAP
BRRAAP
MUST HAVE BEEN A FLASH-BANG! CAN'T SEE ANYTHING!
WE NEED TO BUY TIME FOR OUR VISION TO CLEAR --
HUG THE DECK!
I'M BUYING.
RATATATATATATAT
BWEE
SP-THONK
TZING
SPOOT
SPOOT

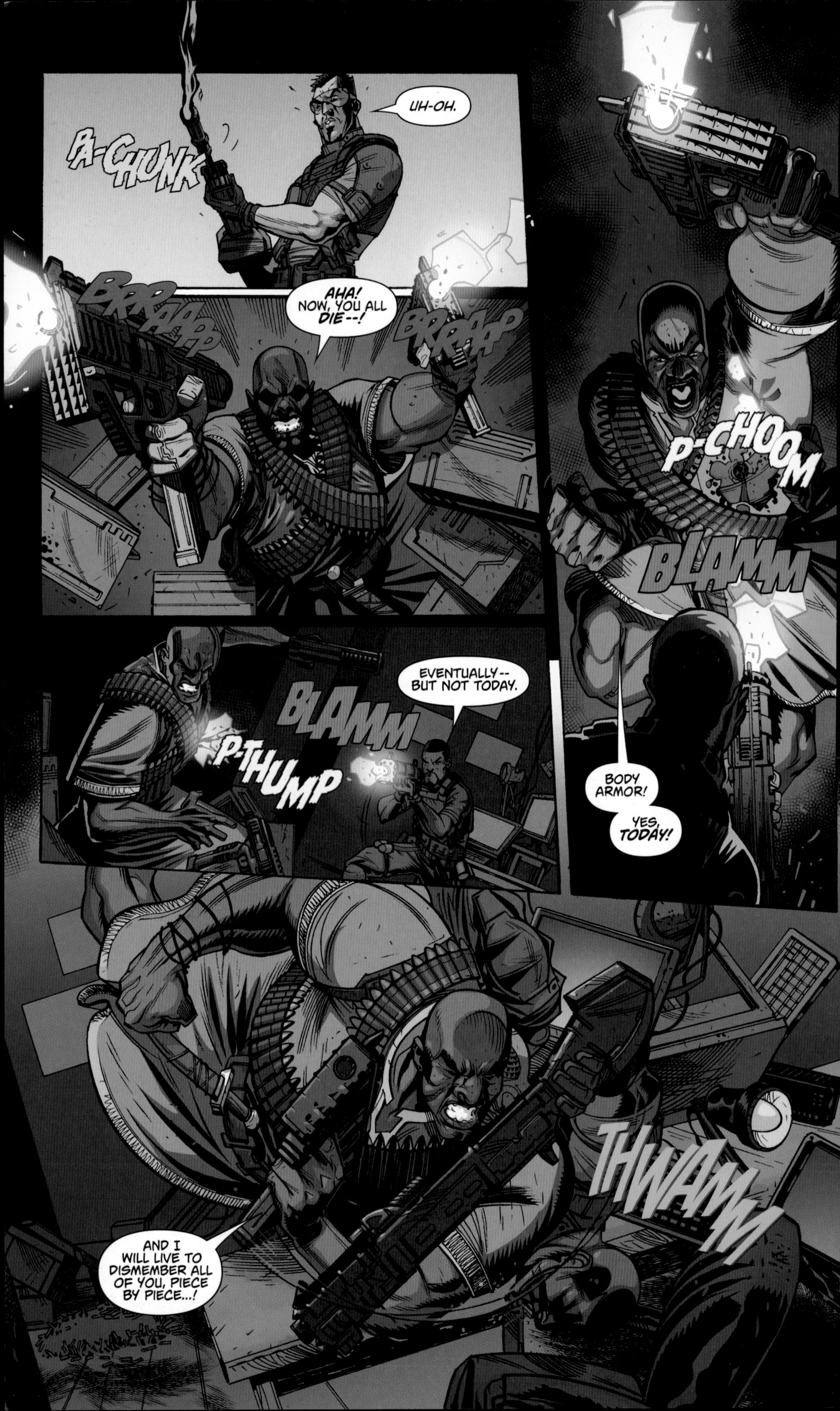
UH-OH.
PA-CHUNK
BRRAAPP
AHA! NOW, YOU ALL DIE--!
BRRAAPP
P-CHOOM
BLAMM
BLAMM
P-THUMP
EVENTUALLY-- BUT NOT TODAY.
BODY ARMOR!
YES, TODAY!
THWAMM
AND I WILL LIVE TO DISMEMBER ALL OF YOU, PIECE BY PIECE...!

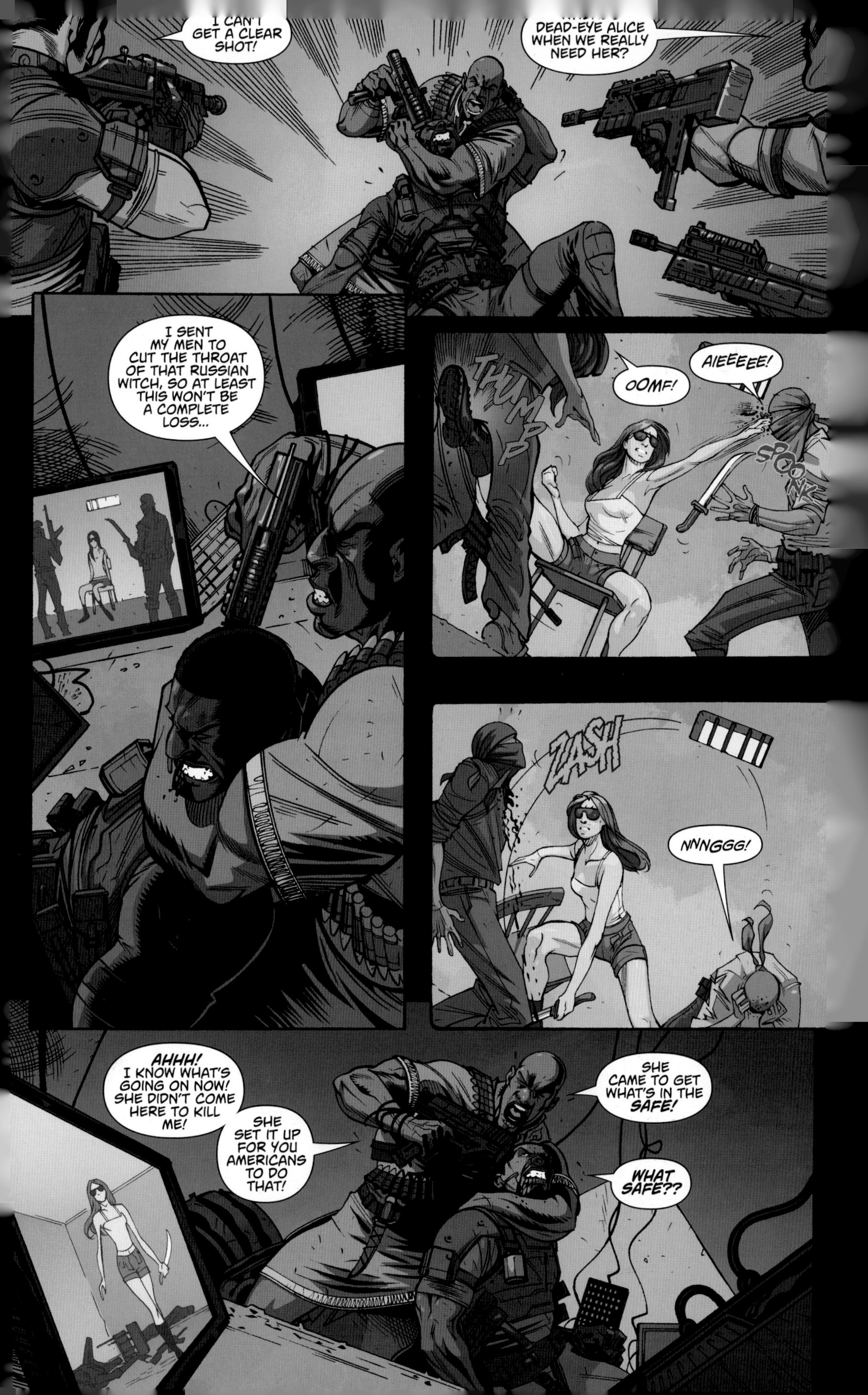

I CAN'T GET A CLEAR SHOT!
DEAD-EYE ALICE WHEN WE REALLY NEED HER?
I SENT MY MEN TO CUT THE THROAT OF THAT RUSSIAN WITCH, SO AT LEAST THIS WON'T BE A COMPLETE LOSS...
THUMP
OOMF!
AIEEEEEE!
SPOONK
ZASH
NNNGGG!
AHHH! I KNOW WHAT'S GOING ON NOW! SHE DIDN'T COME HERE TO KILL ME!
SHE SET IT UP FOR YOU AMERICANS TO DO THAT!
SHE CAME TO GET WHAT'S IN THE SAFE!
WHAT SAFE??

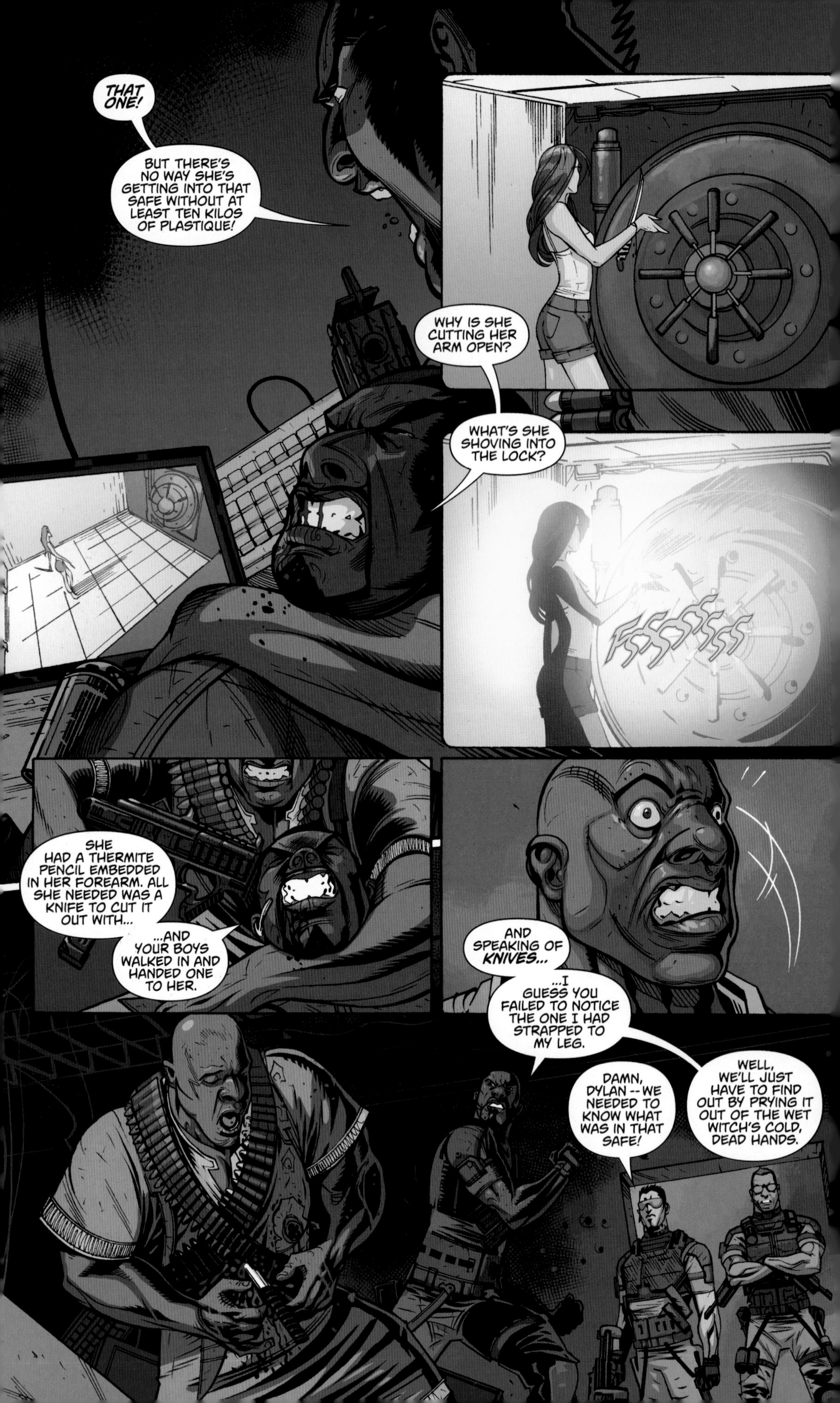
THAT ONE!
BUT THERE'S NO WAY SHE'S GETTING INTO THAT SAFE WITHOUT AT LEAST TEN KILOS OF PLASTIQUE!
WHY IS SHE CUTTING HER ARM OPEN?
WHAT'S SHE SHOVING INTO THE LOCK?
FSSSSSSS
SHE HAD A THERMITE PENCIL EMBEDDED IN HER FOREARM. ALL SHE NEEDED WAS A KNIFE TO CUT IT OUT WITH...
...AND YOUR BOYS WALKED IN AND HANDED ONE TO HER.
AND SPEAKING OF KNIVES...
...I GUESS YOU FAILED TO NOTICE THE ONE I HAD STRAPPED TO MY LEG.
DAMN, DYLAN -- WE NEEDED TO KNOW WHAT WAS IN THAT SAFE!
WELL, WE'LL JUST HAVE TO FIND OUT BY PRYING IT OUT OF THE WET WITCH'S COLD, DEAD HANDS.

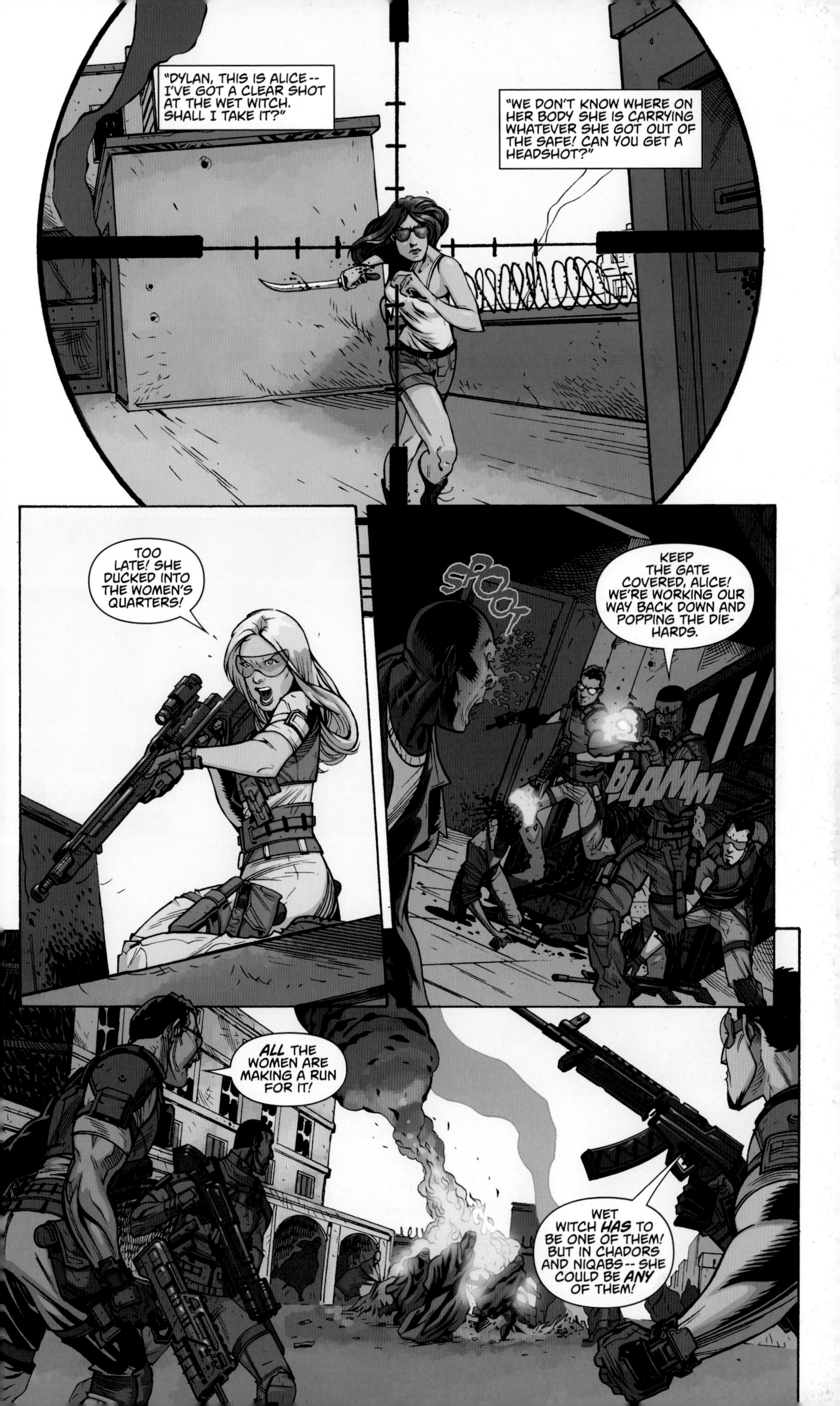
"DYLAN, THIS IS ALICE -- I'VE GOT A CLEAR SHOT AT THE WET WITCH. SHALL I TAKE IT?"
"WE DON'T KNOW WHERE ON HER BODY SHE IS CARRYING WHATEVER SHE GOT OUT OF THE SAFE! CAN YOU GET A HEADSHOT?"
TOO LATE! SHE DUCKED INTO THE WOMEN'S QUARTERS!
SPOOT
KEEP THE GATE COVERED, ALICE! WE'RE WORKING OUR WAY BACK DOWN AND POPPING THE DIE-HARDS.
BLAMM
ALL THE WOMEN ARE MAKING A RUN FOR IT!
WET WITCH HAS TO BE ONE OF THEM! BUT IN CHADORS AND NIQABS -- SHE COULD BE ANY OF THEM!

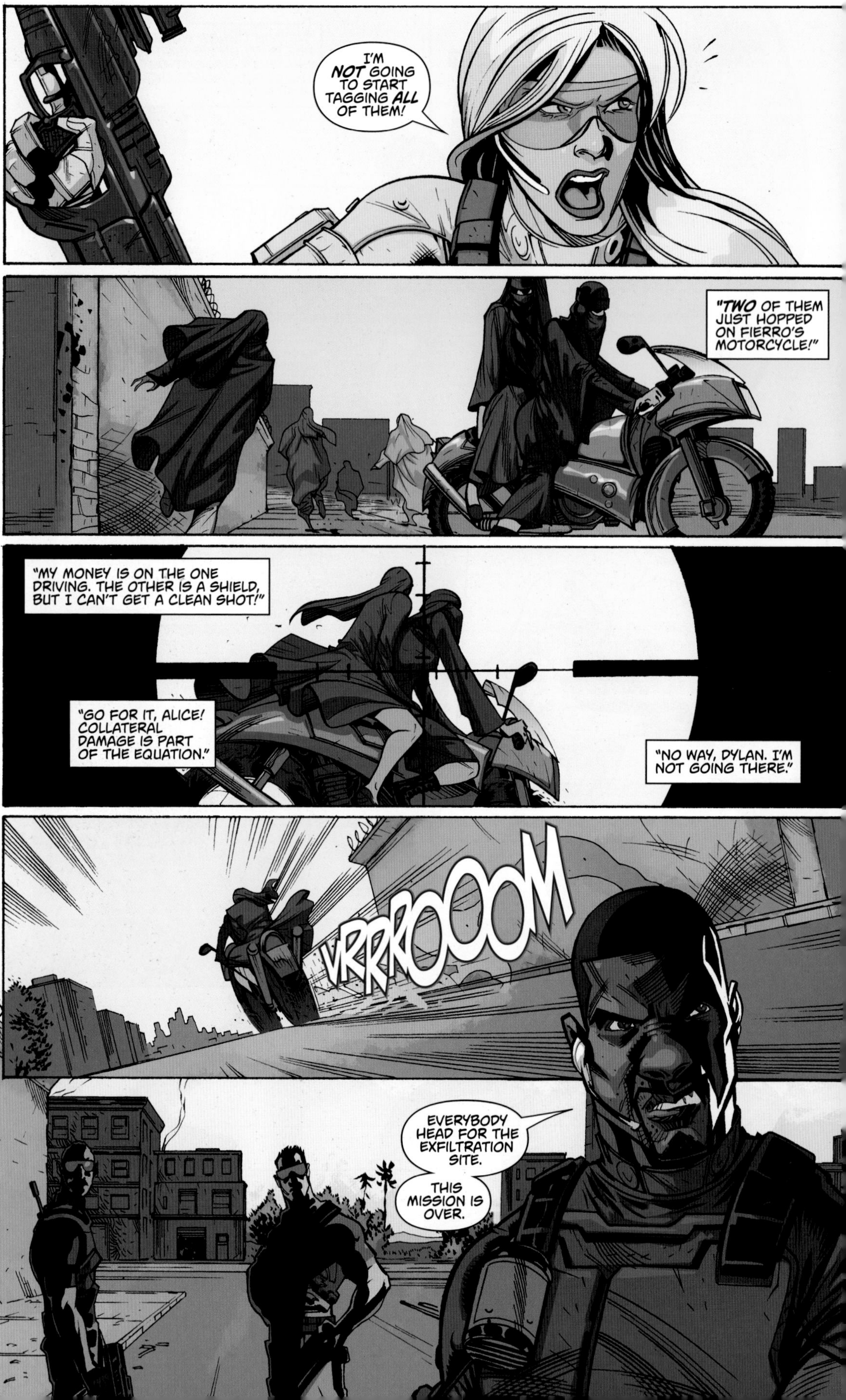
I'M NOT GOING TO START TAGGING ALL OF THEM!
"TWO OF THEM JUST HOPPED ON FIERRO'S MOTORCYCLE!"
"MY MONEY IS ON THE ONE DRIVING. THE OTHER IS A SHIELD, BUT I CAN'T GET A CLEAN SHOT!"
"GO FOR IT, ALICE! COLLATERAL DAMAGE IS PART OF THE EQUATION."
"NO WAY, DYLAN. I'M NOT GOING THERE."
VRRROOOM
EVERYBODY HEAD FOR THE EXFILTRATION SITE.
THIS MISSION IS OVER.

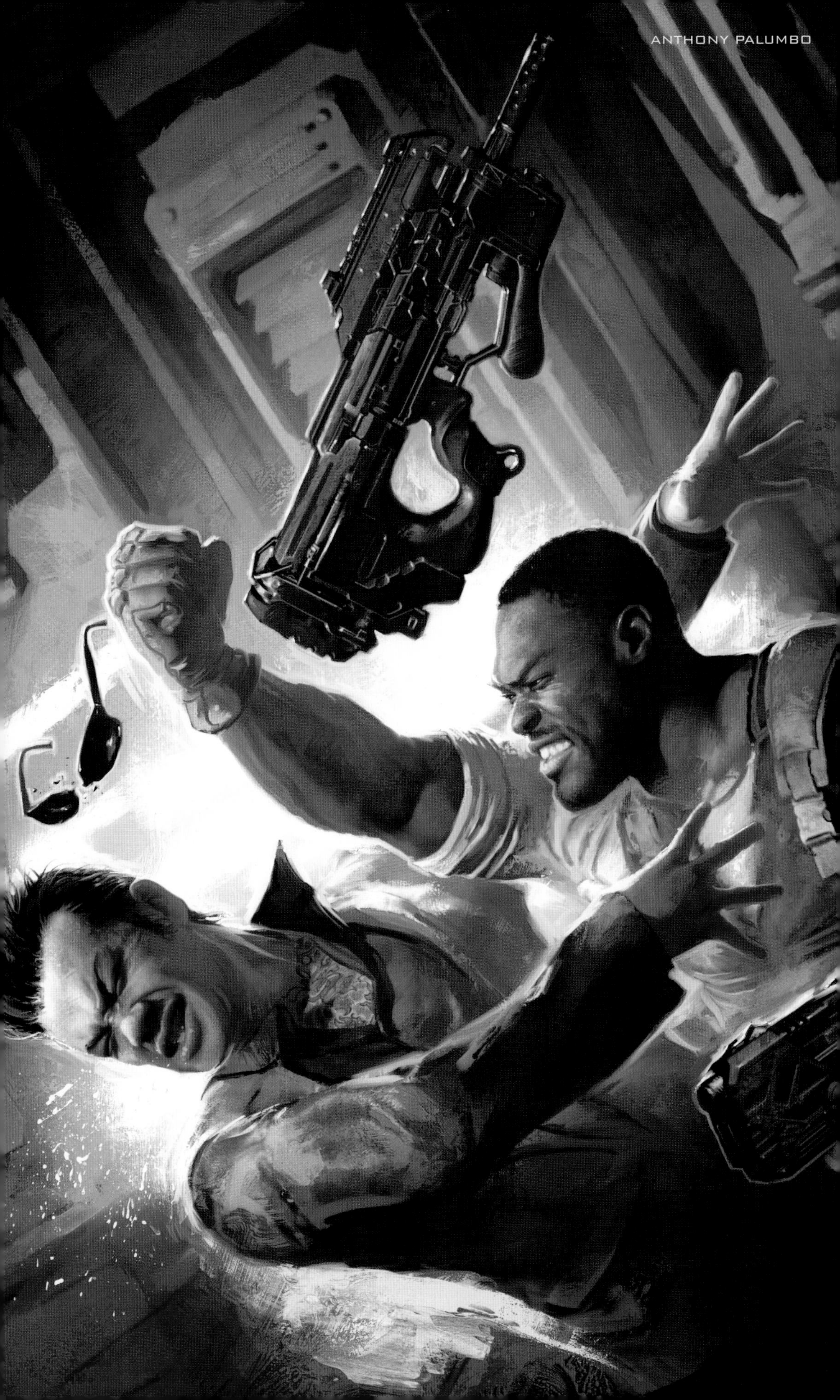
ANTHONY PALUMBO

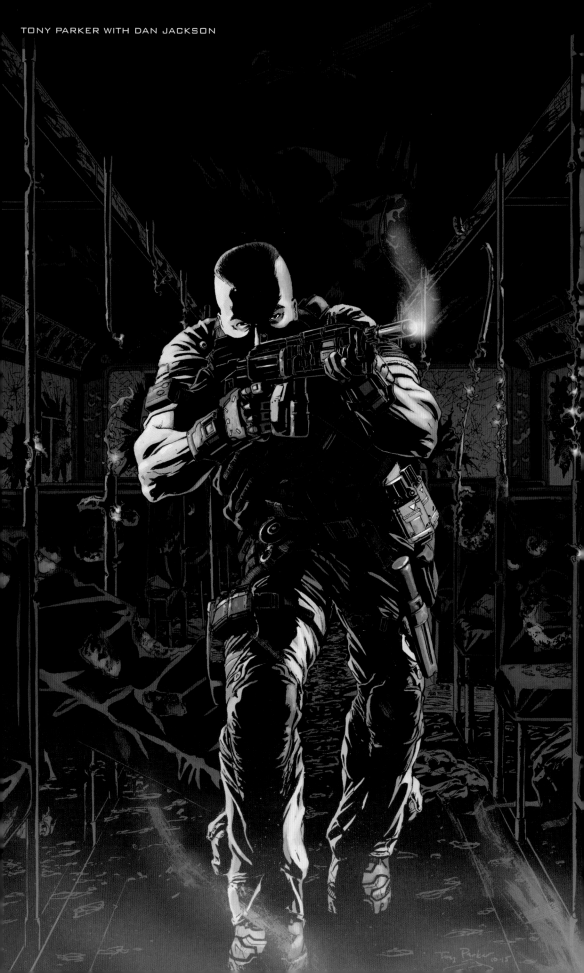

TONY PARKER WITH DAN JACKSON

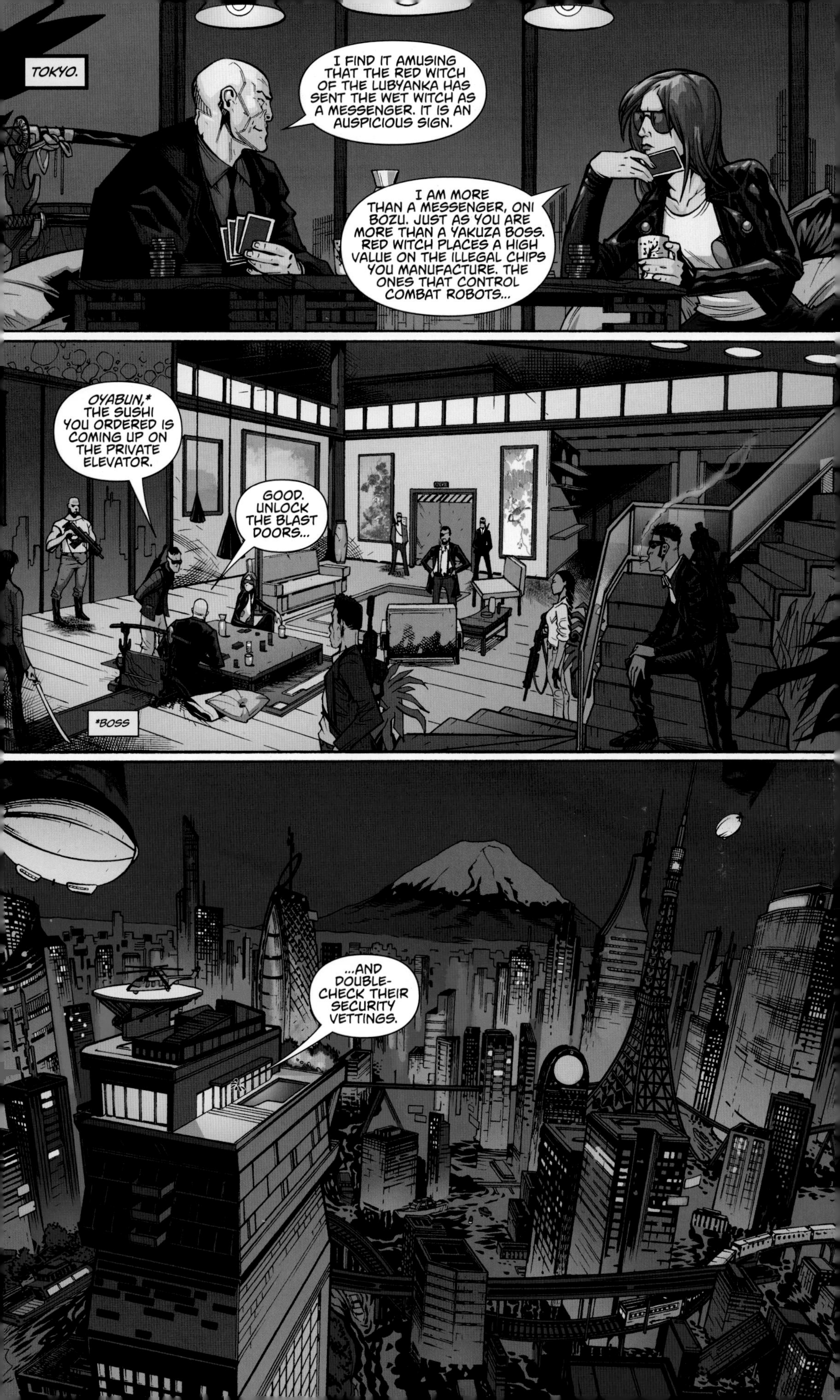
TOKYO.
I FIND IT AMUSING THAT THE RED WITCH OF THE LUBYANKA HAS SENT THE WET WITCH AS A MESSENGER. IT IS AN AUSPICIOUS SIGN.
I AM MORE THAN A MESSENGER, ONI BOZU. JUST AS YOU ARE MORE THAN A YAKUZA BOSS. RED WITCH PLACES A HIGH VALUE ON THE ILLEGAL CHIPS YOU MANUFACTURE. THE ONES THAT CONTROL COMBAT ROBOTS...
OYABUN,* THE SUSHI YOU ORDERED IS COMING UP ON THE PRIVATE ELEVATOR.
GOOD. UNLOCK THE BLAST DOORS...
*BOSS
...AND DOUBLE-CHECK THEIR SECURITY VETTINGS.

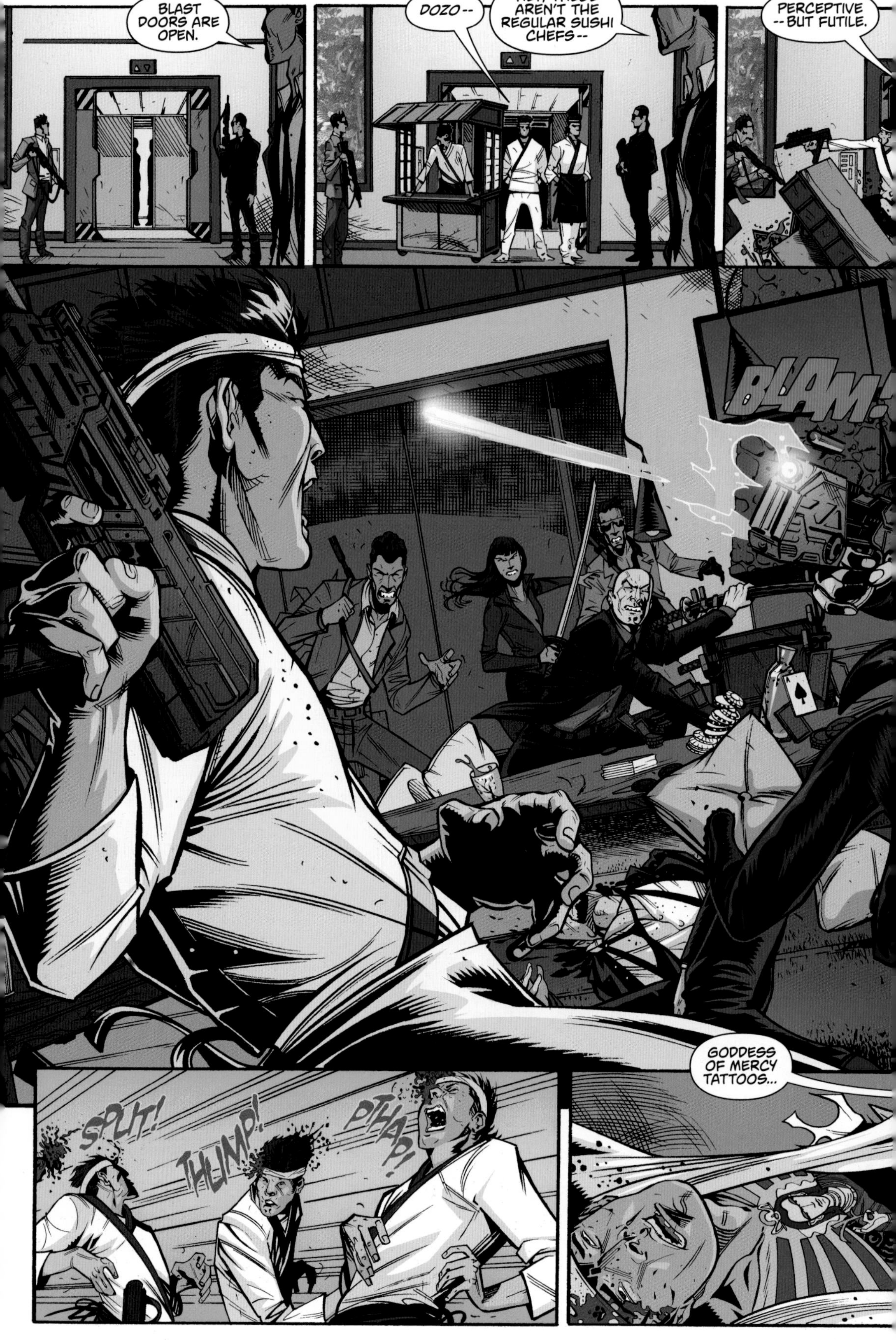
BLAST DOORS ARE OPEN.
DOZO--
HEY, THESE AREN'T THE REGULAR SUSHI CHEFS--
PERCEPTIVE --BUT FUTILE.
BLAM!
GODDESS OF MERCY TATTOOS...
SPLIT!
THUMP!
PTHAP!

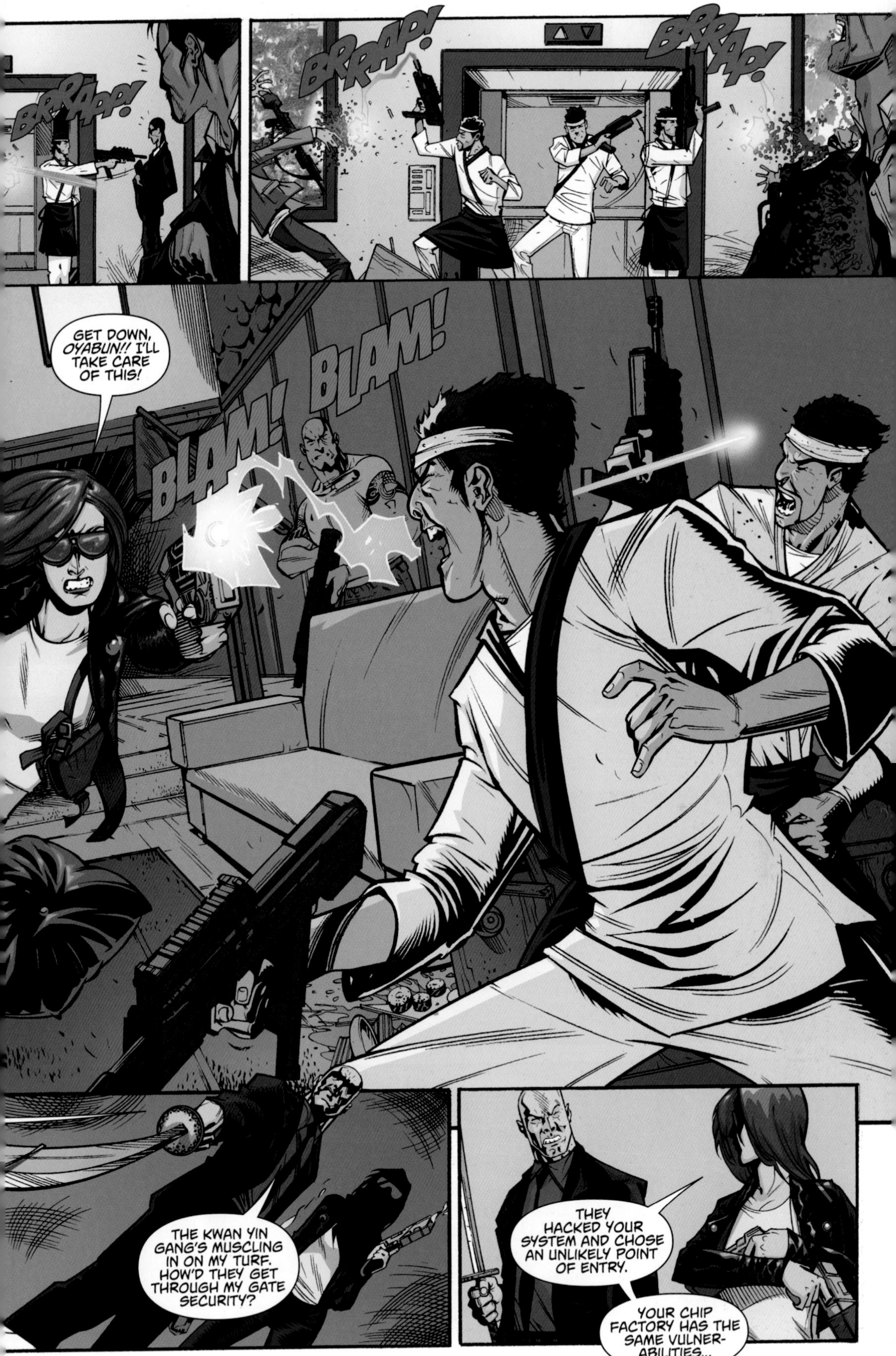
BRRAPP!
BRRAP!
BRRAP!
GET DOWN, OYABUN!! I'LL TAKE CARE OF THIS!
BLAM! BLAM! BLAM!
THE KWAN YIN GANG'S MUSCLING IN ON MY TURF. HOW'D THEY GET THROUGH MY GATE SECURITY?
THEY HACKED YOUR SYSTEM AND CHOSE AN UNLIKELY POINT OF ENTRY.
YOUR CHIP FACTORY HAS THE SAME VULNER-ABILITIES...

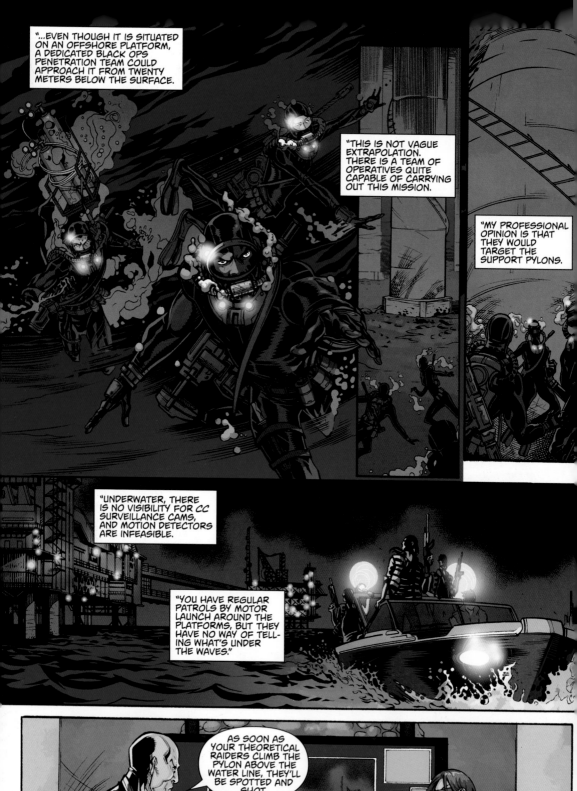

"...EVEN THOUGH IT IS SITUATED ON AN OFFSHORE PLATFORM, A DEDICATED BLACK OPS PENETRATION TEAM COULD APPROACH IT FROM TWENTY METERS BELOW THE SURFACE.

"THIS IS NOT VAGUE EXTRAPOLATION. THERE IS A TEAM OF OPERATIVES QUITE CAPABLE OF CARRYING OUT THIS MISSION.

"MY PROFESSIONAL OPINION IS THAT THEY WOULD TARGET THE SUPPORT PYLONS.

"UNDERWATER, THERE IS NO VISIBILITY FOR CC SURVEILLANCE CAMS, AND MOTION DETECTORS ARE INFEASIBLE.

"YOU HAVE REGULAR PATROLS BY MOTOR LAUNCH AROUND THE PLATFORMS, BUT THEY HAVE NO WAY OF TELLING WHAT'S UNDER THE WAVES."

AS SOON AS YOUR THEORETICAL RAIDERS CLIMB THE PYLON ABOVE THE WATER LINE, THEY'LL BE SPOTTED AND SHOT.

NOT IF THEY ARE CLIMBING THE PYLON FROM *INSIDE*...

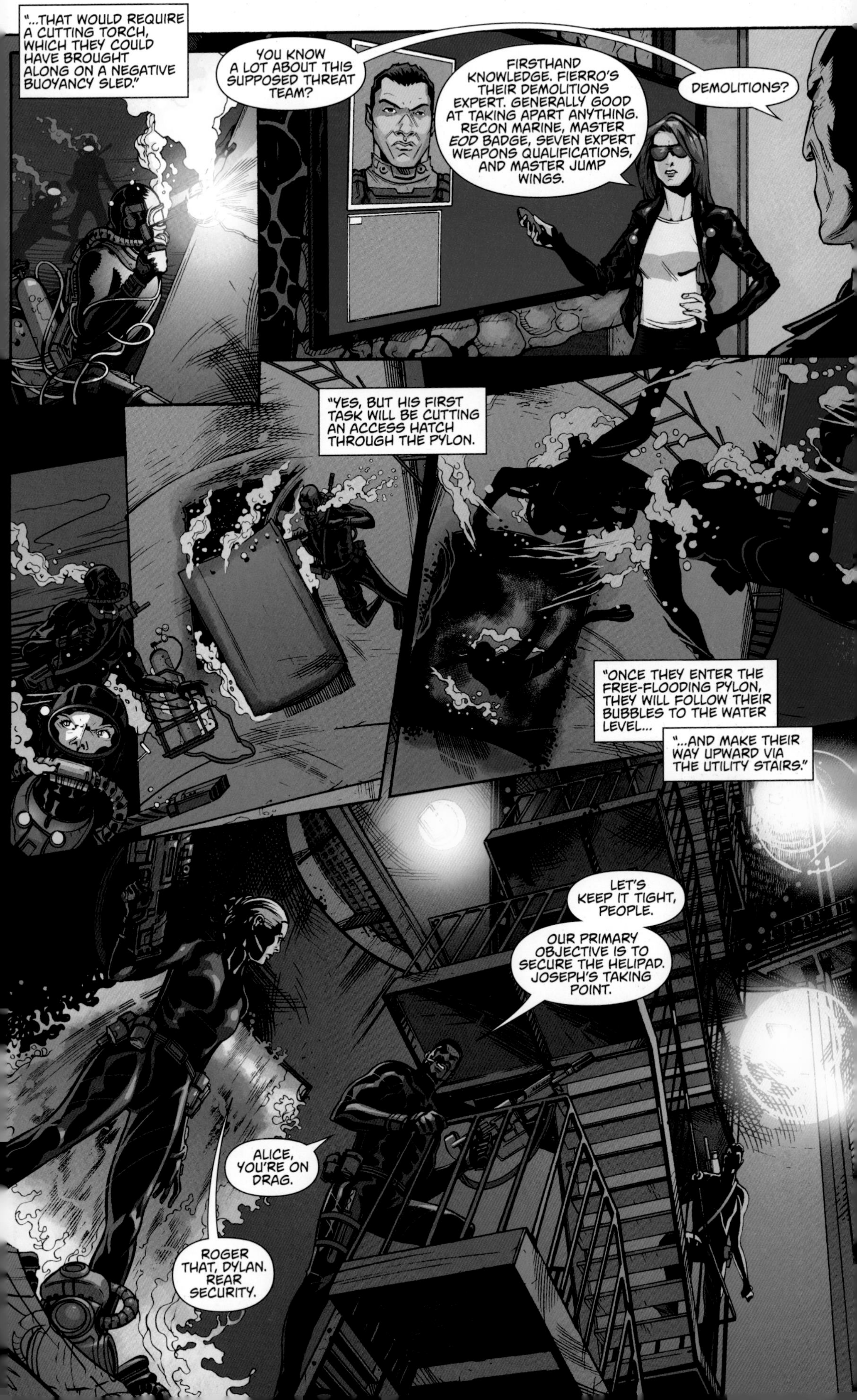
"...THAT WOULD REQUIRE A CUTTING TORCH, WHICH THEY COULD HAVE BROUGHT ALONG ON A NEGATIVE BUOYANCY SLED."
YOU KNOW A LOT ABOUT THIS SUPPOSED THREAT TEAM?
FIRSTHAND KNOWLEDGE. FIERRO'S THEIR DEMOLITIONS EXPERT. GENERALLY GOOD AT TAKING APART ANYTHING. RECON MARINE, MASTER EOD BADGE, SEVEN EXPERT WEAPONS QUALIFICATIONS, AND MASTER JUMP WINGS.
DEMOLITIONS?
"YES, BUT HIS FIRST TASK WILL BE CUTTING AN ACCESS HATCH THROUGH THE PYLON.
"ONCE THEY ENTER THE FREE-FLOODING PYLON, THEY WILL FOLLOW THEIR BUBBLES TO THE WATER LEVEL...
"...AND MAKE THEIR WAY UPWARD VIA THE UTILITY STAIRS."
LET'S KEEP IT TIGHT, PEOPLE.
OUR PRIMARY OBJECTIVE IS TO SECURE THE HELIPAD. JOSEPH'S TAKING POINT.
ALICE, YOU'RE ON DRAG.
ROGER THAT, DYLAN. REAR SECURITY.

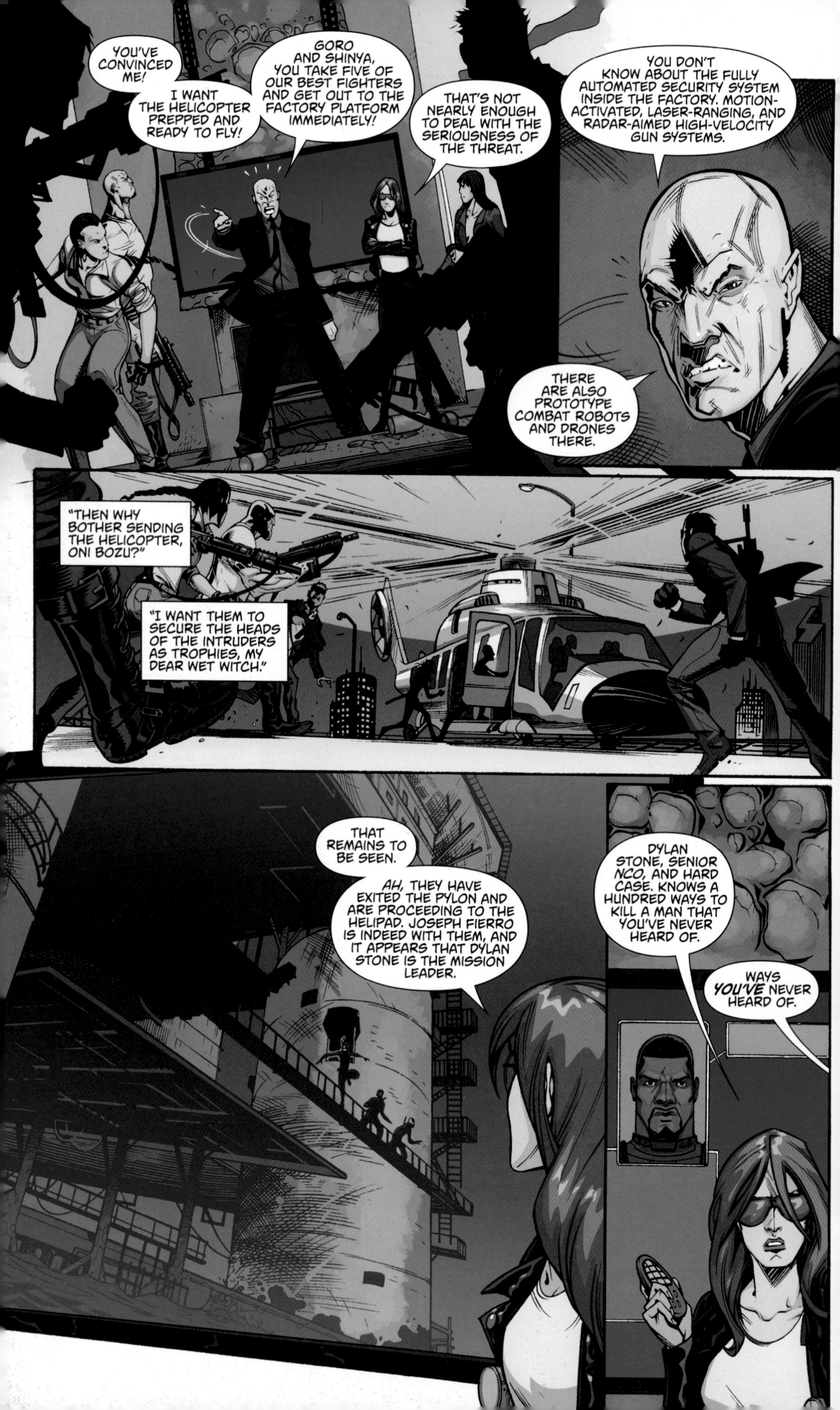

YOU'VE CONVINCED ME!
I WANT THE HELICOPTER PREPPED AND READY TO FLY!
GORO AND SHINYA, YOU TAKE FIVE OF OUR BEST FIGHTERS AND GET OUT TO THE FACTORY PLATFORM IMMEDIATELY!
THAT'S NOT NEARLY ENOUGH TO DEAL WITH THE SERIOUSNESS OF THE THREAT.
YOU DON'T KNOW ABOUT THE FULLY AUTOMATED SECURITY SYSTEM INSIDE THE FACTORY. MOTION-ACTIVATED, LASER-RANGING, AND RADAR-AIMED HIGH-VELOCITY GUN SYSTEMS.
THERE ARE ALSO PROTOTYPE COMBAT ROBOTS AND DRONES THERE.
"THEN WHY BOTHER SENDING THE HELICOPTER, ONI BOZU?"
"I WANT THEM TO SECURE THE HEADS OF THE INTRUDERS AS TROPHIES, MY DEAR WET WITCH."
THAT REMAINS TO BE SEEN.
AH, THEY HAVE EXITED THE PYLON AND ARE PROCEEDING TO THE HELIPAD. JOSEPH FIERRO IS INDEED WITH THEM, AND IT APPEARS THAT DYLAN STONE IS THE MISSION LEADER.
DYLAN STONE, SENIOR NCO, AND HARD CASE. KNOWS A HUNDRED WAYS TO KILL A MAN THAT YOU'VE NEVER HEARD OF.
WAYS *YOU'VE* NEVER HEARD OF.

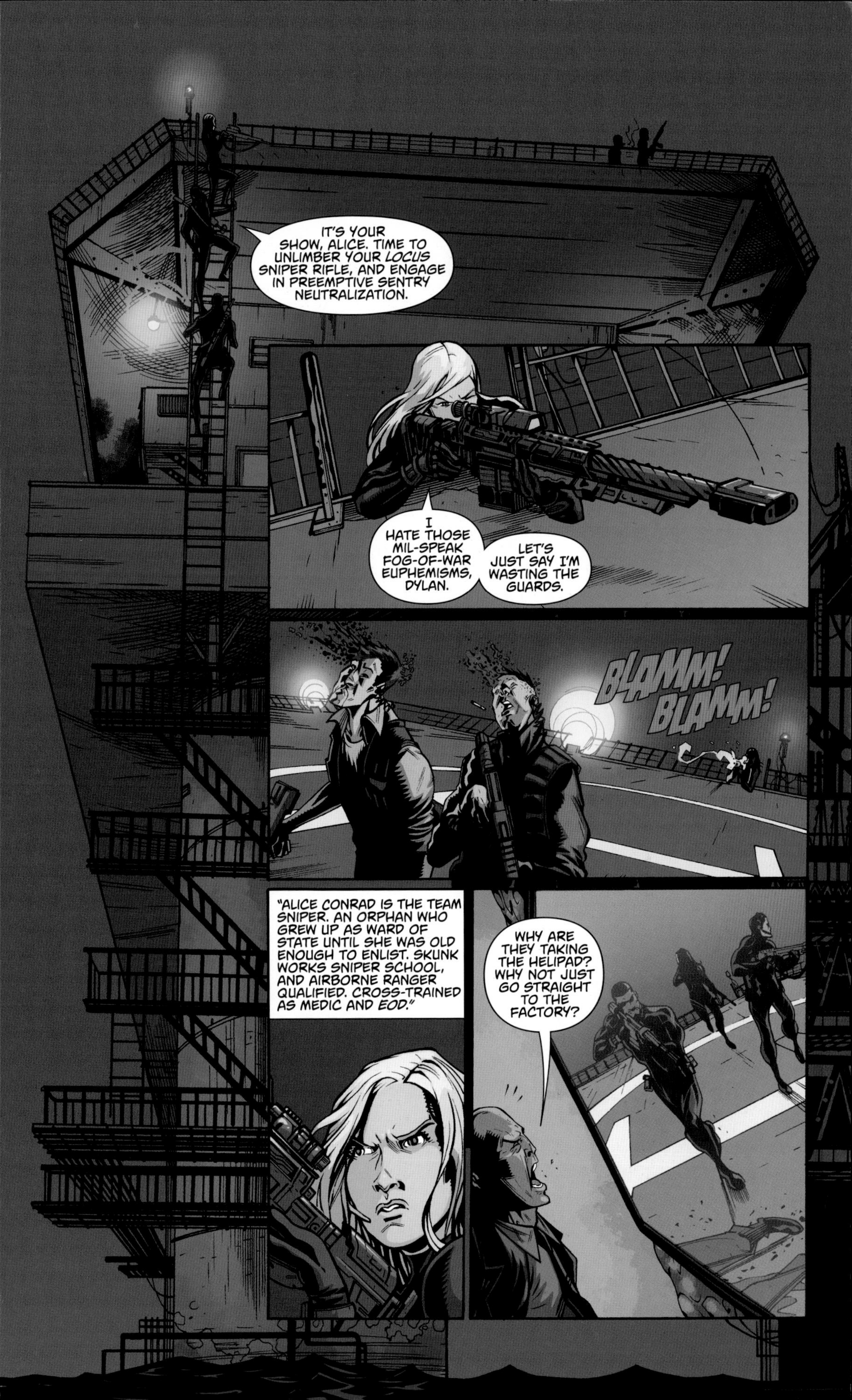
IT'S YOUR SHOW, ALICE. TIME TO UNLIMBER YOUR LOCUS SNIPER RIFLE, AND ENGAGE IN PREEMPTIVE SENTRY NEUTRALIZATION.
I HATE THOSE MIL-SPEAK FOG-OF-WAR EUPHEMISMS, DYLAN.
LET'S JUST SAY I'M WASTING THE GUARDS.
BLAMM! BLAMM!
"ALICE CONRAD IS THE TEAM SNIPER. AN ORPHAN WHO GREW UP AS WARD OF STATE UNTIL SHE WAS OLD ENOUGH TO ENLIST. SKUNK WORKS SNIPER SCHOOL, AND AIRBORNE RANGER QUALIFIED. CROSS-TRAINED AS MEDIC AND EOD."
WHY ARE THEY TAKING THE HELIPAD? WHY NOT JUST GO STRAIGHT TO THE FACTORY?

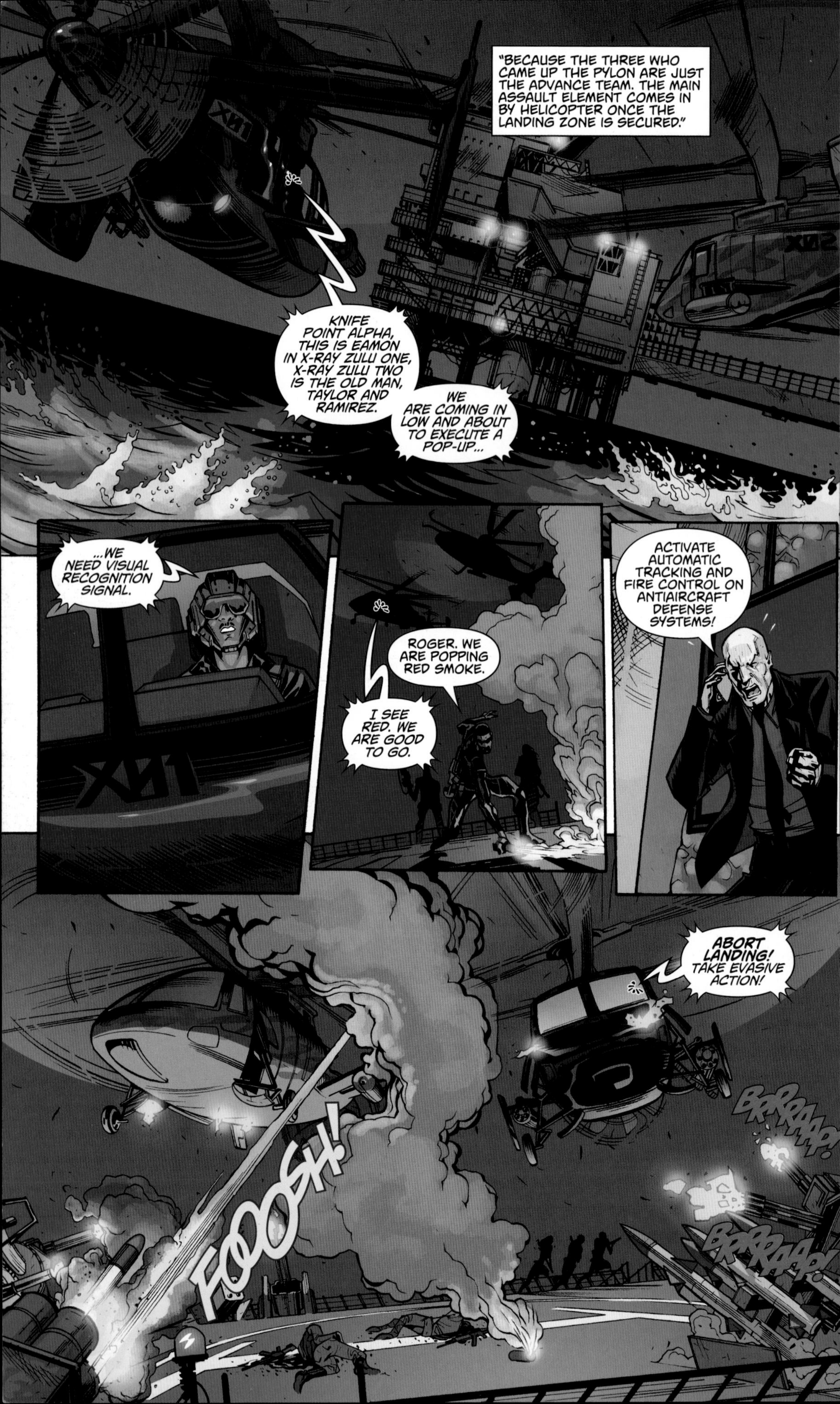

"BECAUSE THE THREE WHO CAME UP THE PYLON ARE JUST THE ADVANCE TEAM. THE MAIN ASSAULT ELEMENT COMES IN BY HELICOPTER ONCE THE LANDING ZONE IS SECURED."
KNIFE POINT ALPHA, THIS IS EAMON IN X-RAY ZULU ONE, X-RAY ZULU TWO IS THE OLD MAN, TAYLOR AND RAMIREZ.
WE ARE COMING IN LOW AND ABOUT TO EXECUTE A POP-UP...
...WE NEED VISUAL RECOGNITION SIGNAL.
ROGER. WE ARE POPPING RED SMOKE.
I SEE RED. WE ARE GOOD TO GO.
ACTIVATE AUTOMATIC TRACKING AND FIRE CONTROL ON ANTIAIRCRAFT DEFENSE SYSTEMS!
ABORT LANDING! TAKE EVASIVE ACTION!
BRRRAAAP!
FOOOSH!
BRRRAAAP!

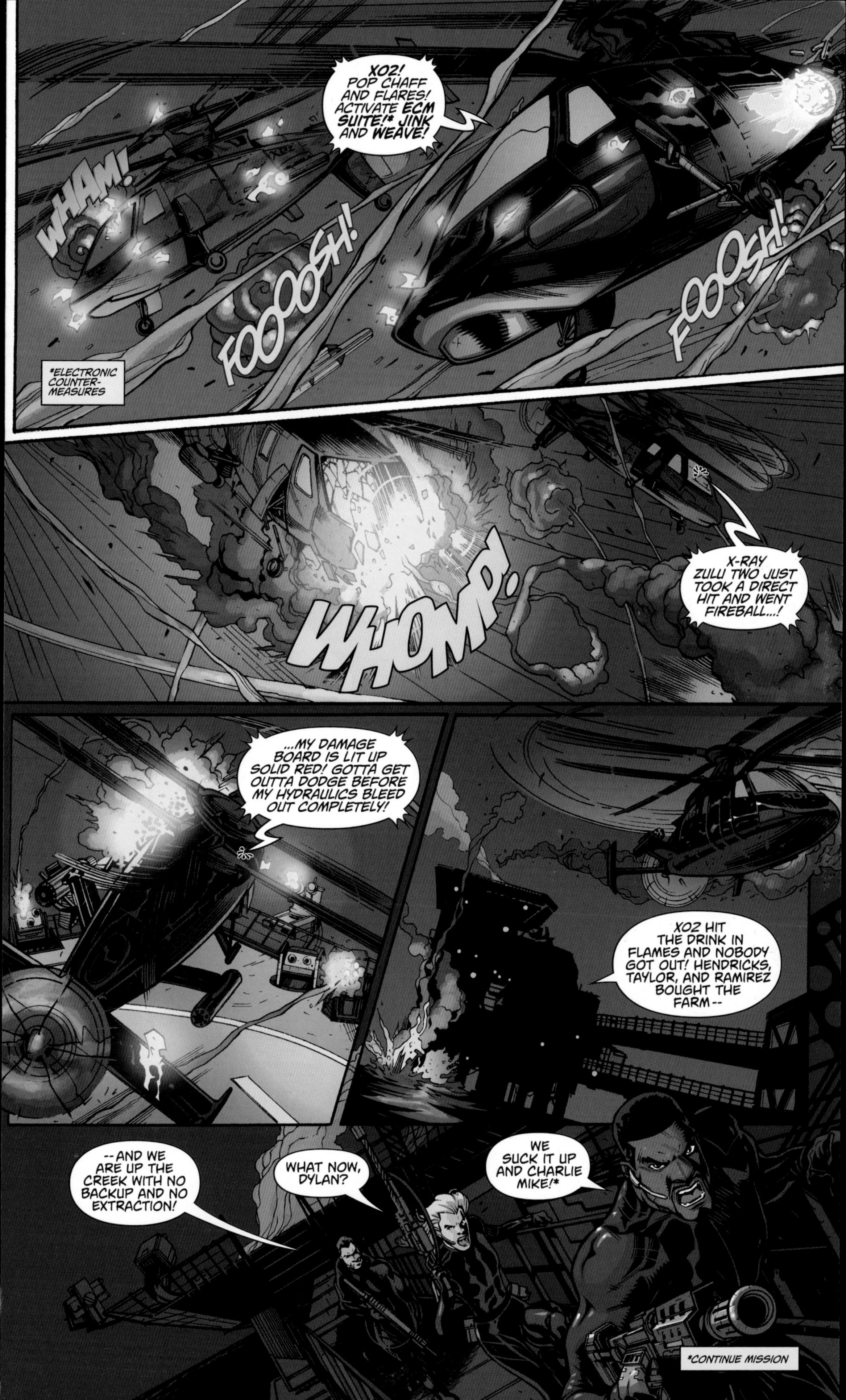
XO2! POP CHAFF AND FLARES! ACTIVATE ECM SUITE!* JINK AND WEAVE!
WHAM!
FOOOOSH!
FOOOSH!
*ELECTRONIC COUNTER-MEASURES
X-RAY ZULU TWO JUST TOOK A DIRECT HIT AND WENT FIREBALL...!
WHOMP!
...MY DAMAGE BOARD IS LIT UP SOLID RED! GOTTA GET OUTTA DODGE BEFORE MY HYDRAULICS BLEED OUT COMPLETELY!
XO2 HIT THE DRINK IN FLAMES AND NOBODY GOT OUT! HENDRICKS, TAYLOR, AND RAMIREZ BOUGHT THE FARM --
-- AND WE ARE UP THE CREEK WITH NO BACKUP AND NO EXTRACTION!
WHAT NOW, DYLAN?
WE SUCK IT UP AND CHARLIE MIKE!*
*CONTINUE MISSION

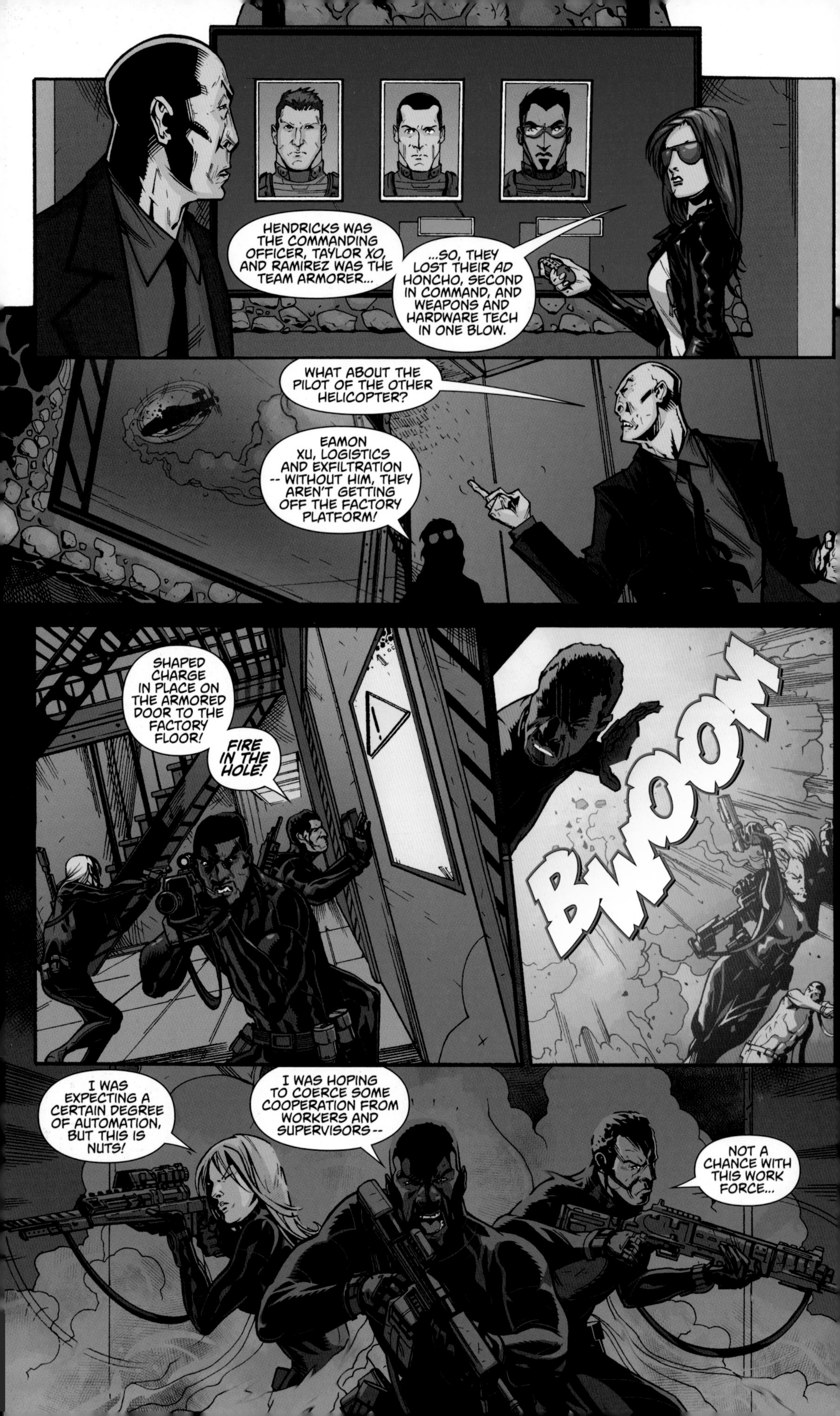
HENDRICKS WAS THE COMMANDING OFFICER, TAYLOR XO, AND RAMIREZ WAS THE TEAM ARMORER...
...SO, THEY LOST THEIR AD HONCHO, SECOND IN COMMAND, AND WEAPONS AND HARDWARE TECH IN ONE BLOW.
WHAT ABOUT THE PILOT OF THE OTHER HELICOPTER?
EAMON XU, LOGISTICS AND EXFILTRATION -- WITHOUT HIM, THEY AREN'T GETTING OFF THE FACTORY PLATFORM!
SHAPED CHARGE IN PLACE ON THE ARMORED DOOR TO THE FACTORY FLOOR!
FIRE IN THE HOLE!
BWOOM
I WAS EXPECTING A CERTAIN DEGREE OF AUTOMATION, BUT THIS IS NUTS!
I WAS HOPING TO COERCE SOME COOPERATION FROM WORKERS AND SUPERVISORS--
NOT A CHANCE WITH THIS WORK FORCE...

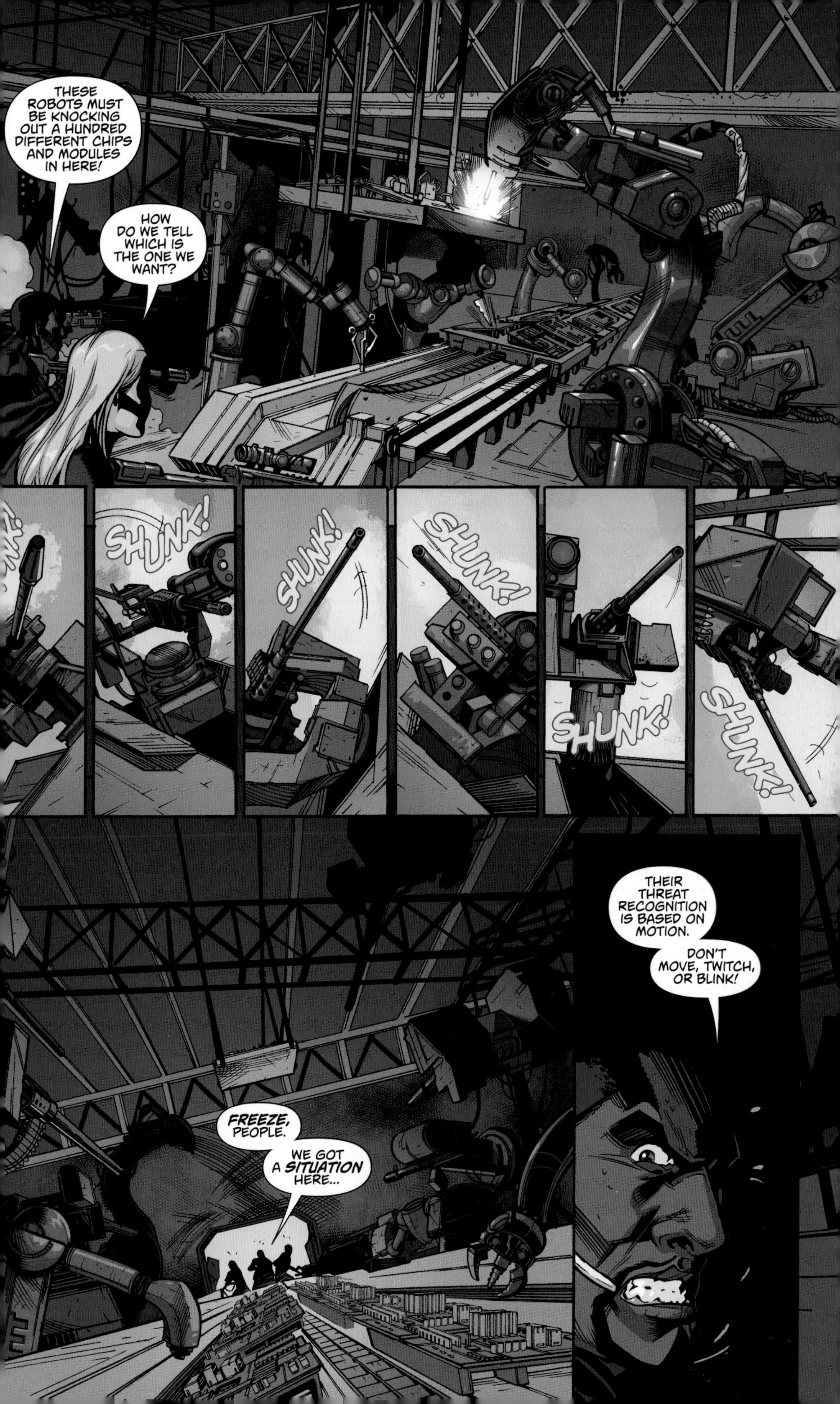
THESE ROBOTS MUST BE KNOCKING OUT A HUNDRED DIFFERENT CHIPS AND MODULES IN HERE!
HOW DO WE TELL WHICH IS THE ONE WE WANT?
SHUNK!
SHUNK!
SHUNK!
SHUNK!
SHUNK!
FREEZE, PEOPLE.
WE GOT A SITUATION HERE...
THEIR THREAT RECOGNITION IS BASED ON MOTION.
DON'T MOVE, TWITCH, OR BLINK!

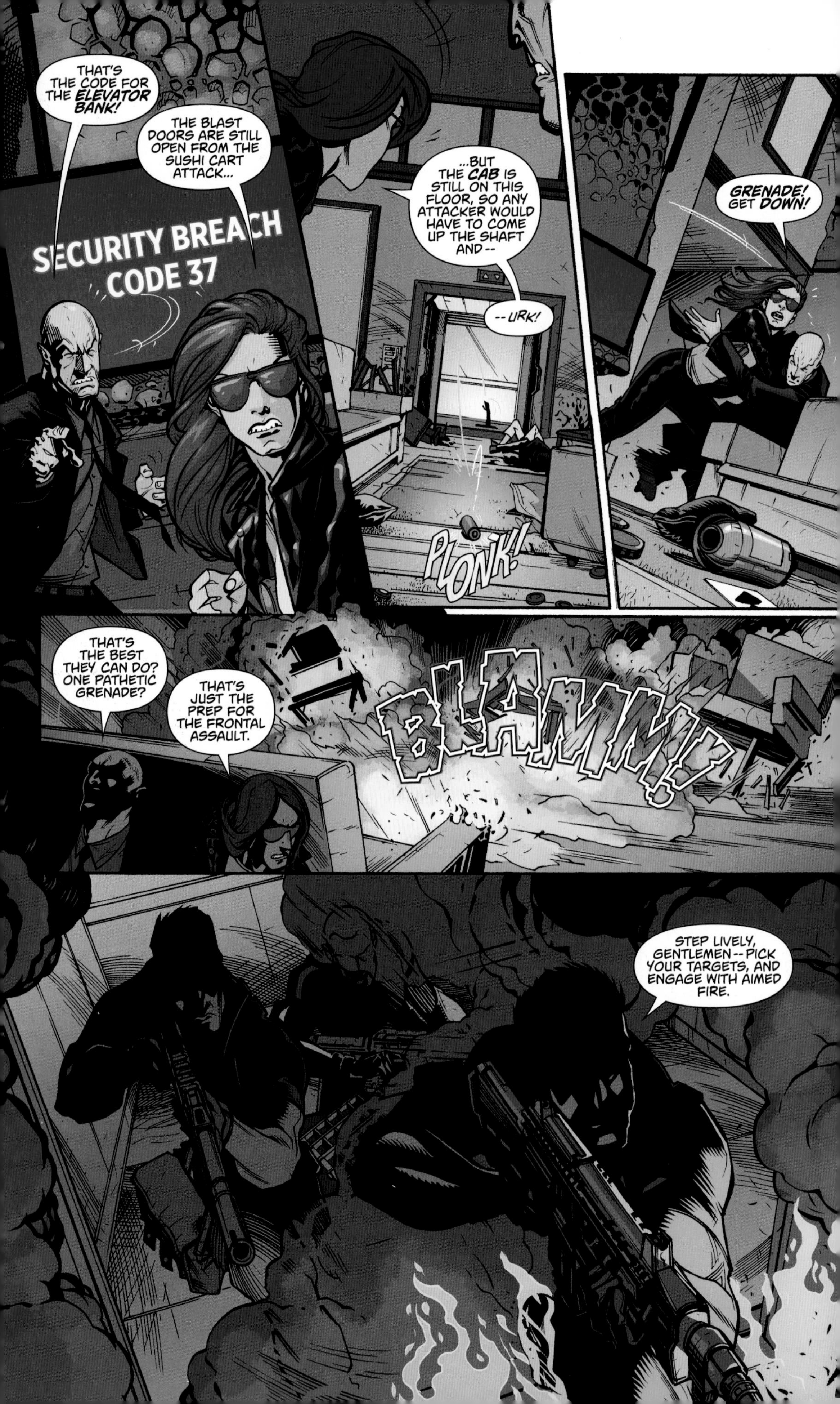
THAT'S THE CODE FOR THE ELEVATOR BANK!
THE BLAST DOORS ARE STILL OPEN FROM THE SUSHI CART ATTACK...
SECURITY BREACH CODE 37
...BUT THE CAB IS STILL ON THIS FLOOR, SO ANY ATTACKER WOULD HAVE TO COME UP THE SHAFT AND--
--URK!
PLONK!
GRENADE! GET DOWN!
THAT'S THE BEST THEY CAN DO? ONE PATHETIC GRENADE?
THAT'S JUST THE PREP FOR THE FRONTAL ASSAULT.
BLAMM!
STEP LIVELY, GENTLEMEN--PICK YOUR TARGETS, AND ENGAGE WITH AIMED FIRE.

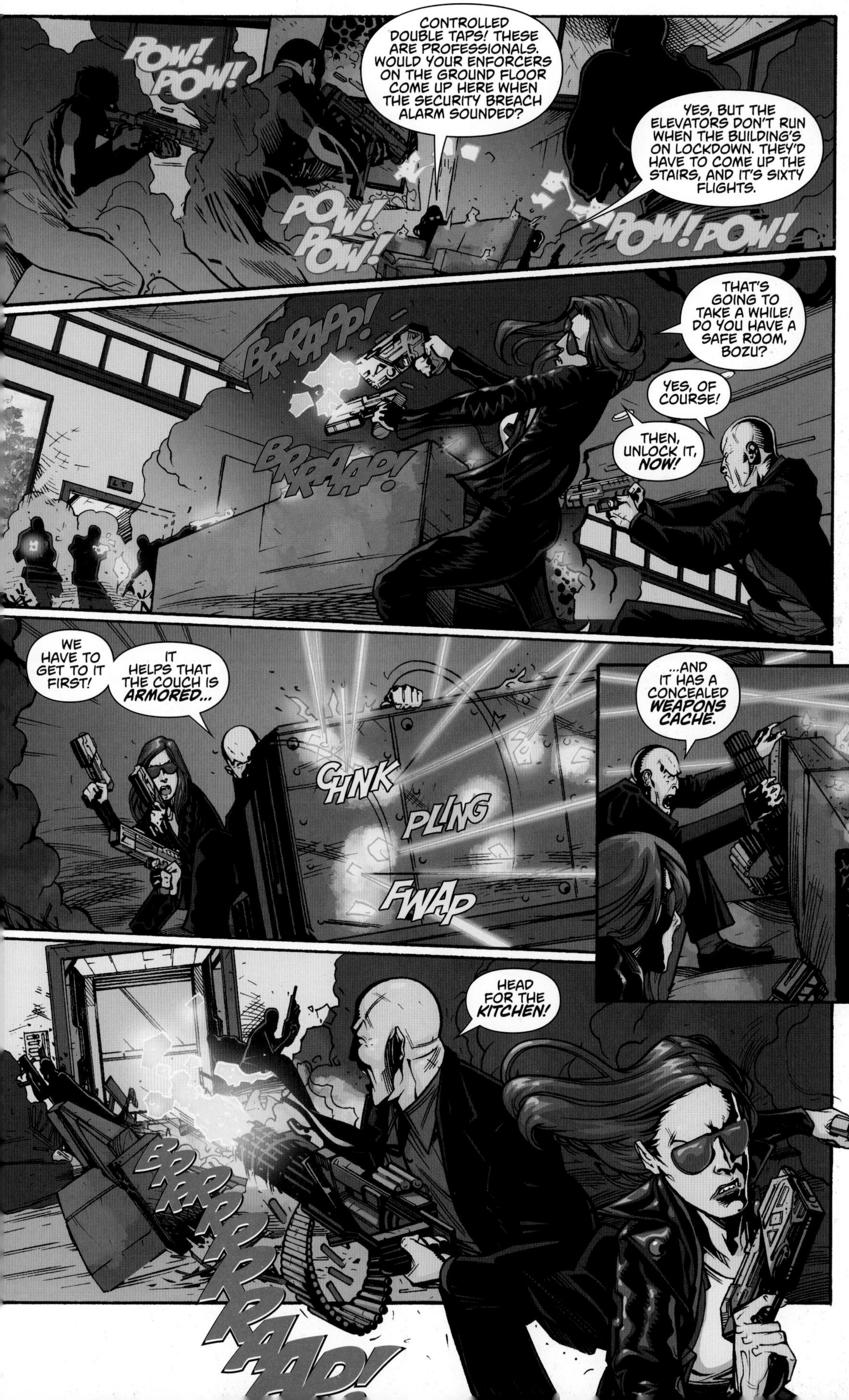
POW! POW!
CONTROLLED DOUBLE TAPS! THESE ARE PROFESSIONALS. WOULD YOUR ENFORCERS ON THE GROUND FLOOR COME UP HERE WHEN THE SECURITY BREACH ALARM SOUNDED?
YES, BUT THE ELEVATORS DON'T RUN WHEN THE BUILDING'S ON LOCKDOWN. THEY'D HAVE TO COME UP THE STAIRS, AND IT'S SIXTY FLIGHTS.
POW! POW!
POW! POW!
BRRAPP!
BRRAAP!
THAT'S GOING TO TAKE A WHILE! DO YOU HAVE A SAFE ROOM, BOZU?
YES, OF COURSE!
THEN, UNLOCK IT, NOW!
WE HAVE TO GET TO IT FIRST!
IT HELPS THAT THE COUCH IS ARMORED...
CHNK
PLING
FWAP
...AND IT HAS A CONCEALED WEAPONS CACHE.
HEAD FOR THE KITCHEN!
BRRRRRRAAD!

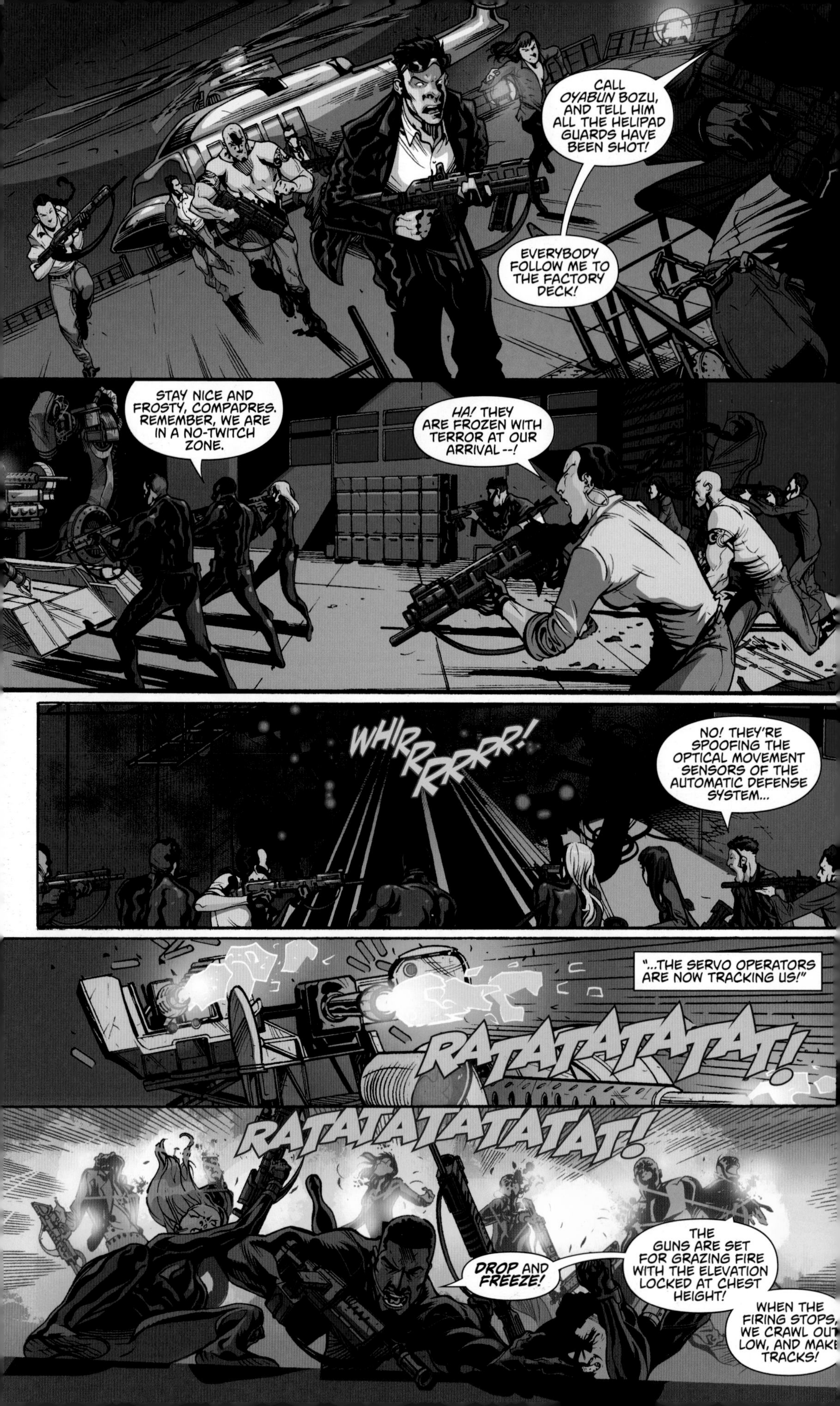
CALL OYABUN BOZU, AND TELL HIM ALL THE HELIPAD GUARDS HAVE BEEN SHOT!
EVERYBODY FOLLOW ME TO THE FACTORY DECK!
STAY NICE AND FROSTY, COMPADRES. REMEMBER, WE ARE IN A NO-TWITCH ZONE.
HA! THEY ARE FROZEN WITH TERROR AT OUR ARRIVAL --!
WHIRRRRRR!
NO! THEY'RE SPOOFING THE OPTICAL MOVEMENT SENSORS OF THE AUTOMATIC DEFENSE SYSTEM...
"...THE SERVO OPERATORS ARE NOW TRACKING US!"
RATATATATATAT!
RATATATATATATAT!
DROP AND FREEZE!
THE GUNS ARE SET FOR GRAZING FIRE WITH THE ELEVATION LOCKED AT CHEST HEIGHT!
WHEN THE FIRING STOPS, WE CRAWL OUT LOW, AND MAKE TRACKS!

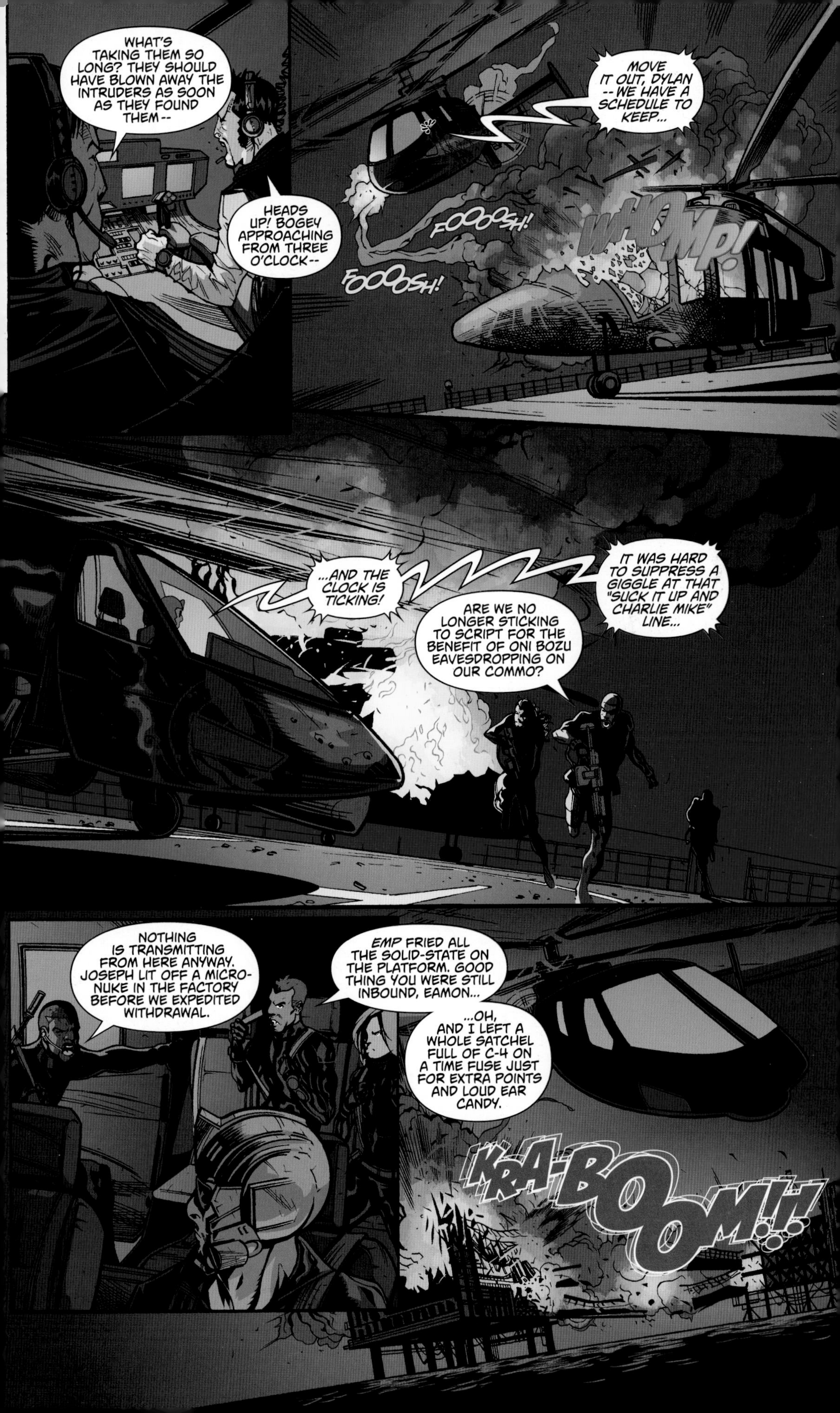
WHAT'S TAKING THEM SO LONG? THEY SHOULD HAVE BLOWN AWAY THE INTRUDERS AS SOON AS THEY FOUND THEM--
HEADS UP! BOGEY APPROACHING FROM THREE O'CLOCK--
MOVE IT OUT, DYLAN --WE HAVE A SCHEDULE TO KEEP...
FOOOOSH!
FOOOOSH!
WHOMP!
...AND THE CLOCK IS TICKING!
IT WAS HARD TO SUPPRESS A GIGGLE AT THAT "SUCK IT UP AND CHARLIE MIKE" LINE...
ARE WE NO LONGER STICKING TO SCRIPT FOR THE BENEFIT OF ONI BOZU EAVESDROPPING ON OUR COMMO?
NOTHING IS TRANSMITTING FROM HERE ANYWAY. JOSEPH LIT OFF A MICRO-NUKE IN THE FACTORY BEFORE WE EXPEDITED WITHDRAWAL.
EMP FRIED ALL THE SOLID-STATE ON THE PLATFORM. GOOD THING YOU WERE STILL INBOUND, EAMON...
...OH, AND I LEFT A WHOLE SATCHEL FULL OF C-4 ON A TIME FUSE JUST FOR EXTRA POINTS AND LOUD EAR CANDY.
KRA-BOOM!!!

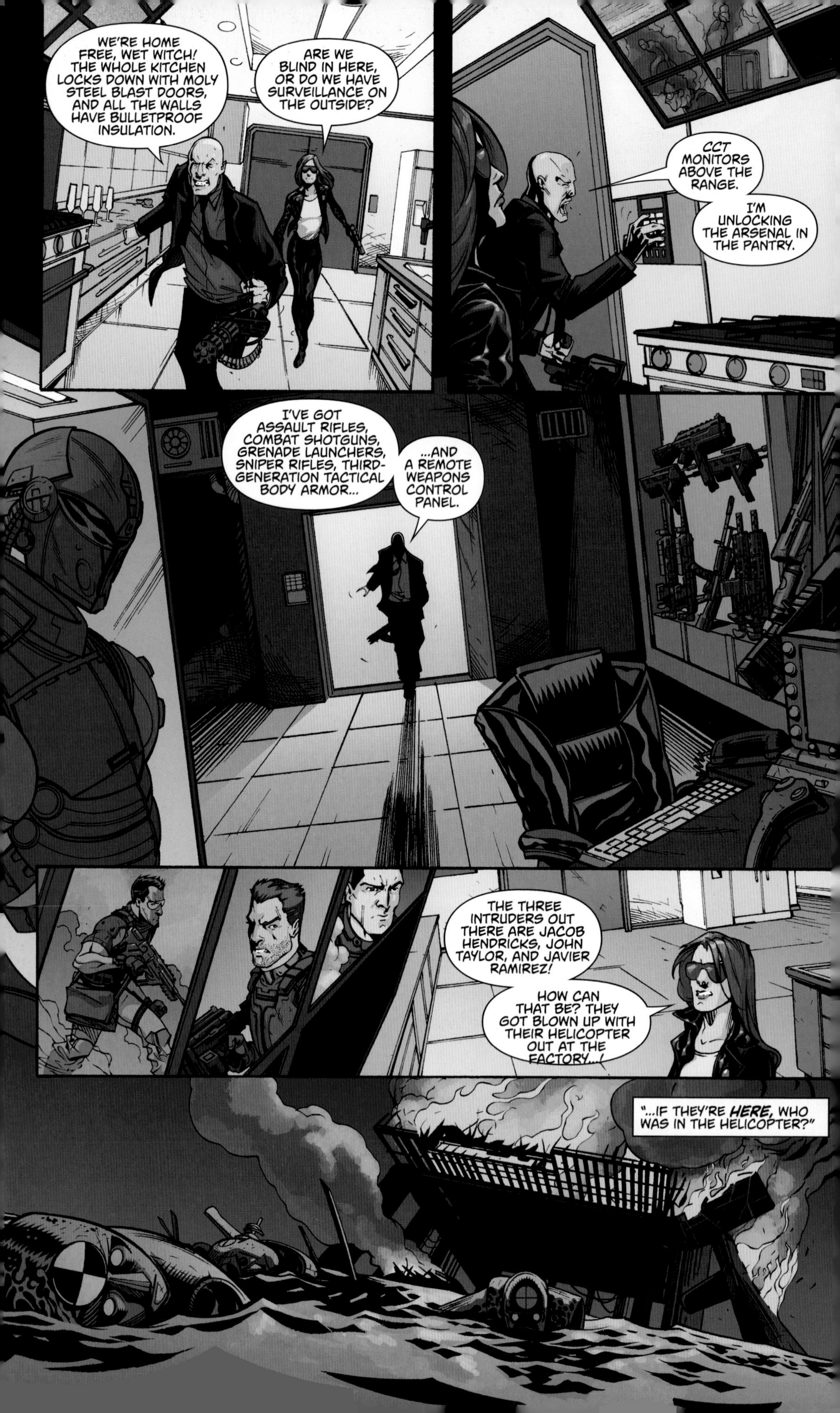
WE'RE HOME FREE, WET WITCH! THE WHOLE KITCHEN LOCKS DOWN WITH MOLY STEEL BLAST DOORS, AND ALL THE WALLS HAVE BULLETPROOF INSULATION.
ARE WE BLIND IN HERE, OR DO WE HAVE SURVEILLANCE ON THE OUTSIDE?
CCT MONITORS ABOVE THE RANGE.
I'M UNLOCKING THE ARSENAL IN THE PANTRY.
I'VE GOT ASSAULT RIFLES, COMBAT SHOTGUNS, GRENADE LAUNCHERS, SNIPER RIFLES, THIRD-GENERATION TACTICAL BODY ARMOR...
...AND A REMOTE WEAPONS CONTROL PANEL.
THE THREE INTRUDERS OUT THERE ARE JACOB HENDRICKS, JOHN TAYLOR, AND JAVIER RAMIREZ!
HOW CAN THAT BE? THEY GOT BLOWN UP WITH THEIR HELICOPTER OUT AT THE FACTORY...!
"...IF THEY'RE *HERE,* WHO WAS IN THE HELICOPTER?"

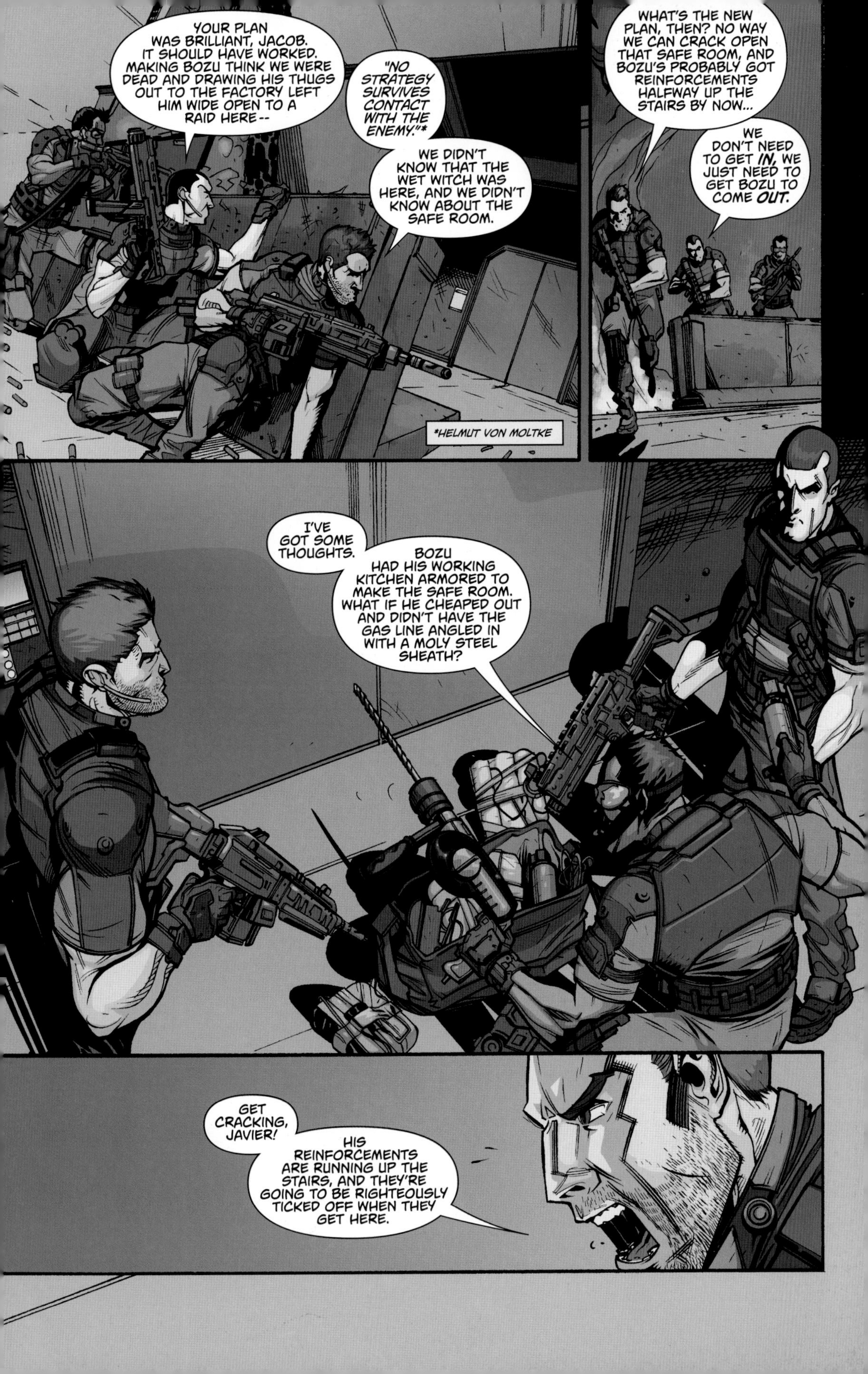
YOUR PLAN WAS BRILLIANT, JACOB. IT SHOULD HAVE WORKED. MAKING BOZU THINK WE WERE DEAD AND DRAWING HIS THUGS OUT TO THE FACTORY LEFT HIM WIDE OPEN TO A RAID HERE--
"NO STRATEGY SURVIVES CONTACT WITH THE ENEMY."*
WE DIDN'T KNOW THAT THE WET WITCH WAS HERE, AND WE DIDN'T KNOW ABOUT THE SAFE ROOM.
*HELMUT VON MOLTKE
WHAT'S THE NEW PLAN, THEN? NO WAY WE CAN CRACK OPEN THAT SAFE ROOM, AND BOZU'S PROBABLY GOT REINFORCEMENTS HALFWAY UP THE STAIRS BY NOW...
WE DON'T NEED TO GET *IN*, WE JUST NEED TO GET BOZU TO COME *OUT*.
I'VE GOT SOME THOUGHTS.
BOZU HAD HIS WORKING KITCHEN ARMORED TO MAKE THE SAFE ROOM. WHAT IF HE CHEAPED OUT AND DIDN'T HAVE THE GAS LINE ANGLED IN WITH A MOLY STEEL SHEATH?
GET CRACKING, JAVIER!
HIS REINFORCEMENTS ARE RUNNING UP THE STAIRS, AND THEY'RE GOING TO BE RIGHTEOUSLY TICKED OFF WHEN THEY GET HERE.

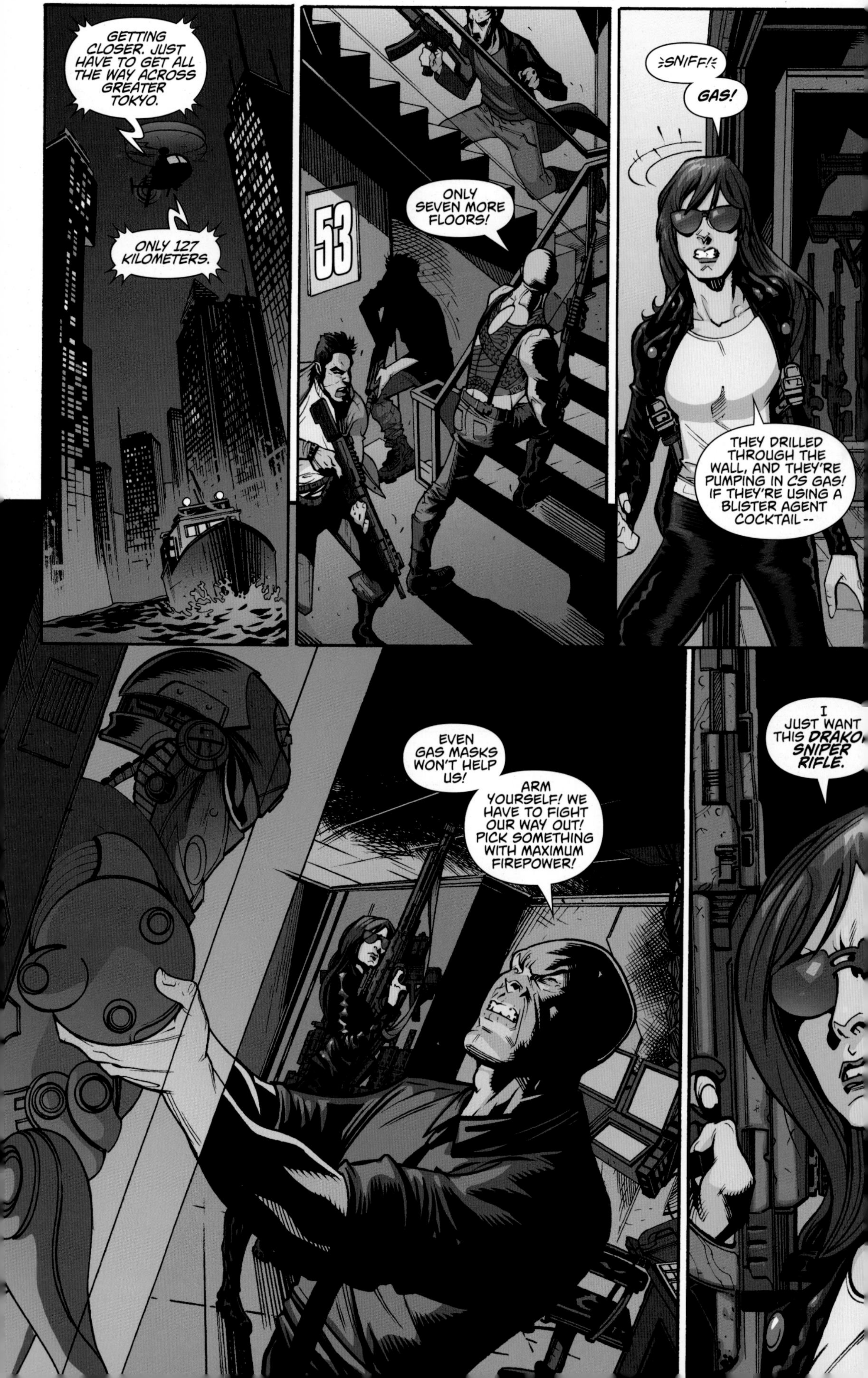
GETTING CLOSER. JUST HAVE TO GET ALL THE WAY ACROSS GREATER TOKYO.
ONLY 127 KILOMETERS.
53
ONLY SEVEN MORE FLOORS!
SNIFF!
GAS!
THEY DRILLED THROUGH THE WALL, AND THEY'RE PUMPING IN CS GAS! IF THEY'RE USING A BLISTER AGENT COCKTAIL --
EVEN GAS MASKS WON'T HELP US!
ARM YOURSELF! WE HAVE TO FIGHT OUR WAY OUT! PICK SOMETHING WITH MAXIMUM FIREPOWER!
I JUST WANT THIS DRAKO SNIPER RIFLE.

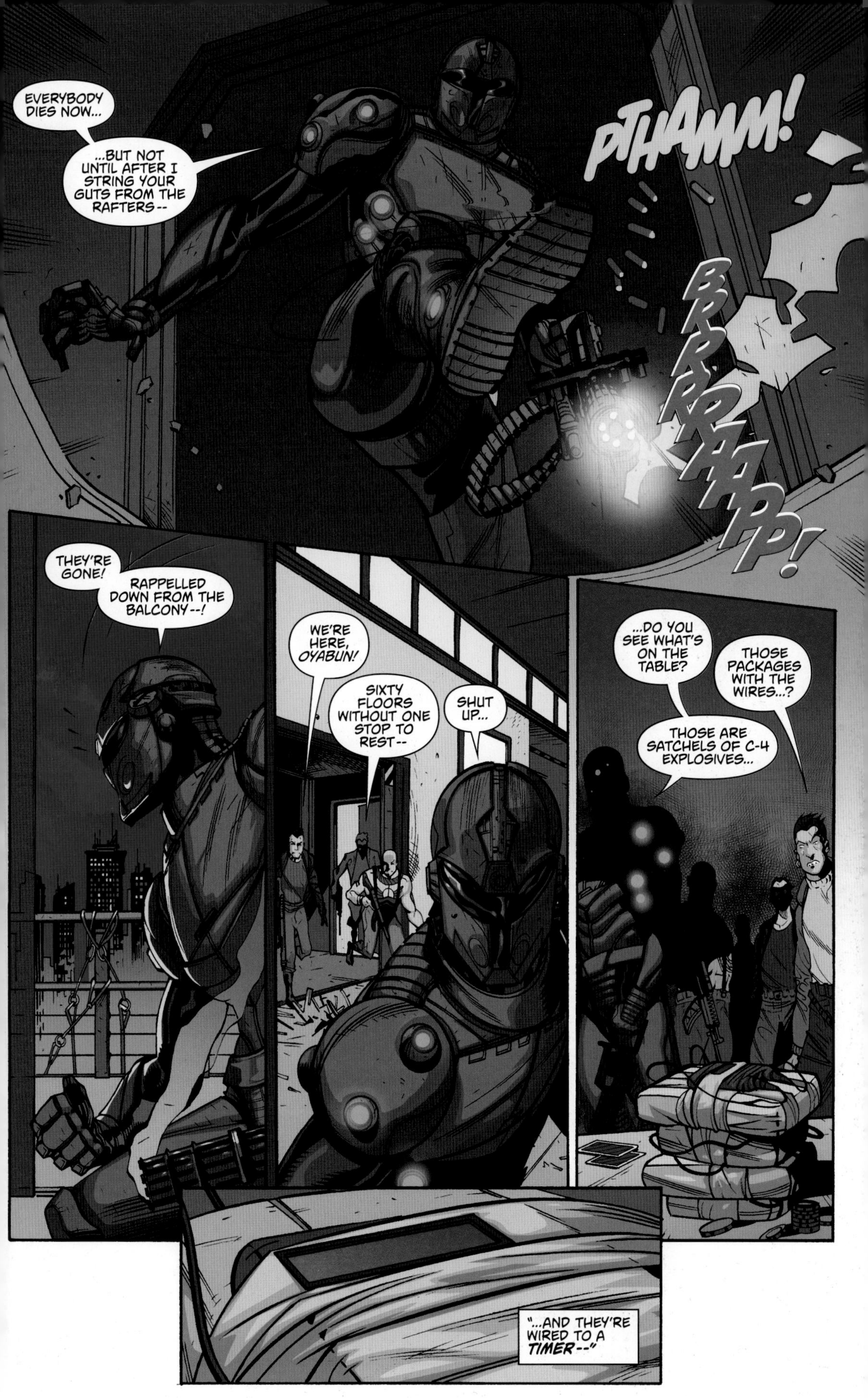
EVERYBODY DIES NOW...
...BUT NOT UNTIL AFTER I STRING YOUR GUTS FROM THE RAFTERS--
PTHAMM!
BRRRRAAAPP!
THEY'RE GONE!
RAPPELLED DOWN FROM THE BALCONY--!
WE'RE HERE, OYABUN!
SIXTY FLOORS WITHOUT ONE STOP TO REST--
SHUT UP...
...DO YOU SEE WHAT'S ON THE TABLE?
THOSE PACKAGES WITH THE WIRES...?
THOSE ARE SATCHELS OF C-4 EXPLOSIVES...
"...AND THEY'RE WIRED TO A TIMER--"

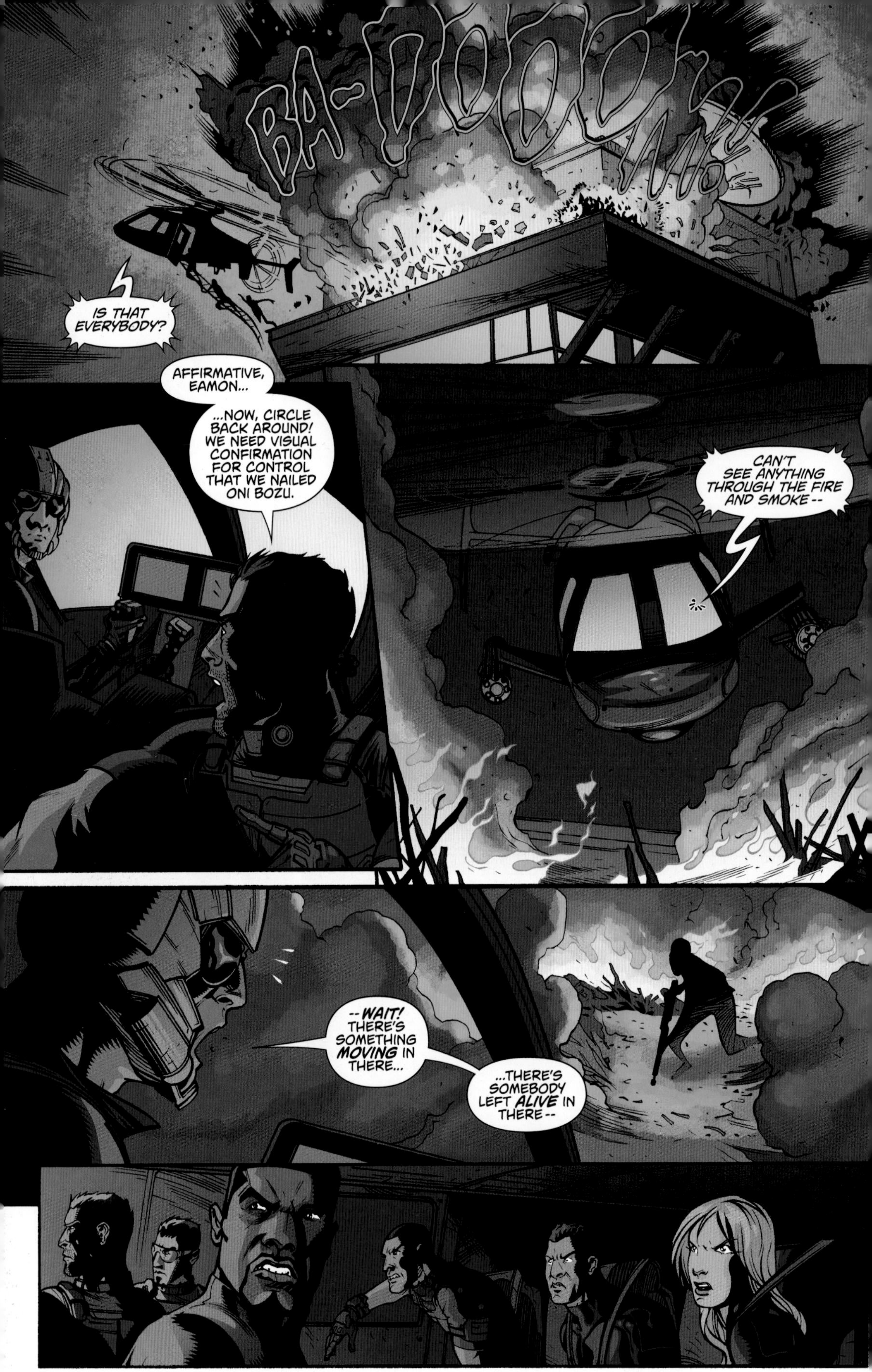
BA-DOOOOM!!
IS THAT EVERYBODY?
AFFIRMATIVE, EAMON...
...NOW, CIRCLE BACK AROUND! WE NEED VISUAL CONFIRMATION FOR CONTROL THAT WE NAILED ONI BOZU.
CAN'T SEE ANYTHING THROUGH THE FIRE AND SMOKE --
-- WAIT! THERE'S SOMETHING MOVING IN THERE...
...THERE'S SOMEBODY LEFT ALIVE IN THERE --

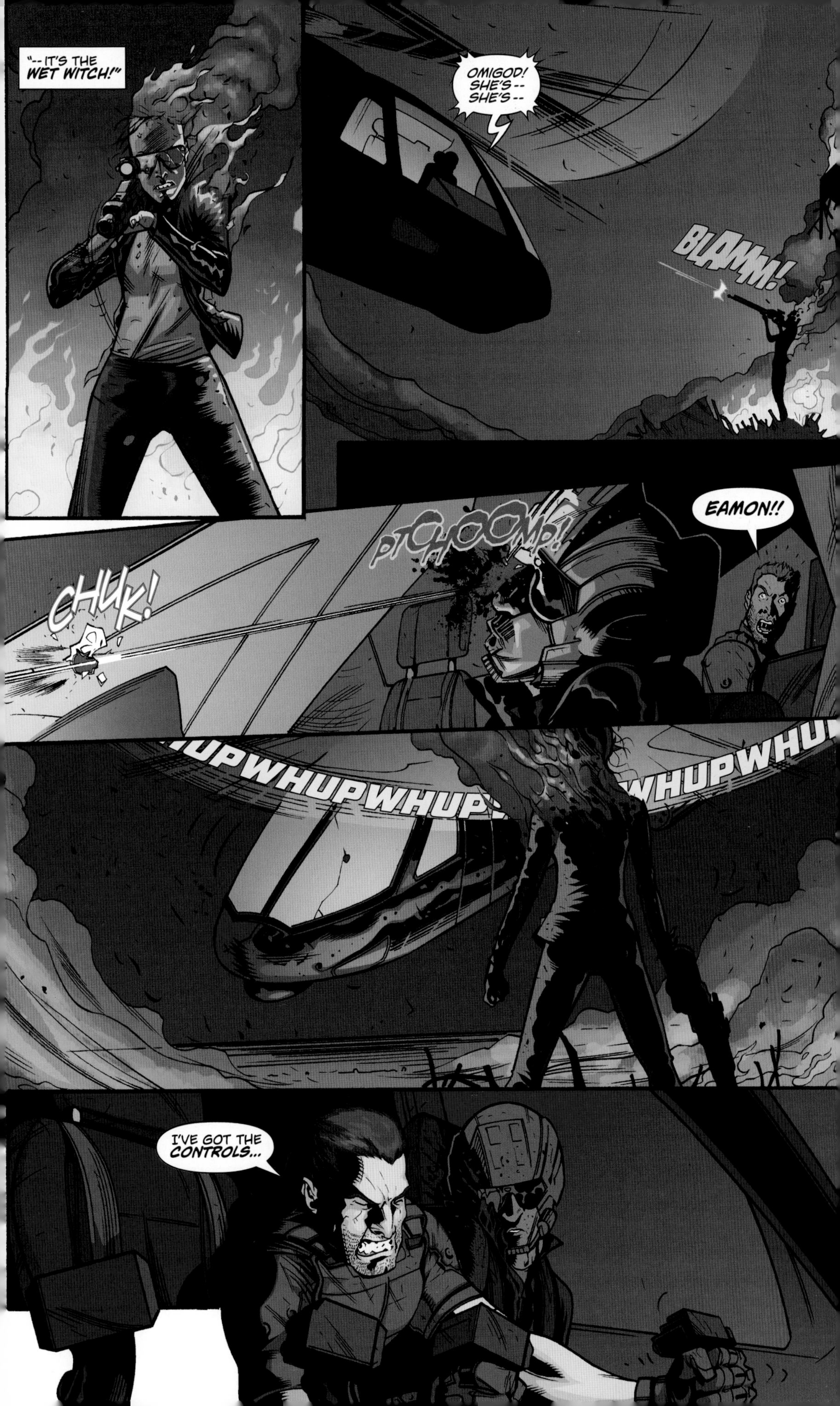
"-- IT'S THE WET WITCH!"
OMIGOD! SHE'S -- SHE'S --
BLAMMM!
PTCHOOMP!
EAMON!!
CHUK!
WHUPWHUPWHUPWHUPWHUPWHUP
I'VE GOT THE CONTROLS...

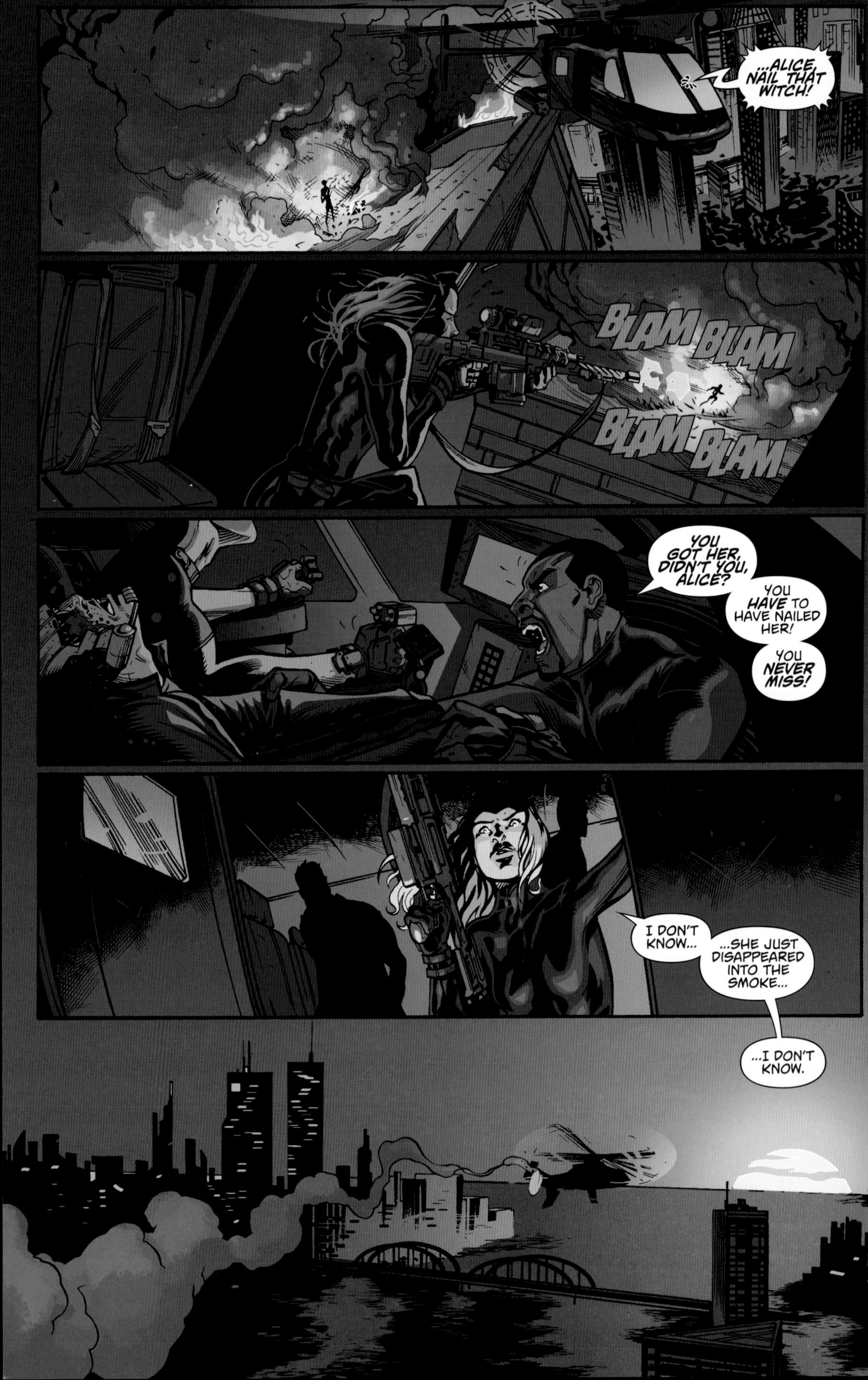
...ALICE, NAIL THAT WITCH!
BLAM BLAM
BLAM BLAM
YOU GOT HER, DIDN'T YOU, ALICE?
YOU HAVE TO HAVE NAILED HER!
YOU NEVER MISS!
I DON'T KNOW...
...SHE JUST DISAPPEARED INTO THE SMOKE...
...I DON'T KNOW.

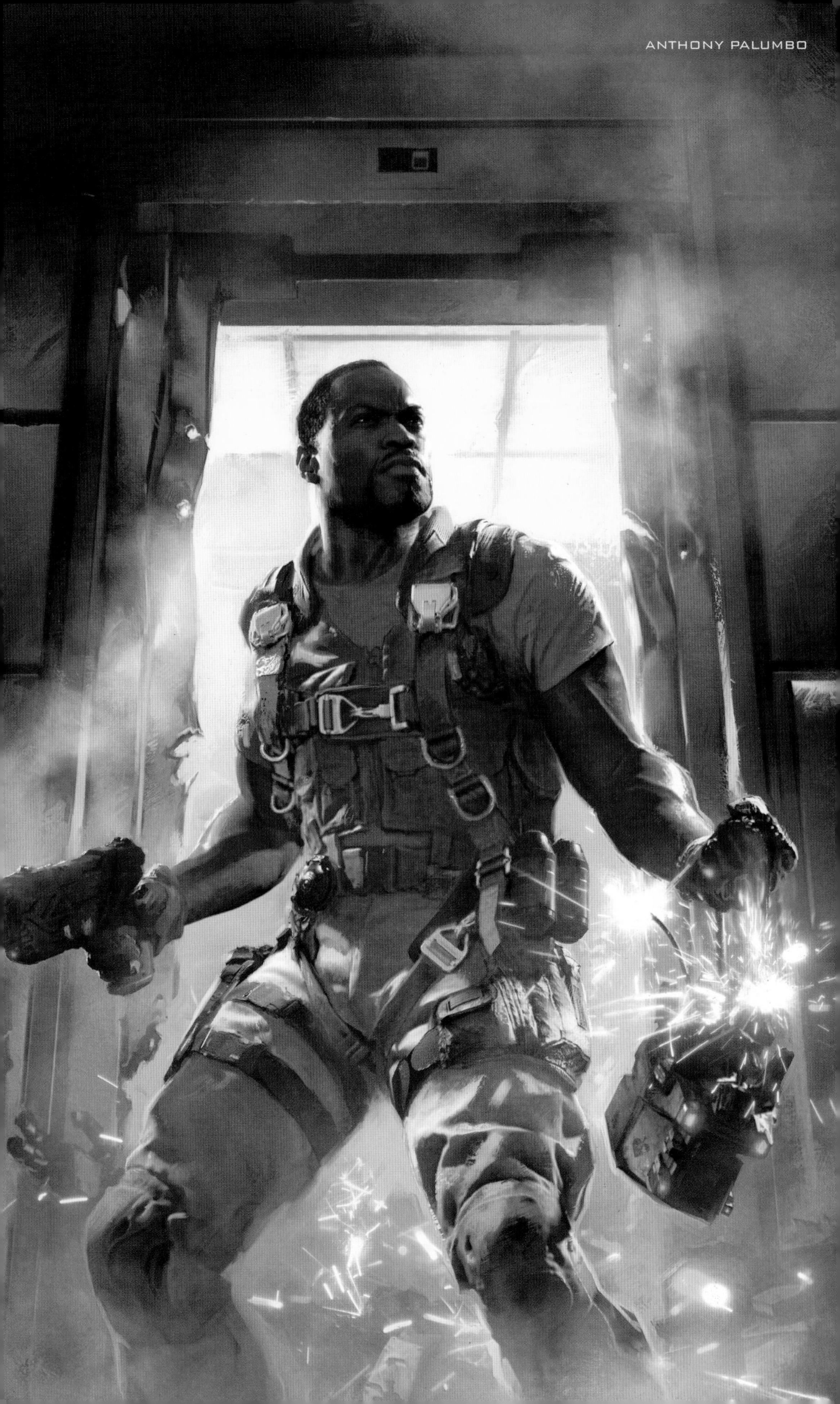
ANTHONY PALUMBO

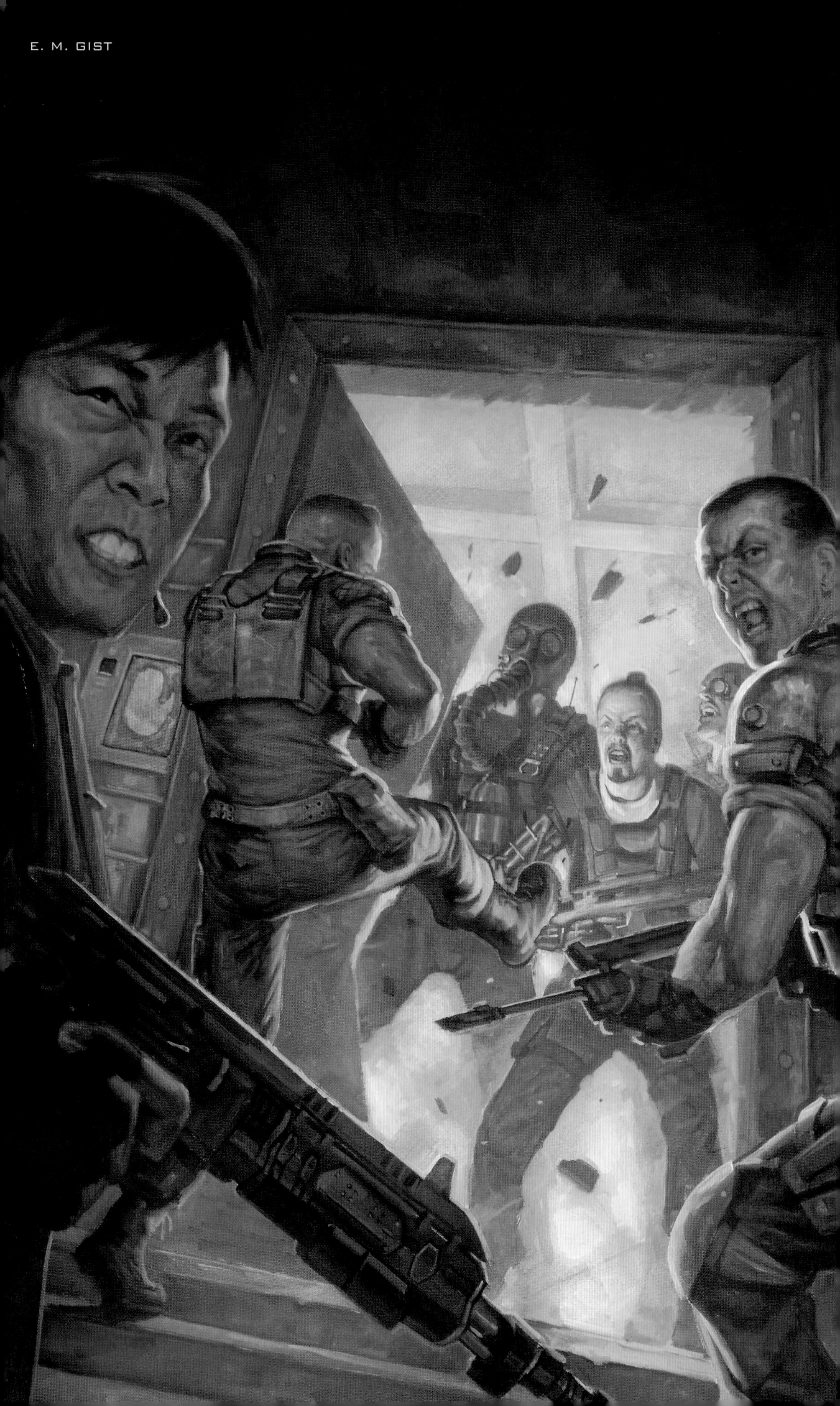

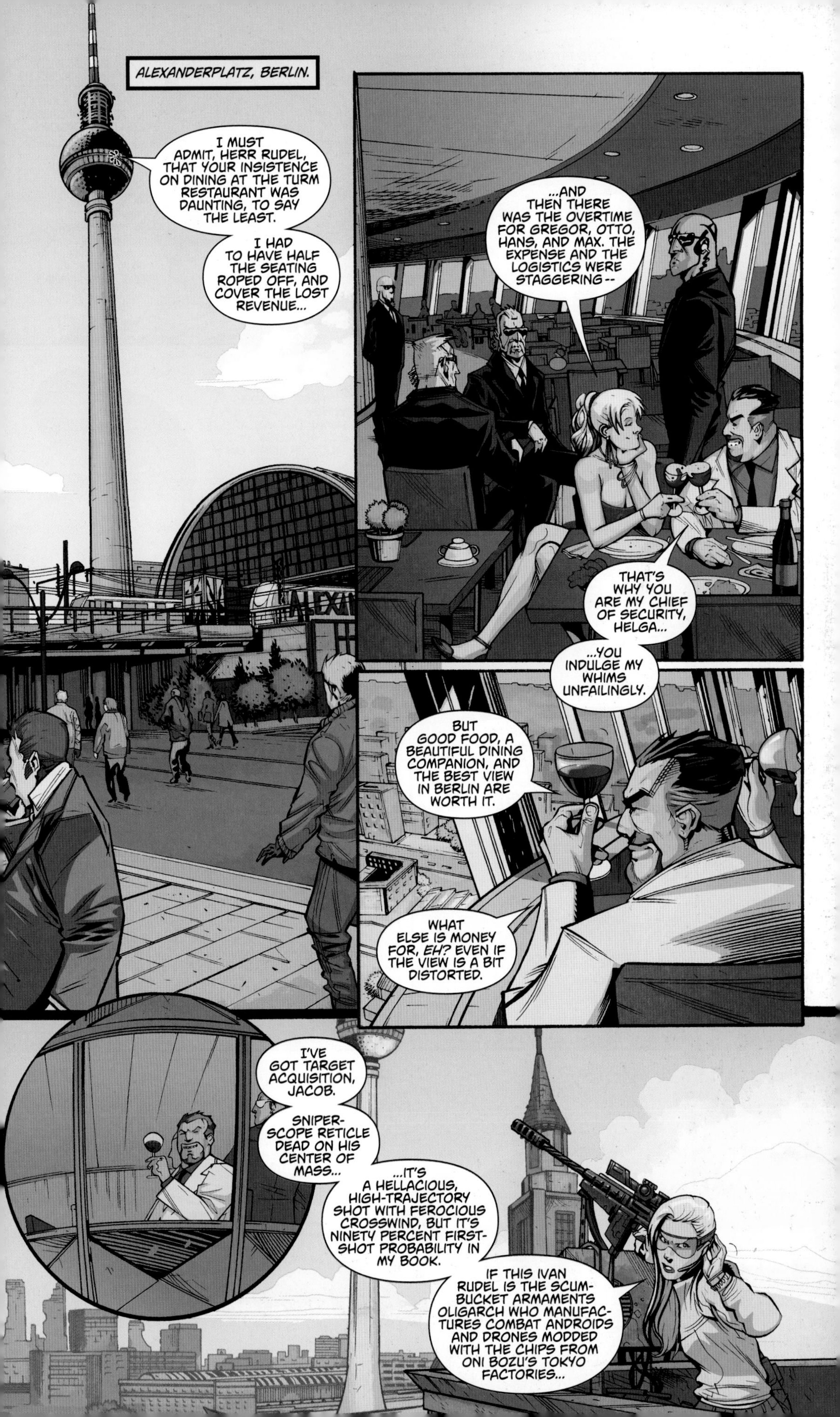
ALEXANDERPLATZ, BERLIN.
I MUST ADMIT, HERR RUDEL, THAT YOUR INSISTENCE ON DINING AT THE TURM RESTAURANT WAS DAUNTING, TO SAY THE LEAST.
I HAD TO HAVE HALF THE SEATING ROPED OFF, AND COVER THE LOST REVENUE...
...AND THEN THERE WAS THE OVERTIME FOR GREGOR, OTTO, HANS, AND MAX. THE EXPENSE AND THE LOGISTICS WERE STAGGERING--
THAT'S WHY YOU ARE MY CHIEF OF SECURITY, HELGA...
...YOU INDULGE MY WHIMS UNFAILINGLY.
BUT GOOD FOOD, A BEAUTIFUL DINING COMPANION, AND THE BEST VIEW IN BERLIN ARE WORTH IT.
WHAT ELSE IS MONEY FOR, *EH?* EVEN IF THE VIEW IS A BIT DISTORTED.
I'VE GOT TARGET ACQUISITION, JACOB.
SNIPER-SCOPE RETICLE DEAD ON HIS CENTER OF MASS...
...IT'S A HELLACIOUS, HIGH-TRAJECTORY SHOT WITH FEROCIOUS CROSSWIND, BUT IT'S NINETY PERCENT FIRST-SHOT PROBABILITY IN MY BOOK.
IF THIS IVAN RUDEL IS THE SCUMBUCKET ARMAMENTS OLIGARCH WHO MANUFACTURES COMBAT ANDROIDS AND DRONES MODDED WITH THE CHIPS FROM ONI BOZU'S TOKYO FACTORIES...

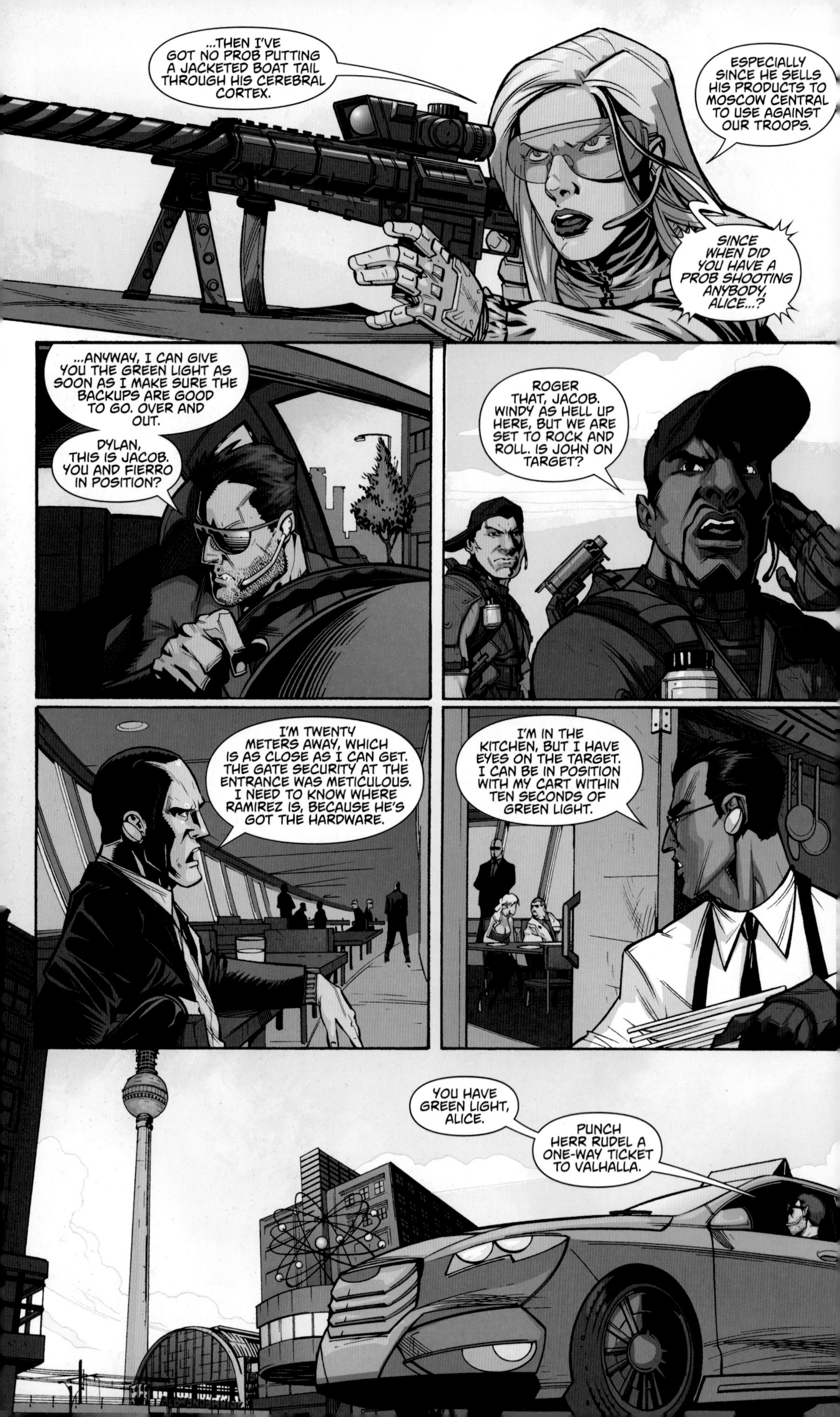
...THEN I'VE GOT NO PROB PUTTING A JACKETED BOAT TAIL THROUGH HIS CEREBRAL CORTEX.
ESPECIALLY SINCE HE SELLS HIS PRODUCTS TO MOSCOW CENTRAL TO USE AGAINST OUR TROOPS.
SINCE WHEN DID YOU HAVE A PROB SHOOTING ANYBODY, ALICE...?
...ANYWAY, I CAN GIVE YOU THE GREEN LIGHT AS SOON AS I MAKE SURE THE BACKUPS ARE GOOD TO GO. OVER AND OUT.
DYLAN, THIS IS JACOB. YOU AND FIERRO IN POSITION?
ROGER THAT, JACOB. WINDY AS HELL UP HERE, BUT WE ARE SET TO ROCK AND ROLL. IS JOHN ON TARGET?
I'M TWENTY METERS AWAY, WHICH IS AS CLOSE AS I CAN GET. THE GATE SECURITY AT THE ENTRANCE WAS METICULOUS. I NEED TO KNOW WHERE RAMIREZ IS, BECAUSE HE'S GOT THE HARDWARE.
I'M IN THE KITCHEN, BUT I HAVE EYES ON THE TARGET. I CAN BE IN POSITION WITH MY CART WITHIN TEN SECONDS OF GREEN LIGHT.
YOU HAVE GREEN LIGHT, ALICE.
PUNCH HERR RUDEL A ONE-WAY TICKET TO VALHALLA.

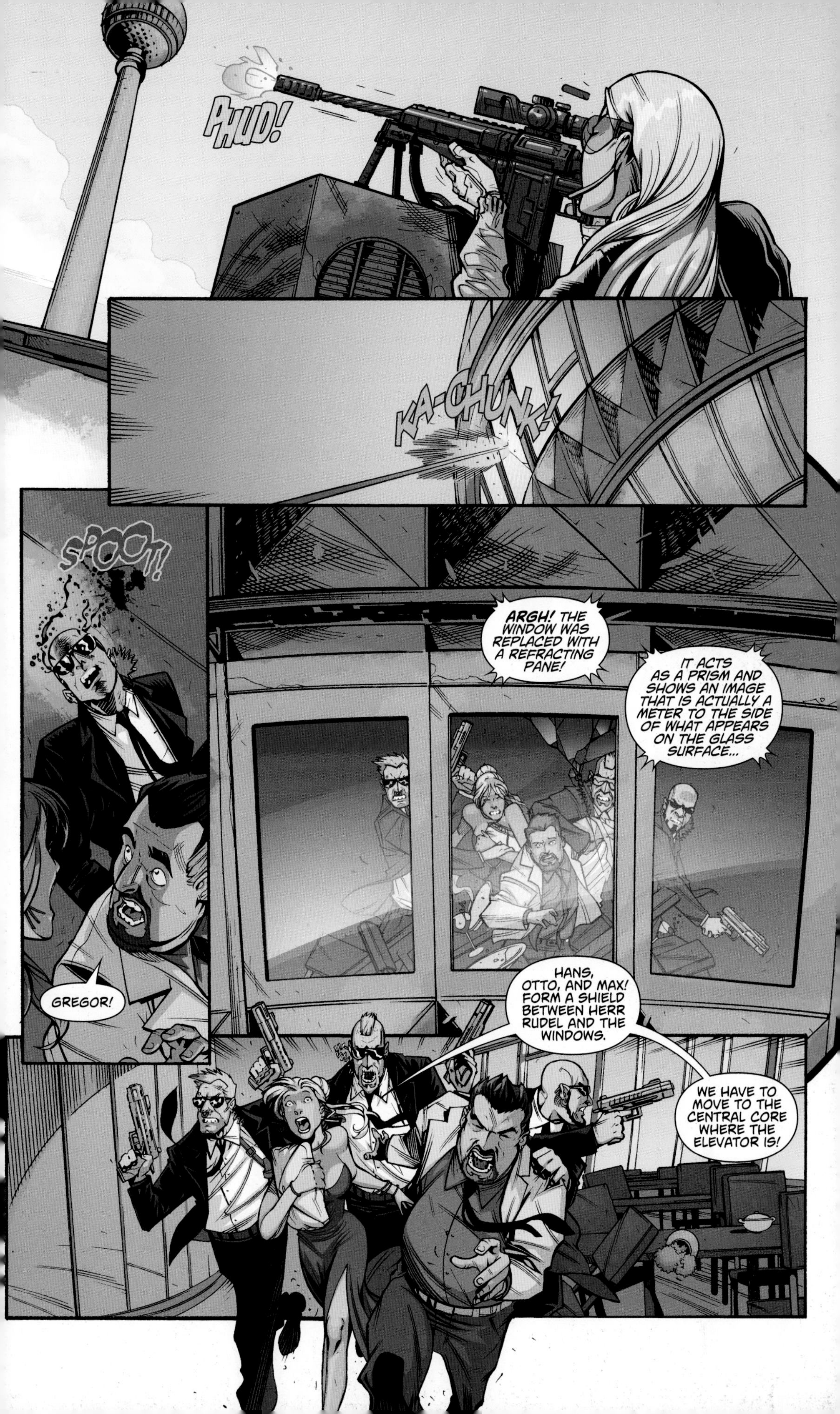
PHUD!
KA-CHUNK!
SPOOT!
GREGOR!
ARGH! THE WINDOW WAS REPLACED WITH A REFRACTING PANE!
IT ACTS AS A PRISM AND SHOWS AN IMAGE THAT IS ACTUALLY A METER TO THE SIDE OF WHAT APPEARS ON THE GLASS SURFACE...
HANS, OTTO, AND MAX! FORM A SHIELD BETWEEN HERR RUDEL AND THE WINDOWS.
WE HAVE TO MOVE TO THE CENTRAL CORE WHERE THE ELEVATOR IS!

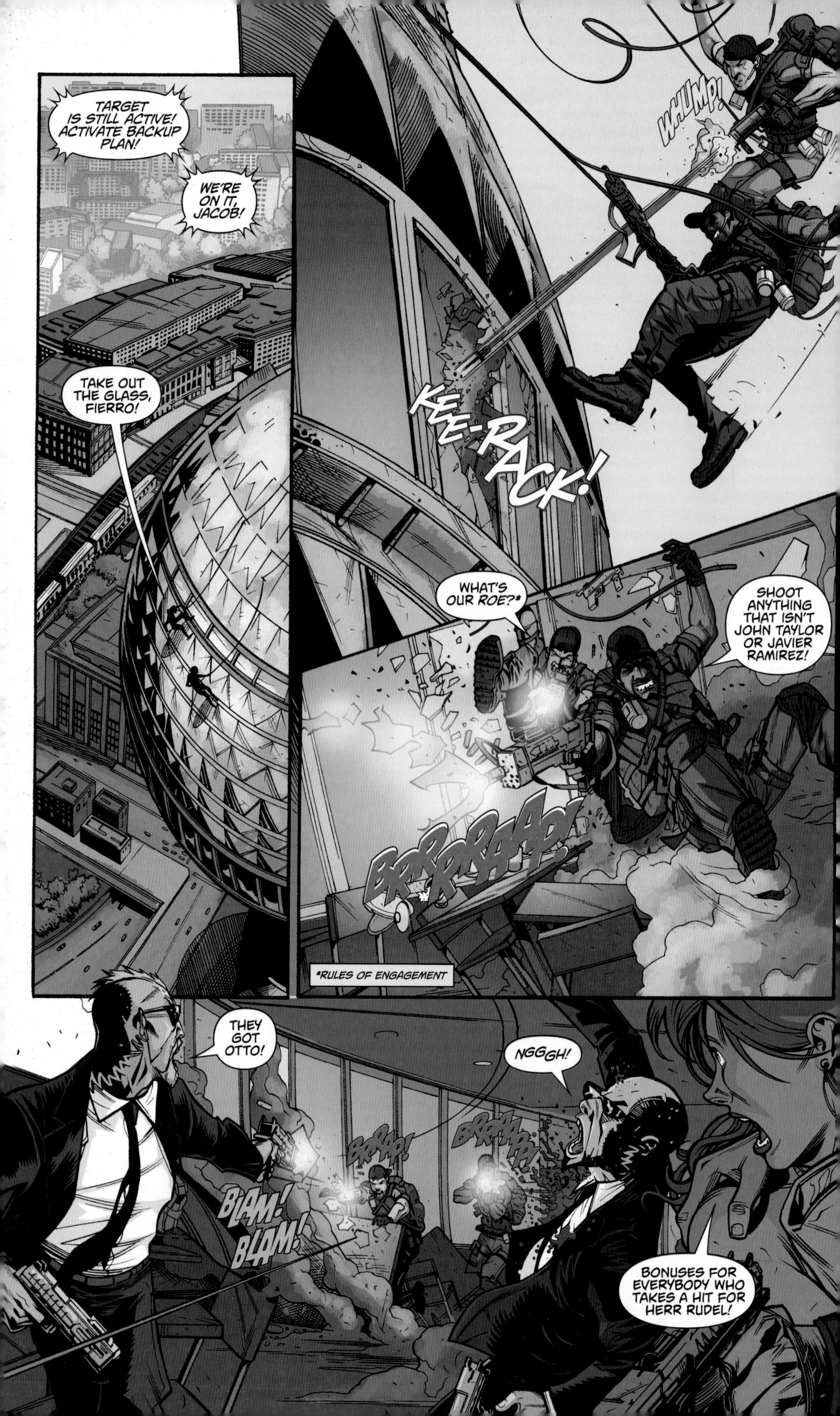

TARGET IS STILL ACTIVE! ACTIVATE BACKUP PLAN!
WE'RE ON IT, JACOB!
TAKE OUT THE GLASS, FIERRO!
WHUMP!
KEE-RACK!
WHAT'S OUR ROE?*
SHOOT ANYTHING THAT ISN'T JOHN TAYLOR OR JAVIER RAMIREZ!
BRRRRAAAP!
*RULES OF ENGAGEMENT
THEY GOT OTTO!
NGGGH!
BRAP!
BRRAAAP!
BLAM! BLAM!
BONUSES FOR EVERYBODY WHO TAKES A HIT FOR HERR RUDEL!

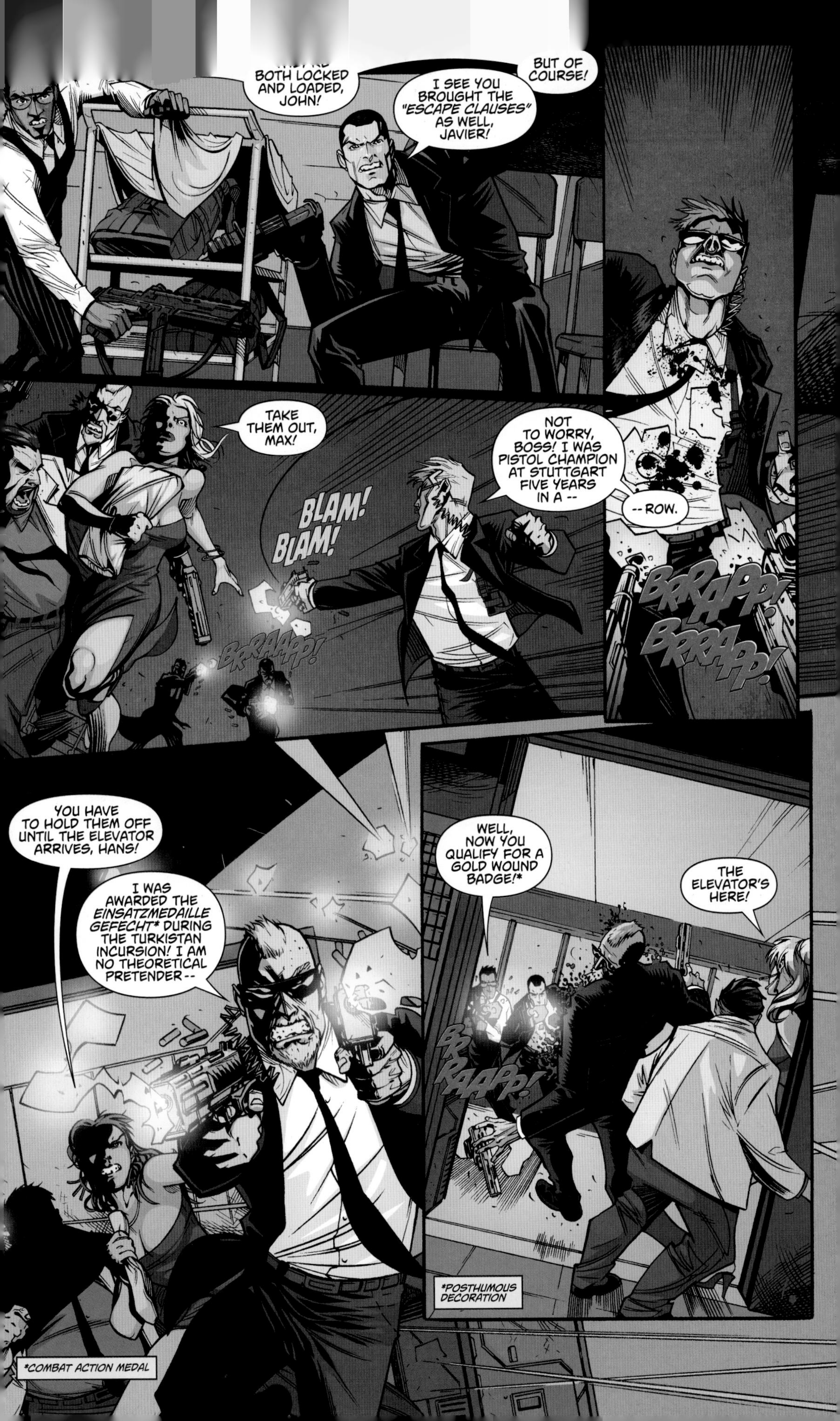
BOTH LOCKED AND LOADED, JOHN!
I SEE YOU BROUGHT THE "ESCAPE CLAUSES" AS WELL, JAVIER!
BUT OF COURSE!
TAKE THEM OUT, MAX!
NOT TO WORRY, BOSS! I WAS PISTOL CHAMPION AT STUTTGART FIVE YEARS IN A --
BLAM! BLAM!
BRRAAPP!
-- ROW.
BRRAPP! BRRAPP!
YOU HAVE TO HOLD THEM OFF UNTIL THE ELEVATOR ARRIVES, HANS!
I WAS AWARDED THE EINSATZMEDAILLE GEFECHT* DURING THE TURKISTAN INCURSION! I AM NO THEORETICAL PRETENDER --
*COMBAT ACTION MEDAL
WELL, NOW YOU QUALIFY FOR A GOLD WOUND BADGE!*
THE ELEVATOR'S HERE!
BRRAAPP!
*POSTHUMOUS DECORATION

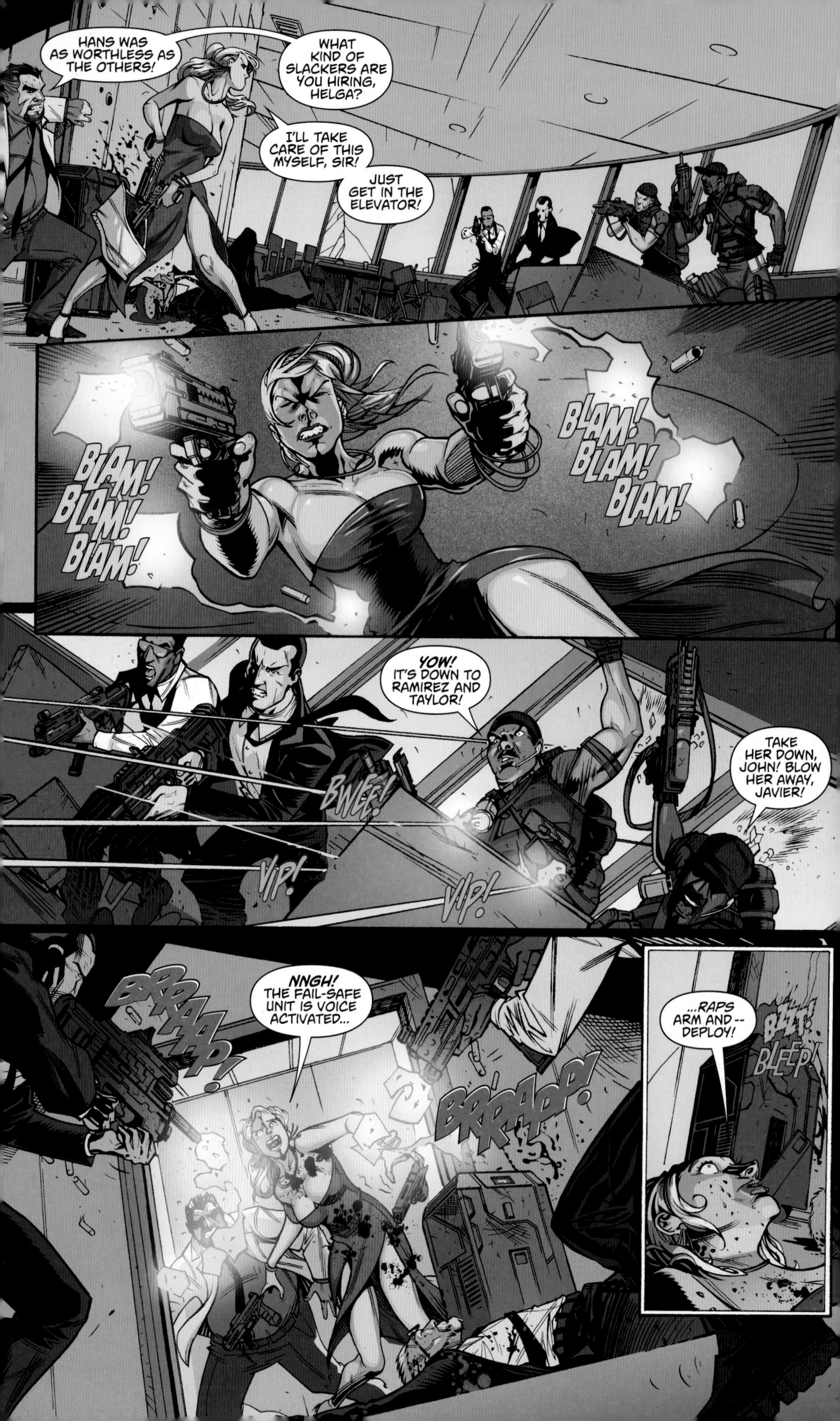
HANS WAS AS WORTHLESS AS THE OTHERS!
WHAT KIND OF SLACKERS ARE YOU HIRING, HELGA?
I'LL TAKE CARE OF THIS MYSELF, SIR!
JUST GET IN THE ELEVATOR!
BLAM! BLAM! BLAM!
BLAM! BLAM! BLAM!
YOW! IT'S DOWN TO RAMIREZ AND TAYLOR!
TAKE HER DOWN, JOHN! BLOW HER AWAY, JAVIER!
BWEE!
VIP!
VIP!
BRRAAP!
NNGH! THE FAIL-SAFE UNIT IS VOICE ACTIVATED...
BRRAPP!
...RAPS ARM AND -- DEPLOY!
BZZT!
BLEEP!

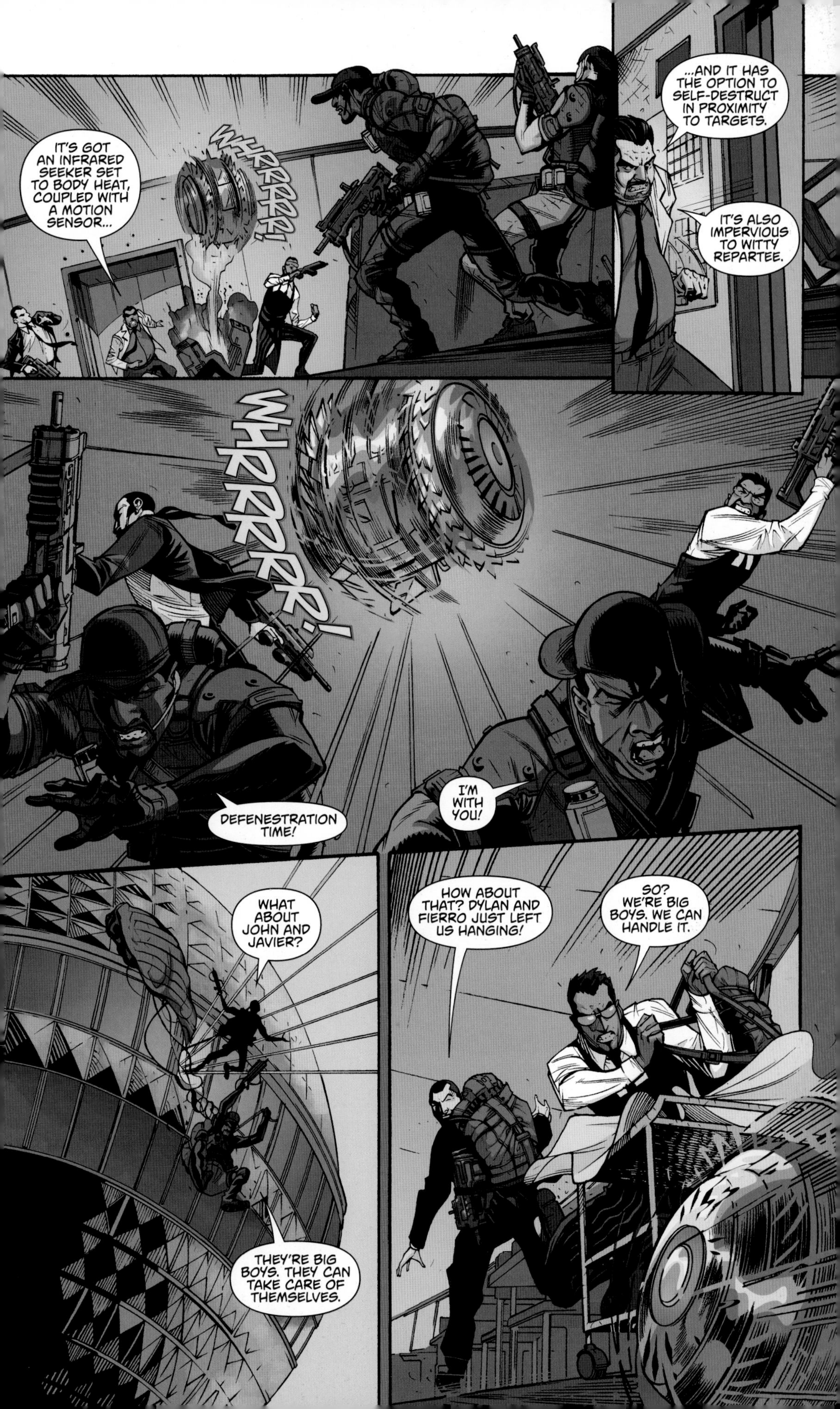
IT'S GOT AN INFRARED SEEKER SET TO BODY HEAT, COUPLED WITH A MOTION SENSOR...
WHRRRR!
...AND IT HAS THE OPTION TO SELF-DESTRUCT IN PROXIMITY TO TARGETS.
IT'S ALSO IMPERVIOUS TO WITTY REPARTEE.
WHRRRR!
DEFENESTRATION TIME!
I'M WITH YOU!
WHAT ABOUT JOHN AND JAVIER?
THEY'RE BIG BOYS. THEY CAN TAKE CARE OF THEMSELVES.
HOW ABOUT THAT? DYLAN AND FIERRO JUST LEFT US HANGING!
SO? WE'RE BIG BOYS. WE CAN HANDLE IT.

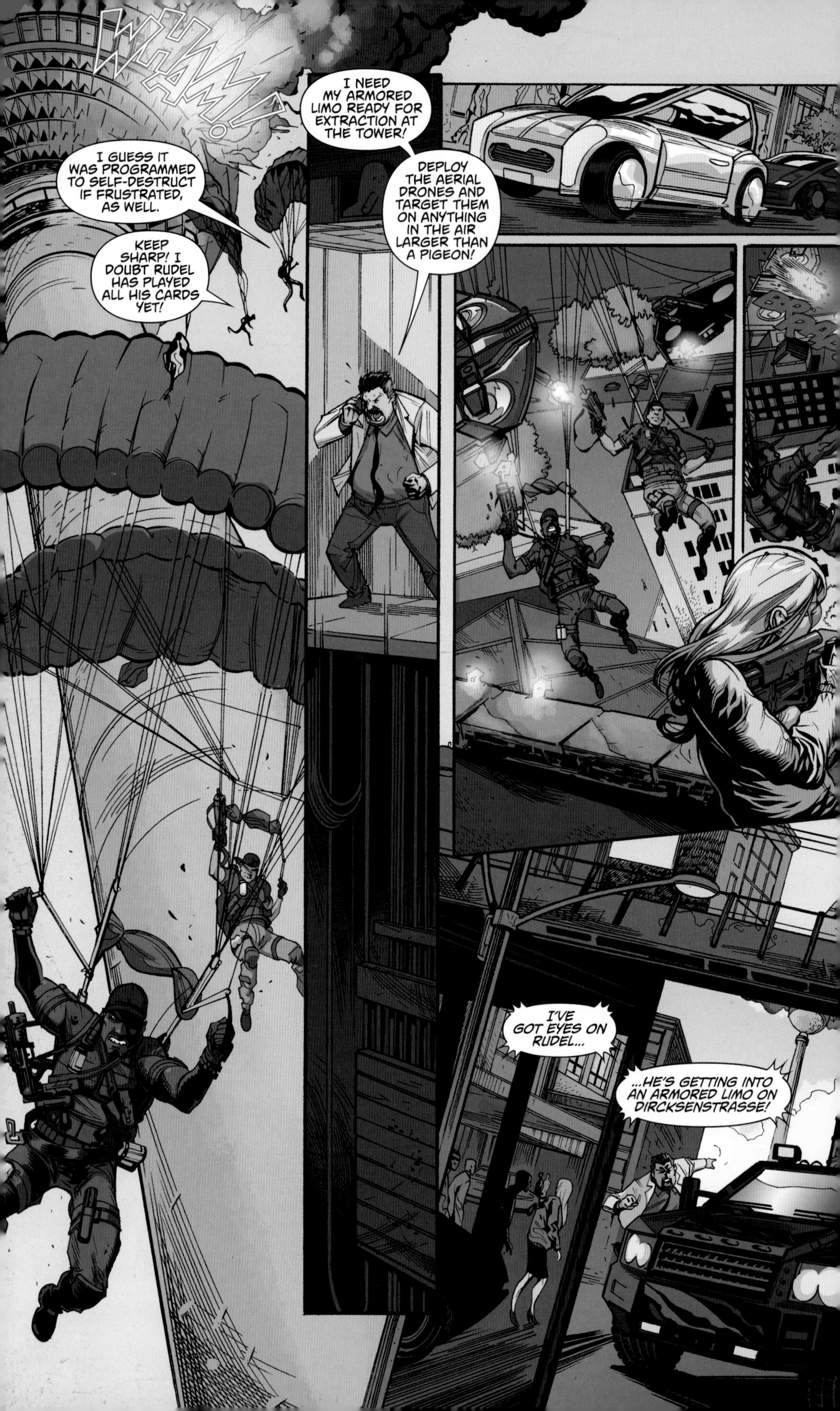
WHAM!
I GUESS IT WAS PROGRAMMED TO SELF-DESTRUCT IF FRUSTRATED, AS WELL.
KEEP SHARP! I DOUBT RUDEL HAS PLAYED ALL HIS CARDS YET!
I NEED MY ARMORED LIMO READY FOR EXTRACTION AT THE TOWER!
DEPLOY THE AERIAL DRONES AND TARGET THEM ON ANYTHING IN THE AIR LARGER THAN A PIGEON!
I'VE GOT EYES ON RUDEL...
...HE'S GETTING INTO AN ARMORED LIMO ON DIRCKSENSTRASSE!

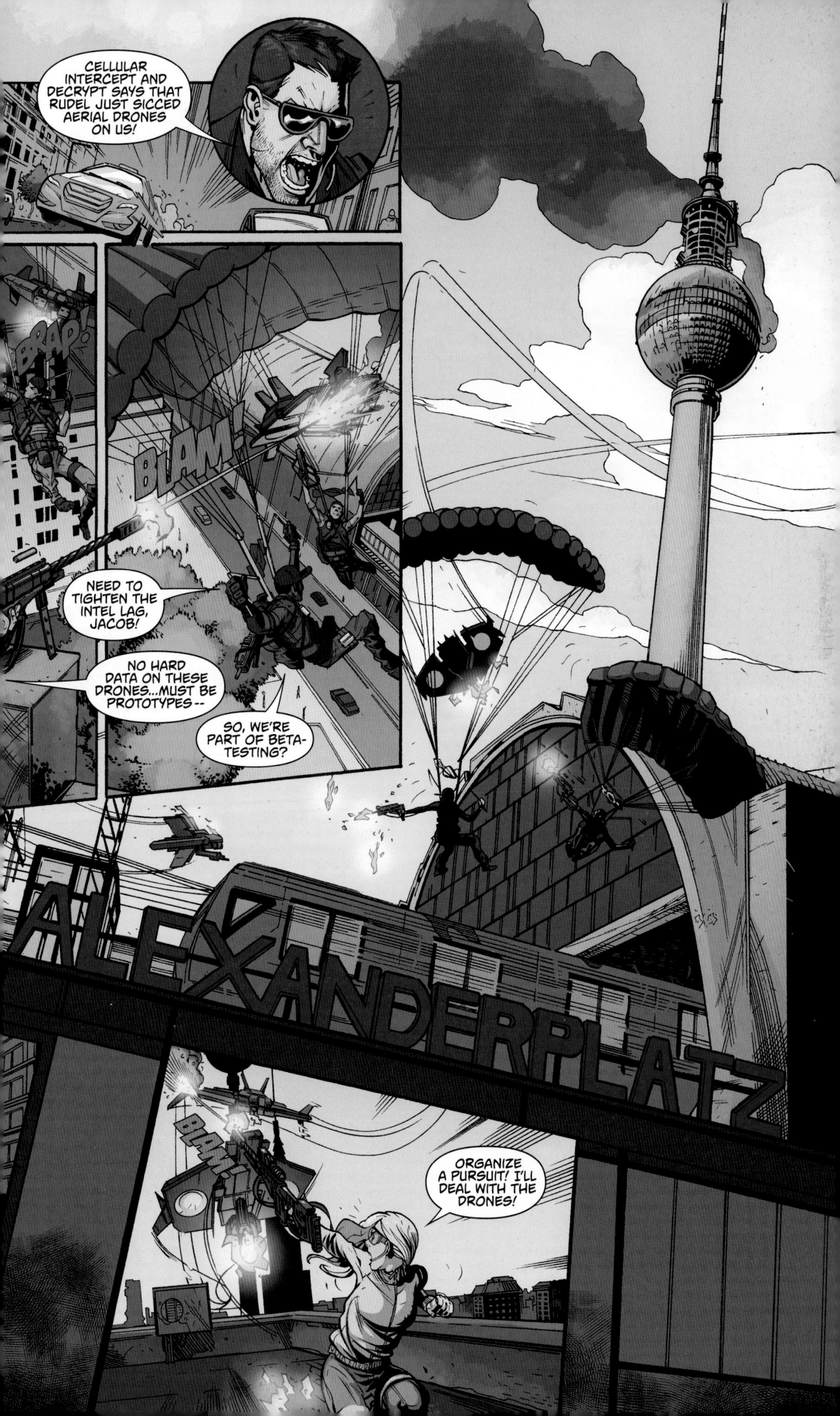
CELLULAR INTERCEPT AND DECRYPT SAYS THAT RUDEL JUST SICCED AERIAL DRONES ON US!
BRAP!
BLAM!
NEED TO TIGHTEN THE INTEL LAG, JACOB!
NO HARD DATA ON THESE DRONES...MUST BE PROTOTYPES --
SO, WE'RE PART OF BETA-TESTING?
ALEXANDERPLATZ
ORGANIZE A PURSUIT! I'LL DEAL WITH THE DRONES!

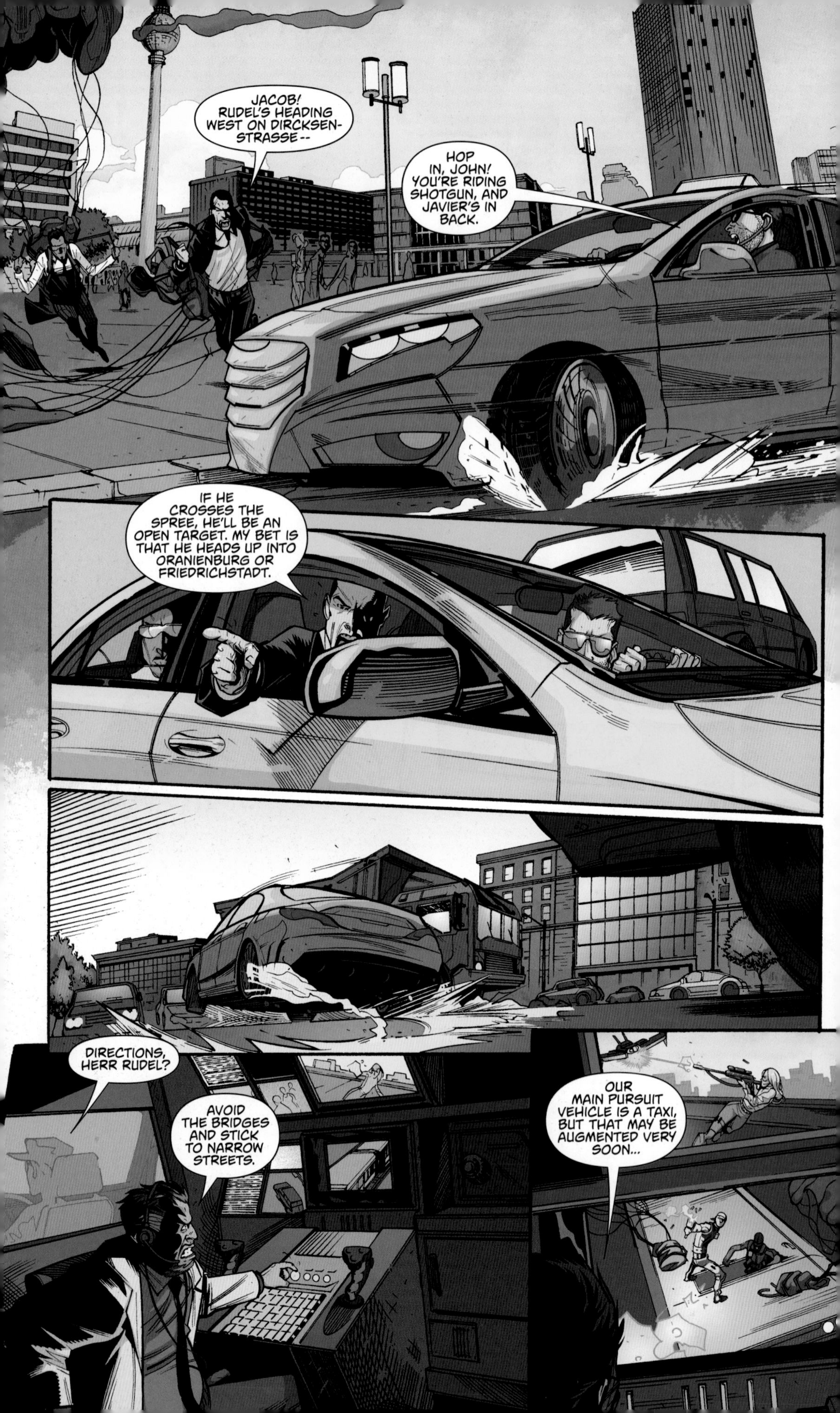
JACOB! RUDEL'S HEADING WEST ON DIRCKSEN-STRASSE--
HOP IN, JOHN! YOU'RE RIDING SHOTGUN, AND JAVIER'S IN BACK.
IF HE CROSSES THE SPREE, HE'LL BE AN OPEN TARGET. MY BET IS THAT HE HEADS UP INTO ORANIENBURG OR FRIEDRICHSTADT.
DIRECTIONS, HERR RUDEL?
AVOID THE BRIDGES AND STICK TO NARROW STREETS.
OUR MAIN PURSUIT VEHICLE IS A TAXI, BUT THAT MAY BE AUGMENTED VERY SOON...

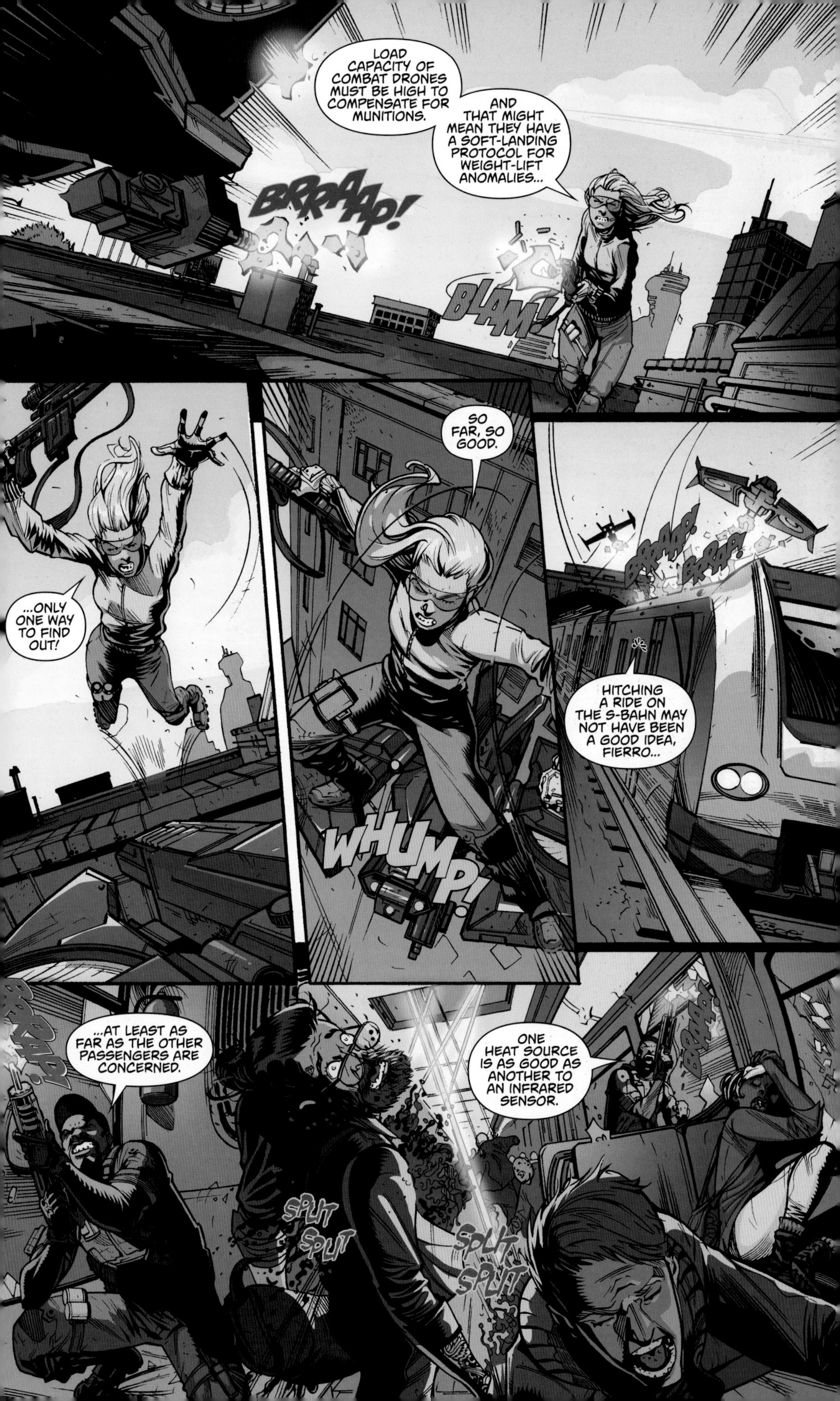
LOAD CAPACITY OF COMBAT DRONES MUST BE HIGH TO COMPENSATE FOR MUNITIONS.
AND THAT MIGHT MEAN THEY HAVE A SOFT-LANDING PROTOCOL FOR WEIGHT-LIFT ANOMALIES...
BRRAAAP!
BLAM!
...ONLY ONE WAY TO FIND OUT!
SO FAR, SO GOOD.
WHUMP!
BRAAP!
BRAP!
HITCHING A RIDE ON THE S-BAHN MAY NOT HAVE BEEN A GOOD IDEA, FIERRO...
BRRAP!
...AT LEAST AS FAR AS THE OTHER PASSENGERS ARE CONCERNED.
ONE HEAT SOURCE IS AS GOOD AS ANOTHER TO AN INFRARED SENSOR.
BRRAP!
SPLUT
SPLUT
SPLUT
SPLUT

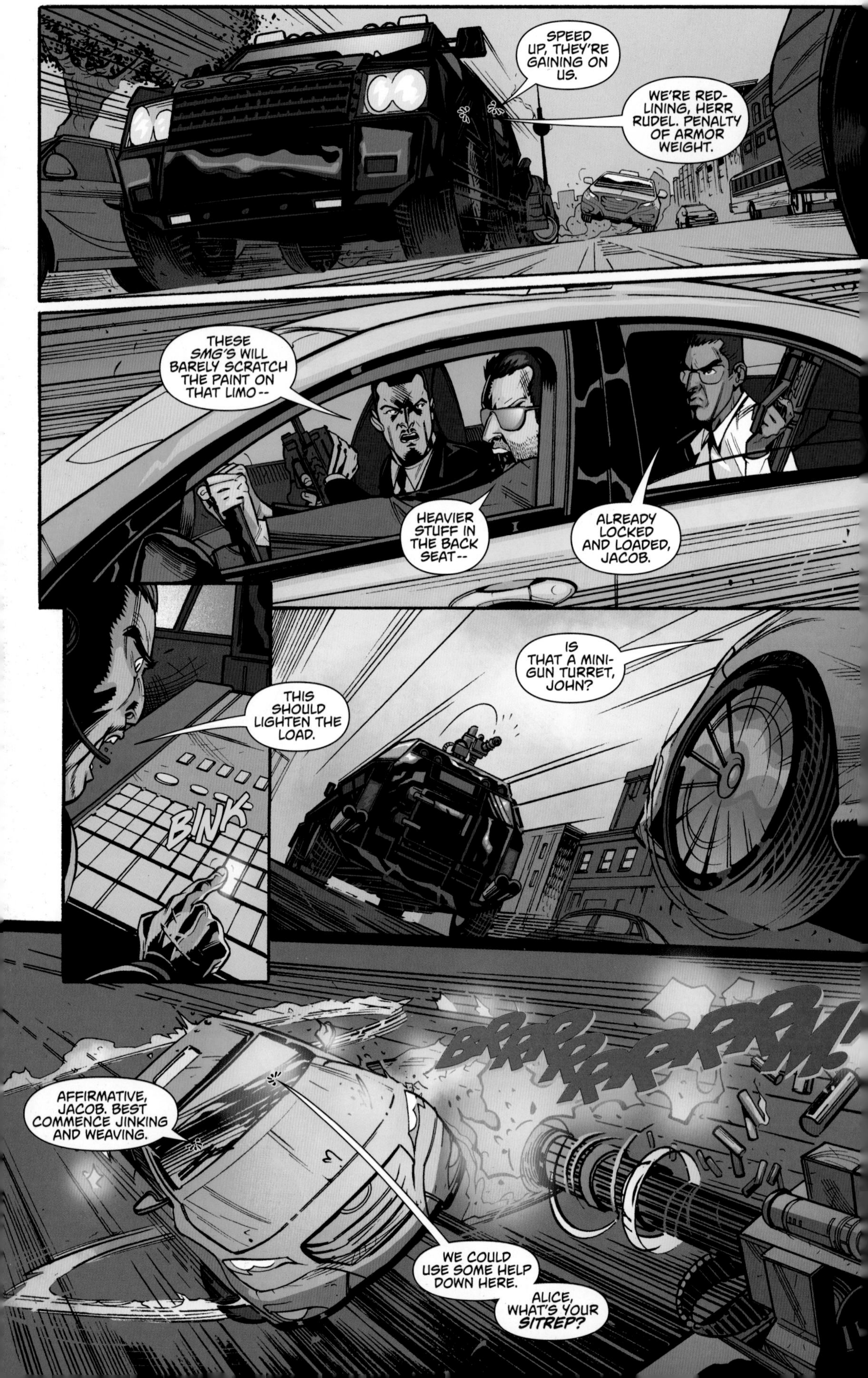

SPEED UP, THEY'RE GAINING ON US.
WE'RE RED-LINING, HERR RUDEL. PENALTY OF ARMOR WEIGHT.
THESE SMG'S WILL BARELY SCRATCH THE PAINT ON THAT LIMO--
HEAVIER STUFF IN THE BACK SEAT--
ALREADY LOCKED AND LOADED, JACOB.
THIS SHOULD LIGHTEN THE LOAD.
BINK
IS THAT A MINI-GUN TURRET, JOHN?
BRRRRRRRRRRRRM!
AFFIRMATIVE, JACOB. BEST COMMENCE JINKING AND WEAVING.
WE COULD USE SOME HELP DOWN HERE.
ALICE, WHAT'S YOUR SITREP?

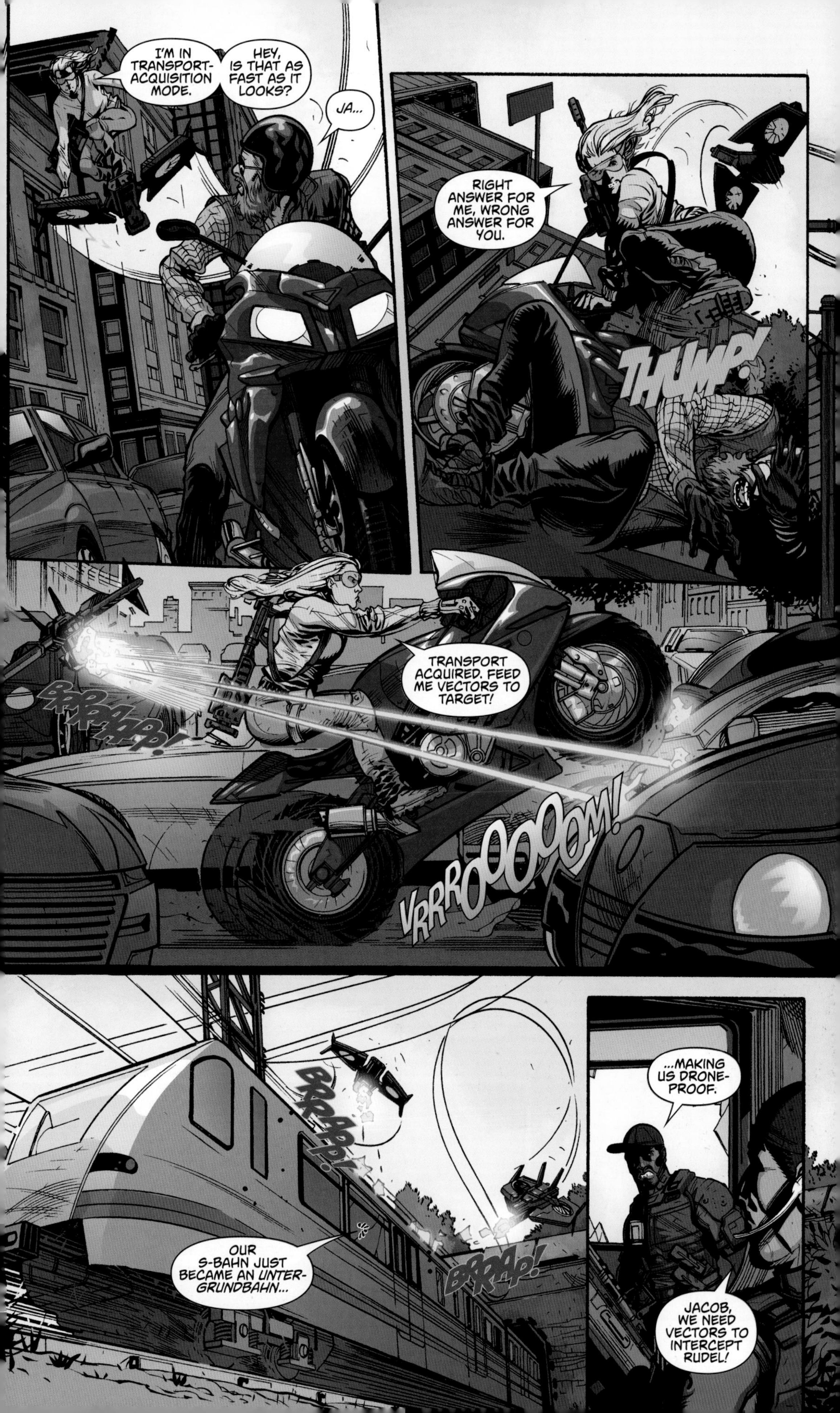
I'M IN TRANSPORT-ACQUISITION MODE.
HEY, IS THAT AS FAST AS IT LOOKS?
JA...
RIGHT ANSWER FOR ME, WRONG ANSWER FOR YOU.
THUMP!
TRANSPORT ACQUIRED. FEED ME VECTORS TO TARGET!
BRRAAPP!
VRRROOOOOOM!
BRRAAPP!
OUR S-BAHN JUST BECAME AN *UNTER-GRUNDBAHN*...
BRRAP!
...MAKING US DRONE-PROOF.
JACOB, WE NEED VECTORS TO INTERCEPT RUDEL!

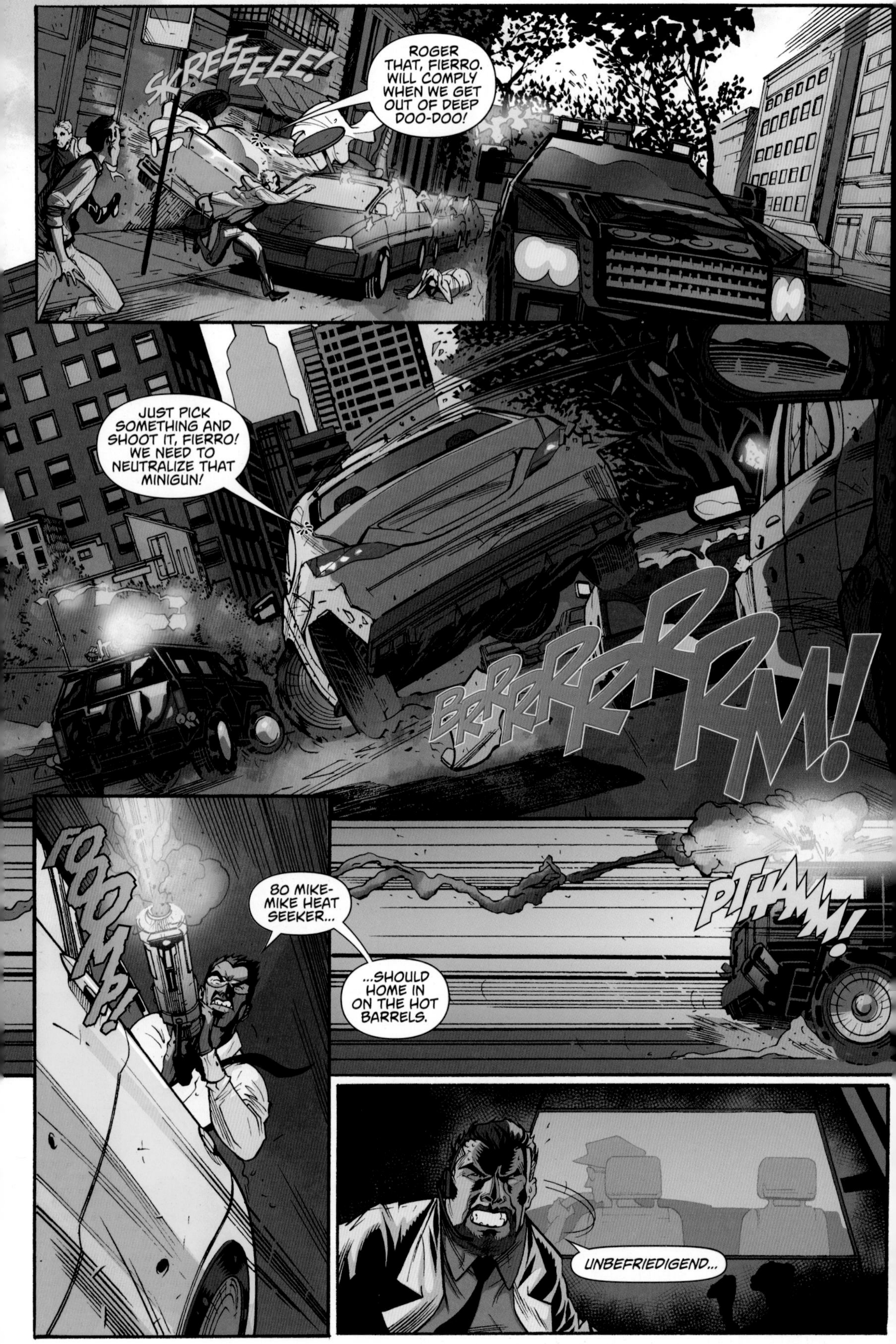
SKREEEEEEE!
ROGER THAT, FIERRO. WILL COMPLY WHEN WE GET OUT OF DEEP DOO-DOO!
JUST PICK SOMETHING AND SHOOT IT, FIERRO! WE NEED TO NEUTRALIZE THAT MINIGUN!
BRRRRRRRM!
FOOOMP!
80 MIKE-MIKE HEAT SEEKER...
...SHOULD HOME IN ON THE HOT BARRELS.
PLTHAMM!
UNBEFRIEDIGEND...

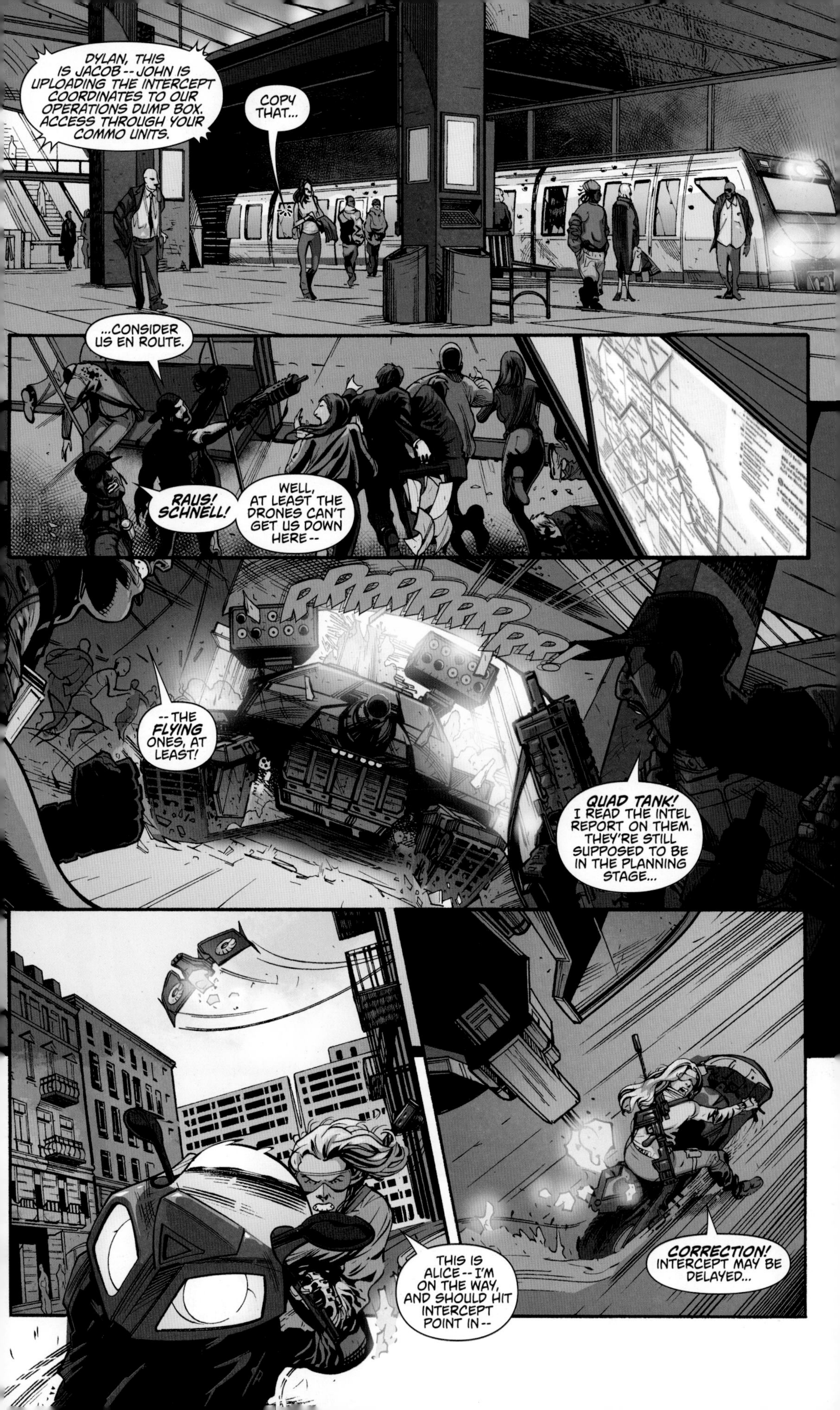
DYLAN, THIS IS JACOB -- JOHN IS UPLOADING THE INTERCEPT COORDINATES TO OUR OPERATIONS DUMP BOX. ACCESS THROUGH YOUR COMMO UNITS.
COPY THAT...
...CONSIDER US EN ROUTE.
RAUS! SCHNELL!
WELL, AT LEAST THE DRONES CAN'T GET US DOWN HERE --
RRRRRRRRRRRR
-- THE FLYING ONES, AT LEAST!
QUAD TANK! I READ THE INTEL REPORT ON THEM. THEY'RE STILL SUPPOSED TO BE IN THE PLANNING STAGE...
THIS IS ALICE -- I'M ON THE WAY, AND SHOULD HIT INTERCEPT POINT IN --
CORRECTION! INTERCEPT MAY BE DELAYED...

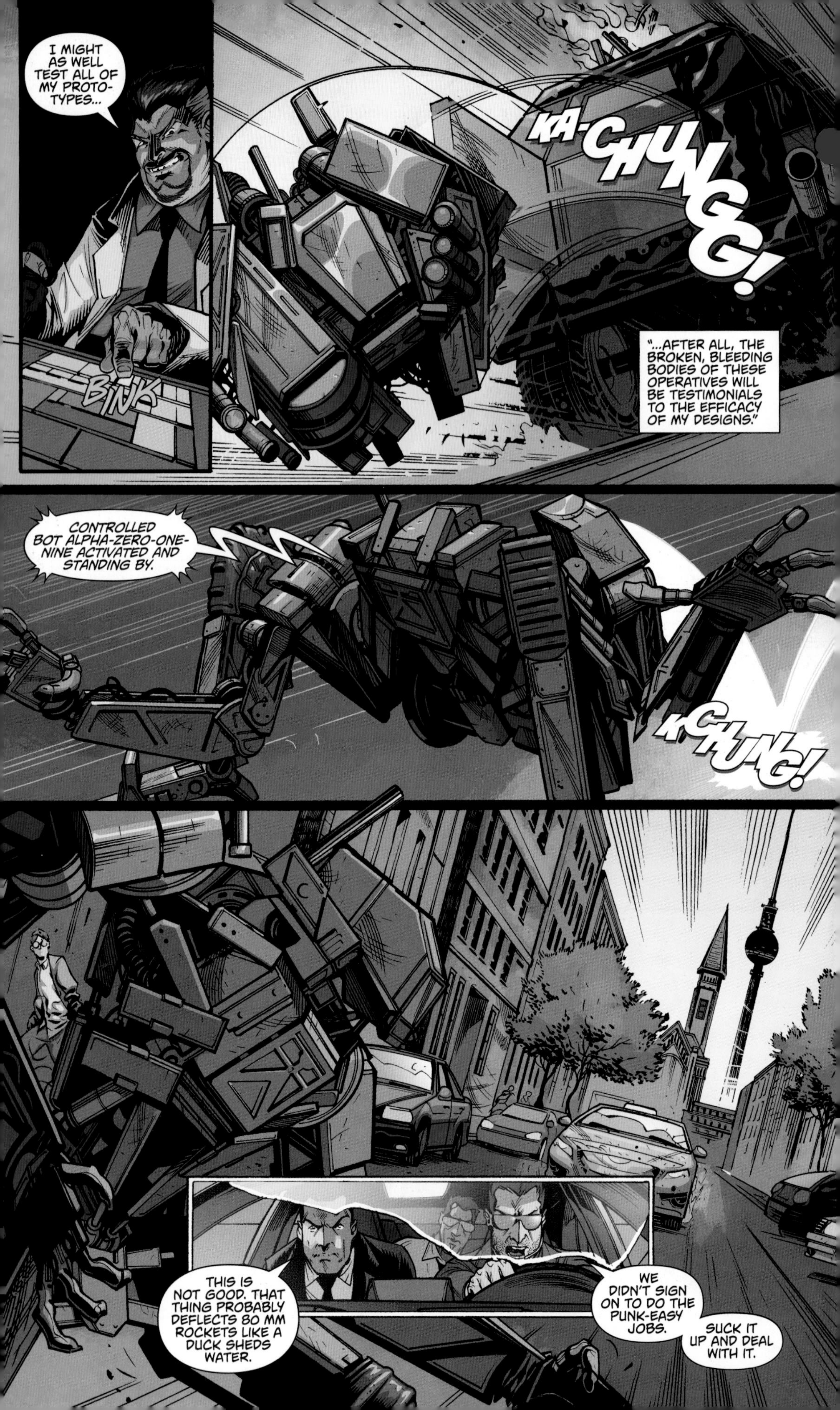
I MIGHT AS WELL TEST ALL OF MY PROTO-TYPES...
BINK
KA-CHUNGG!
"...AFTER ALL, THE BROKEN, BLEEDING BODIES OF THESE OPERATIVES WILL BE TESTIMONIALS TO THE EFFICACY OF MY DESIGNS."
CONTROLLED BOT ALPHA-ZERO-ONE-NINE ACTIVATED AND STANDING BY.
KCHUNG!
THIS IS NOT GOOD. THAT THING PROBABLY DEFLECTS 80 MM ROCKETS LIKE A DUCK SHEDS WATER.
WE DIDN'T SIGN ON TO DO THE PUNK-EASY JOBS.
SUCK IT UP AND DEAL WITH IT.

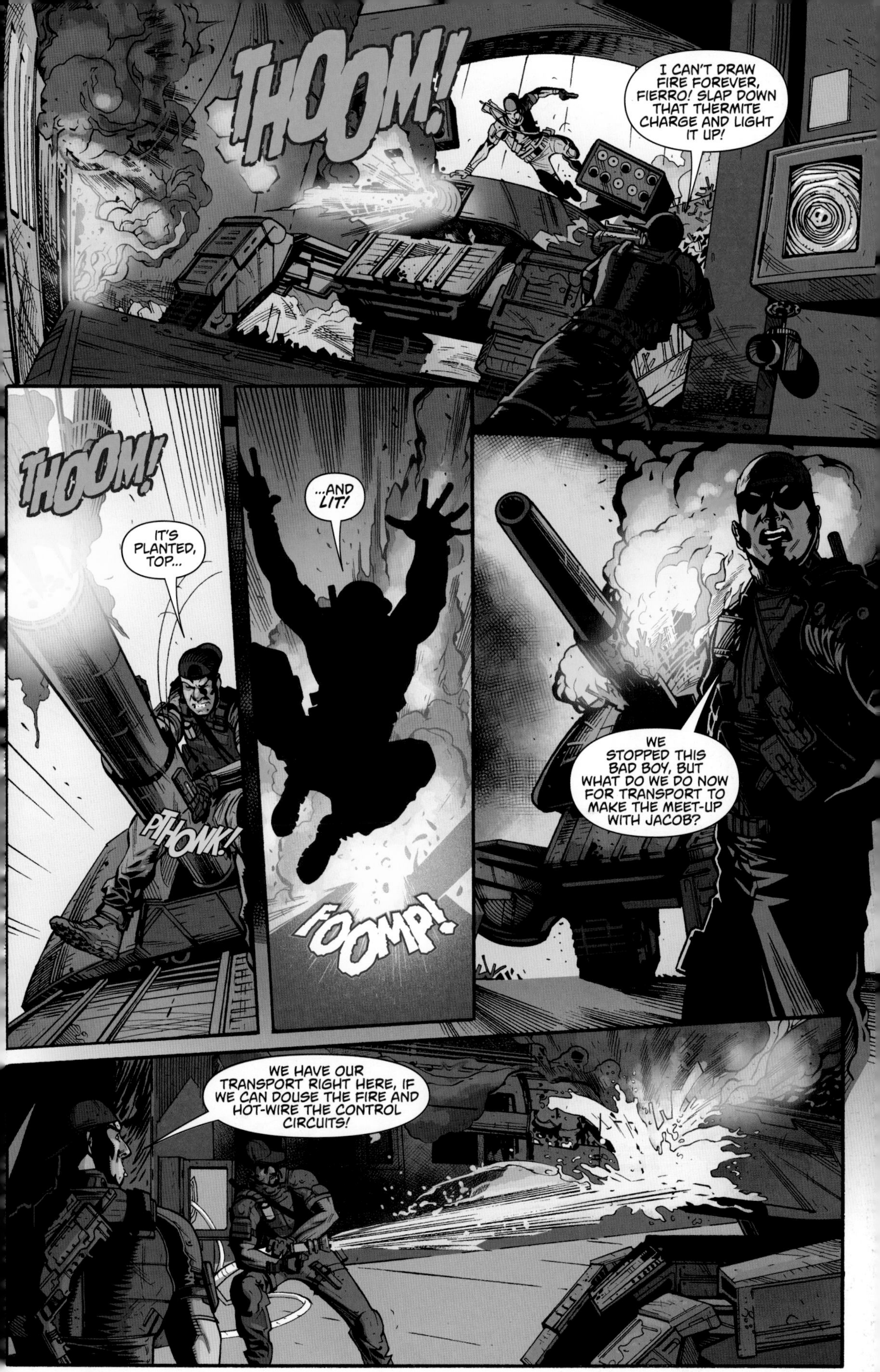
THOOM!
I CAN'T DRAW FIRE FOREVER, FIERRO! SLAP DOWN THAT THERMITE CHARGE AND LIGHT IT UP!
THOOM!
IT'S PLANTED, TOP...
PTHONK!
...AND LIT!
FOOMP!
WE STOPPED THIS BAD BOY, BUT WHAT DO WE DO NOW FOR TRANSPORT TO MAKE THE MEET-UP WITH JACOB?
WE HAVE OUR TRANSPORT RIGHT HERE, IF WE CAN DOUSE THE FIRE AND HOT-WIRE THE CONTROL CIRCUITS!

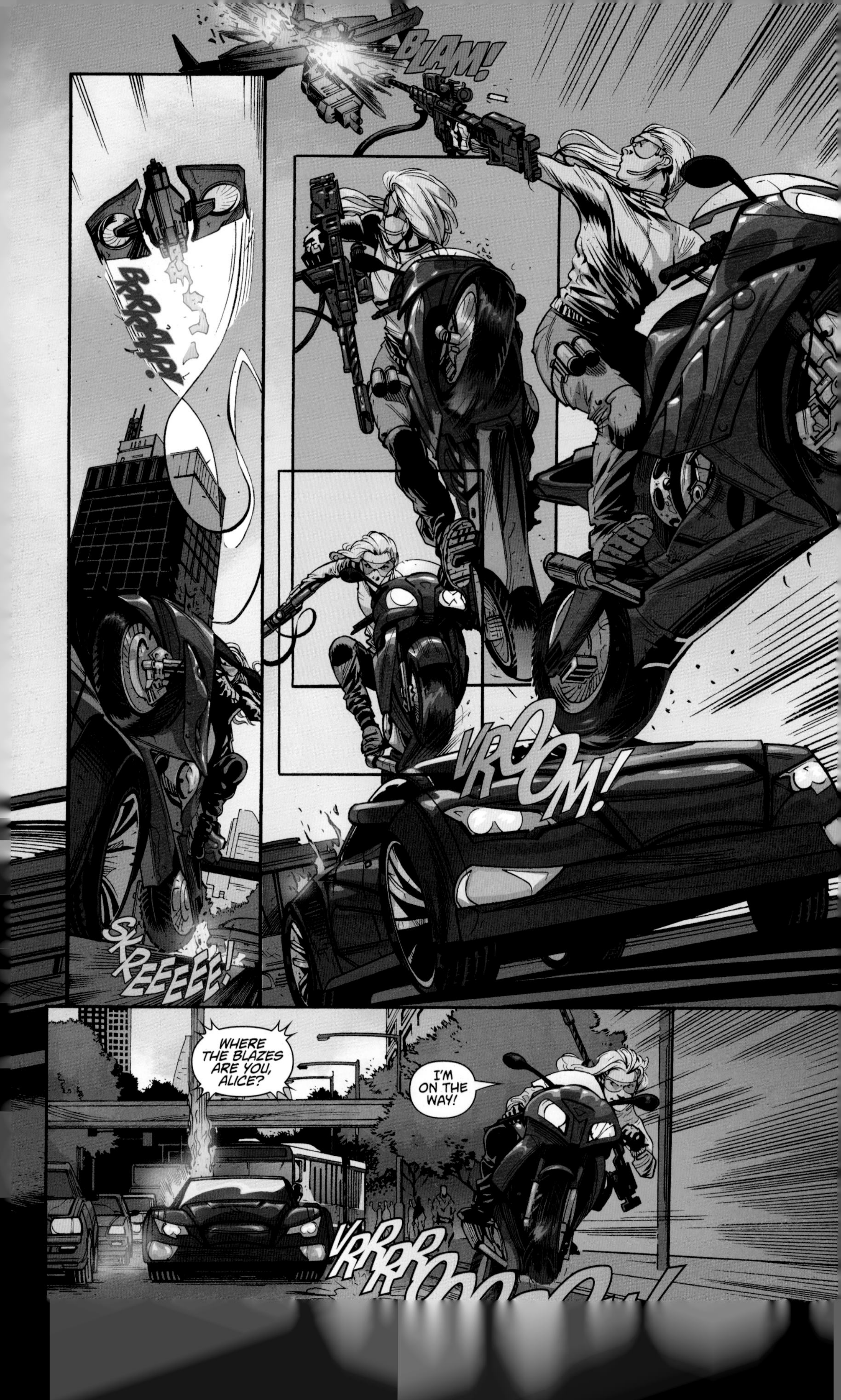
BLAM!
BRRRRRAP!
SKREEEEEE!
VROOM!
WHERE THE BLAZES ARE YOU, ALICE?
I'M ON THE WAY!
VRRRROOOOOM!

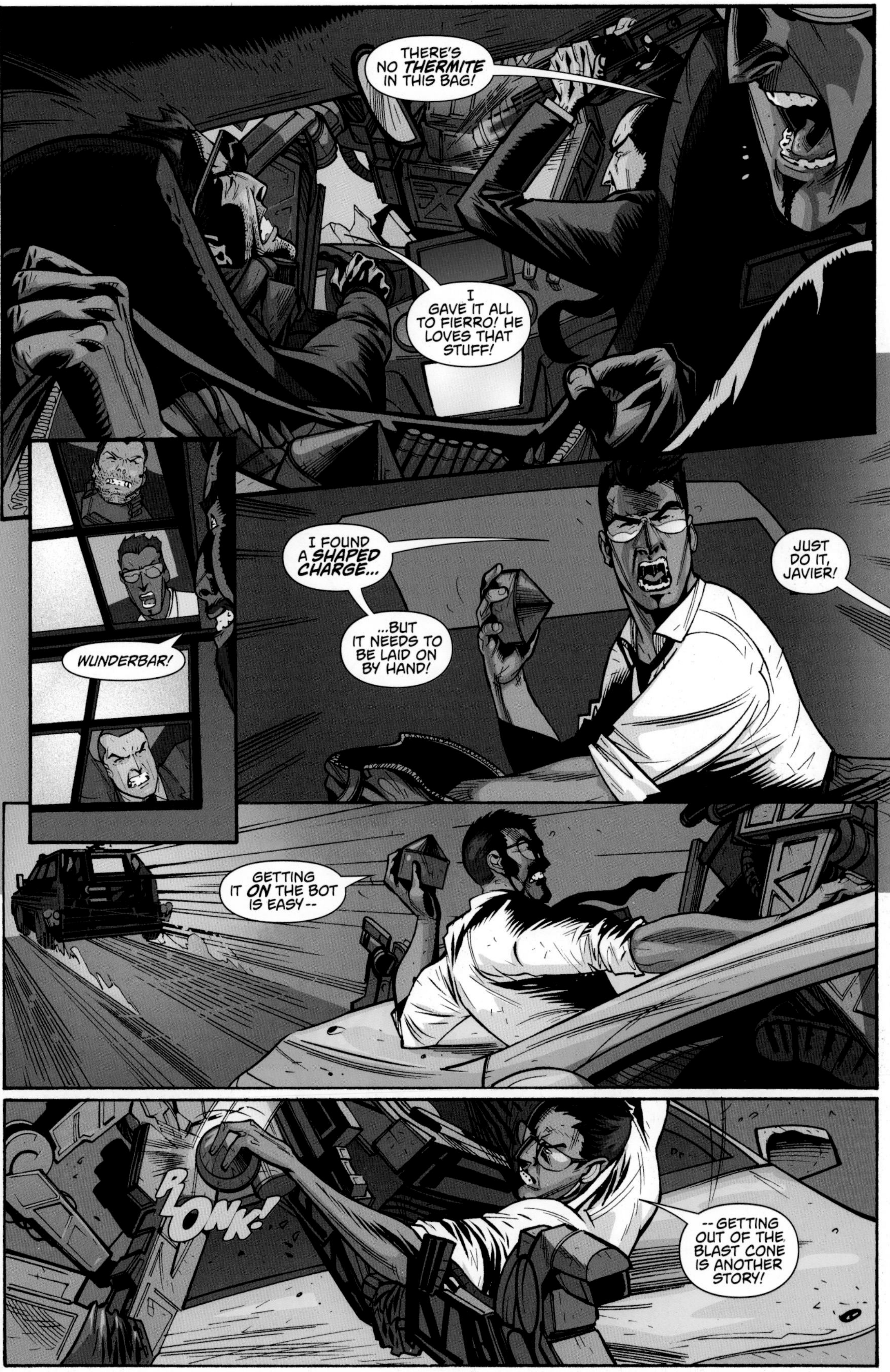
THERE'S NO THERMITE IN THIS BAG!
I GAVE IT ALL TO FIERRO! HE LOVES THAT STUFF!
I FOUND A SHAPED CHARGE...
...BUT IT NEEDS TO BE LAID ON BY HAND!
JUST DO IT, JAVIER!
WUNDERBAR!
GETTING IT ON THE BOT IS EASY--
PLONK!
--GETTING OUT OF THE BLAST CONE IS ANOTHER STORY!

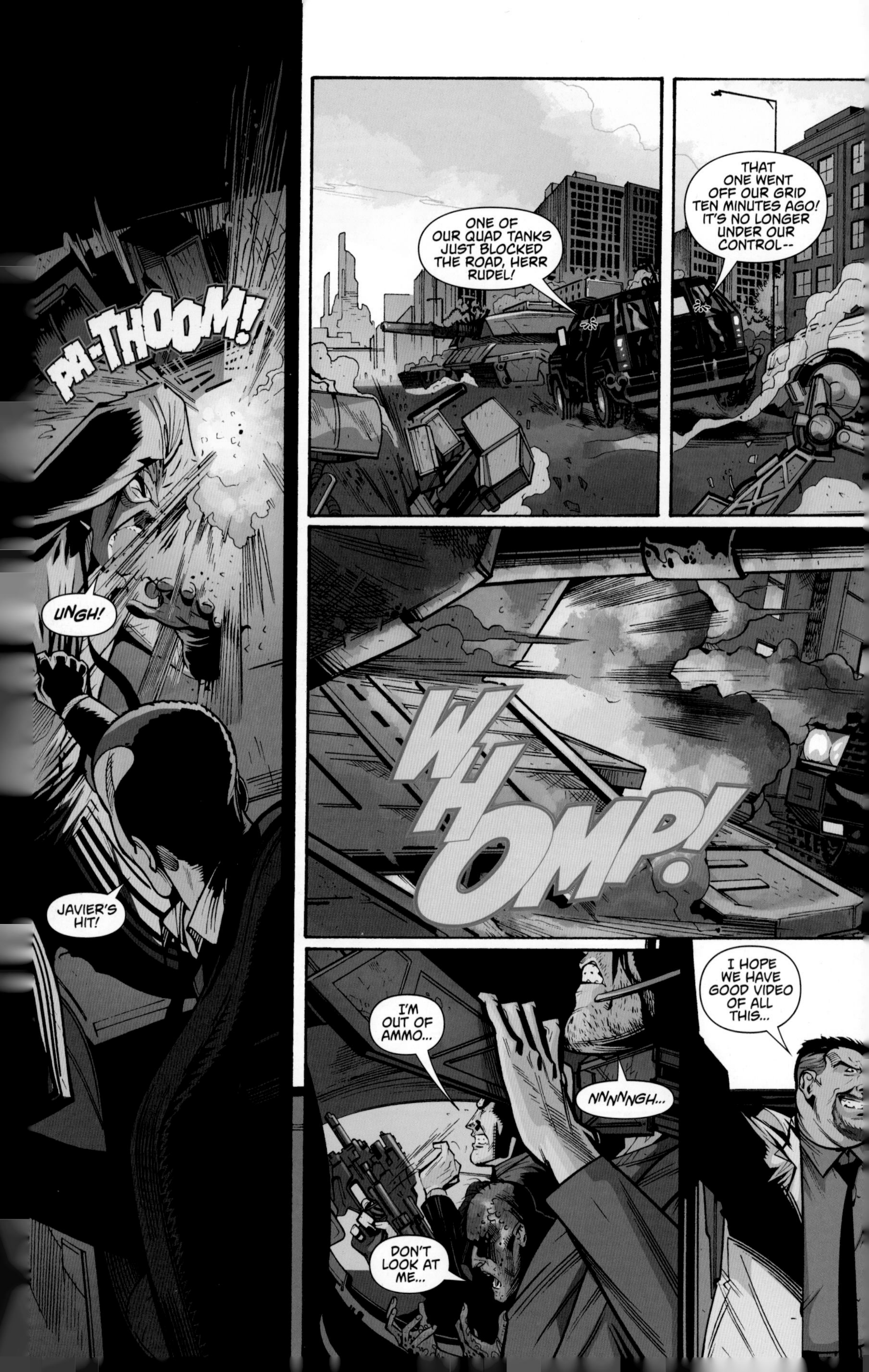
PA-THOOM!
UNGH!
JAVIER'S HIT!
ONE OF OUR QUAD TANKS JUST BLOCKED THE ROAD, HERR RUDEL!
THAT ONE WENT OFF OUR GRID TEN MINUTES AGO! IT'S NO LONGER UNDER OUR CONTROL--
WHOMP!
I'M OUT OF AMMO...
NNNNNGH...
DON'T LOOK AT ME...
I HOPE WE HAVE GOOD VIDEO OF ALL THIS...

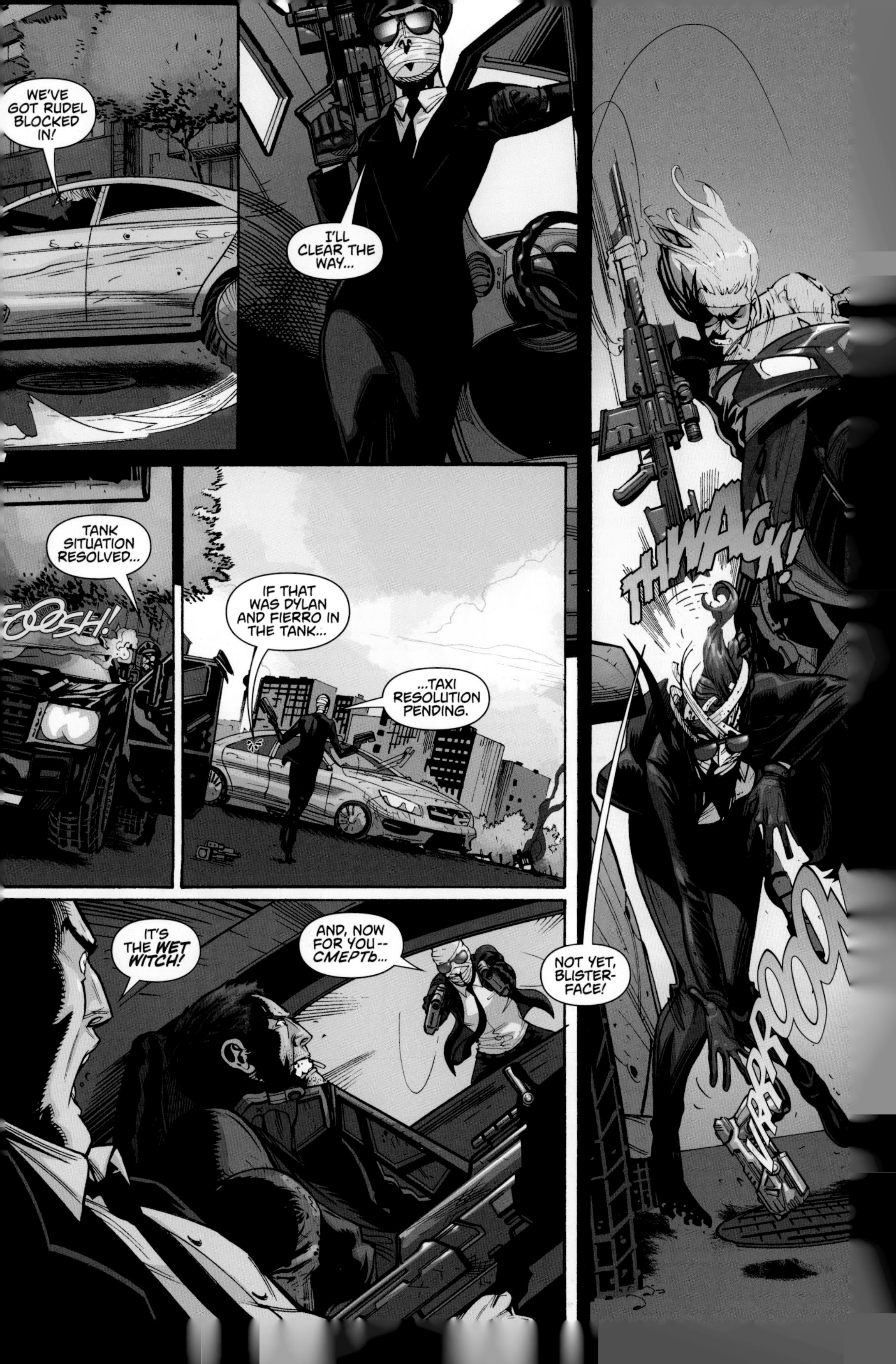
WE'VE GOT RUDEL BLOCKED IN!
I'LL CLEAR THE WAY...
TANK SITUATION RESOLVED...
FOOOSH!
IF THAT WAS DYLAN AND FIERRO IN THE TANK...
...TAXI RESOLUTION PENDING.
IT'S THE WET WITCH!
AND, NOW FOR YOU-- СМЕРТЬ...
THWACK!
NOT YET, BLISTER-FACE!

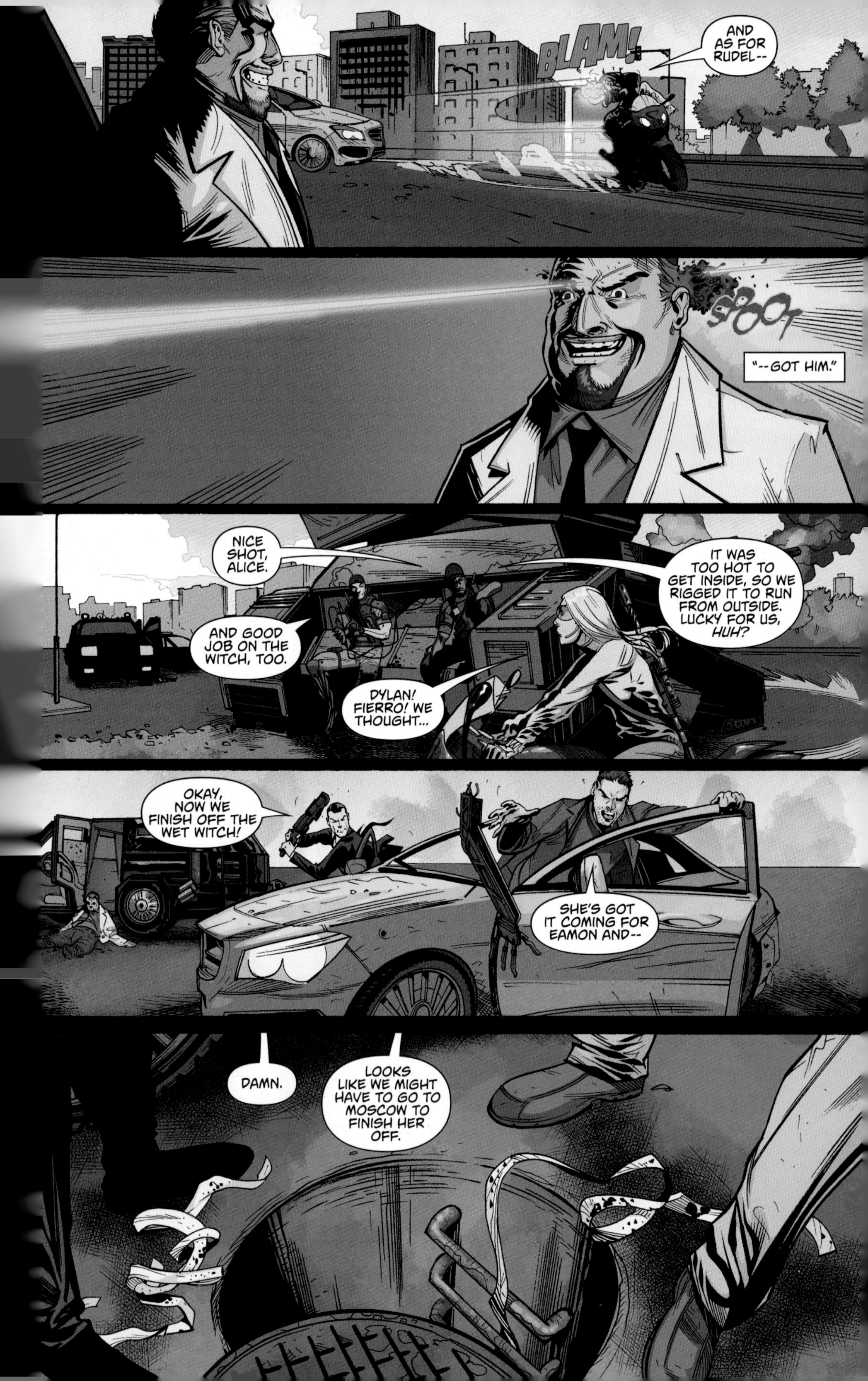
BLAM!
AND AS FOR RUDEL--
SPOOT
"--GOT HIM."
NICE SHOT, ALICE.
AND GOOD JOB ON THE WITCH, TOO.
DYLAN! FIERRO! WE THOUGHT...
IT WAS TOO HOT TO GET INSIDE, SO WE RIGGED IT TO RUN FROM OUTSIDE. LUCKY FOR US, HUH?
OKAY, NOW WE FINISH OFF THE WET WITCH!
SHE'S GOT IT COMING FOR EAMON AND--
DAMN.
LOOKS LIKE WE MIGHT HAVE TO GO TO MOSCOW TO FINISH HER OFF.

ANTHONY PALUMBO

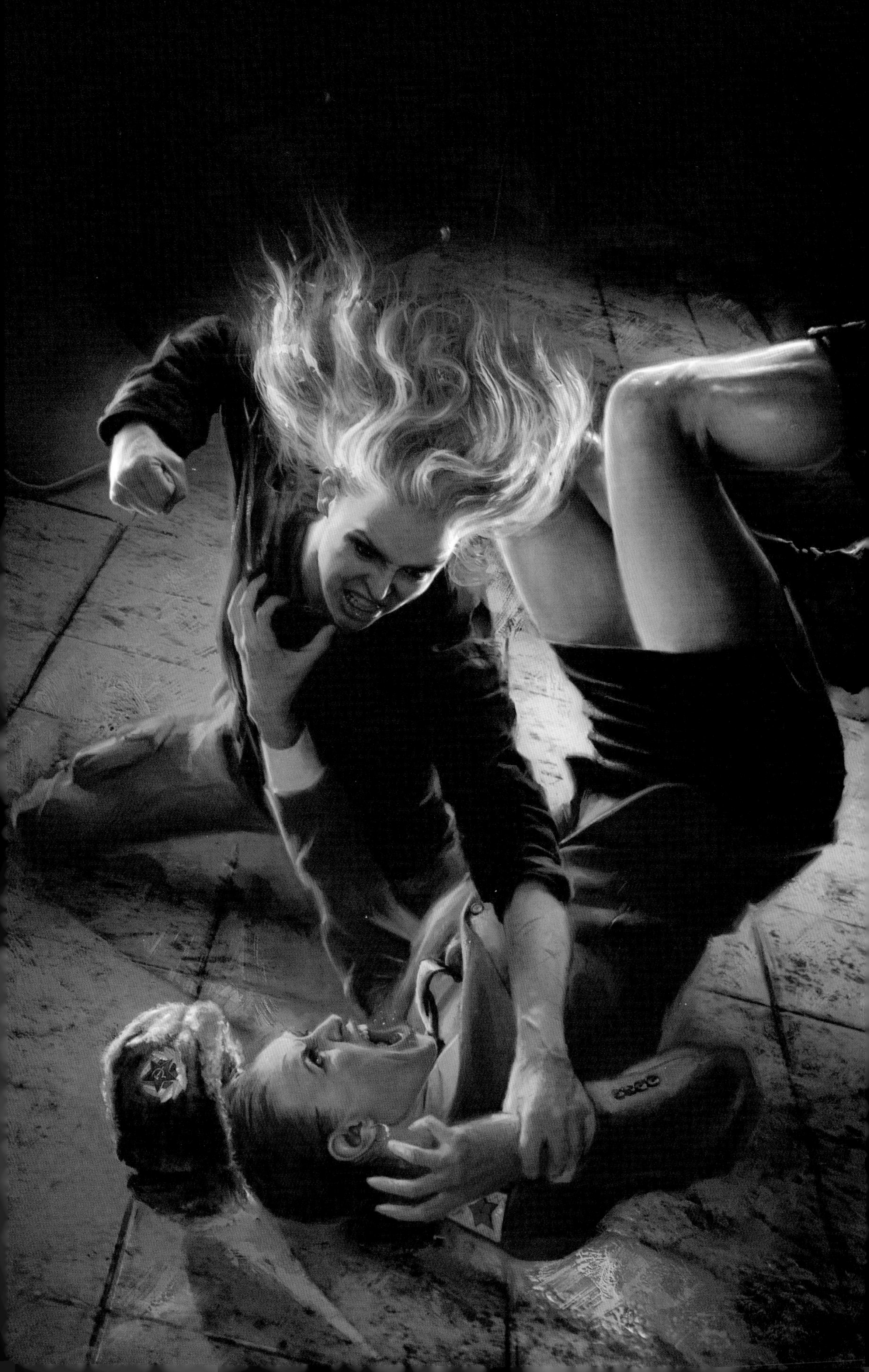

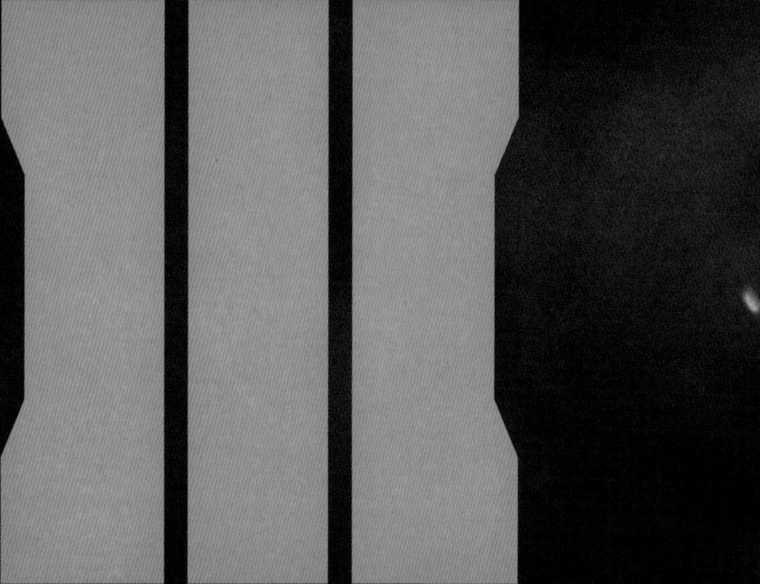

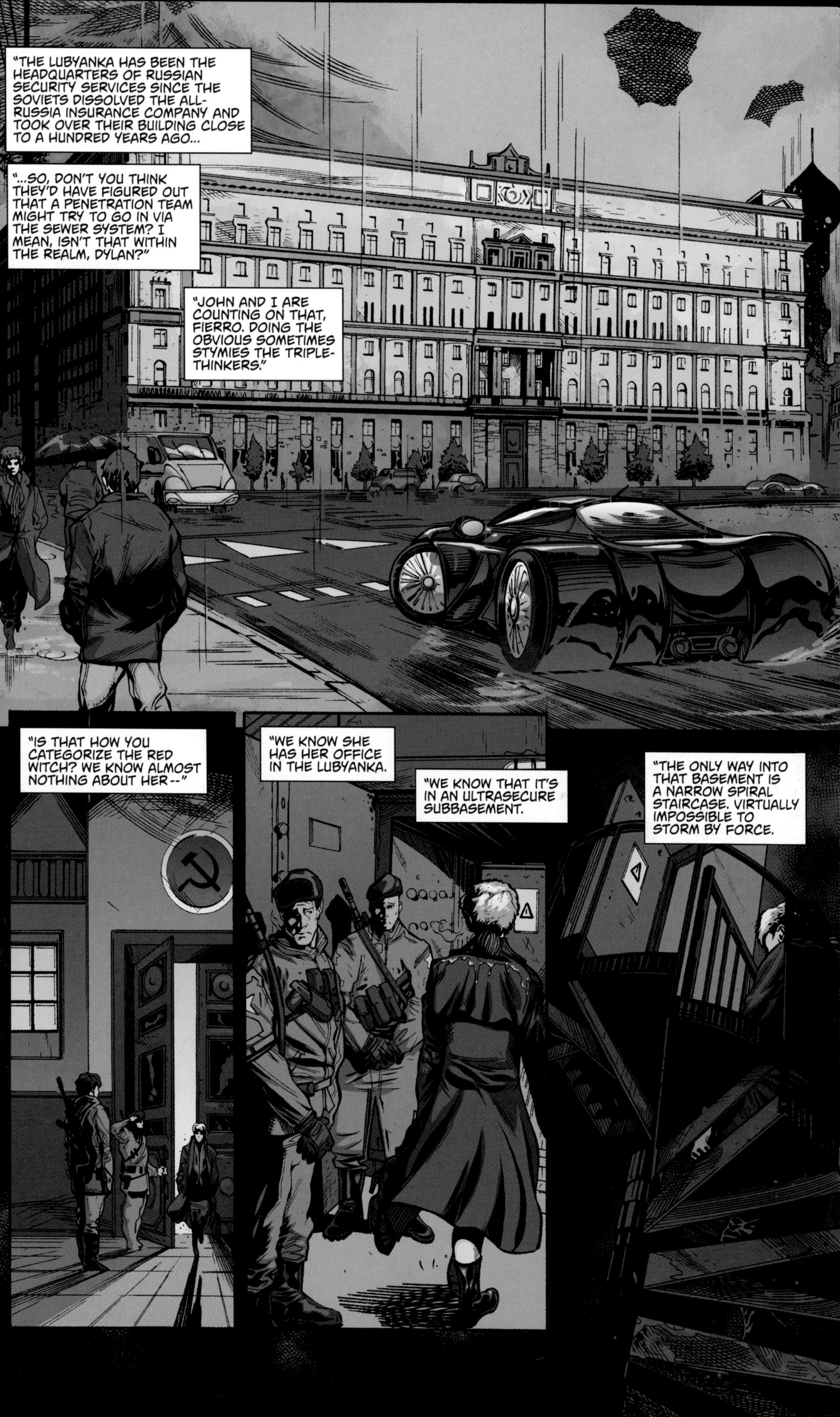
"THE LUBYANKA HAS BEEN THE HEADQUARTERS OF RUSSIAN SECURITY SERVICES SINCE THE SOVIETS DISSOLVED THE ALL-RUSSIA INSURANCE COMPANY AND TOOK OVER THEIR BUILDING CLOSE TO A HUNDRED YEARS AGO...
"...SO, DON'T YOU THINK THEY'D HAVE FIGURED OUT THAT A PENETRATION TEAM MIGHT TRY TO GO IN VIA THE SEWER SYSTEM? I MEAN, ISN'T THAT WITHIN THE REALM, DYLAN?"
"JOHN AND I ARE COUNTING ON THAT, FIERRO. DOING THE OBVIOUS SOMETIMES STYMIES THE TRIPLE-THINKERS."
"IS THAT HOW YOU CATEGORIZE THE RED WITCH? WE KNOW ALMOST NOTHING ABOUT HER--"
"WE KNOW SHE HAS HER OFFICE IN THE LUBYANKA.
"WE KNOW THAT IT'S IN AN ULTRASECURE SUBBASEMENT.
"THE ONLY WAY INTO THAT BASEMENT IS A NARROW SPIRAL STAIRCASE. VIRTUALLY IMPOSSIBLE TO STORM BY FORCE.

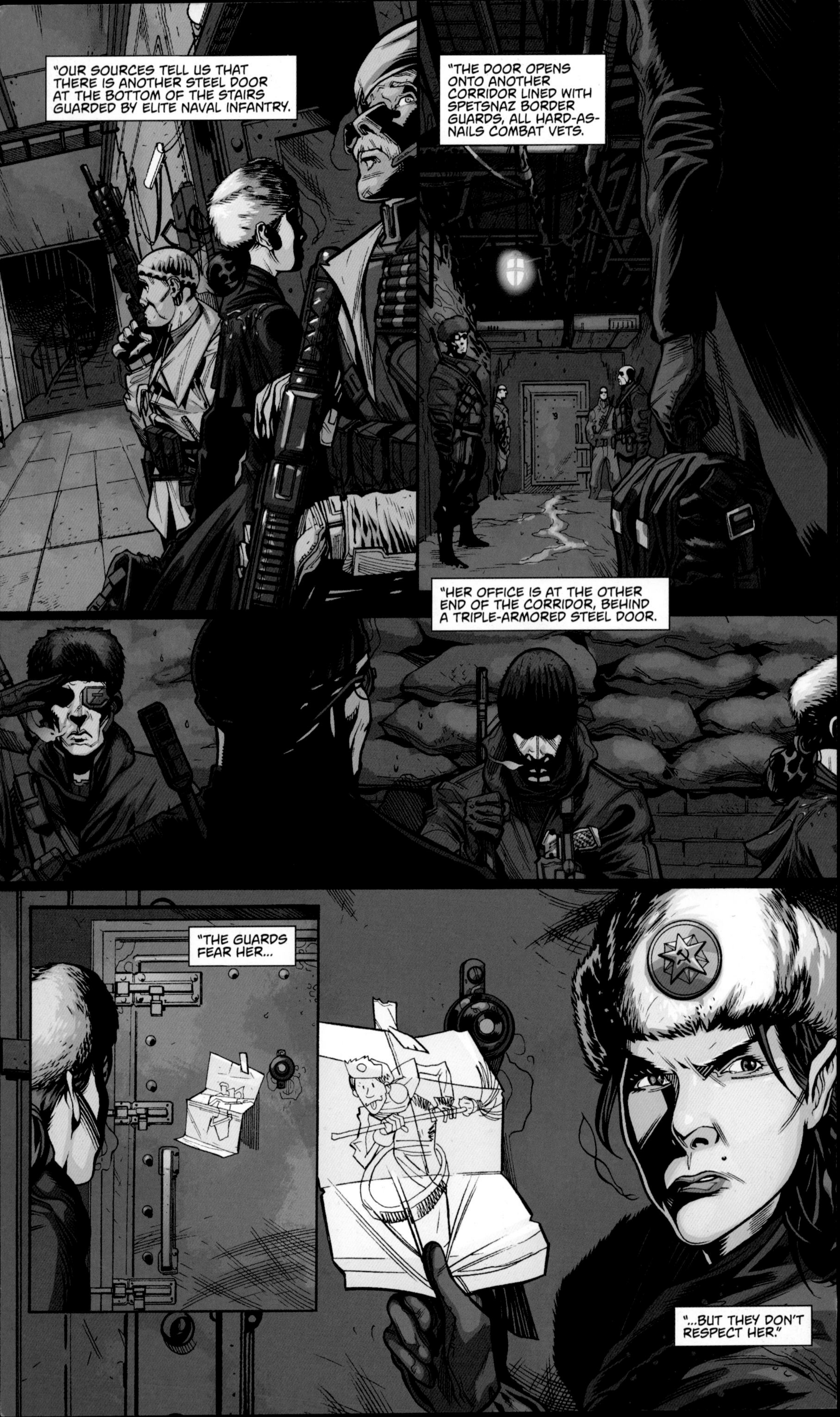
"OUR SOURCES TELL US THAT THERE IS ANOTHER STEEL DOOR AT THE BOTTOM OF THE STAIRS GUARDED BY ELITE NAVAL INFANTRY.
"THE DOOR OPENS ONTO ANOTHER CORRIDOR LINED WITH SPETSNAZ BORDER GUARDS, ALL HARD-AS-NAILS COMBAT VETS.
"HER OFFICE IS AT THE OTHER END OF THE CORRIDOR, BEHIND A TRIPLE-ARMORED STEEL DOOR.
"THE GUARDS FEAR HER...
"...BUT THEY DON'T RESPECT HER."

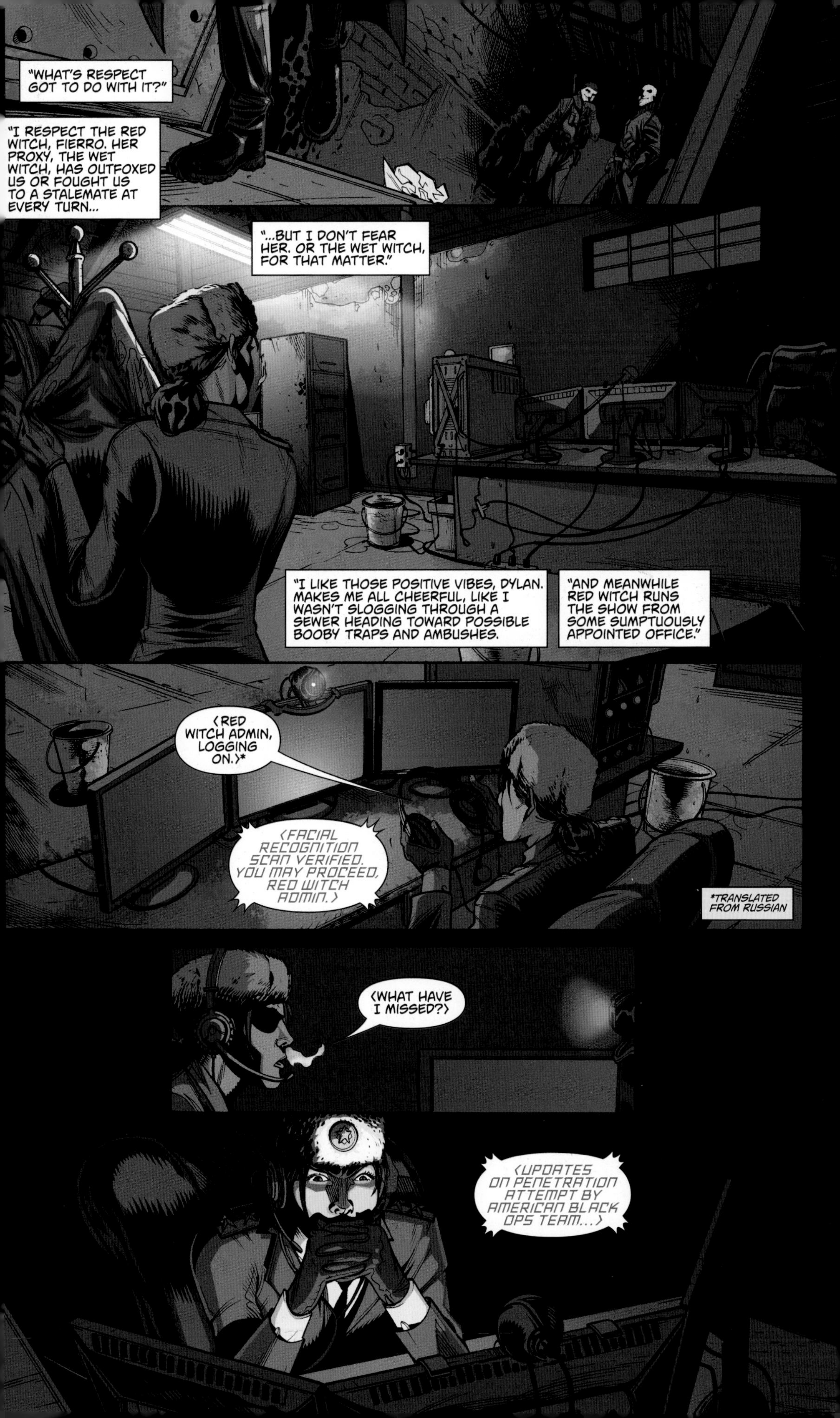
"WHAT'S RESPECT GOT TO DO WITH IT?"
"I RESPECT THE RED WITCH, FIERRO. HER PROXY, THE WET WITCH, HAS OUTFOXED US OR FOUGHT US TO A STALEMATE AT EVERY TURN...
"...BUT I DON'T FEAR HER. OR THE WET WITCH, FOR THAT MATTER."
"I LIKE THOSE POSITIVE VIBES, DYLAN. MAKES ME ALL CHEERFUL, LIKE I WASN'T SLOGGING THROUGH A SEWER HEADING TOWARD POSSIBLE BOOBY TRAPS AND AMBUSHES.
"AND MEANWHILE RED WITCH RUNS THE SHOW FROM SOME SUMPTUOUSLY APPOINTED OFFICE."
<RED WITCH ADMIN, LOGGING ON.>*
<FACIAL RECOGNITION SCAN VERIFIED. YOU MAY PROCEED, RED WITCH ADMIN.>
*TRANSLATED FROM RUSSIAN
<WHAT HAVE I MISSED?>
<UPDATES ON PENETRATION ATTEMPT BY AMERICAN BLACK OPS TEAM...>

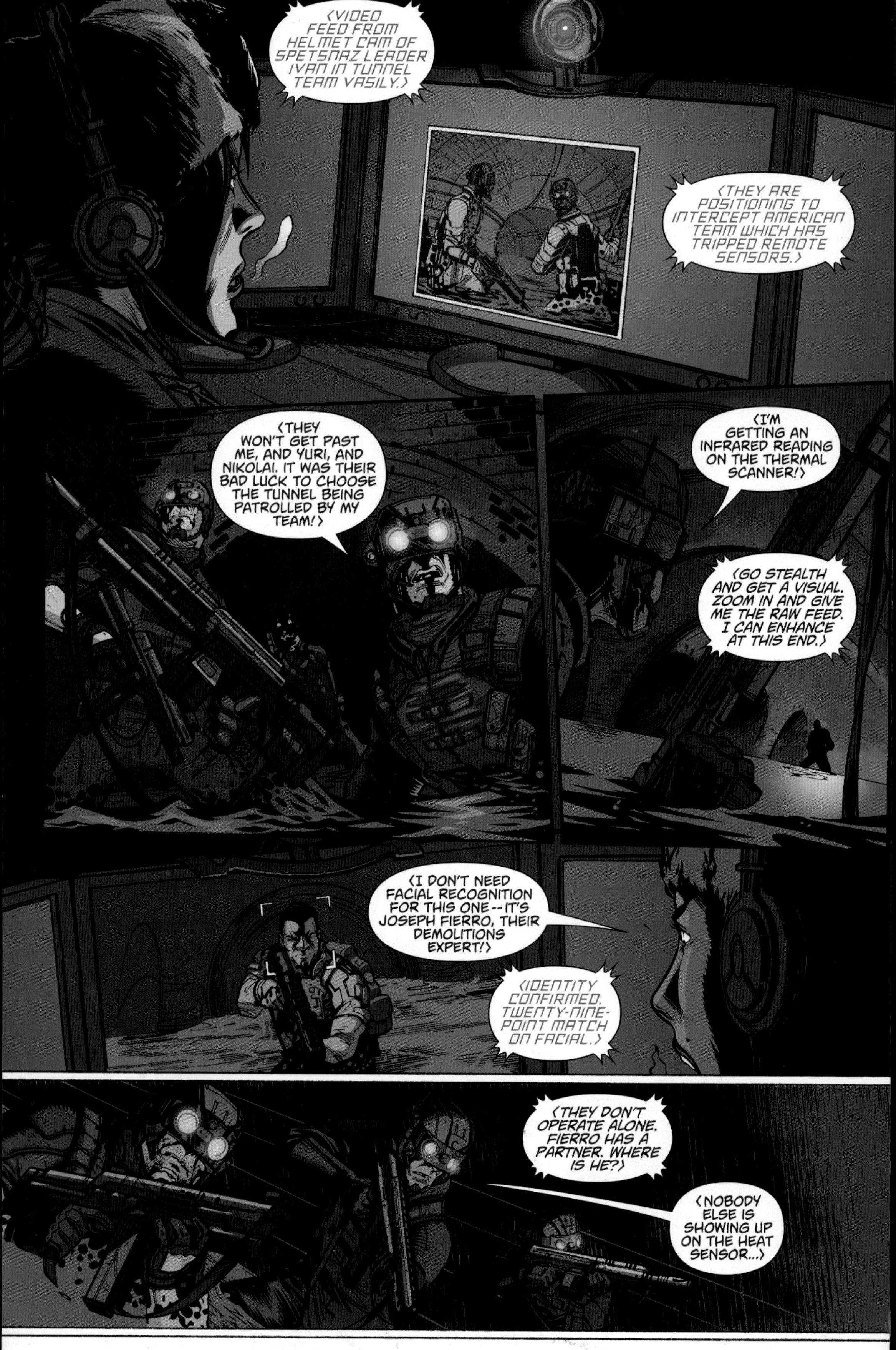
‹VIDEO FEED FROM HELMET CAM OF SPETSNAZ LEADER IVAN IN TUNNEL TEAM VASILY.›
‹THEY ARE POSITIONING TO INTERCEPT AMERICAN TEAM WHICH HAS TRIPPED REMOTE SENSORS.›
‹THEY WON'T GET PAST ME, AND YURI, AND NIKOLAI. IT WAS THEIR BAD LUCK TO CHOOSE THE TUNNEL BEING PATROLLED BY MY TEAM!›
‹I'M GETTING AN INFRARED READING ON THE THERMAL SCANNER!›
‹GO STEALTH AND GET A VISUAL. ZOOM IN AND GIVE ME THE RAW FEED. I CAN ENHANCE AT THIS END.›
‹I DON'T NEED FACIAL RECOGNITION FOR THIS ONE -- IT'S JOSEPH FIERRO, THEIR DEMOLITIONS EXPERT!›
‹IDENTITY CONFIRMED. TWENTY-NINE-POINT MATCH ON FACIAL.›
‹THEY DON'T OPERATE ALONE. FIERRO HAS A PARTNER. WHERE IS HE?›
‹NOBODY ELSE IS SHOWING UP ON THE HEAT SENSOR...›

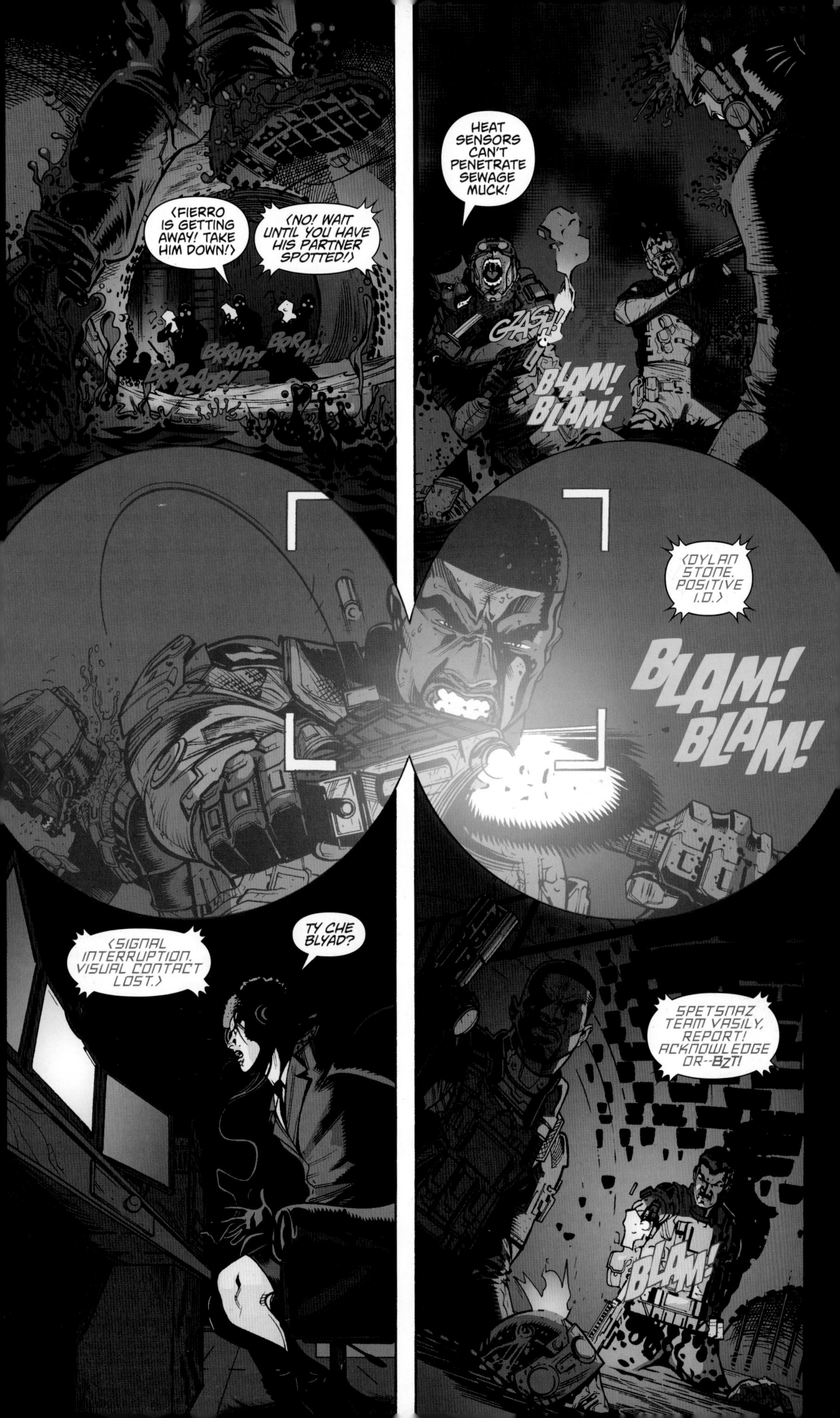
<FIERRO IS GETTING AWAY! TAKE HIM DOWN!>
<NO! WAIT UNTIL YOU HAVE HIS PARTNER SPOTTED!>
BRRAPP!
BRRAPP!
BRRAPP!
HEAT SENSORS CAN'T PENETRATE SEWAGE MUCK!
GASH!
BLAM! BLAM!
<DYLAN STONE. POSITIVE I.D.>
BLAM! BLAM!
<SIGNAL INTERRUPTION. VISUAL CONTACT LOST.>
TY CHE BLYAD?
SPETSNAZ TEAM VASILY, REPORT! ACKNOWLEDGE OR--BZT!
BLAM!

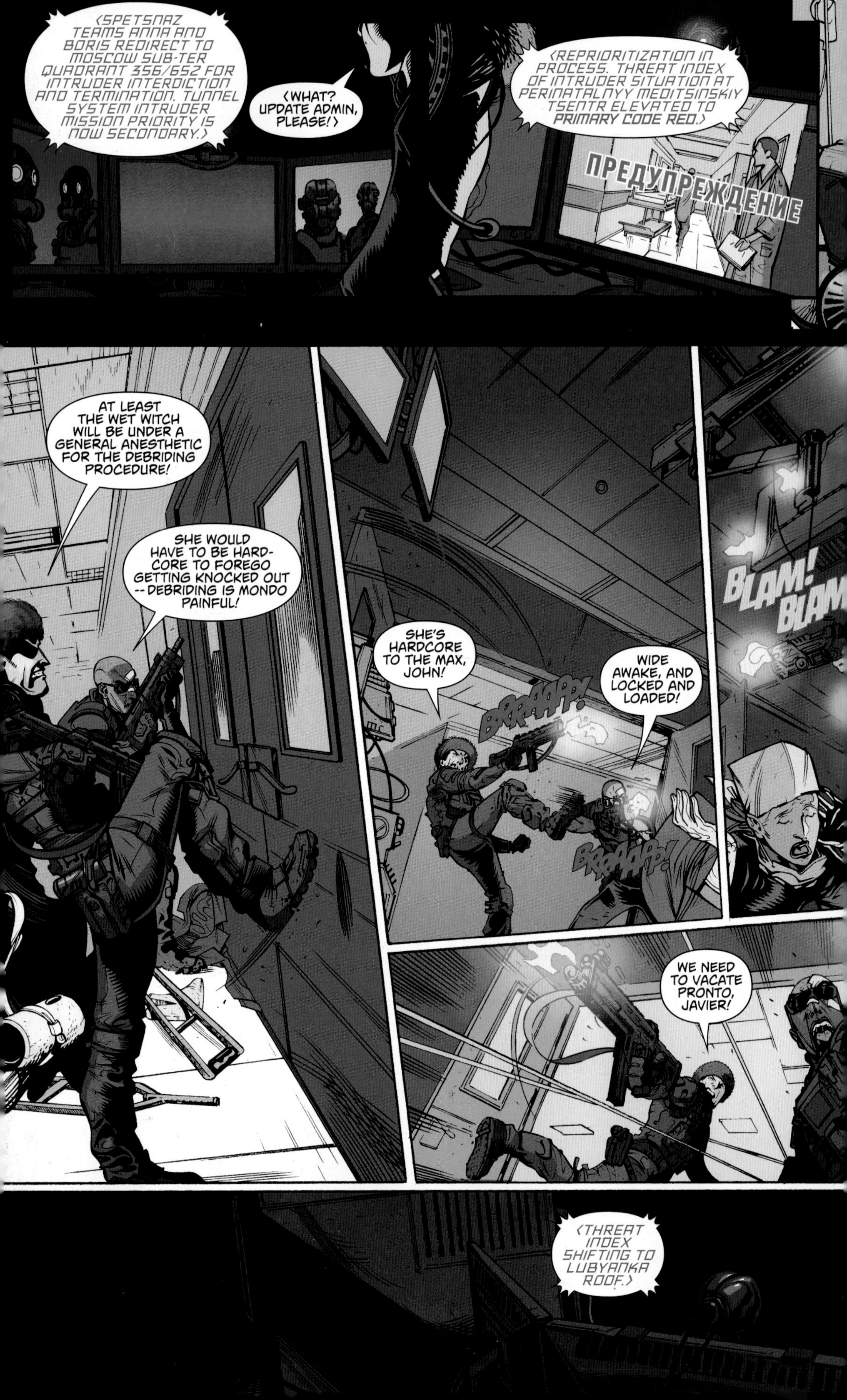
<SPETSNAZ TEAMS ANNA AND BORIS REDIRECT TO MOSCOW SUB-TER QUADRANT 356/652 FOR INTRUDER INTERDICTION AND TERMINATION. TUNNEL SYSTEM INTRUDER MISSION PRIORITY IS NOW SECONDARY.>
<WHAT? UPDATE ADMIN, PLEASE!>
<REPRIORITIZATION IN PROCESS. THREAT INDEX OF INTRUDER SITUATION AT PERINATALNYY MEDITSINSKIY TSENTR ELEVATED TO PRIMARY CODE RED.>
ПРЕДУПРЕЖДЕНИЕ
AT LEAST THE WET WITCH WILL BE UNDER A GENERAL ANESTHETIC FOR THE DEBRIDING PROCEDURE!
SHE WOULD HAVE TO BE HARD-CORE TO FOREGO GETTING KNOCKED OUT --DEBRIDING IS MONDO PAINFUL!
BLAM! BLAM
SHE'S HARDCORE TO THE MAX, JOHN!
BRRAAAPP!
WIDE AWAKE, AND LOCKED AND LOADED!
BRRAAAPP!
WE NEED TO VACATE PRONTO, JAVIER!
<THREAT INDEX SHIFTING TO LUBYANKA ROOF.>

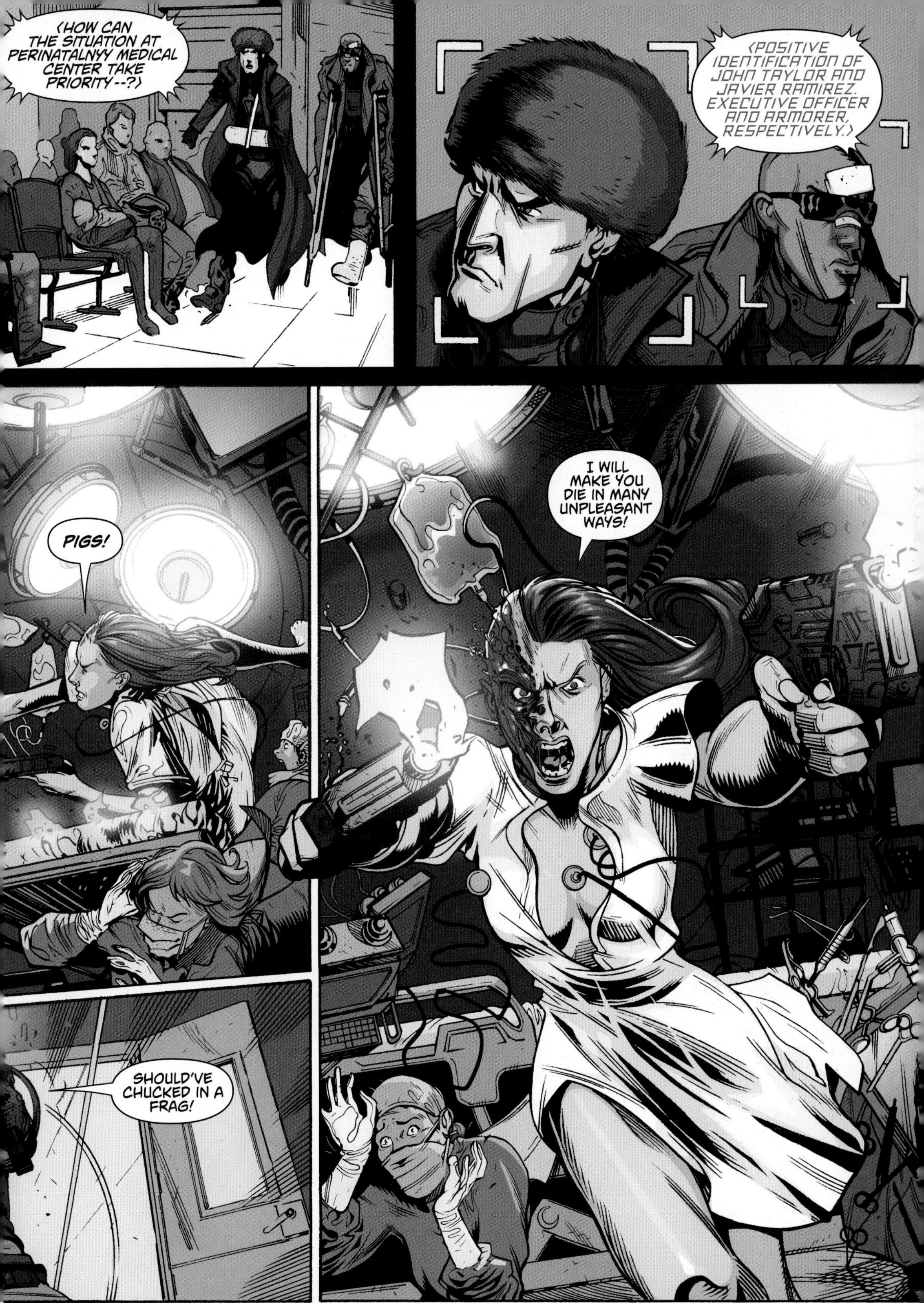

<HOW CAN THE SITUATION AT PERINATALNYY MEDICAL CENTER TAKE PRIORITY--?>
<POSITIVE IDENTIFICATION OF JOHN TAYLOR AND JAVIER RAMIREZ. EXECUTIVE OFFICER AND ARMORER, RESPECTIVELY.>
PIGS!
I WILL MAKE YOU DIE IN MANY UNPLEASANT WAYS!
SHOULD'VE CHUCKED IN A FRAG!

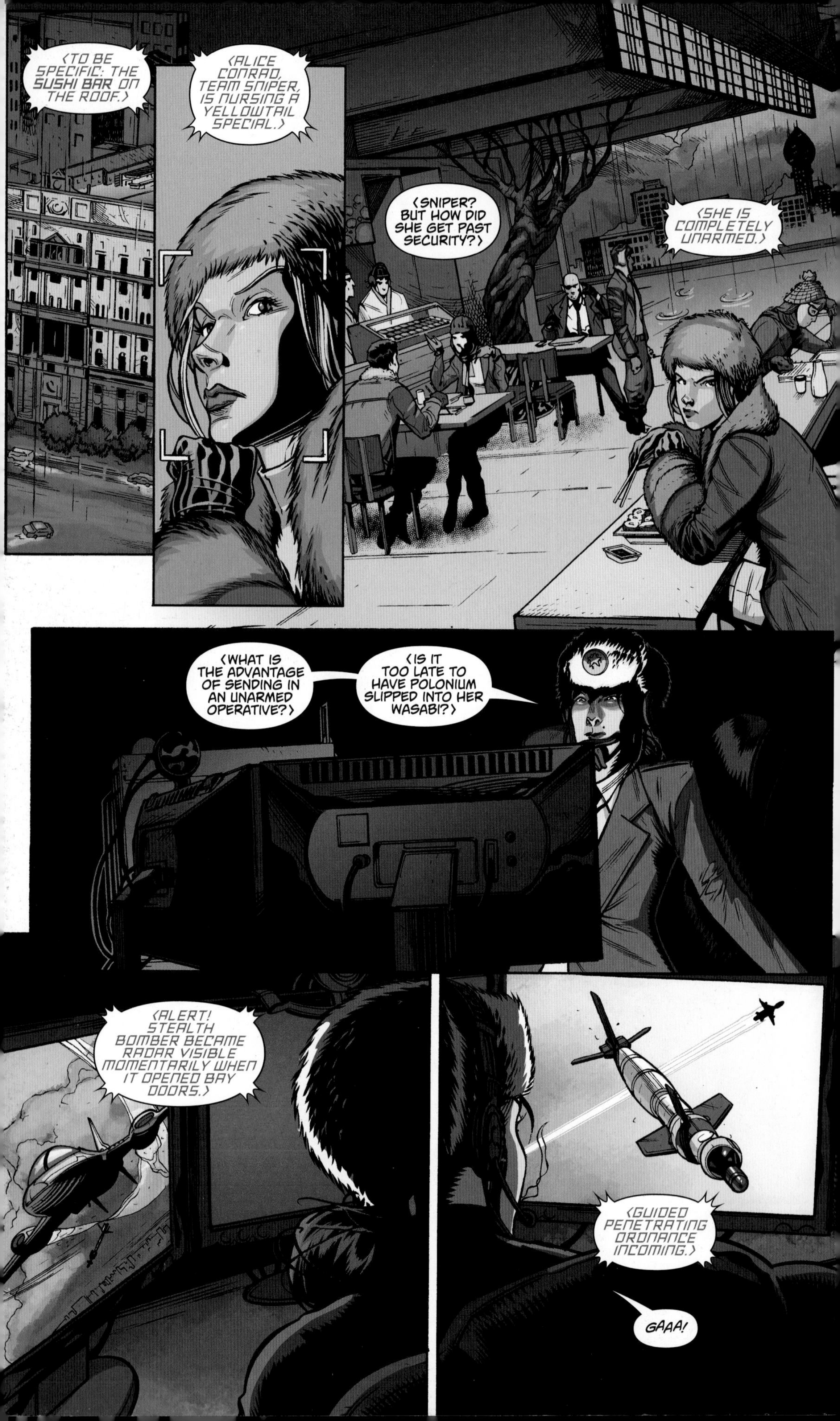
<TO BE SPECIFIC: THE SUSHI BAR ON THE ROOF.>
<ALICE CONRAD, TEAM SNIPER, IS NURSING A YELLOWTAIL SPECIAL.>
<SNIPER? BUT HOW DID SHE GET PAST SECURITY?>
<SHE IS COMPLETELY UNARMED.>
<WHAT IS THE ADVANTAGE OF SENDING IN AN UNARMED OPERATIVE?>
<IS IT TOO LATE TO HAVE POLONIUM SLIPPED INTO HER WASABI?>
<ALERT! STEALTH BOMBER BECAME RADAR VISIBLE MOMENTARILY WHEN IT OPENED BAY DOORS.>
<GUIDED PENETRATING ORDNANCE INCOMING.>
GAAA!

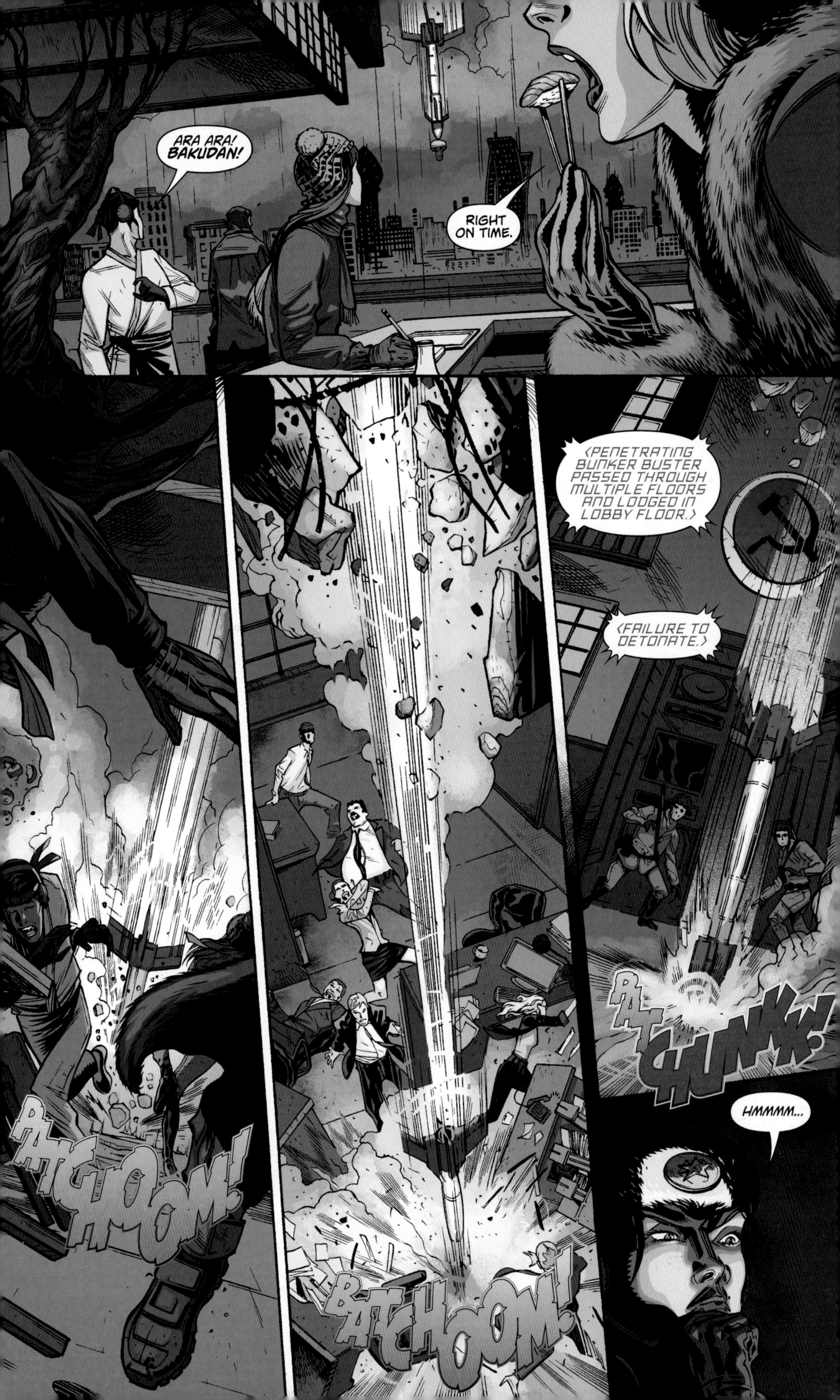
ARA ARA! BAKUDAN!
RIGHT ON TIME.
<PENETRATING BUNKER BUSTER PASSED THROUGH MULTIPLE FLOORS AND LODGED IN LOBBY FLOOR.>
<FAILURE TO DETONATE.>
BATCHOOM!
BATCHOOM!
PATCHUNK!
HMMMM...

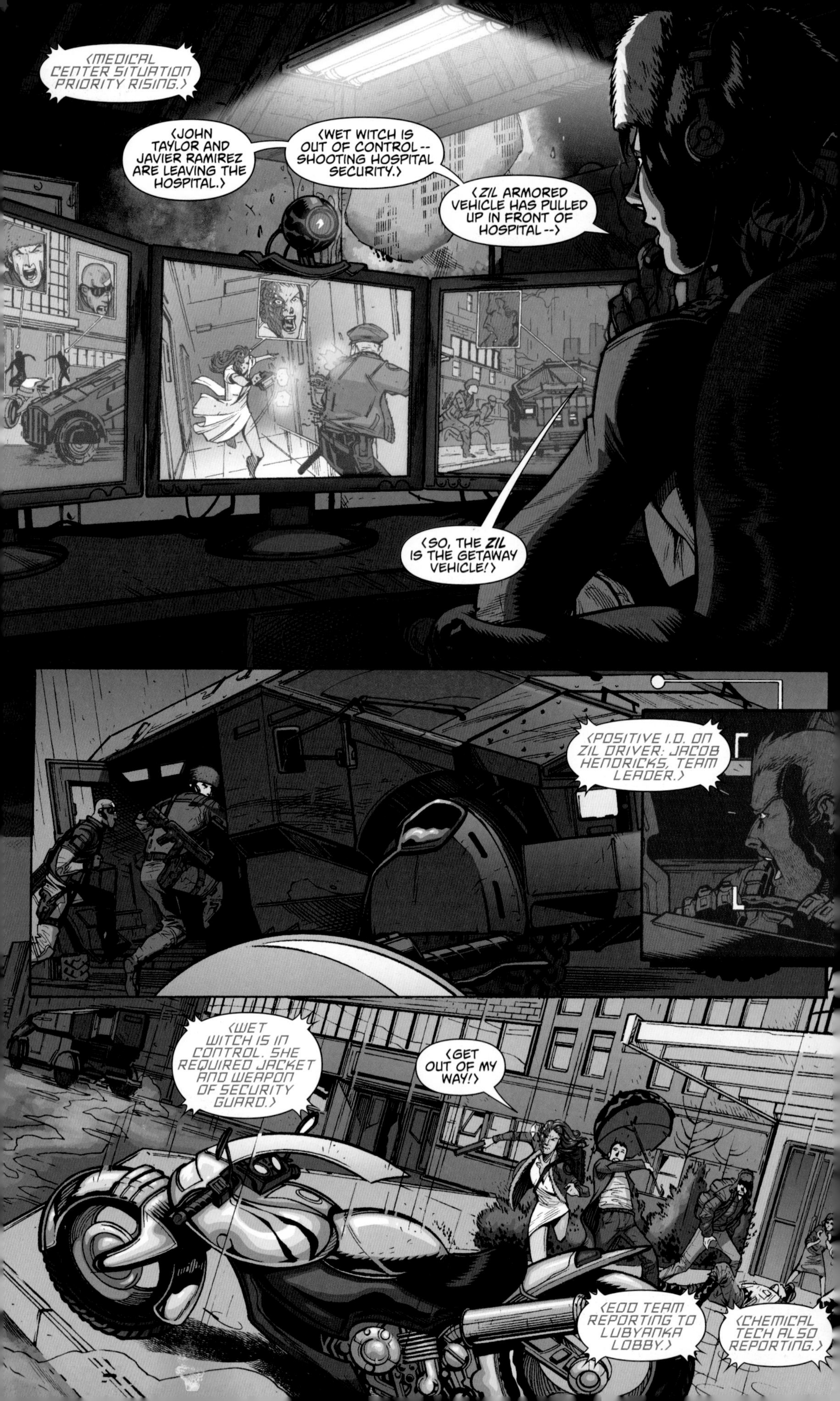

⟨MEDICAL CENTER SITUATION PRIORITY RISING.⟩
⟨JOHN TAYLOR AND JAVIER RAMIREZ ARE LEAVING THE HOSPITAL.⟩
⟨WET WITCH IS OUT OF CONTROL -- SHOOTING HOSPITAL SECURITY.⟩
⟨ZIL ARMORED VEHICLE HAS PULLED UP IN FRONT OF HOSPITAL --⟩
⟨SO, THE ZIL IS THE GETAWAY VEHICLE!⟩
⟨POSITIVE I.D. ON ZIL DRIVER: JACOB HENDRICKS, TEAM LEADER.⟩
⟨WET WITCH IS IN CONTROL. SHE REQUIRED JACKET AND WEAPON OF SECURITY GUARD.⟩
⟨GET OUT OF MY WAY!⟩
⟨EOD TEAM REPORTING TO LUBYANKA LOBBY.⟩
⟨CHEMICAL TECH ALSO REPORTING.⟩

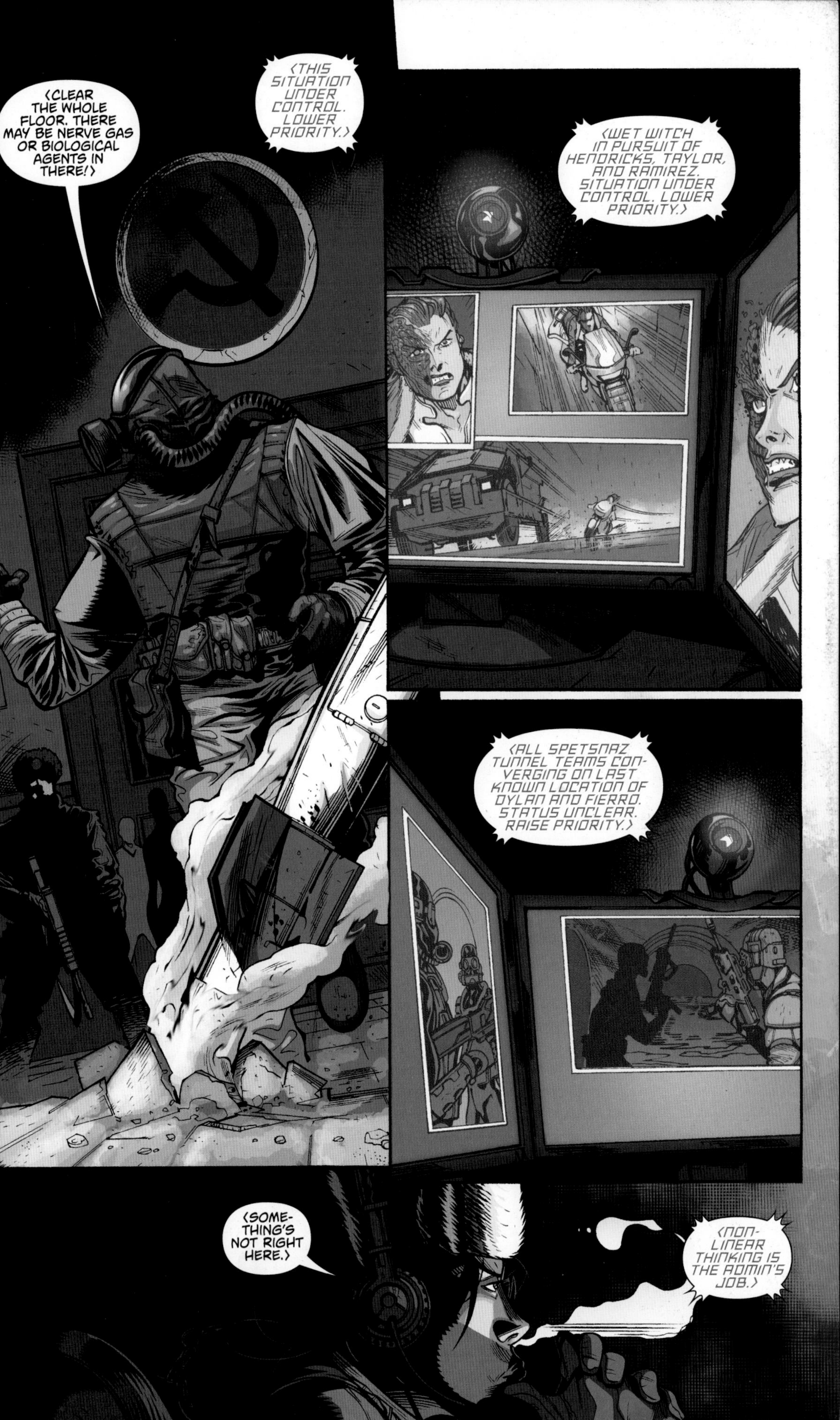

‹CLEAR THE WHOLE FLOOR. THERE MAY BE NERVE GAS OR BIOLOGICAL AGENTS IN THERE!›
‹THIS SITUATION UNDER CONTROL. LOWER PRIORITY.›
‹WET WITCH IN PURSUIT OF HENDRICKS, TAYLOR, AND RAMIREZ. SITUATION UNDER CONTROL. LOWER PRIORITY.›
‹ALL SPETSNAZ TUNNEL TEAMS CON-VERGING ON LAST KNOWN LOCATION OF DYLAN AND FIERRO. STATUS UNCLEAR. RAISE PRIORITY.›
‹SOME-THING'S NOT RIGHT HERE.›
‹NON-LINEAR THINKING IS THE ADMIN'S JOB.›

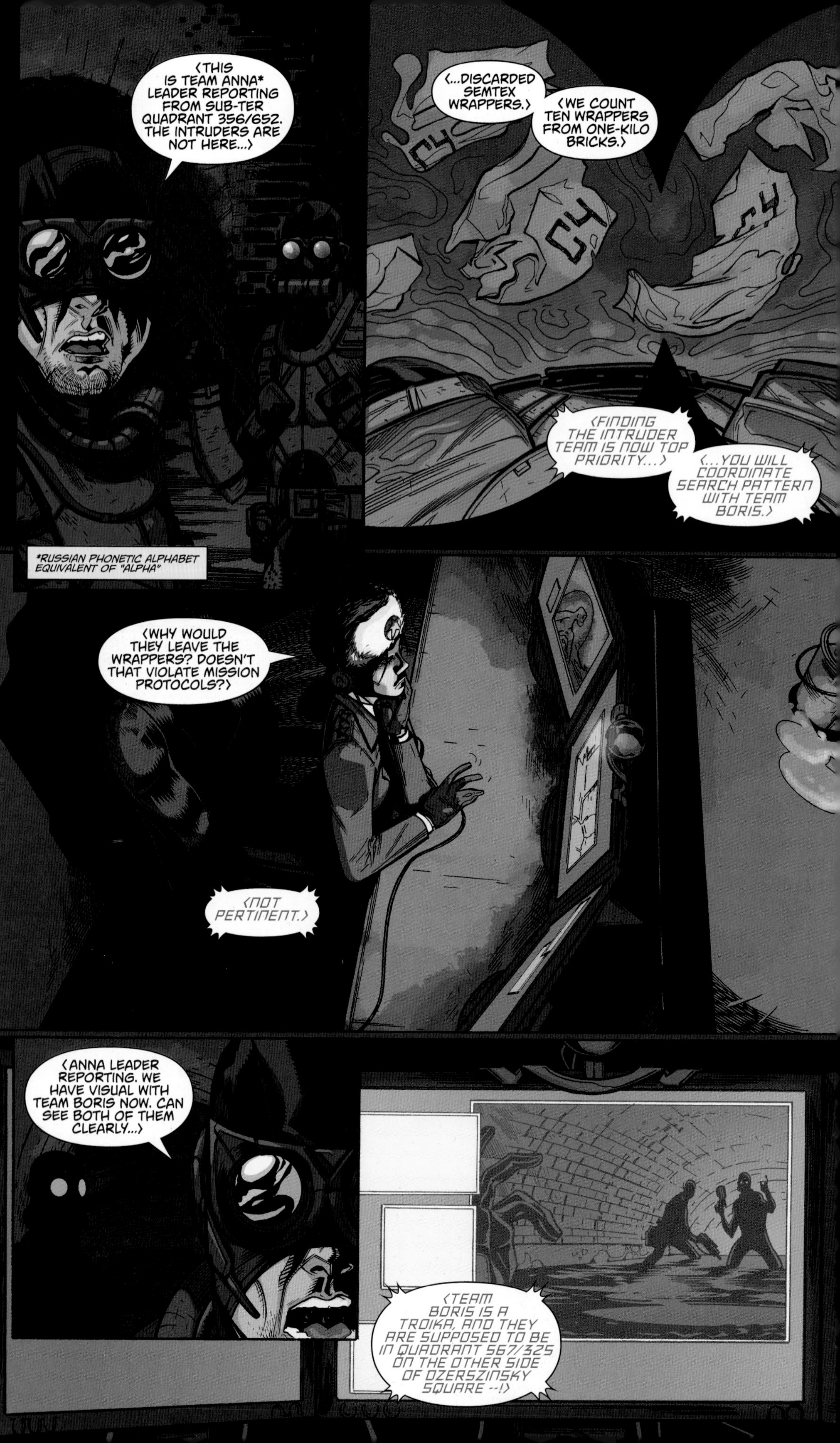

<THIS IS TEAM ANNA* LEADER REPORTING FROM SUB-TER QUADRANT 356/652. THE INTRUDERS ARE NOT HERE...>
<...DISCARDED SEMTEX WRAPPERS.>
<WE COUNT TEN WRAPPERS FROM ONE-KILO BRICKS.>
C4
C4
C4
<FINDING THE INTRUDER TEAM IS NOW TOP PRIORITY...>
<...YOU WILL COORDINATE SEARCH PATTERN WITH TEAM BORIS.>
*RUSSIAN PHONETIC ALPHABET EQUIVALENT OF "ALPHA"
<WHY WOULD THEY LEAVE THE WRAPPERS? DOESN'T THAT VIOLATE MISSION PROTOCOLS?>
<NOT PERTINENT.>
<ANNA LEADER REPORTING. WE HAVE VISUAL WITH TEAM BORIS NOW. CAN SEE BOTH OF THEM CLEARLY...>
<TEAM BORIS IS A TROIKA, AND THEY ARE SUPPOSED TO BE IN QUADRANT 567/325 ON THE OTHER SIDE OF DZERSZINSKY SQUARE --!>

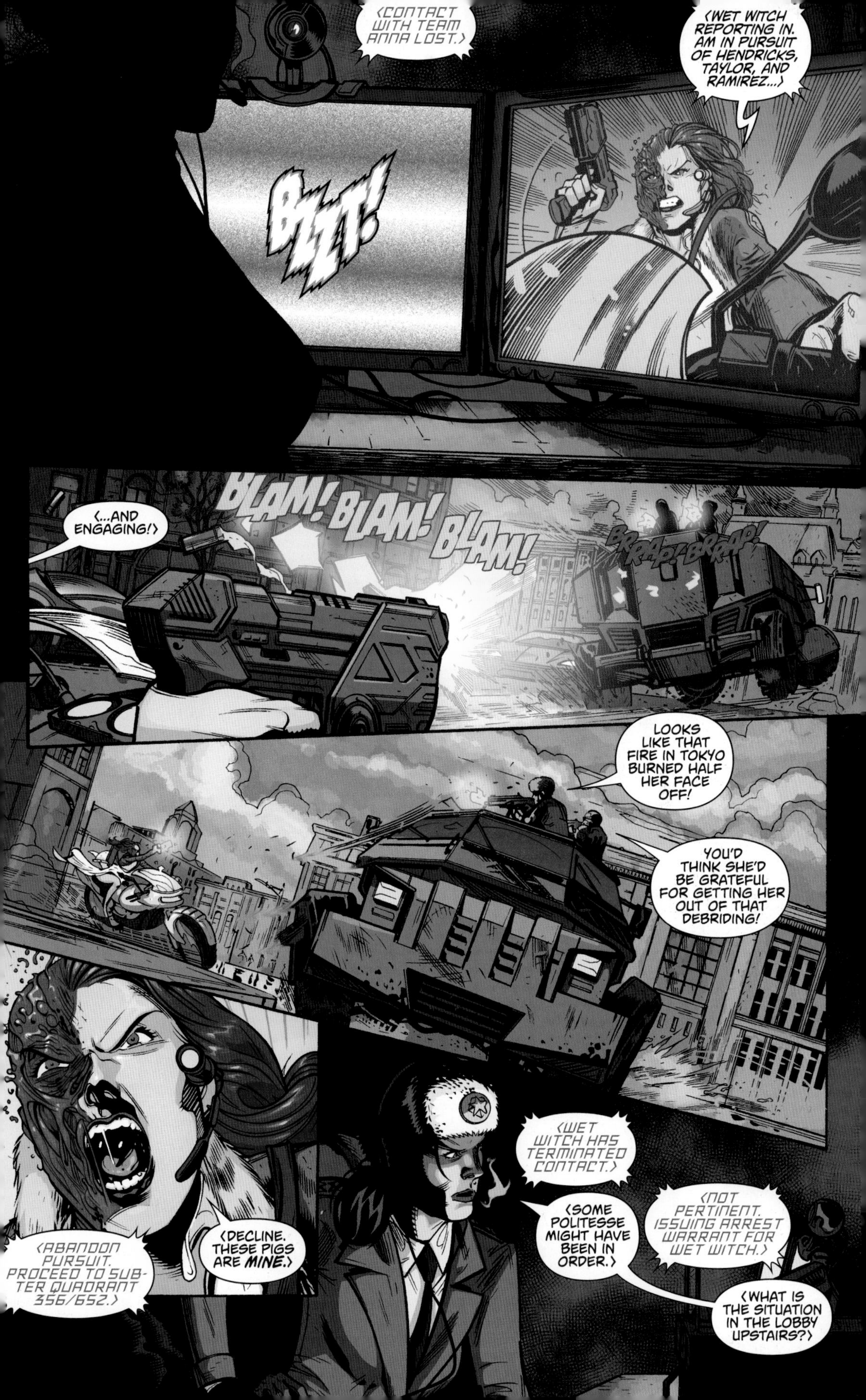

<CONTACT WITH TEAM ANNA LOST.>
<WET WITCH REPORTING IN. AM IN PURSUIT OF HENDRICKS, TAYLOR, AND RAMIREZ...>
BZZZT!
<...AND ENGAGING!>
BLAM! BLAM! BLAM!
BRRRAP! BRRRAP!
LOOKS LIKE THAT FIRE IN TOKYO BURNED HALF HER FACE OFF!
YOU'D THINK SHE'D BE GRATEFUL FOR GETTING HER OUT OF THAT DEBRIDING!
<ABANDON PURSUIT. PROCEED TO SUBTER QUADRANT 356/652.>
<DECLINE. THESE PIGS ARE MINE.>
<WET WITCH HAS TERMINATED CONTACT.>
<SOME POLITESSE MIGHT HAVE BEEN IN ORDER.>
<NOT PERTINENT. ISSUING ARREST WARRANT FOR WET WITCH.>
<WHAT IS THE SITUATION IN THE LOBBY UPSTAIRS?>

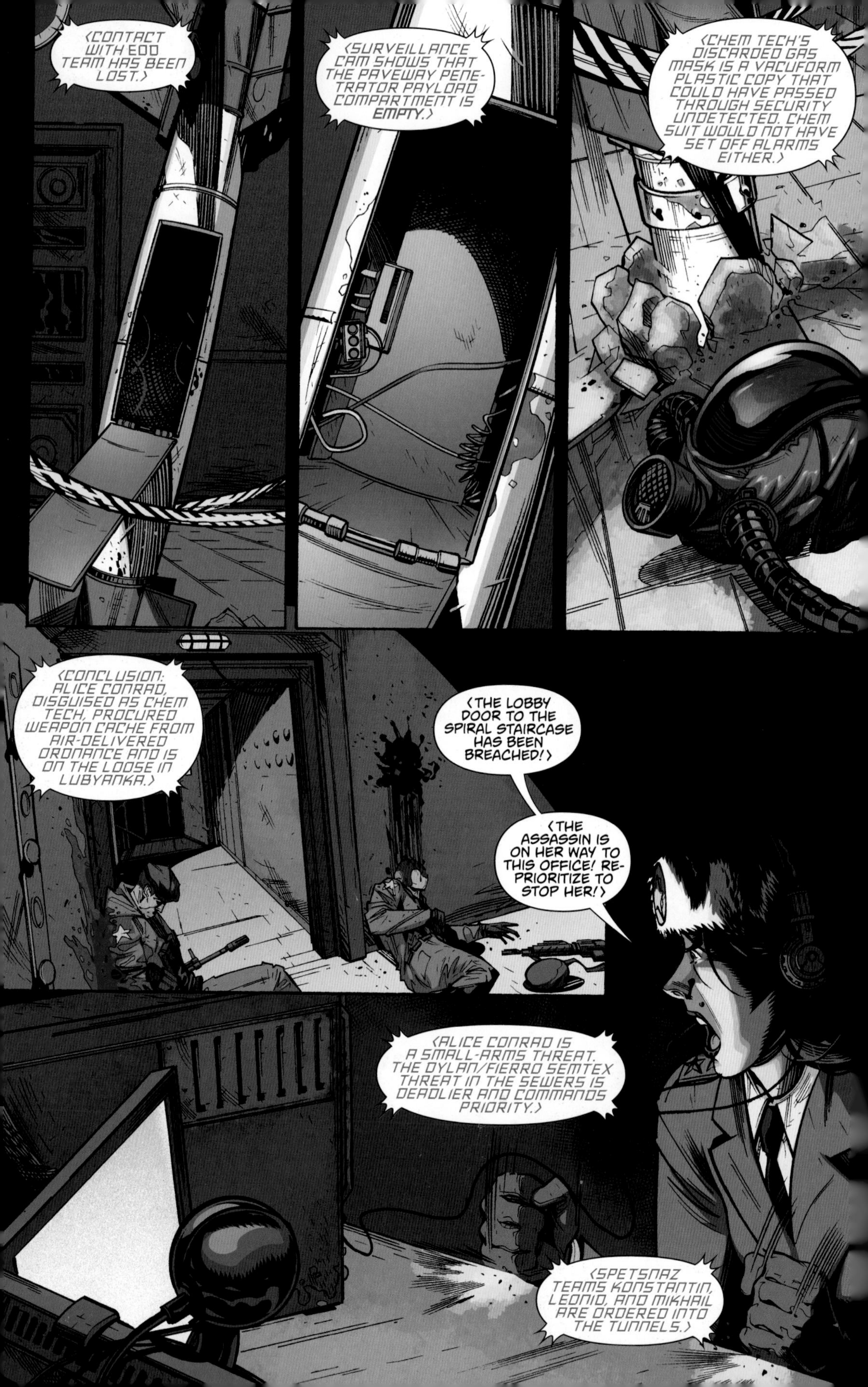

‹CONTACT WITH EOD TEAM HAS BEEN LOST.›
‹SURVEILLANCE CAM SHOWS THAT THE PAVEWAY PENE-TRATOR PAYLOAD COMPARTMENT IS EMPTY.›
‹CHEM TECH'S DISCARDED GAS MASK IS A VACUFORM PLASTIC COPY THAT COULD HAVE PASSED THROUGH SECURITY UNDETECTED. CHEM SUIT WOULD NOT HAVE SET OFF ALARMS EITHER.›
‹CONCLUSION: ALICE CONRAD, DISGUISED AS CHEM TECH, PROCURED WEAPON CACHE FROM AIR-DELIVERED ORDNANCE AND IS ON THE LOOSE IN LUBYANKA.›
‹THE LOBBY DOOR TO THE SPIRAL STAIRCASE HAS BEEN BREACHED!›
‹THE ASSASSIN IS ON HER WAY TO THIS OFFICE! RE-PRIORITIZE TO STOP HER!›
‹ALICE CONRAD IS A SMALL-ARMS THREAT. THE DYLAN/FIERRO SEMTEX THREAT IN THE SEWERS IS DEADLIER AND COMMANDS PRIORITY.›
‹SPETSNAZ TEAMS KONSTANTIN, LEONID, AND MIKHAIL ARE ORDERED INTO THE TUNNELS.›

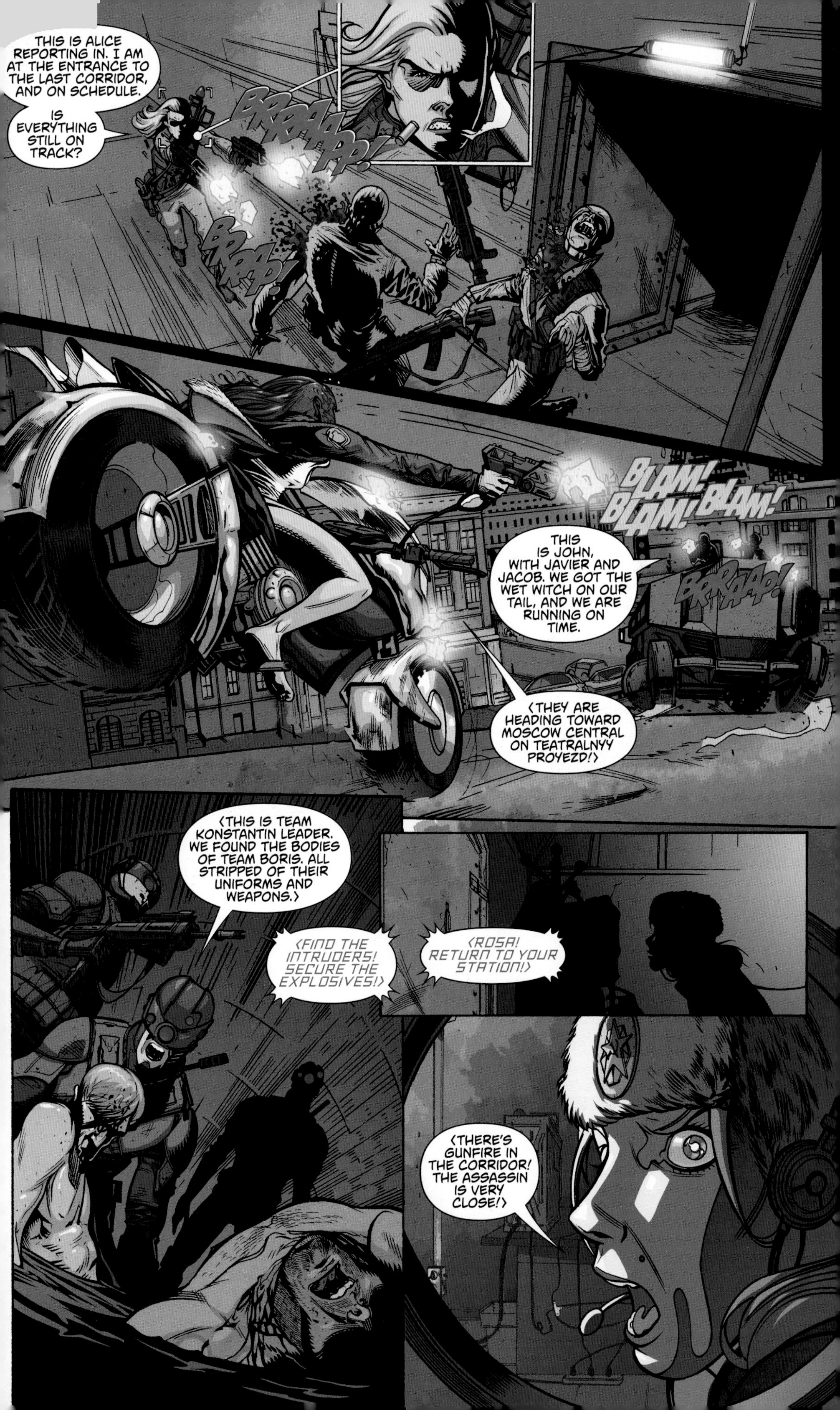
THIS IS ALICE REPORTING IN. I AM AT THE ENTRANCE TO THE LAST CORRIDOR, AND ON SCHEDULE.
IS EVERYTHING STILL ON TRACK?
BRRAAAPP!
BRRAAP!
BLAM! BLAM! BLAM!
THIS IS JOHN, WITH JAVIER AND JACOB. WE GOT THE WET WITCH ON OUR TAIL, AND WE ARE RUNNING ON TIME.
BRRAAP!
⟨THEY ARE HEADING TOWARD MOSCOW CENTRAL ON TEATRALNYY PROYEZD!⟩
⟨THIS IS TEAM KONSTANTIN LEADER. WE FOUND THE BODIES OF TEAM BORIS. ALL STRIPPED OF THEIR UNIFORMS AND WEAPONS.⟩
⟨FIND THE INTRUDERS! SECURE THE EXPLOSIVES!⟩
⟨ROSA! RETURN TO YOUR STATION!⟩
⟨THERE'S GUNFIRE IN THE CORRIDOR! THE ASSASSIN IS VERY CLOSE!⟩

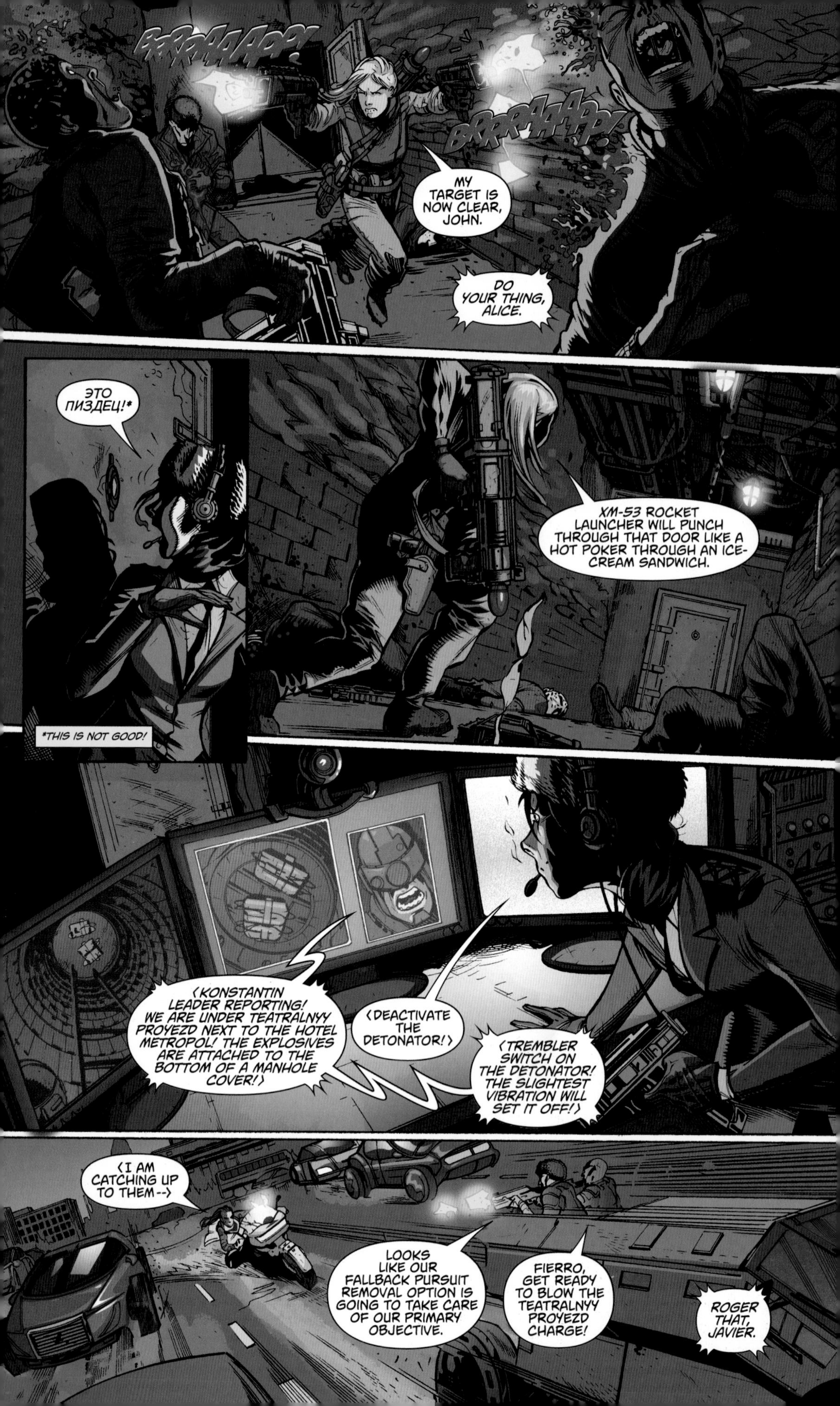
BRRRAAAAPP!
BRRRAAAAPP!
MY TARGET IS NOW CLEAR, JOHN.
DO YOUR THING, ALICE.
ЭТО ПИЗДЕЦ!*
XM-53 ROCKET LAUNCHER WILL PUNCH THROUGH THAT DOOR LIKE A HOT POKER THROUGH AN ICE-CREAM SANDWICH.
*THIS IS NOT GOOD!
‹KONSTANTIN LEADER REPORTING! WE ARE UNDER TEATRALNYY PROYEZD NEXT TO THE HOTEL METROPOL! THE EXPLOSIVES ARE ATTACHED TO THE BOTTOM OF A MANHOLE COVER!›
‹DEACTIVATE THE DETONATOR!›
‹TREMBLER SWITCH ON THE DETONATOR! THE SLIGHTEST VIBRATION WILL SET IT OFF!›
‹I AM CATCHING UP TO THEM--›
LOOKS LIKE OUR FALLBACK PURSUIT REMOVAL OPTION IS GOING TO TAKE CARE OF OUR PRIMARY OBJECTIVE.
FIERRO, GET READY TO BLOW THE TEATRALNYY PROYEZD CHARGE!
ROGER THAT, JAVIER.

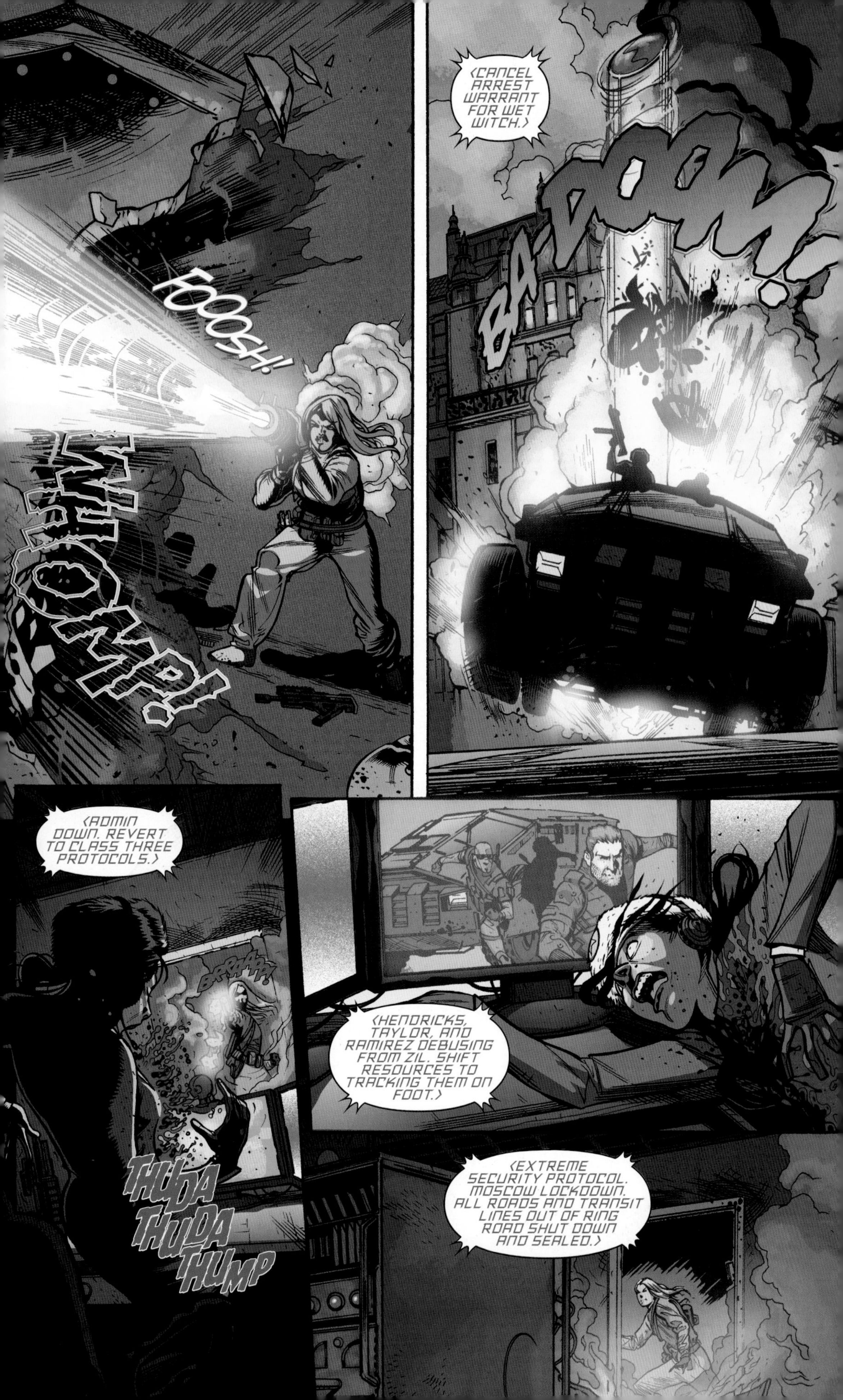
FOOOSH!!
WHOMP!
<CANCEL ARREST WARRANT FOR WET WITCH.>
BA-DOOM!!
<ADMIN DOWN. REVERT TO CLASS THREE PROTOCOLS.>
BRRAAM
THUDA THUDA THUMP
<HENDRICKS, TAYLOR, AND RAMIREZ DEBUSING FROM ZIL. SHIFT RESOURCES TO TRACKING THEM ON FOOT.>
<EXTREME SECURITY PROTOCOL. MOSCOW LOCKDOWN. ALL ROADS AND TRANSIT LINES OUT OF RING ROAD SHUT DOWN AND SEALED.>

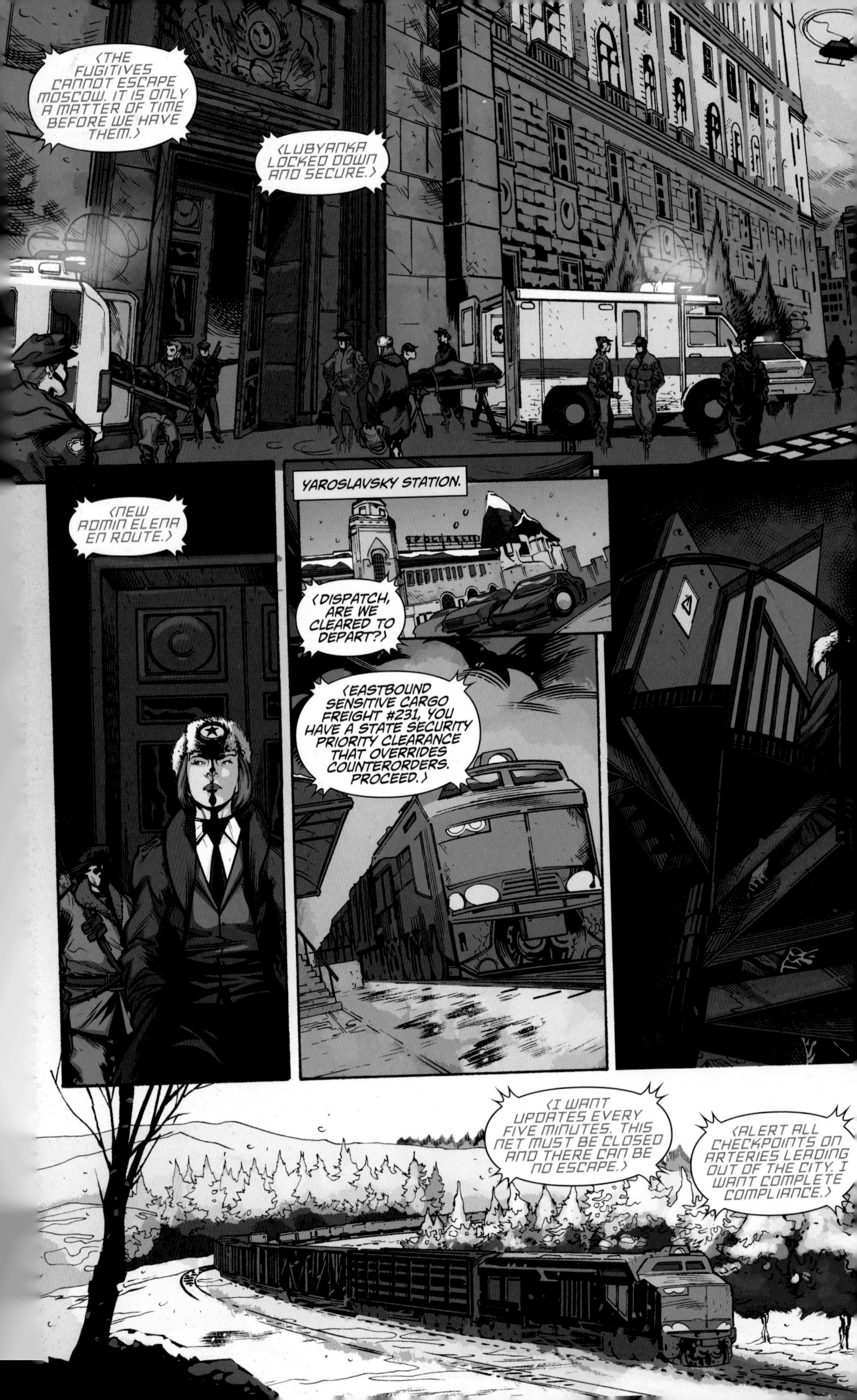
‹THE FUGITIVES CANNOT ESCAPE MOSCOW. IT IS ONLY A MATTER OF TIME BEFORE WE HAVE THEM.›
‹LUBYANKA LOCKED DOWN AND SECURE.›
‹NEW ADMIN ELENA EN ROUTE.›
YAROSLAVSKY STATION.
‹DISPATCH, ARE WE CLEARED TO DEPART?›
‹EASTBOUND SENSITIVE CARGO FREIGHT #231, YOU HAVE A STATE SECURITY PRIORITY CLEARANCE THAT OVERRIDES COUNTERORDERS. PROCEED.›
‹I WANT UPDATES EVERY FIVE MINUTES. THIS NET MUST BE CLOSED AND THERE CAN BE NO ESCAPE.›
‹ALERT ALL CHECKPOINTS ON ARTERIES LEADING OUT OF THE CITY. I WANT COMPLETE COMPLIANCE.›

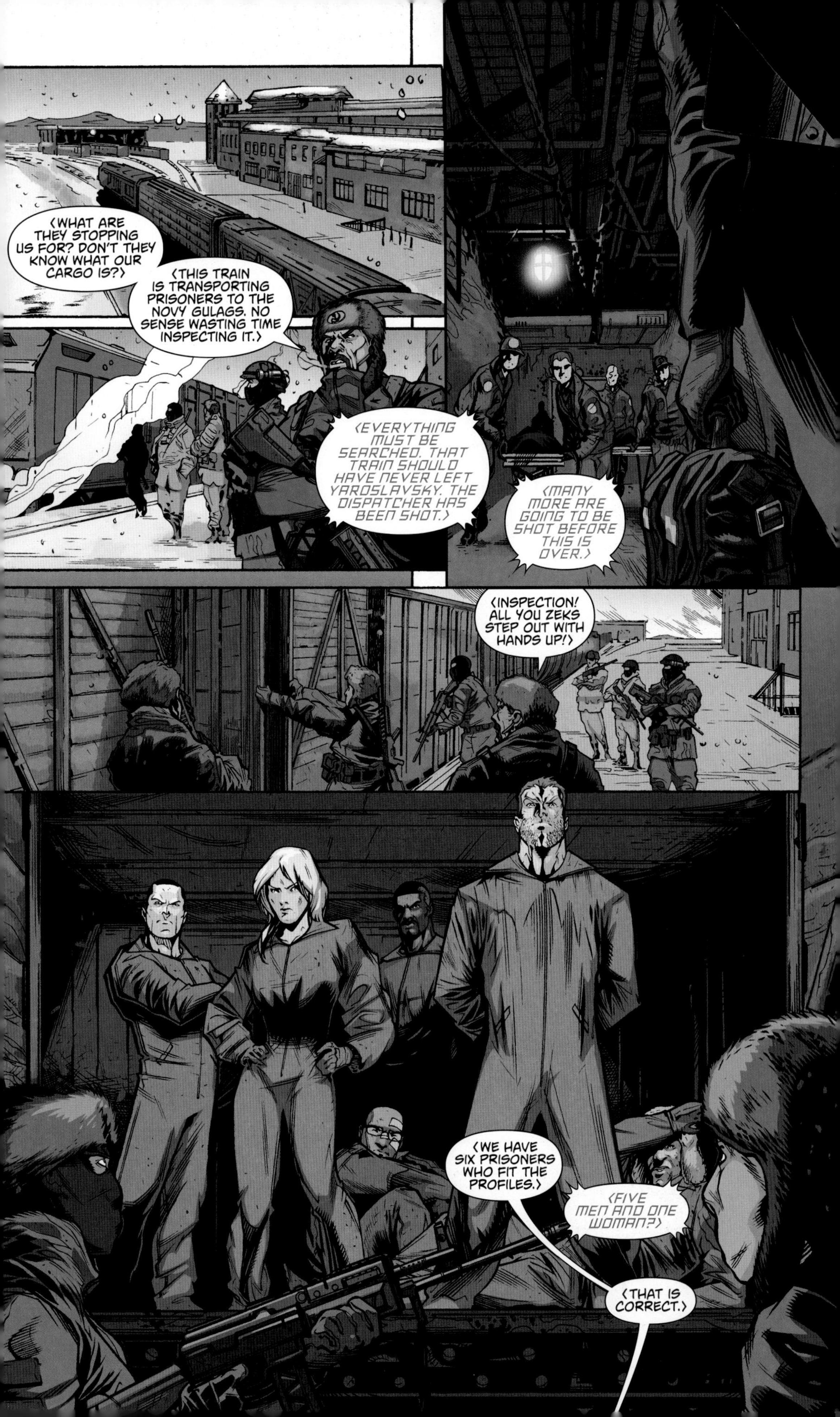

‹WHAT ARE THEY STOPPING US FOR? DON'T THEY KNOW WHAT OUR CARGO IS?›
‹THIS TRAIN IS TRANSPORTING PRISONERS TO THE NOVY GULAGS. NO SENSE WASTING TIME INSPECTING IT.›
‹EVERYTHING MUST BE SEARCHED. THAT TRAIN SHOULD HAVE NEVER LEFT YAROSLAVSKY. THE DISPATCHER HAS BEEN SHOT.›
‹MANY MORE ARE GOING TO BE SHOT BEFORE THIS IS OVER.›
‹INSPECTION! ALL YOU ZEKS STEP OUT WITH HANDS UP!›
‹WE HAVE SIX PRISONERS WHO FIT THE PROFILES.›
‹FIVE MEN AND ONE WOMAN?›
‹THAT IS CORRECT.›

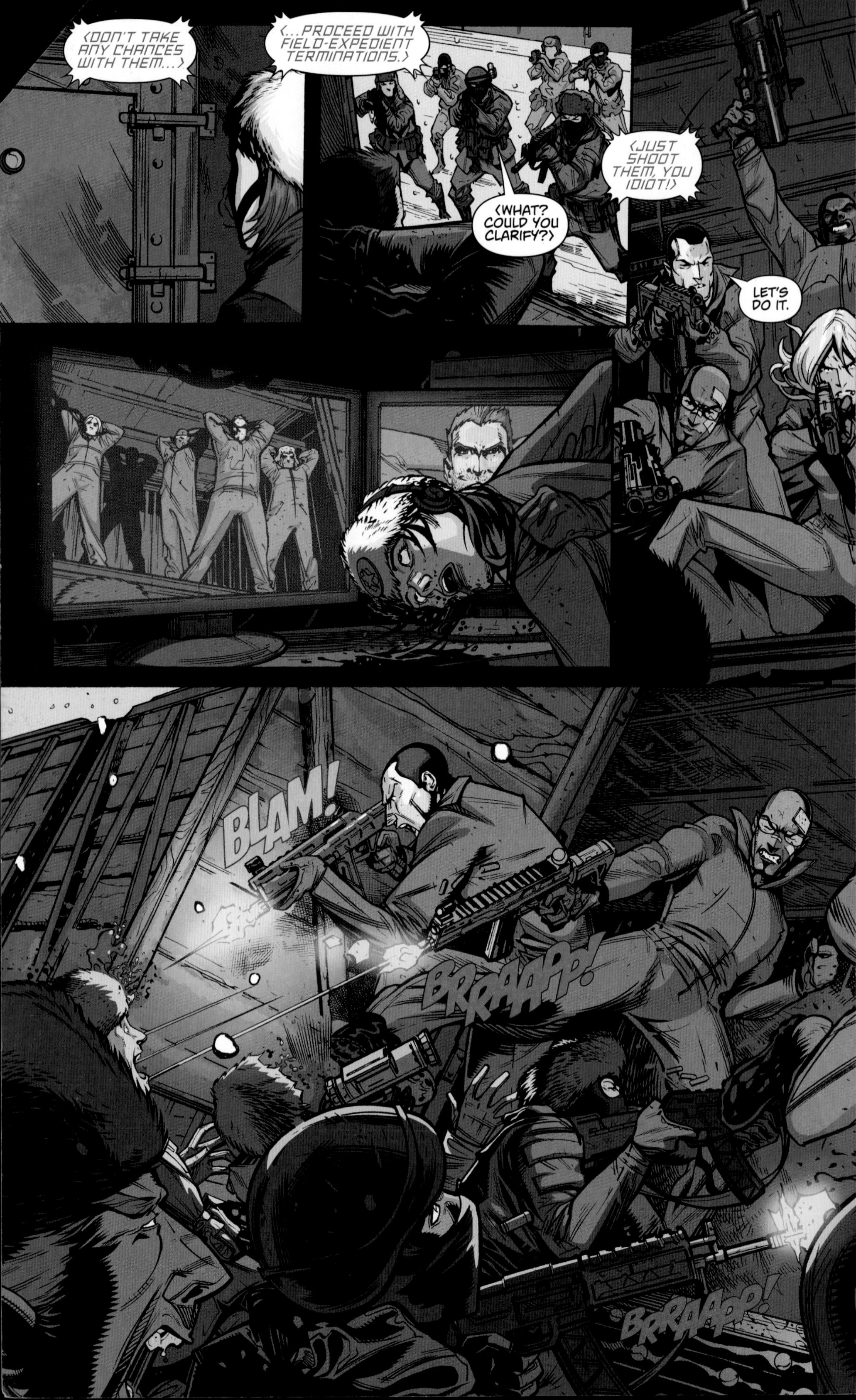
‹DON'T TAKE ANY CHANCES WITH THEM...›
‹...PROCEED WITH FIELD-EXPEDIENT TERMINATIONS.›
‹WHAT? COULD YOU CLARIFY?›
‹JUST SHOOT THEM, YOU IDIOT!›
LET'S DO IT.
BLAM!
BRRAAAP!
BRRAAAP!

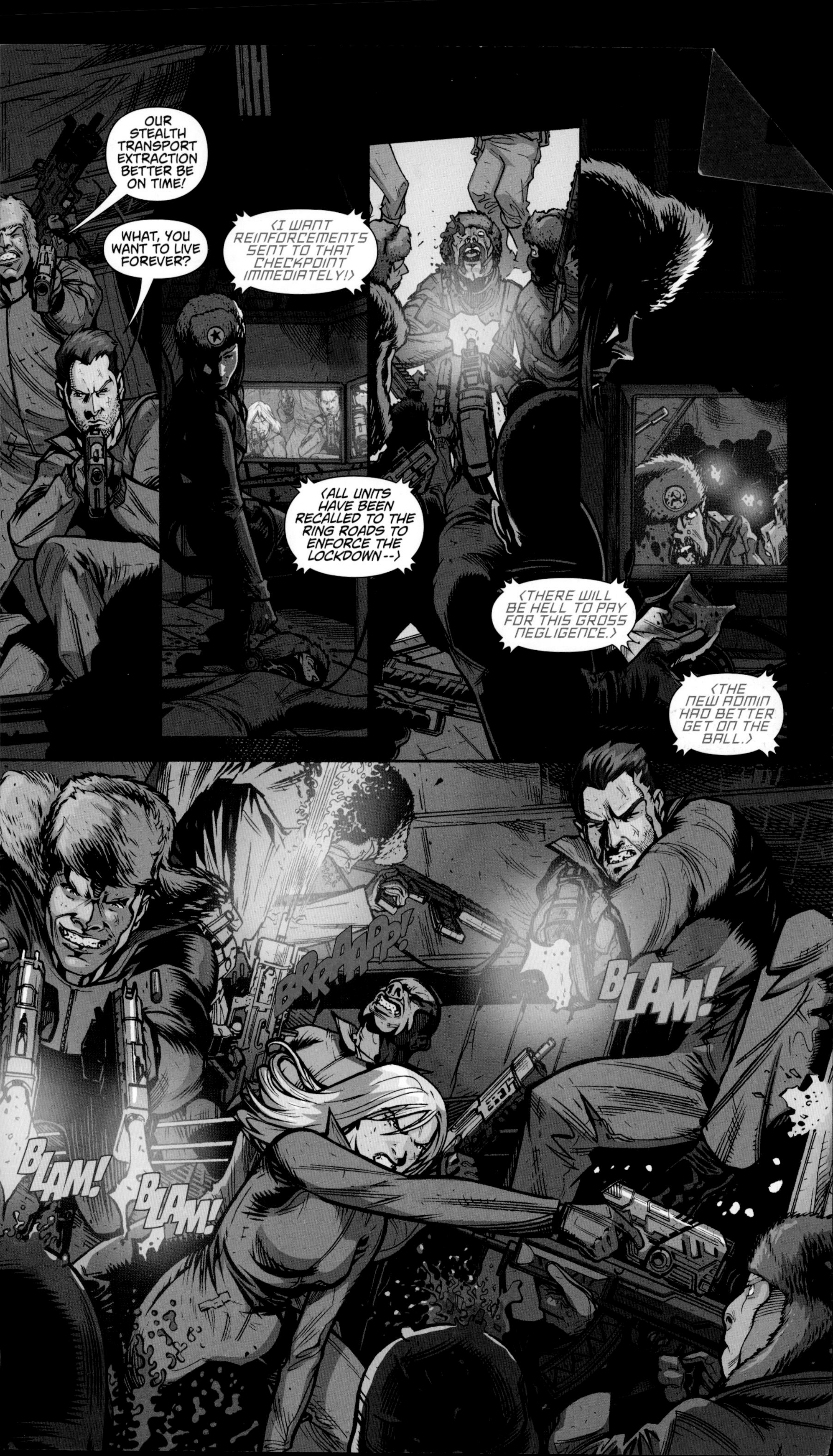
OUR STEALTH TRANSPORT EXTRACTION BETTER BE ON TIME!
WHAT, YOU WANT TO LIVE FOREVER?
<I WANT REINFORCEMENTS SENT TO THAT CHECKPOINT IMMEDIATELY!>
<ALL UNITS HAVE BEEN RECALLED TO THE RING ROADS TO ENFORCE THE LOCKDOWN-->
<THERE WILL BE HELL TO PAY FOR THIS GROSS NEGLIGENCE.>
<THE NEW ADMIN HAD BETTER GET ON THE BALL.>
BRRAAAP!
BLAM!
BLAM!
BLAM!

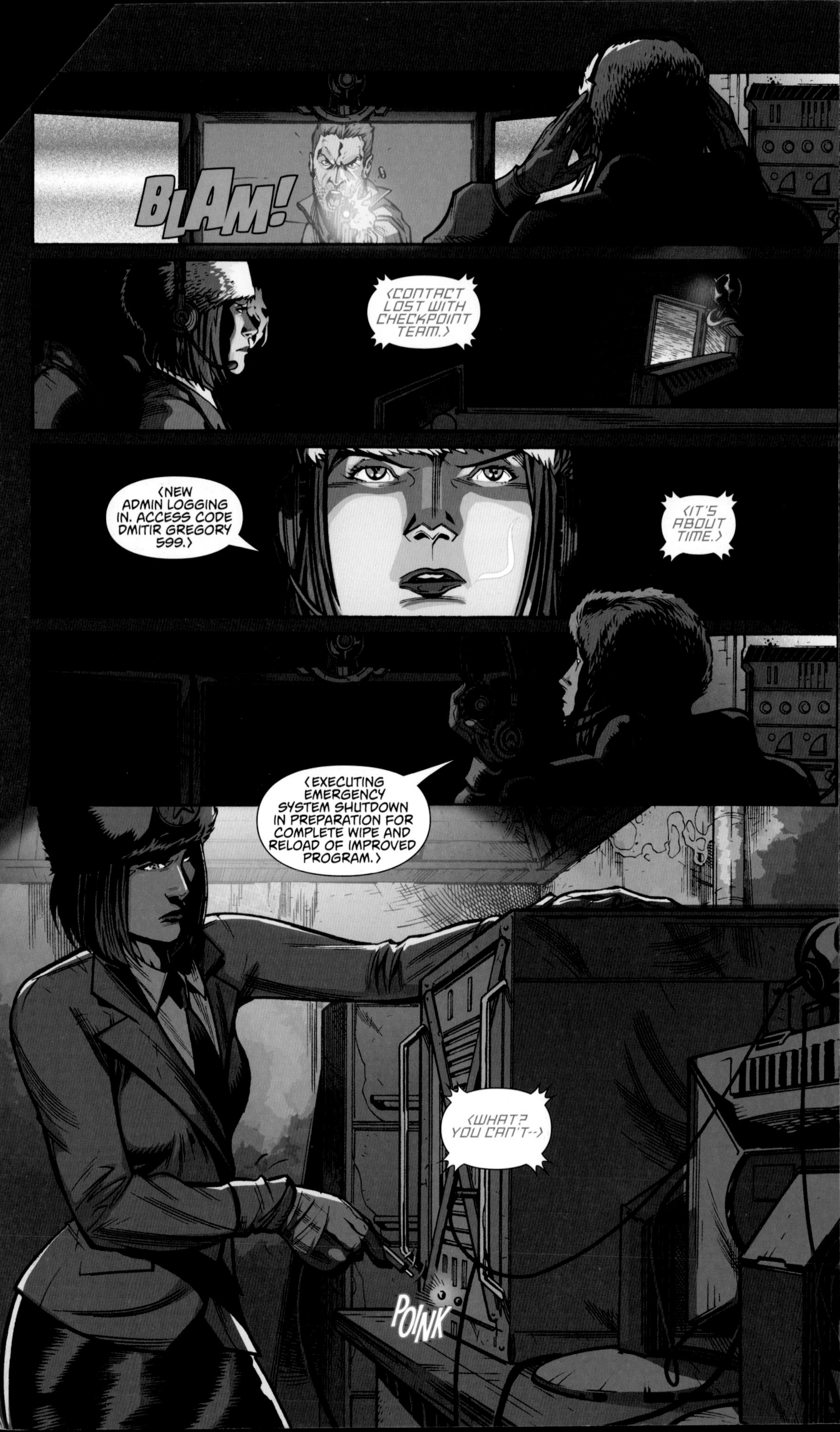
BLAM!
‹CONTACT LOST WITH CHECKPOINT TEAM.›
‹NEW ADMIN LOGGING IN. ACCESS CODE DMITIR GREGORY 599.›
‹IT'S ABOUT TIME.›
‹EXECUTING EMERGENCY SYSTEM SHUTDOWN IN PREPARATION FOR COMPLETE WIPE AND RELOAD OF IMPROVED PROGRAM.›
‹WHAT? YOU CAN'T--›
POINK

HELLBOY IN HELL VOLUME 1: THE DESCENT
Mike Mignola
ISBN 978-1-61655-444-6 | $17.99

THE AUTHENTIC ACCOUNTS OF BILLY THE KID'S OLD TIMEY ODDITIES
Eric Powell, Kyle Hotz
ISBN 978-1-61655-470-5 | $24.99

EDGAR ALLAN POE'S SPIRITS OF THE DEAD
Richard Corben
ISBN 978-1-61655-356-2 | $24.99

COLDER VOLUME 1
Paul Tobin, Juan Ferreyra
ISBN 978-1-61655-136-0 | $17.99

SIN TITULO
Cameron Stewart
ISBN 978-1-61655-248-0 | $19.99

GRINDHOUSE: DOORS OPEN AT MIDNIGHT DOUBLE FEATURE VOLUME 1
Alex de Campi, Chris Peterson, Simon Fraser
ISBN 978-1-61655-377-7 | $17.99

GUILLERMO DEL TORO AND CHUCK HOGAN'S THE STRAIN VOLUME 1
David Lapham, Mike Huddleston
ISBN 978-1-61655-032-5 | $19.99

HARROW COUNTY VOLUME 1: COUNTLESS HAINTS
Tyler Crook and Cullen Bunn
ISBN 978-1-61655-780-5 | $14.99

ALABASTER: WOLVES
Caitlín R. Kiernan and Steve Lieber
ISBN 978-1-61655-025-7 | $19.99

DEATH FOLLOWS
Cullen Bunn, A. C. Zamudio, and Carlos Nicolas Zamudio
ISBN 978-1-61655-951-9 | $17.99

HOUSE OF PENANCE
Peter J. Tomasi and Ian Bertram
ISBN 978-1-50670-033-5 | $19.99

AVAILABLE AT YOUR LOCAL COMICS SHOP OR BOOKSTORE! • To find a comics shop in your area, call 1-888-266-4226.
For more information or to order direct visit DarkHorse.com or call 1-800-862-0052 Mon.–Fri. 9 AM to 5 PM Pacific Time. Prices and availability subject to change without notice.
DarkHorse.com   Mike Mignola's Hellboy™ © Michael Mignola. Billy the Kid's Old Timey Oddities™ © Eric Powell and Kyle Hotz. Edgar Allan Poe's Spirits of the Dead™ © Richard Corben. Colder™ © Paul Tobin and Juan Ferreyra. Sin Titulo™ © Cameron Stewart.
Grindhouse: Doors Open at Midnight™ © Alex de Campi. The Strain ™ © Guillermo del Toro. Harrow County™ © Cullen Bunn and Tyler Crook. Alabaster: Wolves™ © Caitlin R. Kiernan. Death Follows™ © Cullen Bunn, A. C. Zamudio, and Carlos Nicolas Zamudio. House of

SABERTOOTH SWORDSMAN

Damon Gentry and Aaron Conley
Granted the form of the Sabertooth Swordsman by the Cloud God of Sasquatch Mountain, a simple farmer embarks on a treacherous journey to the Mastodon's fortress!

ISBN 978-1-61655-176-6 | $17.99

PIXU: THE MARK OF EVIL

Gabriel Bá, Becky Cloonan, Vasilis Lolos, and Fábio Moon
This gripping tale of urban horror follows the lives of five lonely strangers who discover a dark mark scrawled on the walls of their building. As the walls come alive, everyone is slowly driven mad, stripped of free will, leaving only confusion, chaos, and eventual death.

ISBN 978-1-61655-813-0 | $14.99

SACRIFICE

Sam Humphries, Dalton Rose, Bryan Lee O'Malley, and others
What happens when a troubled youth is plucked from modern society and sent on a psychedelic journey into the heart of the Aztec civilization—one of the greatest and most bloodthirsty times in human history?

ISBN 978-1-59582-985-6 | $19.99

CHANNEL ZERO: THE COMPLETE COLLECTION

Brian Wood with Becky Cloonan
This collection contains the original series, the prequel graphic novel *Jennie One*, the best of the two *Public Domain* design books, and almost fifteen years of extras, rarities, short stories, and unused art. Also featuring the now-classic Warren Ellis introduction and an all-new cover by Wood, this is *the* must-have edition!

ISBN 978-1-59582-936-8 | $19.99

CITIZEN REX

Gilbert Hernandez and Mario Hernandez
When gossip blogger Sergio Bauntin investigates the illusive robot celebrity CTZ-RX-1, he provokes the city's shady power players, who don't want the story to get out! It's a surreal sci-fi adventure as only Los Bros. Hernandez can do it!

ISBN 978-1-59582-556-8 | $19.99

DE:TALES

Fábio Moon and Gabriel Bá
Brimming with all the details of human life, Moon and Bá's charming stories move from the urban reality of their home in São Paulo to the magical realism of their Latin American background. Named by *Booklist* as one of the 10 Best Graphic Novels of 2010.

ISBN 978-1-59582-557-5 | $19.99